1994

W9-AOX-616

The Legislative Drafter's

Desk Reference

The Legislative Drafter's
Desk Reference

Lawrence E. Filson

Congressional Quarterly Inc.
Washington, D.C.

Book and cover design: Paula Anderson

Printed in the United States of America

Library of Congress Cataloging-in-Publication Data

Filson, Lawrence E.
The legislative drafter's desk reference / Lawrence E. Filson.
p.   cm.
Includes bibliographical references and index.
ISBN 0-87187-670-1 -- ISBN 1-56802-008-2 (pbk.)
1. Bill drafting--United States.   I. Title.
KF4950.F55   1992
328.73'0773--dc20   92-16062
                                                                 CIP

Contents

151, 596

Contents

Preface

A statute consists of written words, appropriately arranged on pages. Anyone who reads the daily papers or listens to news broadcasts soon learns that the process by which those words come into being—the process by which laws achieve their physical existence—is called "legislative drafting". When a bill is introduced or a law is enacted there has to have been someone, somewhere, who "drafted" it.

This seems simple and straightforward enough; after all, when words are found on a page there must be an author lurking somewhere. However, when that page happens to be part of a bill or a law the situation becomes more complicated, because someone who never lifted a pencil—a legislator who introduced, sponsored, or supported the bill or even an outsider who promoted it—is certain to be occupying center stage, loudly proclaiming authorship. And authorship of ideas is, of course, every bit as real as authorship of words.

Nevertheless, someone did write the actual language. Just who was it? What exactly did the writer do to make the words appear, and how did the writer's activities fit into the overall legislative picture? It seldom occurs to most people even to ask these questions; but legislative drafting is a highly specialized form of writing and there are widespread misconceptions about just what it involves.

Legislative drafting does not include the gestation of the ideas to be incorporated in a bill or the formulation of the bill's policy, purposes, and objectives; but it is not merely an editorial or clerical activity either. Standing midway between the birth of the raw ideas and the actual incorporation of those ideas into a finished legislative document, it is in many ways the central element in the making of a law. The sponsor's initial generalities must be converted into specifics; any gaps in the proposal as originally presented must be filled; any substantive, legal, administrative, and technical questions that may arise must be answered; and an arrangement of the bill's various elements that will effectively communicate its message to the intended audience must be found.

The responsibility for doing these things without leaving any loose ends, as well as converting the end product into the proper legislative form and style, is primarily the drafter's. And if the drafter has done the preliminary work correctly, the actual writing of the words is likely to be relatively quick and easy.

▼ ▼ ▼

Legislative drafting is not an esoteric skill, but neither is it just another routine form of writing. It is a uniquely demanding craft.

The ability to draft legislation properly, however, is a skill that can be acquired. The special approach to legislative problems that the drafter must take, and the special techniques and devices needed to handle those problems, can be learned. And it is a skill that should be thoroughly understood by anyone with a serious interest in how the legislative process works.

Some individuals draft bills on a regular basis as an integral part of the legislative process, but many others also participate. Executive-branch officials and members of public interest groups, for example, frequently need to formulate legislative proposals or at least be able to understand and evaluate proposals already on the table. And State legislative technicians need a familiarity with the ins and outs of drafting at the Federal level, because State objectives can often be best achieved through modifications of the Federal law (or can only be achieved, through modifications of the State law, after particular changes have been made in the Federal law).

Presenting a legislative proposal without accompanying legislative language to carry it out simply postpones the initial drafting stage, although it is sometimes the only way to get the ball rolling. This approach almost certainly fails to address some of the problems involved, since it is hard to see them all until you have tried to solve the ones that are obvious. And of course a poorly written or inadequately thought-out draft is often worse than none at all.

From a broader perspective, the ability to draft well is invariably accompanied by an ability—or an increased ability—to identify problems in legislation and to comprehend legislative language. This is significant to anyone who needs to understand what a particular legislative proposal would do to or for some group or interest and who wants to know how best to enhance the proposal's prospects.

Anyone who needs to understand legislation—whatever the reason—can benefit from a better feel for the drafting process; and that is what *The Legislative Drafter's Desk Reference* is all about.

▼ ▼ ▼

This book's primary objective is to provide an all-purpose drafting manual for individuals who, by choice or necessity, may be called upon to draft legislation, and to serve the needs of those individuals without regard to their background, the setting in which they operate, and the extent (if any) of their previous training. It is aimed at experienced and occasional drafters alike and is intended to serve as a reference document for desk-side use.

A second objective—in many ways equally important—is to paint a realistic and meaningful picture of what legislative drafting involves and how it fits into the legislative process as a whole. In this sense, it is intended for individuals who simply have a serious interest in government and are seeking a better understanding of the overall process as well as for individuals who actually draft bills.[1]

Despite the differences that exist between individual drafters with varying degrees of experience and between the legislative settings in which they work, the author firmly believes that it is both possible and desirable to address the subject broadly, because the drafter's basic approach and most of the practical problems to be faced will be the same for both the occasional drafter and the full-time professional, regardless of setting. And the author has made every effort to take the special disadvantages of occasional drafters fully into account, since most readers will fall into that category. (Relatively speaking, there are very few full-time professional drafters today.)

▼ ▼ ▼

Much of what has previously been written about legislative drafting is regrettably of little practical use to the aspiring legislative drafter or to this author. Most of the works in the field fall into one of several categories—(1) those that emphasize the more abstruse legal, scholarly, and philosophical aspects of drafting, too often in a purely academic or overly ponderous way, (2) those that have a particular ax to grind ("laws are too complicated" or "any drafter who would renumber a section of existing law should be shot"), and (3) those that contain interminable lists of drafting rules in the form of "dos and don'ts" and very little else (attributing to each rule the status of holy writ, but usually without any indication of why).

Occasionally one of these works will have something significant to say, but more often than not its author is either engaging in a purely academic exercise or just "letting off steam". The one thing they seem to have in common is their failure to recognize the everyday practical problems that the typical drafter faces.

Fortunately there are some works on the subject that are both useful and practical, and three of them deserve special mention at the outset:

(1) *The Fundamentals of Legal Drafting,* by Reed Dickerson (to be cited as *Dickerson*)[2]—probably the classic in the field,

---

[1] An accurate, complete, and concise treatment of the process is *The Legislative Process,* by John M. Kernochan, published in 1981 by the Foundation Press; it concentrates on the Federal level but includes a good summary of State procedures as well. Another brief but informative source at the Federal level is *How Our Laws Are Made,* revised and updated by Edward R. Willet, Jr., published every few years by the House of Representatives and available from the House document room or the Government Printing Office.

[2] Published for the American Bar Foundation by Little, Brown, and Co. (1965).

and an example of a scholarly work that does not shortchange the practical side;

(2) *Drafting Federal Law,* by Donald Hirsch (to be cited as *Hirsch*)[3]—a highly instructive book that is altogether practical, often to the point of irreverence; and

(3) *Style Manual; Drafting Suggestions for the Trained Drafter* (to be cited as HOLC)[4]—the everyday working manual of the Office of the Legislative Counsel, U.S. House of Representatives, often characterized as the country's premier professional drafting office.

The cited works are frequently referred to, paraphrased, or quoted verbatim in this book; the author sees no point in trying to rephrase things that have already been well said. All three reflect extensive professional drafting experience, and in the author's judgment (although they do not always agree with each other or with him) the views they express are invariably rational and seldom very far from the target.

Indeed, the existence of the three cited works would render this book largely unnecessary were it not for two facts: They are aimed at specialized audiences, and they all make the frequently unwarranted assumption that their readers are already familiar with the mechanical and environmental difficulties that the typical drafter faces every day. And, of course, the author of this book occasionally has definite opinions of his own to express about matters on which they do disagree.

This book grinds enough axes and lists enough "dos and don'ts" to satisfy anyone, but hopefully it does so in a way that reflects the realities of the legislative process and leaves the reader with an understanding of the drafter's everyday practical problems as a participant in that process.

▼ ▼ ▼

The main portion of this book—that is, everything after the introductory material contained in Part I—consists of six parts.

Part II (chapters 4 through 6) deals with the preliminary stage of any drafting operation—the things that have to be done before the actual writing begins: pinning down the sponsor's problem and its intended solution, identifying and dealing with any collateral questions which that solution may raise, and organizing the bill.

Part III (chapters 7 through 9) discusses some of the broader considerations that bear upon legislative form and style—the mechanics of good writing, the Roman rule, and the quest for readability.

---

[3] Published for the Department of Health and Human Services, Office of the General Counsel, Legislation Division (1980), and (with revisions) for the use of the Office of the Legislative Counsel, U.S. House of Representatives (1989).

[4] Published by the Office of the Legislative Counsel, U.S. House of Representatives (1989).

Part IV (chapters 10 through 13) begins the more specific treatment of the writing process, enumerating the various provisions that might be found in a typical freestanding bill and discussing their form and style and the alternatives available to the drafter.

Part V (chapters 14 through 18) deals with the writing of amendatory bills, addressing the basic amendatory forms and styles, the proper organization and arrangement of amendments, and a number of problems unique to the amendatory approach.

Part VI (chapters 19 through 28) deals with legislative style and usage generally, setting forth a list of the drafting rules, principles, and techniques that would normally apply without regard to the type of bill involved or its setting.

Part VII (chapters 29 through 32) addresses matters of form, style, and procedure that are important in Federal bill drafting but which could not appropriately be included in the preceding parts because of the wide variety of circumstances and requirements in the different States.

When reading this manual, you should keep in mind the following:

(1) In a number of instances the same point is made, or the same steps in the legislative process are retraced, in two or more places. This is intentional; and it is done so that readers who are interested only in the subject covered by a particular chapter can get the full picture without having to look elsewhere. The sort of clear-cut compartmentalization that would make repetition unnecessary is not really possible in a book of this kind.

(2) Each of the examples and models in this book illustrates a particular point. It should be read as addressing only that point and should not be taken as an endorsement or criticism of anything else that may be contained in it.

(3) Most of the examples and models assume the continued existence of the legislative rules, procedures, and forms currently in effect; but these things do change—often rapidly and with no advance notice. The author can only express the hope, if any such example or model should become obsolete before its time, that the point he was trying to make is still valid.

▼ ▼ ▼

On the subject of pure editorial style, in legislative drafting as in other forms of prose composition, any standard dictionary, read in conjunction with *The Chicago Manual of Style* or its equivalent, should be regarded as the basic authority. This primarily involves such things as spelling, capitalization, hyphenation, and punctuation, as well as the uses of words and numerals in particular circumstances.

When a more specialized manual on the writing or printing of public documents in the context involved (such as the *Government Printing Office Style Manual* or one of its State counterparts) provides a different rule, however, that rule should be followed instead.

And when the unique needs of legislative drafting demand the application of a rule that is different from any of the cited authorities, that rule should be applied even if it violates the otherwise-established practice.

The style in which this book is written—like the style in which the author would normally write legislation—reflects this hierarchy of choices. It generally follows the dictionary and the *Chicago Manual,* but it deviates from them (for example, by capitalizing governmental terms like "State", "Federal", and "President") when that is what the *GPO Style Manual* does. And it deviates from all of the cited authorities whenever that is the only way to meet the drafter's overriding need for absolute clarity and precision; see chapters 21, 22, and 27 for examples.

▼ ▼ ▼

In an ideal world you would always be able to draft under circumstances that give you every opportunity to do it right, with plenty of time and resources and with no possibility of having overlooked anything important. As a practical matter, however, this does not occur as frequently as you might wish.

For reasons quite beyond your control you must often be satisfied with just "doing the best you can" in the hope that that will be sufficient to accomplish the desired result without causing the foundations of the Republic to crumble. It should always be remembered that as a practical matter you will almost never have the option of flatly refusing to be of assistance to a sponsor simply because you have problems—even insoluble ones—so you need to know how to face those problems cheerfully and with some hope of success. The author knows only too well about the difficulties you are likely to encounter and will always try to suggest ways of handling them.

There are horror cases, of course, but they are largely the province of the on-the-scene professionals. For the occasional drafter the outlook is far less forbidding; most of your drafting assignments will involve one-shot proposals of limited scope, being developed in friendly territory. Very few of you will ever be solely responsible for a massive and complex piece of legislation, or find yourself in the middle of the legislative storm, or have to deal regularly with waves of frantic sponsors going in opposite directions.

And you should take comfort in the thought that the legislative process is self-correcting in the sense that early mistakes and technical shortcomings are almost always taken care of, one way or another, in the later stages.

▼ ▼ ▼

For their assistance in the development and preparation of this book the author is indebted to his former colleagues in the House Legislative Counsel's Office—especially Roger Young (the Deputy Legislative Counsel), Doug Bellis, John Buckley, Stan Grimm, Ed Grossman, Larry Johnston, Fred Dichter, and Lynne Richardson—who always responded when called upon for help. Special thanks are due Steve Cope, who actually waded through the entire manuscript (at an early stage), making constructive suggestions and only occasionally recoiling in horror.

The author is also deeply appreciative of the moral support provided by Ward Hussey (the longtime former Legislative Counsel of the House), David Meade and Frank Burk (the current Legislative Counsels of the House and Senate), and Don Hirsch (whose views pervade the book).

This book could not have been written without the assistance and support of these people. To the extent that it turns out to have been a worthwhile endeavor, the author will be eternally grateful to them. To the extent that it stumbles, however, they should not be held responsible; the author insists on his right to blunder without help from anyone.

Part I

General Overview

Approaching
the Subject

▶ **1.1   The approach in general**

Middleton Beaman, the first Legislative Counsel of the House of Representatives, once said that a legislative drafter must be an intellectual eunuch. Reed Dickerson, in commenting on this statement some years later, added that the drafter must be an emotional oyster as well.[1] Each of them had a point, but overstated the case by a considerable margin. Almost anyone with writing ability and a modicum of analytical judgment can become a respectable legislative drafter, and need not secede from the human race to do it.

After all, when reduced to its simplest terms legislative drafting is nothing more than the process of converting ideas into language that will effectively carry them out—not altogether different from other kinds of writing. The fact that it is a highly specialized and uniquely demanding kind only means that the skills needed to do it properly (and a realistic understanding of what it involves) may be somewhat harder to acquire.

To help you develop those skills (and that understanding), this book consciously endeavors to do better in several ways than previous works on the subject:

(1) Without minimizing the intellectual and journalistic aspects of the craft, it treats legislative drafting as the

---

[1] The Beaman statement was made during hearings on H. Con. Res. 18, 79th Congress, 1st Session (1945), 413, 416; the Dickerson addition appears in *Dickerson* at page 9.

highly pragmatic activity it is rather than as a merely academic exercise.

(2) Without "writing down" to the reader (and thereby minimizing its usefulness to more experienced drafters), it places special emphasis upon the problems of the occasional drafter who needs help the most.

(3) And without apologizing for its emphasis on *Federal* legislative drafting, it recognizes the needs of individuals whose interests or drafting activities lie in non-Federal areas and includes material relevant to those needs whenever possible.

A word of warning, however. Neither this book nor any other can turn you into an accomplished legislative drafter. Only experience, and the imitation of good models under expert guidance, can do that. What this book can do is give you some basic rules and teach you an approach that will equip you with techniques to solve drafting problems for yourself as you encounter them.

▶ **1.2**   **The importance of understanding the rules, and of knowing when to ignore them**

Most of the rules and principles that you should follow in drafting a bill would be self-evident to any good writer, and many others would become evident upon a little reflection, simply as a matter of common sense. But good drafting also involves the application of specialized rules, unique to that form, which would not be likely to occur to a nondrafter spontaneously; and it is important that you understand what they are and why they matter.

It would be possible, of course, to apply these rules without having learned anything about them in advance, simply by using this book or its equivalent as a reference manual and consulting its index frequently whenever you sit down to draft. But knowing something about them *before* sitting down to draft is important if you want to do the job right.

Without some understanding of their purpose you may not recognize a drafting problem when it stares you in the face, and you won't always know what to look for in the index. And more importantly, you can seldom afford to spend a lot of time on the mechanics of a drafting job when you need that time to deal with the substantive and legal aspects of the proposal. The mechanical aspects of legislative drafting— approach, organization, form, style, and technique—should become second nature simply so you can forget about them when you need to focus on real problems.

But there is another side to the coin. In real life, the drafter often must choose between conflicting rules or find the lesser of several evils. No drafting rule is written in stone; there are cases where not applying one of the time-honored rules will in fact increase clarity or otherwise improve the product. And when the application of one stylistic rule would conflict with another that is more important, the rule in question, however useful and sensible it may otherwise be, must give way.

▶ 1.3   Terminology

A number of concepts involved in legislative drafting will surface over and over again in this book, as will several frequently used terms to which somewhat arbitrary meanings are assigned. Fairness to the reader requires that they receive special mention at the outset.

To keep things as simple as possible, the author adopts the following definitions and conventions and uses them throughout the book:

Classification of drafters. It will often be necessary or desirable to distinguish individuals who draft bills regularly, and should already be thoroughly familiar with legislative drafting and its problems, from those who only occasionally draft bills and consequently may need special help.

The term "professional drafter" will be used to refer to an individual, such as an employee of a legislative body, executive agency, or private organization whose job-related duties consist wholly or primarily of drafting bills. All others will be arbitrarily referred to as "occasional drafters", with full recognition that some of them may in fact be better drafters than many of the "professionals".

Types of legislative vehicles. Except when otherwise indicated, the term "bill" will be used broadly to refer to any measure designed to be introduced in and acted upon by a legislative body, including joint, concurrent, and simple resolutions as well as actual bills, and also to refer to any amendment (or other isolated piece of language) designed to be incorporated into a bill. With respect to the latter, the term "introduced" should be read as meaning "offered" or "proposed".

Policy. The term "policy" will be used to refer primarily to the sponsor's basic objective in introducing a bill and seeking its enactment (the "main thrust"), but it also includes the sponsor's intent with respect to any subsidiary or collateral questions that may be involved in achieving the basic objective.

A policy question that is not part of the sponsor's main thrust will be described as "subsidiary" if—

(1) it is integral to the basic policy and must be answered, one way or another, in order to make the bill complete and coherent, or

(2) it involves matters so closely related to the main thrust that failure to address it would leave an obvious gap in the bill.

A policy question will be described as "collateral" if the bill would be complete and coherent (though not necessarily correct) if it were not addressed at all; the most common examples involve the way in which existing laws would affect how the bill operates and vice versa. Subsidiary policy questions are discussed in chapter 4, collateral questions in chapter 5.

The principle that policymaking and drafting are separate functions applies even in those cases where (because of the nature of your position) you can afford the luxury of being your own policymaker. But the objectivity required for good legislative drafting may be jeopardized when you are also an open advocate for the intended policy, unless you remember that you are wearing two quite different hats and that opponents of the policy will be looking for flaws in your drafting.

Sponsors. The term "sponsor" (with respect to a bill) will be used to refer to the individual or entity who requests the drafter to prepare the bill, who determines its policy, and who will be responsible for proposing or introducing it.

If you work for the legislature itself, the sponsor is usually a legislator or a committee. If you work for any other agency or organization, the sponsor is usually an official of that agency or organization (although when the bill is drafted and turned over to a legislator for introduction, the latter becomes the sponsor insofar as subsequent drafters are concerned).

Normally the terms "sponsor" and "policymaker" are synonymous. From your immediate point of view as a drafter, however, there is often a distinction. When you deal with a member of the sponsor's staff rather than directly with the sponsor, you are entitled to treat the staff member as the policymaker. Indeed, a sponsor may instruct you to take the policy from a third party outside the legislative process, such as a consultant or a constituent (although this is tricky, since the sponsor may not like the policy after seeing it).

If you are acting as your own policymaker, you probably have a sponsor in the wings, or are looking for one.

Setting and context. The terms "setting" and "context" will be used to distinguish the physical situations in which different drafters operate—an acknowledgment that at least some of the circumstances you will face, and at least some of the factors that bear upon how you should do your job, will be unique to your particular situation. The distinction is often critical because the external factors that determine your choices as a drafter—institutional structure, procedural rules, constitutional provisions, and all manner of long-standing practices both substantive and stylistic—differ widely from one jurisdiction to another, from one legislative entity to another within the same jurisdiction, and even from one time to another within the same entity.

Audience. The term "audience" (with respect to a bill) will be used to refer to the particular people or entities to whom the bill is primarily directed and who will have to read, understand, and apply it. Thus a bill revising the benefit formula under some existing program (though its primary effect would of course be upon the intended beneficiaries) normally consists of what amounts to instructions to the administrators responsible for calculating the benefits involved, while a bill making specified conduct unlawful is normally addressed directly to the individuals who might be tempted to engage in that conduct. The differences between an audience consisting of administrators and an audience consisting of the affected individuals can be important to you as a drafter.

Readability and clarity. Language is "readable" if it can be read comfortably and comprehended with a minimum of effort. Language has "clarity" if it says precisely what it is supposed to say, leaving no doubt about what it means. Both qualities are virtues but, as will be stressed later (especially in chapter 9), either may exist without the other.

Readability is desirable, but clarity is indispensable.

What Is Legislative Drafting?

2.1 *In general*

2.2 *Legislative drafting as a unique form of writing*

2.3 *Getting the policy right*

2.4 *Nonpartisanship and impartiality*

2.5 *Confidentiality and privilege*

▶ **2.1 In general**

The terms "legislative drafting" and "bill drafting" are commonly used to describe simply the act of writing legislation. Used more accurately, however, they describe the entire process of taking raw ideas, refining them and developing the language to carry them out, and then organizing that language so as to achieve the sponsor's objective exactly—a process in which analysis and perspective are immeasurably more important than style.

The final product must address any problems, omissions, and ambiguities that may have existed in the sponsor's original proposal or that may subsequently arise as a result of refinements in the sponsor's policy. It must be cast in language that is clear, consistent, legally effective, technically sound, administrable, enforceable, and constitutional; is correct in form and style; and is as readable and aesthetically pleasing as possible. And, of course, it must not inadvertently create any new problems or cause any unintended side effects.

Although legislative drafting does not include the origination of the ideas to be incorporated in the bill, a major part of your work as a drafter does consist of helping to clarify the sponsor's concepts and raising policy issues that the sponsor may not have considered. The drafting process thus involves far more than just writing; in many cases it actually provides the principal mechanism for substantive policy development.

Your efforts to convert the sponsor's general policy objectives into specific legislative language often constitute the best way—and sometimes the only way—to identify the aspects of that policy needing further refinement; in the words of one of the author's former colleagues, you have to turn over the stones before you can find the snakes.

Too many people miss the point completely and regard legislative drafting as solely "a search for the accurate and felicitous phrase" or just "legal packaging or ornament", thereby encouraging practitioners and students of the craft to think of it as the kind of exercise that can safely be minimized when the going gets tough (*Dickerson,* pages xiii, 4, and 7). At the other extreme, some people still confuse drafting with policymaking; newspapers frequently report that a government agency or official, a legislator, or even a private organization, in sponsoring or publicly supporting a particular bill, was the "drafter" of that bill or one of its major provisions. This misuse of terms is probably harmless, but it illustrates a common misconception.

HOLC (page 1), with characteristic succinctness, summarizes the basic skills of the trained drafter this way:

1. Finding out what the client *really* wants to do;

2. analyzing the legal and other problems involved;

3. helping the client come up with solutions to those problems that will—

   A. be administrable and enforceable, and

   B. keep hassles and litigation to a minimum; and

4. getting the client's message across.

There are many simple bills, of course, that involve little more than *HOLC's* first step followed immediately by the actual writing; but even then your decision to bypass the other preliminaries must be a conscious one, and must be made before you start to write.

▶ **2.2   Legislative drafting as a unique form of writing**

Many people regard legislative drafting as just another kind of writing, like a term paper, office memorandum, or business letter, except for its subject matter and format. They understand that there may be a few specialized requirements of style and form, but they assume that any good writer's instincts will be sufficient for the task, at least with the aid of

9

an elementary drafting manual. After all, term papers, memoranda, and business letters need to be carefully phrased too.

Others believe that it is an arcane skill that should be undertaken, and can be mastered, only by a select few.

Neither view is completely realistic. Legislation does resemble other forms of written communication in most important respects, but there are differences which are sufficiently critical to require that the drafter possess special qualifications and training and to demand of the drafter a significantly different approach.

First and foremost, legislative drafting possesses elements of complexity and imposes requirements of accuracy and precision that are "unknown in other forms of writing outside of the language of mathematics and logic" (*Dickerson,* page 154); and the attention to structure and detail that it demands is unique. The differences in degree are so great as to constitute practical differences in kind.

Statutory language is frequently criticized and caricatured by learned commentators as well as by the citizenry at large because it is too "complicated". In some cases the critics are right—there are plenty of laws that could have been written more simply. But for the most part these critics fail to appreciate the difficulties that any language would face in attempting to carry out policies which—necessarily or unnecessarily—are complex and convoluted themselves to begin with (see chapter 9).

Laws that are inherently and inescapably complex are of course favorite targets—the Internal Revenue Code (one of the most skillfully written laws on the books) has been reviled for its "colossal nebulosity and impenetrable density", and the Social Security Act has been described as a statute that "might have been less confusing if it had been written in Arabic" [1]—but less complicated laws regularly suffer as well.

Efforts to require that all laws be written in "plain English" are a recurring fad; and many impressive-sounding projects to do this have been undertaken in recent years (by the American Bar Association, State governments, and various other public and private entities). Some succeeded in bringing about localized improvements in form and style; but most of them aborted, largely because they too overlooked the fact

---

[1] *American Bar Association Journal,* December 1956 (p. 1119) and April 1957 (p. 319).

that complex and poorly thought-out policies—not the niceties of form and style—are the real source of the problem.

Second, legislative language is intended to become the law of the jurisdiction involved and must coexist amicably with the other provisions of that law. This means that (in order to make sure it is written correctly) it must be developed with one eye firmly fixed on the existing law in the field involved and in related fields, and also on the existing law in more general areas whose provisions impose administrative, budgetary, procedural, constitutional, or other requirements affecting substantive rights and duties across the board. Meanwhile (in order to make sure it will work after it is written) the other eye must be focused on the possible legal consequences of the specific words the drafter plans to use.

A related point is that while some laws may be totally self-executing, most cannot be; and as a drafter you must keep in mind that regulations will probably have to be written by the agency responsible for administering your product. Future regulations are something over which you have no control, of course; but you must recognize the areas in which administrative discretion will be required and try to make life as easy as possible for both the regulation-writers and the regulation-readers.

Major legislation is invariably crammed with complications of this kind, and failure to identify and deal with them may affect the rights of large numbers of people for decades. Every drafter must learn to recognize them instinctively.

Third, nearly all of the bills with which you may be concerned as a drafter are general in their application, but more often than not the problems that caused them to be proposed in the first place were highly specific—the sponsor has simply become aware of a situation in which the operation (or nonapplicability) of some existing law or program is adversely affecting a particular individual or group in which the sponsor is interested.

But no matter how narrowly the bill is written (unless it is cast in the form of a private relief bill), it will unavoidably cover many people in addition to those whose specific problems triggered the proposal. Most of them usually should be covered (because their situations are sufficiently similar to the triggering situation), but it is easy to overlook the differences and to cover some people whose situations are really dissimilar enough to warrant quite different treatment—see 4.5.

These questions arise even when the proposal involves a matter of broad public policy like a general tax increase or funding reduction. A broad impersonal proposal of this kind will almost always affect different people and situations in different ways, and the legislature will not have done its job unless it considers whether and to what extent the proposal should be modified in order to deal with specific cases. Efforts to amend the proposal for this purpose will almost certainly be made, and some drafter will have to face the problem after all.

Unlike the typical practicing lawyer who looks at specific legal controversies during or after the fact, as a drafter you must look before the fact at all of the possible situations to which the bill might conceivably apply and all of the possible variations which might exist in the types and contexts of those situations.

Fourth, legislation has its own form and style as well as its own specialized vocabulary, and every drafter must learn to use them correctly. Form and style usually have no substantive effect, but they can be critically important nonetheless. Consistently following the proper form and style will aid in organizing the legislative product, in achieving precision, and in reaching the intended audience.

And using the accepted style and terminology in a bill will make the Members and committees who must determine the bill's fate (and their staffs) feel more comfortable with it, and consequently more favorably disposed toward it, when they are considering what action to take. They may not be trained drafters themselves, but the sight of language that is written in an unfamiliar form and style (or uses unfamiliar terminology) is bound to make them feel uneasy. They are likely to equate what they perceive as stylistic shortcomings with substantive defects.

There is no excuse for not getting the form and style right, even without a drafting manual such as this book. It may require a little effort, but just observing the standard forms and following the past practice will usually guarantee a respectable product.

Learning the terminology of the field in which you are working, however, can be more demanding. Drafters and other legislative technicians frequently refer to key provisions of existing law by their alphanumeric designations and to key concepts in colloquial, descriptive terms. Such references are an indispensable form of verbal shorthand—convenient "terms of art" precisely alluding to complicated statutory provisions. They are completely unambiguous to the technicians who must work with and talk about the concepts involved (and should not be confused with the casual descriptive terms which are commonly and often misleadingly used in newspaper accounts); but their meaning and significance will almost never be clear at the outset to anyone not already familiar with the field involved.

Finally, the setting in which legislation is considered and enacted is like nothing else on earth, and you as a drafter must always have in mind the forces that will affect your product as it moves through the legislative process. Writers of other kinds of documents are usually aware of the factors that will determine how their words will be understood and evaluated; they can adjust those words to fit the situation, and remain more or less in control. Drafters cannot, and they must always be on the lookout for ways to protect themselves against unexpected amendments and adverse procedural turns.

Sometimes legislative language that effectively carries out the desired policy will be totally nullified by parliamentary or procedural restrictions if written in one way, but will survive unscathed if written in another. The latter option may not be available in a particular case, of course, for any one of a number of reasons; but it is your job as a drafter to find it if it is.

▶ 2.3   **Getting the policy right**

Most readers will expect this book to serve primarily as a manual that teaches legislative form and style; these are, after all, the aspects of bill drafting on which special instruction seems most necessary. In fact, the bulk of this book does concern itself with matters of form and style. Why then the repeated suggestion that the policy-related aspects of drafting are more important? The answer is simple: If a choice must be made, they *are* more important. As mentioned earlier, the technical aspects of drafting are straightforward objective matters, but getting the policy right is how drafters justify their existence. The ability to effectuate policy, rather than mere stylistic facility, is what separates the skilled drafter from the run-of-the-mill.

A bill may be full of stylistic and technical shortcomings, but if it clearly and correctly carries out the desired policy (without creating new substantive problems) it is far better than a beautifully crafted piece of work that doesn't.

▶ 2.4   Nonpartisanship and impartiality

A professional drafter who serves legislators of varying political persuasions must present a nonpartisan and nonpolitical image, and must maintain an impartial attitude concerning the policies to be converted into legislative language. This seems natural and proper enough to the author, since it reflects his own personal drafting experience; but he recognizes that other drafters will often be in a quite different position.

The typical drafter (operating outside of the congressional drafting offices and the corresponding offices in State legislatures) is more likely to serve a single person or entity who consistently advocates particular partisan policies. Obviously that drafter cannot be expected to be nonpartisan or nonpolitical, or to maintain an impartial attitude about the wisdom of the policies.

All drafters, however, must maintain an impartial attitude about their tasks in the sense that their professional concern with any assignment is solely to make sure that the bills they write will accurately reflect the sponsors' policies and will work. If you are an active player in a partisan environment, you must always remember, when wearing your drafter's hat, to be scrupulously objective in implementing that concern.

None of this should be taken to mean that the drafter has no part at all to play in the policy area, of course. As indicated earlier (and expanded upon in 4.7), helping to develop and refine the sponsor's policy is an integral part of your job as a drafter; the problem is how to do it without imposing your own substantive views upon the sponsor. The line is often fine but it is always there.

▶ 2.5   Confidentiality and privilege

Any legislative drafter who is an attorney and serves policymakers in an attorney-client relationship must of course treat everything that transpires between them as absolutely privileged and confidential. The attorneys in the congressional drafting offices and in nearly all of the corresponding State drafting offices fall within this category.

However, not every drafting relationship involving an attorney is attorney-client in nature, and many legislative drafters are not attorneys at all. Although every drafter is subject to some requirement of confidentiality, at least part of the time, the requirement is most often imposed simply as a means of protecting the sponsor's interests and promoting trust between sponsor and drafter.

Any strict requirement of confidentiality is likely to limit the drafter's access to needed information, of course. But if the sponsor refuses to permit an outside contact because the source of the information would be hostile, is considered untrustworthy, or would be a possible "leak", the drafter must live with it.

Because most professional drafters are subject to some requirement of confidentiality, they develop what is often described as a "passion for anonymity". If you are working on a bill but are forbidden to reveal what provisions it contains or to talk to anyone about your dealings with the sponsor, you're much better off (and can work more efficiently) if no one knows who you are. The legislative corridors are full of lobbyists and other partisans who will descend en masse on anyone they think they might influence; and professional drafting offices routinely try to keep their participation in particular legislative activities from becoming public knowledge or (failing that) to somehow prevent the partisans from congregating outside their doors. Surprisingly enough they usually succeed.

3

The Drafting
Process Itself

▶ **3.1   Preliminary comments**

The typical bill starts on its way because someone—usually a legislator or an agency official—believes that there is a problem that can be solved by legislation, and turns to a drafter for help. Whether the proposal is simple or complex, the drafter has a number of steps to take before actually writing a bill that will accomplish what the sponsor has in mind. This chapter offers only a general outline of the overall process—the details come later, beginning in part II with the preliminary steps—but a couple of comments are in order at the outset.

The first is that this book (except when addressing specific practical problems) always assumes what might be called the ideal drafting situation—one in which the sponsor provides a clear policy along with all necessary background information, the sponsor and the drafter can fully discuss the issues, and the drafter has carte blanche to write the bill in the way that seems best.

Unfortunately, except in States where all introduced bills are required to be drafted by the legislature's own in-house professional drafters (and such a requirement is not imposed by Congress or by most State legislatures), any sponsor may write a bill without calling upon a drafter at all. Or the sponsor may limit the drafter's function to a quick review of form and style—an unsatisfactory assignment for the drafter, who will usually detect more serious problems during the process. Obviously, in such cases the ideal situation does not exist.

The second is that most bills don't go anywhere after they are introduced, and their sponsors are usually realistic enough to understand this. Very few introduced bills are "taken seriously" (that is, actually considered by a committee or subcommittee). But you should never use this as an excuse for sloppy drafting, because sponsors want to make their points effectively and have their products admired and because some unlikely bills do become law despite the odds. As an example, the author worked on a bill, which was introduced in 1953, to make Ohio a State. The initial request was treated lightly and the bill was drafted amid great hilarity; but it eventually became Public Law 204 of the 83rd Congress, providing (effective as of March 1, 1803) that—

> the State of Ohio . . . is hereby declared to be one of the United States of America, and is admitted into the Union on an equal footing with the original States, in all respects whatsoever.

As it turned out, there had been an irregularity in Ohio's original admission, and some legal scholars felt that there were questions about Ohio's status that needed to be put to rest. The point, of course, is that the drafters' early flippancy could have caused substantial problems.

▶ **3.2** **Bill drafting as a multistep operation; a checklist**

Drafting any bill can be viewed simplistically as a continuous process divided into successive steps. Viewed this way you would—

> 1. make sure you understand the factual and legal problems to be dealt with—the problems that led the sponsor to seek legislative relief in the first place;
>
> 2. make sure you understand the main thrust of the sponsor's policy—how the sponsor proposes to deal head-on with those problems;
>
> 3. explore with the sponsor the possible ways of achieving the goal, pointing out the alternatives and their consequences;
>
> 4. identify and deal with any related questions that the implementation of the sponsor's policy may create, giving

particular attention to any provisions of existing law that may already deal with the subject and to the bill's effective date if it would play a significant part in implementing that policy;

5. decide upon the general approach to be taken in drafting the bill—whether it should be broad or narrow in scope, and whether it should be self-executing or rely heavily on administrative discretion and regulation;

6. decide upon the organization of the bill—what provisions need to be included, and how they should be arranged;

7. take account of the legislative context—the type of vehicle to be used and the effect of any parliamentary or constitutional restrictions; and

8. write the bill.

The tasks described in steps (1) through (5) might be regarded as primarily policy-related, and those described in steps (6) through (8) as primarily technical.

▶ **3.3**   **Bill drafting as a two-stage operation**

A checklist of the type described in 3.2 may have some instructional value, but it would be more realistic to view the drafting process as simply a two-stage operation, consisting of a preliminary (or preparatory) stage and a final (or writing) stage. The two stages can usefully be thought of as consecutive, even though they almost always overlap.

The preliminary stage of any legislative drafting effort involves the things you must do before beginning to write. This is usually the most important and demanding stage, encompassing all of the matters set forth in steps (1) through (7) of the checklist in 3.2; and the quality of the final product seldom rises above the quality of the work done at this stage.

These matters (which are the subject of chapters 4, 5, and 6) can often be disposed of quickly and easily, of course, but in major bills they constitute the heart of the drafting process. Needless to say, they are seldom addressed in any precise or preestablished order; and in many cases they can be dealt with more or less simultaneously.

Besides making certain that you correctly carry out the sponsor's policy, you must always remember that the bill is an effort to communicate that policy to a particular audience, and the nature of the audience has a great deal to do with the concepts you choose and the way you arrange them. A bill whose message is addressed primarily to government officials may need to be written differently from one addressed to the public, and a bill addressed to a specialized segment of the public (such as a particular industry) may need to be written differently from one addressed to the public at large. (As indicated earlier, in some fields it is often necessary to treat the relevant government officials as the audience even though the bill is being written for and about particular individuals or groups.) And you must often make a distinction between audiences even within a single bill.

Finally, you should constantly ask yourself, "If this were a statute addressed to me, how exactly would I go about carrying it out?", putting yourself in the shoes of the person who will have to administer the bill once it becomes law. The administrative world is full of esoteric requirements about which no drafter could be expected to know; and even professional drafters occasionally write bills that are unworkable simply because existing procedures (of which they were unaware) make it impossible for anyone to take the actions needed to achieve the desired result. If you don't understand the administrative ins and outs of the field you are working in, you should always know how to reach someone who does.

The final stage is of course the actual writing. This stage is usually the easiest and least time-consuming part of the process. Nevertheless it is obviously a critical stage, since the words once written do constitute the entire result of the process. No matter how sound the concept or how brilliant the analysis and treatment of the problems involved, the cause is lost if the language as finally drafted is inadequate to carry out the policy or is otherwise unsuitable. (And it goes without saying that the writing itself, like any other kind of writing, can present major problems in terms of how to start, what to say, how to say it, and how to finish it off.)

You should never forget that although your main objective—clarity—is primarily a matter that is achieved in the preliminary stage, it cannot be finally realized without careful attention to form and style. *Dickerson* (page 52) emphasizes that clarity does not come from the isolated application of any one stylistic rule but as the cumulative effect of all of them—"the aggregate result of a myriad of small operations"—and stresses (at pages 49-52) that the transition to the writing stage is not usually abrupt; the two stages blend imperceptibly, because substance and form cannot altogether be functionally divorced. The shift is mainly in emphasis. You will continue to be interested in substance up to the last minute, particularly since you will want to take full advantage of the substantive improvements that a systematic attention to matters of form and style inevitably makes possible. And you must avoid becoming so style-conscious that the more fundamental matters of substance are neglected; indeed, any sharp distinction between form and substance can do more harm than good, because it diverts attention from the fact that clarity and simplicity are more than sentence-deep.

In any event, despite the blurred nature of the line between the two drafting stages, this book will continue to emphasize the very real difference between them. But it is important to remember that the really crucial parts of a bill are often concocted hastily at the last minute, and that sometimes the greatest contribution you can make during both of the early stages is just to provide a workable framework for them.

▶ **3.4**   **An institutional drafter's perspective**

This book generally treats the drafter-sponsor relationship as one in which the drafter is responsible to an individual sponsor, such as a Member of Congress or a specific agency official, but in many (perhaps most) cases the potential reader will be an institutional drafter, responsible to an agency or organization as a whole. Everything that has been said about drafting for individual sponsors normally applies in institutional cases; but the institutional situation has a special flavor along with some unique problems that result from the hydra-headed nature of the sponsor.

If you are an institutional drafter, you receive your initial marching orders from an individual official of the agency or organization for which you work, and are entitled to think of that official as the primary policymaker; but before you are finished you will have had to deal with a number of different policymakers, and there is often no single source to which you can turn to mediate their conflicting positions. Although the policy specifications at the outset are usually no more vague and incomplete than the typical initial request of an individual sponsor, the drafter-sponsor relationship can become quite unmanageable when there are multiple policymakers to satisfy.

Since the policy comes from a number of different sources, some parts of the specifications may be more complete and precise than others, which may make resolving conflicts in policy positions more difficult for the drafter. In addition, at least some of the policymakers—those who had nothing to do with originating the proposal but who will nonetheless be called upon to sign off on the part that concerns them—may have little or no enthusiasm for the project and are likely to be significantly less helpful (and less accessible) than the others.

Institutional drafters do have two advantages over their non-institutional counterparts, however: Their policymakers almost always know the subject and understand the agency's probable position on it, and they are likely to have easier access to the future administrators.

▶ **3.5**   **The drafter at different stages of the legislative process**

The drafter's basic objective—carrying out the sponsor's policy accurately and effectively—is the same regardless of the stage of the legislative process; but the way the drafter functions, and the problems and difficulties likely to be encountered, will differ significantly from one stage to another. Indeed, for many drafters the ability to participate at all will diminish and may disappear altogether in the later stages.

Working on a bill to be introduced tends to be relatively leisurely. Nothing has yet been fed into the legislative mill, and most sponsors do want their product to be admired when it surfaces. Unless there are external pressures of a personal, political, or tactical nature, the sponsor will understand the drafter's need for time and information and will normally try to be accommodating.

The situation can quickly change after the bill is actually introduced. The drafter then begins working on amendments to be offered to the bill in subcommittee, in full committee, on the floor, or in conference; the work is likely to be fraught with time requirements, hidden agendas, and external factors over which no one has complete control.

Policymaking in committee or in conference is a collective operation; in a sense drafters become more "institutional" and their chief function is often just integrating suggestions that have been hastily thrown on the table rather than analyzing and refining any one sponsor's ideas. This is especially true when the committee is trying to operate on the basis of "consensus" rather than sheer political muscle.

One of the author's longtime colleagues was fond of saying

that the quality of the drafting in the early stages of a long and complicated bill is always better than in the later stages, and that good drafting toward the end of the process—when the bill is on the floor or in conference—is more the result of serendipity (and instinct based on experience) than of skill. This is probably true; and it emphasizes again the fact that good drafting in the early stages—especially good structure and organization—always gives the drafter a real advantage throughout the entire process.

▶ **3.6   Easing the task**

An experienced drafter regularly uses a number of techniques to make the job of planning, organizing, and writing a bill easier and less time-consuming. Some of these have been mentioned already (and all of them will be dealt with more fully later); but a few are particularly useful and deserve to be summarized in passing.

Working drafts and outlines.   If a bill is lengthy or at all complex, you should make an outline or working draft at the earliest possible moment. It need not be complete or include language on all the matters to be covered, as long as it leaves a slot for each provision which (so far as you can tell at the time) will eventually have to be included. Working from an outline or rough draft not only helps you arrange and integrate your materials properly, it also protects you against oversights and saves time.

Revisions.   You should expect to revise the working draft as often as may be necessary in order to perfect the language already written, correct your mistakes, fill in the empty slots, and otherwise keep things current; and you should plan your work on the basis of that expectation. Multiple revisions (with gradually increasing accuracy and completeness) are the hallmark of a sound drafting operation and should never be regarded as a cause for embarrassment or an indication of incompetence.

When you go through a series of discrete revisions, it is a good idea to designate each version as a "Tentative Draft" or "Working Draft", with a number or date to indicate its place in the succession. And be sure to save a copy of each version; not only will a complete collection of successive working drafts help you answer questions about where particular provisions came from, but sometimes provisions that were stricken in earlier revisions will be restored in later ones.

Definitions.   Whenever a bill repeatedly uses a crucial term that might be unclear or ambiguous, you should define it, placing the definition where it may most easily be found—at the place where it first occurs or in a special section or subsection devoted exclusively to definitions. This will not only clarify the meaning of the term; it also will help you express complex thoughts in an understandable way and promote "drafting economy" (*Hirsch*'s term), making the bill shorter and less repetitious and its language less cumbersome.

Although a number of writers have expressed reservations about the excessive use of definitions in statutes, you should use them whenever the occasion arises. The types and uses of definitions in drafting (along with the reservations of the doubters) are fully addressed in 11.7 and 23.2.

Cross-references.   In spite of the current tendency to make fun of legislative language that contains frequent incorporations by reference or purely informative cross-references, you should use them freely. There is no rational reason why a drafter who wants to invoke or refer to a particular provision by name or number shouldn't do so. Used correctly, cross-references save time, shorten the bill by avoiding repetition, and promote internal consistency. They are addressed more fully in 22.4 and 23.3.

Tables and tabulation.   You should freely use columnar tables to show relationships between numerical quantities, tabulated lists to enumerate items, and tabulated sentences in provisions that necessarily include several interrelated concepts or elements. These devices are among your most useful tools for dealing with complex concepts and avoiding ambiguity. They are discussed in depth in chapter 23.

Headings.   Section and subsection headings are highly visible when flipping through the pages of a draft and aid the reader in understanding the arrangement of the bill. They can also be of great value to you as a drafter, giving you an excellent road map that will help you locate provisions quickly and thereby save time and irritation, and helping you organize the bill by forcing you to provide logical places in advance for all the pieces. Chapter 20 contains a detailed discussion of headings and how to construct them; and chapter 31 sets forth literal examples of the types of headings used in all of the various Federal drafting styles.

Models and boilerplate forms.   In a surprising percentage of drafting assignments you will be able to find a previously written law, bill, or draft which (in its entirety or in one or more of its key provisions) is similar enough to what you are working on to serve as a useful model. The extent to which it will have to be modified before it can be used will differ from case to case, of course, but a good model can get you started and be your salvation in a difficult situation.

Both as a time-saver and as an accuracy-promoter, you should develop and maintain a reasonably complete file, based on your own previous efforts and other sources, of all the recurring forms you are likely to find useful in the field or fields in which you work (10.4 addresses the subject in detail).

Compilations and similar resource documents. When you work regularly in a particular field you should have at your side at all times a reliable compilation or other up-to-date version of the relevant law in that field. You should never have to stop what you are doing and go elsewhere to find a literal copy of a crucial provision if you can avoid it.

In addition, when your work involves a particular provision of existing law you will frequently need to know what other provisions of law may affect or be affected by it. A good cross-reference table, listing all the places (both within and without the statute involved) where that provision is cited can be a real lifesaver.

When a published compilation or cross-reference table is not available in your field, you would be well advised to make your own and keep it current—see 29.6. The time and effort required will repay you many times over.

Checking and polishing the draft. Needless to say, you should double-check your work periodically, and go through it one final time (after you are sure it is substantively correct) for the sole purpose of smoothing out any rough edges. It is particularly important that you look it over carefully each time you complete a major revision, checking the new or revised portions against the unchanged portions to make sure that the revision itself has not created any new internal inconsistencies. An absolutely perfect provision can sometimes be rendered inaccurate or inappropriate by new or revised language in a totally different part of the draft, and this is a kind of error that is very easy to miss.

Getting specialized help. When you need technical or other specialized assistance you should seek it from any source that is readily available to you. And you should never hesitate to seek help on specific *drafting* problems—all experienced drafters do. But beware of group drafting sessions, as *Dickerson* (page 49) emphasizes:

> [W]riting by conference . . . wastes time and talent. Groups can mull over ideas, they can criticize, and they can give or withhold approval, but they cannot compose concisely, consistently, or clearly. The wise draftsman refuses [when he can] to participate in such an endeavor.

The value of a nonspecialized sounding board. Totally apart from any technical or specialized needs you may have, as you go through the drafting process you should periodically seek someone who can serve as a sounding board. It is not necessary that the person be an expert on what you are trying to do; for everyday working purposes it is sometimes better not to have an expert, since what you are looking for is someone to help you see the forest as well as the trees. The author has often said (only partly in jest) that every drafter should acquire a deskside dressmaker's dummy just to have a good listener off whom ideas can be bounced; it is amazing how often the sound of your own voice explaining an idea can call its gaps and flaws to your consciousness.

Most of the suggestions contained here are just matters of common sense. It is true that a few of them—devices such as tabulated provisions, cross-references, and interrelated definitions—may occasionally intimidate people who are not used to reading statutes. But you should never forget that the target audience of most bills these days consists of administrators and legislative specialists, and they *are* used to reading statutes. For them these devices will actually improve readability.

15 / 5-96

Part II

The First Stage: Preparing
to Put Pen to Paper

Defining the Problem
and Its Solution

▶ **4.1 In general**

A sponsor who is a legislator, when seeking a drafter's help, is probably acting simply as a matter of personal philosophy or party policy, or as the result of a constituent's request. A sponsor who is an official of an agency or organization is more likely acting to carry out an institutional policy (and will have to find a sympathetic legislator to introduce the bill and take over the role of primary sponsor).

In either case the problem may be broad (like the need for a new national program) or narrow (like the need for an additional Assistant Secretary), or anything in between. But most bills taken seriously in any legislative forum are simply designed to clear up difficulties that have come to light in the everyday administration of some existing law or program. The impetus for such a bill, which might be viewed as being essentially a "housekeeping" measure even though it can have major substantive impact, usually comes from the agency that administers the program involved and is responsible for making it work properly, from a legislator who serves on the committee that is responsible for monitoring its operation, or from a private organization whose interests are affected.

And occasionally the "problem" is not really a problem at all, but simply a perceived need to make a statement of some kind, to give recognition to some person or circumstance, to call attention to some situation, or just to tidy up the law. Common examples are "sense of Congress" resolutions, bills changing the names of existing public buildings, and bills providing for new national holidays or celebrations.

Your job as a drafter, of course, is to help the sponsor put into legislative form what the sponsor wants in substance, and to accomplish it as smoothly and effectively as possible. Your first instinct (after receiving the sponsor's request) may be to reach for a pencil, but experienced drafters know that the first instinct *should* be to look for questions to ask. In many cases the sponsor's substantive ideas are imperfectly formed, providing no more than a set of general objectives; and you must help to refine those objectives before you can hope to develop a practical means for carrying them out.

You ideally should be brought into the picture long before the writing begins in order to find out as much as possible about what the sponsor is trying to accomplish and about how the sponsor wants to attack the problem. You must be fully informed on both the underlying policy and its factual setting in order to discharge your central responsibility.

You must often engage in a continuing exchange of ideas with the sponsor or the sponsor's staff in order to be sure that your understanding is correct and complete and that the sponsor can live with the consequences. You must help the sponsor think the problem through, pointing out any substantive inconsistencies and any administrative, legal, constitutional, and practical difficulties that the sponsor ought to know about.

In addition, since you may need more information than can be supplied by the sponsor, you must often pick the brains of whatever expert advisers (legislative, executive, or nongovernmental) may be available to you in order to fill in the substantive, legal, and technical gaps.

As statute law becomes more and more complex, you are almost *required* to develop a good working knowledge of the substantive field in which you are working. You must know the statutory environment, just as an architect must know the building site, so that what you draft will fit smoothly and workably in that environment. More often than not the initial stage of your work on any bill requires a thorough examination and analysis of the laws already on the books in the field involved, with the objective of making absolutely certain that all of your legal ducks are neatly in a row before the actual writing begins. In most well-run legislative drafting offices each drafter specializes in one or two substantive areas, because that is the only way to develop the necessary substantive expertise.

The drafter's relationship with the sponsor in the process of learning about the problem and working out the desired solution is the most critical element in the drafting of any bill. It is the purpose of this chapter to examine some of the things which are commonly involved in that process (4.2 and 4.3 address the subject head-on; 4.4-4.9 deal with specific aspects of the subject that deserve separate mention).

▶ **4.2   Recognizing the problem**

In most cases you will have no trouble grasping what the problem is and what you are supposed to do about it. The sponsor simply says in effect "here is my problem—fix it"; and in its broad outlines, at least, the challenge seems clear. But in many cases a little thought reveals that it is not clear at all.

If the proposal is very broad or the subject matter is unusually complicated, so that only a specialist would be likely to understand all the ramifications, the remedy is plain (if the sponsor is willing): Find someone who does understand them, and pick that person's brains.

But when the sponsor is acting on a complaint or suggestion from someone else and simply passes the matter along to the drafter with a request for legislation to take care of the situation, life can be more difficult. In most such cases neither the sponsor nor the drafter questions the facts as presented; but surprisingly often the drafter's analysis raises doubts about what they really are. The approach that immediately suggests itself, of course, is to keep badgering the sponsor until you are satisfied that you have all the facts—the sponsor will usually have better access to them than you do—but unfortunately this is not always feasible or politic.

Uncharitable persons might be tempted to say that sponsors should do their homework better before disturbing the drafter's repose, but this would not be entirely fair. Legislators and agency officials are not specialists, investigators, or drafters, and within limits they are entitled to rely on those who are to deal with the details involved in carrying out their objectives.

And in many cases the situation as presented to them will have been incomplete, misunderstood, or misstated by the complainant or other source, or at least "edited" by someone so as to characterize the situation in the light most favorable to the complainant's case.

Making sure of the factual situation that gives rise to a particular proposal is critically important, however, both for the sponsor (who wants to avoid subsequent regrets about having taken on the project) and for the drafter (who needs to be sure the problem has actually been solved). What can you do when there is a question about the correctness of the information you have been given?

Obviously, you should not proceed without doing whatever you can as a practical matter to make sure (through conversations with the sponsor or the sponsor's staff, consultations with experts, contacts with the persons on whose behalf the sponsor is acting, or otherwise) that you have the true picture. If circumstances prevent a full investigation, you may have no choice but to accept the facts as given to you, despite your suspicions about their incompleteness or possible distortion. At a minimum, however, you should alert the sponsor to these suspicions so that the matter can be further looked into, making it clear that the bill as you propose to write it, based on the information at hand, may in fact not achieve its intended purpose.

▶ 4.3   Understanding the policy

Types of policy questions.   As indicated in 1.3, a sponsor's basic policy (which defines the general objective) is only part of the policy picture; it often presents the drafter with questions of subsidiary policy and collateral policy that can be equally troublesome.

In a proposal to provide for the establishment of a commission to study fraud and abuse in a major Federal program, for example, the question of just what should be studied and the question of what should be done with the information gathered would of course constitute "basic" policy questions; but such things as the makeup and organization of the commission, the compensation of its members, the timing of the study, and whether the Federal Advisory Commission Act should apply are policy questions as well.

The questions about makeup and organization, compensation, and timing are "subsidiary" policy questions for our purposes because (although they are not part of the main thrust of the basic policy, and may not even matter to the sponsor) they are integral to the basic policy and must necessarily be answered in the bill, one way or another, in order to complete it. They cannot simply be ignored.

The question about the application of the Federal Advisory Commission Act is "collateral", since the basic policy would seem to be complete and coherent even if the question were totally overlooked—the Advisory Commission Act would simply apply or not apply in accordance with its terms. (Note, however, that that Act could so integrally restrict the functioning of the commission if it did apply that the question takes on a strongly "subsidiary" flavor.)

Extracting the policy.   Once the problem is clear, the next order of business is its solution. And it goes without saying that, since the policy to be carried out (basic, subsidiary, and collateral) is the sponsor's choice, the drafter must look to the sponsor in order to understand it.

The typical drafting operation involves a colloquy between the drafter and the sponsor or the sponsor's staff that may take 30 seconds or may continue over a period of days, weeks, or months, resurfacing intermittently as new questions arise. And if the subject or its factual setting is highly technical and complicated, and the sponsor is willing, most of the colloquy may turn out to be with experts and specialists. The process continues until everything is clear, however long that takes.

Actually, the drafter will seldom experience any difficulty understanding the *basic* policy to be carried out in a bill, since a sponsor typically does not seek drafting help to solve a problem without a reasonably firm idea of what the solution is. The sponsor's main thrust is the one thing you will always be told about up front; and a few well-chosen questions will almost always clear up any ambiguity.

But being clear about the subsidiary and collateral policy issues, which can be extremely important to sponsors (once they are reminded of them, at least), is not quite so automatic. Usually sponsors are preoccupied with the main thrust, and often do not even think about these issues until prodded, either because it never occurs to them to do so or because they assume that the drafters will identify and present them for consideration in due time.

Since the subsidiary and collateral issues are easy for sponsors to overlook or postpone, drafters must focus on them; and doing this is frequently their most important single contribution. These issues generally fall into one of three categories:

1. Questions about the individual pieces of the puzzle—the separate elements that combine to make up the basic policy as a whole. Examples are the questions about makeup, organization, compensation, and timing in the study commission case discussed earlier.

2. Substantive questions that result from what the basic policy does. When you tamper with any provision of law that affects another provision of law, for example, it is likely that changes in the other provision will be needed to repair the damage; and when you write any totally new provision there may be existing provisions that will be rendered ineffective or inconsistent (or will prevent the new provision from working in the intended way) unless they are changed to reflect it. The changes involved (which are sometimes called "cleaning up the debris" by drafters) are often of a purely technical and conforming nature, but many of them involve serious substantive considerations too.

3. Questions involving breadth and specificity. These are discussed more fully in 4.5.

Policy alternatives.   It is certainly true that many problems might be rationally addressed in any one of several ways. A particular kind of undesirable conduct could be flatly prohibited and made subject to criminal or civil penalties, for example, or regulated, subjected to strict licensing requirements, or taxed. Or abstinence from that kind of conduct could be made a condition of eligibility for related benefits. Or a study commission could be established to look into the problem and make recommendations (thereby postponing the evil day when something actually has to be done about it).

If you think a particular approach might carry out the stated objective better than the one suggested by the sponsor, you should diplomatically make sure that the sponsor understands the alternatives. Remember that different approaches can have different consequences, and make sure that the sponsor is aware of them. A prohibition is a prohibition, but whether the penalty is criminal or civil has a good deal to do with how enforceable it is. And attacking undesirable conduct by licensing or taxing it, or rewarding abstinence, may discourage that conduct by making it more expensive but has the effect of legitimizing it.

A case study of what can happen when the problem is complicated and the possible consequences of the policy adopted are not fully thought out is presented in 4.8.

Lack of policy altogether. The message contained in the preceding paragraphs is, of course, that the actual writing of a bill cannot progress very far (and sometimes cannot even be properly begun) until the sponsor has made the policy clear.

But the hard practicalities of political life often make it more important for the sponsor to have something on paper that can be waved about—an "idea draft" setting forth the main thrust without frills—than for all of the policy questions to be resolved immediately. And when the sponsor demands that a bill be drafted overnight to accomplish some vaguely described objective, you cannot simply abdicate but must do the best you can.

If the sponsor wants to introduce a bill or offer an amendment primarily to make a political point (and doesn't care whether it is technically correct), or to introduce the bill or offer the amendment immediately for tactical or procedural reasons and let others clean it up at a later stage, the sponsor may be quite unwilling (or unable) to accommodate the drafter's needs.

It is sad but true that gaps and defects in a bill (unless they would defeat the main thrust or are highly visible) do not usually matter as much to the sponsor as they do to the drafter. The sponsor appreciates technical perfection, of course, but is well aware of the fact that the media will support the effort, and give credit, on the basis of the main thrust alone; technical shortcomings are not very newsworthy (at least until the bill becomes law and some spectacular misfire occurs). There is nothing really wrong with this; proper timing and political support are the things that make a bill move, and in addition the necessary perfecting can almost always be done at a later stage.

Some sponsors seem to believe that simply asking a drafter for a bill will automatically produce one on their desk the following morning, as if by magic. But even those who understand full well what the drafter faces, when tormented by tight time schedules or tactical dilemmas, sometimes say in effect "You're the drafter, and I've told you what I want to do—just give me a bill I can use and don't bother me with all these trivial questions''. It happens more frequently than you might suspect.

What do you do? Sometimes you must simply resign yourself (if you want to keep your job) to being a good stenographer instead of a good legal technician. Often, though, you can still do a creditable job by following these suggestions:

1. If the unanswered question is collateral in the sense that it can be ignored without making the bill incomplete or internally inconsistent (even though you think the sponsor might regard it as important), ignore it.

2. If the unanswered question leaves a gap that would make the bill incomplete or inconsistent, and you can fill the gap with language that is fairly neutral and is commonly used in similar situations, do so. With any luck you can find a respectable model to use. But make sure the sponsor knows you are simply offering that language for consideration as one of several possible rational approaches—not recommending it.

3. If the gap is one that could conceivably be filled by administrative fiat and there is an appropriate administrator in the picture somewhere, explicitly leave the matter to that administrator's regulations.

In any event you should make absolutely certain that the sponsor is aware of what you have done, and why; and for your own protection, when you deliver the bill, you should attach a note spelling out your misgivings unless you are completely secure about your lines of communication and about how the sponsor will handle the bill. It's not a bad idea to designate the bill itself a "TENTATIVE DRAFT" even though it is as "final" as you can make it, and let the sponsor cross out those words if it is introduced or otherwise made public without first resolving its problems.

▶ **4.4**　　**Clarity, consistency, and organization**

The one overriding requirement of all good legislative drafting is clarity, and there are two basic principles or techniques that are of particular importance in achieving it:

1. You must relentlessly strive for complete internal consistency in all respects—form, style, terminology, expression, and arrangement. Nothing will do more to obscure the intended meaning than failure to do this. The subject is addressed in more detail in chapter 7.

2. You must make certain that the bill—both in its overall contours and in particular sections, subsections, and paragraphs—is organized and arranged in a systematic and logical manner, so as to clearly indicate the nature and relative position of each element in the hierarchy of the sponsor's ideas. This is the subject of chapter 6.

Each of these techniques facilitates comparison and recognition, making it easier for you to uncover substantive problems and policy considerations that would otherwise have been missed and enabling you to exert the constructive influence on policy formulation described in 4.7.

▶ **4.5   Approach, breadth, and specificity**

When sponsors mull over the approach they ought to take in solving a problem through legislation, they are thinking about the main thrust: What exactly should the proposal accomplish?

On the other hand, when you, the drafter, are considering the approach to be taken, you already know what the sponsor's basic policy will be. What you should be thinking about is the way in which you might best carry out that policy: Should the bill be broad or narrow in its coverage? Should it be general or specific in its administrative details? How should it be organized? Should it amend existing law or be freestanding? These are questions that have a technical flavor, since the sponsor's policy can be effectively carried out regardless of how they are answered, and they can fairly be considered to be (at least concurrently) within the drafter's province; but they themselves may raise a new and totally different set of policy questions.

Questions of this kind pose a common dilemma for the drafter, who may legitimately participate in the process of answering them but (as always in the case of policy questions, even minor ones) must still leave the final decision to the sponsor unless it is certain that there are no substantive or tactical overtones. Every drafter should be conscious of them, and it may be worthwhile to examine a few of them briefly.

How broad or narrow?   Some bills are broad or narrow in their scope as a matter of necessity. A bill to establish a comprehensive system for reducing the Federal deficit across the board just cannot be approached narrowly, while a bill to simply extend some expiring Federal program for one additional year (without making substantive changes) is narrow and specific by its very nature. In these cases the scope of the bill is conclusively determined by the sponsor's main thrust, and neither the sponsor nor the drafter has to face a decision on whether the approach should be broad or narrow.

Many proposals, however, present both the sponsor and the drafter with a wide range of possible choices. As indicated earlier, in most instances a bill is triggered by a very specific case but will nonetheless be general in its application, so that a decision has to be made about the extent to which the bill's coverage might be extended to other cases that are similarly situated. This in turn requires a decision about which similarities are sufficiently important to warrant the extension—that is, a decision about what "similarly situated" means (which is a matter of the sponsor's policy).

Assume, for example, that the sponsor requests a bill to overhaul the appeals procedure in disability cases based on mental illness under the social security program. The request almost certainly arises out of the denial of one specific mentally ill individual's claim for disability benefits under that program, but several questions of breadth immediately suggest themselves:

1. Should the bill also cover appeals involving other kinds of disability under the same program? Maybe; it would probably depend on the specific grounds for the denial— that is, on the nature of the alleged procedural defects that caused it. Some kinds of defects would be unique to mental disability cases, some would not. (And some kinds of defects might be uniquely related to the particular kind of mental disorder involved in the constituent's case, creating the possibility that the bill should be narrowed instead.)

2. Should consideration be given to extending the bill to include appeals in disability cases under the supplemental security income (SSI) program? Probably yes, because the administrative provisions of the two programs are similar and in many respects identical (and in fact are largely shared, with one administrative determination being effective under both programs).

3. What about including appeals under still other disability-related programs—railroad retirement, medicare, medicaid, and various programs under the public health laws? Probably not; although the railroad retirement and social security programs are closely interrelated in many ways

(including disability determinations), there is very little symmetry in the other cases. And in addition the inclusion of any of them would raise serious questions of committee jurisdiction. The sponsor would probably not want to extend the bill's coverage that far unless the alleged defect is thought to be so widespread that an across-the-board attack is justified despite the jurisdictional problems.

And all of this may be only the beginning, since cost, politics, tactics, and strategy, which in many cases could be important considerations to the sponsor, have been ignored.

In any event, the bill could be written narrowly to cover only cases exactly like the sponsor's case—limiting it to a single type of disability under a single set of circumstances within a single program—or it could be written more broadly so as to cover other cases (few or many) that are similar but not identical. The former would be easier to draft (and probably to get through Congress) but might create an entirely new and different set of problems by providing discriminatorily different treatment for substantially similar cases. The latter might be more equitable but would cost more, raise jurisdictional questions, and risk covering at least some situations that ought to be governed by quite different considerations.

As a drafter you cannot make these decisions for yourself, since they would have very real substantive consequences. But you must always make sure that the sponsor is aware of the choices and their rationales and understands the consequences. And when the sponsor's decision is based on cost or on political considerations, you must of course take that into account in any advice you give.

Specific or general? An apparently similar but actually quite different dilemma (also briefly mentioned earlier) involves the degree of specificity with which you should describe how the proposal is to work in practice.

On the one hand, you cannot possibly provide a specific answer to every question that could conceivably arise under the bill—indeed you cannot even identify them all—and the harder you try the more likely it is that you will introduce impediments to sensible administrative judgment.

On the other hand, if the sponsor's policy has been well crystallized, most of the individually important questions that will arise often enough to be significant can usually be foreseen; and the bill can (if the sponsor so desires) spell out in detail exactly how the administering agency is to carry it out, specifying such things as the standards to be applied, the procedures to be followed, and any organizational changes within the agency that may be required.

There are several factors to consider. Some situations are best left to future administrative (or judicial) determination. And if the sponsor's policy has intentionally or unavoidably been left in general terms, the development of more specific guidelines may have to be left to the administering agency. In addition, elaborate legislative structures almost always require complex administrative procedures to give them effect, and the more these are expressly included in the bill the less likely the bill is to work as the sponsor intended. It may be desirable to phrase the bill in general (and even deliberately vague) terms, simply telling the agency what it is supposed to accomplish and leaving the specifics to its rules, regulations, and administrative practices.

The general approach is easier and less time-consuming to draft, covers a multitude of sins (it is very useful when there is no time to work out the details), and avoids interfering with flexible good-faith administration by imposing too many restrictions. Most legislators, however, feel that undue reliance on administrative discretion is dangerous, and they generally prefer to see most of the necessary standards and procedures (to the extent they can agree on them) spelled out. In the end, most bills result in a compromise of these approaches (as they do on the question of breadth discussed earlier).

▶ **4.6**   **Different bills, different challenges**

Bills come in all sizes, shapes, and textures, and all policies are not equally burdensome to the drafter. The way in which you approach your task can differ markedly from one assignment to another depending on the nature and scope of the proposals involved; and naturally enough the differences are most significant during the preliminary stage, while you are trying to figure out just what to put into the bill and how to arrange it.

The policy involved in a relatively straightforward and specific proposal is likely to be quite clear, with few subsidiary or collateral problems; but the policies involved in a broader or relatively nonspecific proposal, or one that intimately affects or is affected by a complicated body of existing law, may be another story altogether. Drafting assignments range from one extreme to the other, of course, but most of them fall easily into the somewhat arbitrary hierarchy of difficulty which follows.

One-shot proposals of limited scope, without predictable complications. In such a proposal the policy is likely to be quite clear; there may be problems to deal with, and there may be a few collateral questions, but there should be nothing that can't be handled with relative ease.

Assume for example that you are asked to draft a bill to provide a one-year authorization of funds for an existing program. The basic policy is perfectly clear, and its factual background is almost immaterial. You are presumably told the amount to be authorized and the fiscal year involved, and you can easily locate the provision of law that contains the program's existing authorization of funds. Normally all that remains is to make a simple amendment to that provision.

If for example the authorization provision is located in section 8(c) of the ABC Act and currently reads:

> (c) To carry out the program under this Act there is authorized to be appropriated—
>
>> (1) $1,000,000 for the fiscal year 1991; and
>>
>> (2) $2,000,000 for the fiscal year 1992.

your amendment might read something like this:

> SEC. _____. Section 8(c) of the ABC Act is amended—
>
>> (1) by striking "and" at the end of paragraph (1);
>>
>> (2) by striking the period at the end of paragraph (2) and inserting "; and"; and
>>
>> (3) by adding after paragraph (2) the following new paragraph:
>>
>> "(3) $3,000,000 for the fiscal year 1993.".

The only other thing you would normally need to do is make sure there are no time-related or amount-related provisions in the ABC Act that might be affected by what you have done—for example, a specific cutoff date for the filing of applications, or a provision limiting the amount of any grant to a specified percentage of the funds currently available (in which case your amendment taken by itself could result in an increase in the maximum grant amount). You should scan the rest of the Act; and if you find any such provision you should either conform it or (if your course is not clear) raise the question with the sponsor.

One-shot proposals of limited scope, with predictable complications. The complications most often arise because the proposal must be woven into a statutory tapestry which is already complicated and the various parts of which are extensively interrelated. The subsidiary policies are likely to be only partially clear, and you must be especially wary of collateral problems.

Assume that you are asked to draft a bill increasing social security benefits for widows by a specified percentage. Superficially the request sounds quite straightforward; but in fact it is not clear at all.

Aside from a few esoteric questions involving mathematics and computation formulas that must normally be left to the specialists, there are a number of policy questions (basic, subsidiary, and collateral) on which you need to inform yourself at the outset. For example:

1. What kind of widows are we talking about? There are several types that can receive social security benefits. Probably the sponsor has had complaints from one or more widows receiving "widow's insurance benefits", which are derivative benefits payable to widows (on the work records of their deceased husbands) because they are aged or disabled. But there are also widows (age and physical condition immaterial) who receive derivative benefits—called "mother's insurance benefits"—because they have minor children in their care. In addition, there are still some very elderly widows on the rolls who are getting nonderivative widow's benefits (gratuitously) because their husbands' working lifetimes ended before social security coverage became available.

And there may even be a question about whether the sponsor means to include women who are receiving nonderivative benefits (as retired workers or otherwise) and who just happen to be widows, as well as individuals receiving derivative benefits because they are widows.

Most sponsors would probably limit their proposals to the first category of widows—aged or disabled widows receiving "widow's insurance benefits"—since that is what most people mean when speaking of widows under social security.

2. What about widowers and their benefits? This is a collateral question, of course, but the Supreme Court has made the equal treatment of widows and widowers under the program a matter of constitutional necessity, so it needs to be raised. Most sponsors would include them.

3. What about the effect of the proposal on the rest of the widow's family? The "family maximum" provisions in the social security law place a ceiling on the total amount of monthly benefits that can be paid (to all family members) on the basis of any one individual's work record. Thus if you increase the widow's benefits but the family includes other beneficiaries who are eligible on the same work record, she will indeed get more but the others will get less—since the total would have to remain the same—unless you do something about it.

Once you are clear about what you are supposed to do and who you are supposed to do it to, the actual writing should present no major problems.

(The author recognizes that social security is a complicated and specialized field, and that you could not be expected to recognize these problems without developing more expertise in it than you have any use for. But the problems it presents are typical of the approach you must frequently take before beginning to write midsized bills in many fields—nothing is truly simple anymore.)

One-shot proposals of broader scope, within a single statutory area. Such a proposal normally involves several different basic policies—the typical "reform bill" is a good example—rather than being limited to just one or two specific points. Although the general objectives are usually clear, the specific policy is likely to be fuzzy everywhere, with related collateral problems in abundance.

Assume that you are asked to draft a bill establishing a major new program in an area not covered by any existing law. This is not necessarily more difficult just because it is broader; but it is demanding because you will be starting from scratch, with no existing framework in which to put it, and you will need many questions answered before you can begin:

1. The most basic questions involve the main thrust itself, of course: What is the purpose of the program, and how is it supposed to work? For example:

A. If it is a loan or grant program, who can qualify for

assistance, and how do they go about getting it? For what activities can the proceeds be used? How should you set the amount of the assistance? What should the other terms and conditions of the assistance be?

B. If it is a construction program, what exactly is to be built, and where? Who is to do it? What should the specifications, cost limits, and time requirements be? How should the work be contracted for, and what should the contracts contain?

C. If it is a regulatory program, who is to be regulated, and what activities? How is the regulatory process to be conducted? Are there constitutional difficulties, and if so what can be done about them?

2. The new program will obviously need funding: How much should be authorized to be appropriated, and for what period? If it is a loan program, should repayments (and interest earned) be available for making new loans, through a revolving fund or otherwise?

3. There will be a number of subsidiary and collateral policy questions that involve organization and administration: Who will administer the new program? If an existing officer or agency is to do it, are the existing administrative procedures adequate, should new offices or positions be created, and how will the new functions fit into the agency's existing framework? If a new agency is to do it, what organizational and operating characteristics should it be given?

4. It is important that the administering officer or agency possess the capacity to actually carry out the functions conferred: What general powers and operating authorities should that officer or agency be given? If the program is placed within an existing agency, will that agency's existing enumeration of general powers (which would automatically apply) be sufficient? And if a new agency is to be created to run the program, what everyday operating powers should it have? (Since enumerations of agency powers typically have an element of boilerplate in them, a good model would be very useful here, and one can generally be found).

5. The new program must actually work, of course: How will it be monitored and its requirements enforced? Should beneficiaries or other participants be required to give

specified assurances before qualifying, or report periodically on their use of the funds made available? Should the administering officer or agency be required to report periodically on the operation of the program generally or on the extent to which it is achieving its objectives? Should there be penalties (over and above any existing penalties that may apply automatically) for misuse of funds or failure to comply with the applicable requirements?

This is a sampler only, of course, because the variations among programs are wide even when they are of the same general type, and obviously every bill creating a program of any substance will require provisions that are unique to that program. Thus a bill involving scientific research or a new technology (like NASA) will normally contain provisions relating to patents, while a bill involving particularly sensitive subjects (like defense or nuclear energy, or commercial trade secrets) is likely to contain provisions relating to matters of security. And a bill establishing any kind of Federal-State operating arrangement (under State plans or otherwise) must of course spell out the details.

Multipurpose and omnibus bills.   Such a bill combines proposals in totally different statutory areas and typically consists entirely of individual segments (related or unrelated), each of which falls into one of the other three categories. As a drafter you would normally treat each of those segments as a separate project.

It may be worthy of mention in passing that most bills which are taken seriously at the Federal level are amendatory rather than freestanding, and that the amendatory approach itself will often involve special problems even in bills that are otherwise quite uncomplicated—see part V.

It is not always possible to predict the specific problems that will surface in any drafting assignment—collateral policy questions are particularly elusive—but anyone who drafts regularly soon learns (too often the hard way) to sense the probable difficulties that will be involved in the assignments that come along. Actually, of course, most bills are relatively uncomplicated, and whenever you conclude that a particular drafting assignment is truly simple and straightforward you can relax somewhat. But be careful—some of the simplest-looking assignments turn out to be riddled with problems.

▶ **4.7**   **The drafter as a participant in policy formulation**

In its repeated emphasis upon the distinction between policy-making and drafting, this book may sometimes give the impression that neither has anything to do with the other. Nothing could be further from the author's intention, so a few words on the subject may be in order.

How far can you, the drafter, be legitimately concerned with substantive policy? You do not make the policy, of course, but you can quite properly influence it in many ways. And while it would be wrong to intrude yourself into matters of policy that are the sponsor's prime responsibility, it would be equally wrong to let yourself be relegated to the status of a mere stenographer. In practice there is a considerable gray area.

A request from a sponsor usually focuses on the main thrust; it seldom includes everything that you need to know about the specifics of the proposal, and one of your most important functions as a drafter is the questioning which is necessary to complete the picture. The questions you ask, no matter how neutrally they are phrased, inevitably have the effect of suggesting (without actually recommending, of course) policy positions for the sponsor to take.

In addition, it is your professional obligation as a drafter to advise the sponsor on the workability of the proposal as well as to devise the language to carry it out; most sponsors find it hard to visualize the impracticability of a favorite proposal or to recognize and evaluate all the problems it raises. You must always be prepared to confront the sponsor with the legal and practical consequences of the proposal.

You must do these things, of course, in a way that does not encroach upon the sponsor's prerogatives; you cannot inject your own substantive views into the sponsor's policy formulation, and must act with scrupulous objectivity to carry out the sponsor's purpose even when you strongly disagree with it. And if in some respects you find yourself leading the sponsor, you must always be sure you are leading in the direction in which the sponsor wants to go.

There are some risks, of course, in playing the devil's advocate to sponsors who are accustomed to having their own way without question. It requires a high degree of tact and diplomacy. But you must always be sure both that you understand what the sponsor is trying to accomplish and that the sponsor understands the problems. Be deliberate and don't be afraid to ask questions. What you are seeking is a meeting of the minds, enabling you to "fill in the chinks" without overstepping your proper function.

People who are accustomed to black-and-white choices may be uncomfortable with the drafter's peculiar shade of gray; but it is important to understand that your contributions, especially during the initial stages, can have a salutary effect on the sponsor's policy formulation even though you are not a policymaker yourself. Always remember that your specialized approach, training, and experience will often enable you to discover fundamental problems (substantive, legal, adminis- trative, or practical) that the sponsor has overlooked.

The important thing is this: Simply asking sensible questions at the outset and then using good drafting practices—com- plete consistency and rational arrangement above all—will do more to uncover ambiguities, contradictions, gaps, and other policy-related discrepancies in a proposal than all the mental gymnastics in the world.

▶ 4.8   **Case study of a policy gone awry**

As a means of putting some flesh on the bones of what has just been said, it may be instructive to look briefly at a well- known Federal statute that is operating today, for better or worse, in a way which (in the judgment of the author and many others) bears little resemblance to the way it was originally intended to operate.

In the 1960s the nation was preoccupied with organized crime, and Congress undertook to do something about it. There was no consensus on just what constituted "organized crime", but it was generally agreed that it involved such things as drug dealing, prostitution, and extortion and was carried on primarily by labor bosses, undesirable foreigners, and racketeers.

Under the Constitution most crime is a State responsibility, but a basis for Federal action was found in the assumption that organized crime crosses State lines, requiring a central- ized effort to coordinate the fight in a manner analogous to the antitrust laws (which had also involved the Federal Government in matters previously left to the States). The result was the addition of a new chapter 96 in title 18 of the United States Code, entitled "Racketeer Influenced and Cor- rupt Organizations" (RICO).

RICO (having nothing more concrete to fall back on in the way of a definition) set forth a list of Federal and State crimes thought to be characteristic of organized criminal conduct, and defined a "racketeer" to mean anyone who engaged in any two or more of those crimes. The list did not stop with the crimes mentioned above, however, but (presumably in an exercise of caution) added literally dozens of unrelated offenses, major and minor (including a raft of unidentified and undefined State crimes). And in order to supplement the criminal penalties and aid in enforcement, RICO also picked up a provision from the Clayton Act for payment of treble damages (as a civil penalty) to any private person harmed by a violation.

For years the law lay more or less dormant—it didn't seem to help much in the fight against organized crime after all—and the treble damage remedy was largely forgotten. But the utility of that remedy in some of the more mundane legal disputes covered by the overly broad list (along with the broadened opportunities it provided for legal discovery) was eventually noticed, and RICO gradually came to be used in a number of garden-variety business fraud cases, including disputes between competing religious organizations and between pro-abortion and anti-abortion factions. RICO today is more often used as a means of settling everyday legal disputes than as a means of combatting organized crime.

Some of the original policymakers still claim they planned it this way, but that seems unlikely to the author. Eminent jurists (including several members of the Supreme Court) have suggested that the law may be unconstitutionally vague, considering the possibility of such expansive interpretations, and Congress regularly takes a stab at limiting its application.

To say the least, Congress did not sufficiently dwell upon the implications of inserting the treble damage remedy or take fully into account the effect of defining organized crime so broadly.

▶ 4.9   **Some everpresent real-life drafting problems**

When you, as a drafter, find that you are prevented by circumstances beyond your control from doing the job right, it is as certain as death and taxes that you either don't understand the policy or are facing one or more of the following problems (which may, of course, be the reason *why* you don't understand the policy):

Lack of substantive expertise.   A hundred years ago there were relatively few Federal laws on the books, and the ones that existed were relatively simple. Those times are gone.

Today Government at every level generates vast quantities of legislation in areas that were left untouched not too long ago, and it is increasingly complex, specialized, and interrelated. And the number of court cases and regulations interpreting and implementing that legislation has risen by an even greater degree.

In order to work effectively in any substantive field, you need a reasonably good knowledge and understanding of the existing law (statutes, court cases, and regulations) in that field; without it you can never be certain that you have identified and understood all the problems and have found all the cross references and interrelated provisions in the relevant existing law. This is true whether the bill you are writing is amendatory or freestanding.

It is difficult to work in an unfamiliar field or amend an unfamiliar statute, regardless of your qualifications. But if you actually read the relevant laws and seek expert help wherever you can find it, you should survive. And if all else fails and you must simply do the best you can and hope for divine guidance, you should cling to the thought that you are not alone—*most* bills when introduced have gaps and flaws that have to be corrected later. Just be sure to warn the sponsor of any potential problems that you know about.

Lack of legal training. Legal and constitutional questions do, of course, come up in the drafting process, and when they arise you must confront them. You must always be certain that the legal effect of the words you use is the desired effect, and that those words will not cause unnecessary litigation or other avoidable legal problems in the future. Naturally, attorneys have an advantage over nonattorneys in this area, but it is not as great as you might think.

For one thing, most bills do not involve any significant legal or constitutional questions at all, and common sense plus a reasonable familiarity with legislation will go a long way in helping you identify those that do. A bill to establish a new national holiday is unlikely to have any problems of this kind while a bill to revise the antitrust laws would almost certainly be full of them. And most drafters are likely to have access to legal help within their agency or organization, and can seek that help whenever there is reason to suspect legal complications.

For another, since they tend to be the thorniest problems that a drafter faces, legal problems in a bill (unless they are very simple) are the ones that even professional drafters most often leave unresolved, to be worked out at a later date by the legal staff of the committee to which the bill is referred.

And finally, just being an attorney does not automatically give a drafter complete mastery over the legal aspects of a bill. An attorney-drafter who is a specialist in one field may still be totally unfamiliar with cases and legal principles that are important in another, and thus face the same disadvantages as one who is not an attorney.

Lack of time.   Drafting bills in a fraction of the time needed is the story of the drafter's life in far too many cases. Drafters do not control legislative schedules; bills are introduced, taken up, and acted upon when the legislators themselves think it best, and they have no choice but to be ready when the gavel falls.

If what you have been called upon to prepare is a bill for introduction, there is often a deadline because of committee schedules or simply because the sponsor (for political or tactical reasons) wants the bill to burst upon an unsuspecting public on a certain day or in connection with a certain event. If it is a revision of a bill which has already been introduced and is due for consideration in a committee or on the floor, or it is an amendment to such a bill, it must of course be ready by the time that bill is taken up. And legislators are notoriously prone to wait until the last minute before asking the drafter to prepare a bill.

When the sponsor must have a draft of a bill within a specified but insufficient period, you should make sure the sponsor understands the time problem, do the best you can within the limits imposed, inform the sponsor about any known problems that may remain unsolved (with a warning that others may exist), and be willing to continue with the project after the draft is delivered by preparing any necessary amendments.

A substantial percentage of the bills in Congress (and presumably in State legislatures) have serious substantive, legal, or practical problems in them when they are introduced, usually left there because of lack of time and with the knowledge of both drafter and sponsor. The conscious expectation is that the difficulties will be taken care of "in the committee report" or just "at a later stage"; and they usually are.

Lack of closeness to the legislative process.   Even if a bill has been perfectly drafted by every other standard, the job has not been done right if it collapses because it violates some procedural rule of the legislative body involved, or because its timing is wrong, or because it does not take into account any one of a number of other factors that control the way bills and amendments are considered in that body.

These matters have their greatest importance when you are working on amendments to be offered to a bill already moving through the legislative process. But you should always make a conscious effort to foresee the parliamentary and procedural obstacles prior to the bill's introduction, since the contents of the original bill often determine whether or not such obstacles will exist (and it may be too late to do anything about them when they are actually confronted).

The relevant procedural rules and statutory provisions are available in published form and are more or less permanent, and even an occasional drafter can keep abreast of them with a little effort. But a more difficult problem arises when temporary rules and procedures govern the way in which a bill will be taken up and considered on the floor of the legislative body involved.

In the House of Representatives, for example, the way in which particular bills are to be considered is governed by ad hoc "special rules" (see 32.3). The corresponding decisions in the Senate are usually made by unanimous consent, or simply by leadership action. In either case the decisions involved are frequently made at the last minute and are not reported in any publicly available document; but they can be critical to the drafter of an amendment since they may determine the form it should take (or even whether it can be offered at all).

If you have no way of keeping up with these matters on a minute-by-minute basis, you should do your best to establish a connection with someone who does. And you must at least be certain that the sponsor of the bill or amendment you are working on is aware of any possible procedural problems and is prepared to modify it, or switch to a different approach, if necessary.

Searching Out the Collateral Questions

▶ **5.1   In general**

When you are clear about what the problem is and about how you are supposed to solve it, you are theoretically ready to write a bill that is complete and coherent. But bills do not exist in a vacuum; as often as not there are provisions of existing law that bear upon or would be affected by what your bill purports to do and that could result in consequences the sponsor didn't intend. Although these "collateral" questions can be ignored without affecting the internal coherence of the bill, you cannot be said to have carried out the sponsor's policy correctly (and you may be putting him at some risk) if you do ignore them.

Thus collateral questions should not be treated as poor relations. It will often be critically important to the sponsor that you recognize them, and deal with them in a way that promotes the intended policy or at least minimizes the damage. And simply recognizing that one exists is often harder than figuring out what to do about it.

Chapter 4 unavoidably addressed collateral questions along with "subsidiary" questions in its general treatment of policy development (see especially 4.3)—there is obviously overlap between the two. And the "real-life drafting problems" mentioned most often in 4.9 often involve collateral questions. They come in infinite varieties, so this chapter will attempt only to give you an idea of how to identify collateral questions and some guidelines for handling them.

▶ **5.2   Collateral questions within the substantive area involved**

The easiest collateral questions to identify in connection with any bill are those that relate more or less directly to the subject matter of that bill, because you have already had to become familiar with that subject matter and with the relevant existing laws in order to deal with the sponsor's basic policy.

Easiest of all, of course, are questions arising under the very law that you are amending or the law that governs the field involved. Questions that arise under related laws may be a little harder to pinpoint, but the necessity of looking for them should be obvious. A few brief examples should suffice to illustrate the point:

1. In the hypothetical bill increasing social security benefits for widows that was used as an example in 4.6, the questions involving widowers and the "family maximum" limitation are collateral questions arising under other provisions of the same law; you ought to be aware of them, or at least suspect their existence. You might not know whether there are any collateral questions in the SSI, medicare, or railroad retirement laws, but you would know that those laws are interrelated with the social security law in many ways and accordingly check out the possibilities.

2. If you were called upon to draft a bill changing the timing of deficit reports and sequestration orders under the Emergency Deficit Control Act, you would expect to make many collateral changes throughout that Act since most of its procedures and sanctions assume the existing timing. And you would also know that similar changes will be required in the Congressional Budget Act to reflect both the new timing and the other changes made in the Deficit Control Act, since the two are extensively interwoven. In fact, the collateral changes would quickly become the tail that wags the dog. Most of the collateral changes required in these cases will be merely technical and conforming amendments (see 5.4), but some will involve important policy considerations as well and indeed can turn out to be more complicated than, and just as substantive as, the basic policy itself.

▶ **5.3   Collateral questions elsewhere**

Identifying collateral questions that arise in areas totally unrelated to the main thrust is harder, because you may have no reason to suspect they even exist. But there are some general guidelines that may be helpful:

> 1. The nature of the main thrust will often suggest the possibility of collateral questions in other areas. For example, a bill establishing a new antipoverty program might reasonably be expected to raise questions under the AFDC, SSI, food stamp, and housing laws. And a bill regulating the interstate transportation of potentially disease-bearing insects might be expected to have ramifications under the public health and agriculture laws.

> 2. The more administrative actions are required for the bill's implementation (whether or not you propose to spell them out in the bill itself), the more likely it is that the APA provisions of title 5 of the United States Code, and other laws affecting administrative procedures generally, will be involved.

> 3. Laws of general applicability—such as those involving interstate commerce, the budget, and criminal and judicial procedure as well as the various regulatory laws, for example, depending on the nature of the proposal— should be regarded as potential candidates.

You may be able to find a suitable model, in another similar bill or in an existing law, that addresses some of the otherwise-hidden collateral questions (see 10.4). Or you may find that the collateral provisions are actually cited in related existing laws, which would automatically lead you to them (see 5.5).

Remember, however, that you will seldom know in the beginning whether there are any collateral questions of this kind to worry about. If you suspect that such questions exist but you can't identify them, you should seek out a specialist— ideally one with practical operating experience in the field involved. But if you are pressed for time and there is no obvious reason to suspect a problem, save your energy. Any collateral questions that do exist will surface eventually (and can be dealt with then). Don't waste your time rummaging through Federal statutes looking for them now.

▶ 5.4   **Technical and conforming changes**

In theory, technical and conforming amendments are never substantive—they are merely the device the drafter uses to clean up the debris created by the substantive things the bill does. And since they involve no policy questions, they do not need to be thought about in the early stages of drafting. They may raise collateral questions, but not collateral policy questions.

When a bill repeals or renumbers a section referred to in another provision of existing law, the reference to that section becomes meaningless or incorrect and must be either eliminated or conformed. So, if a section being repealed is referred to in 20 other provisions of law, the bill must include (at a minimum) 20 "technical and conforming amendments" eliminating those references and possibly making further conforming amendments to compensate for their elimination. And if the bill adds a new section that needs to be taken into account under another law, or does anything that constitutes a hidden or implied exception or addition to a general rule set forth in another law, the insertion of an appropriate cross-reference in the other law is clearly indicated.

Amendments of this kind are usually simple, mechanical, and purely technical. But not always. In a surprising number of cases, cleaning up the debris raises its own substantive and tactical problems.

When your bill has the effect of repealing or nullifying a section of existing law, for example, and an unrelated provision of law contains a cross-reference to that section, simply striking the now obsolete cross-reference is not enough if the unrelated provision *depends* upon that cross-reference for its effectiveness. Unless you also want to repeal or nullify the unrelated provision, you will have to rewrite it so as to incorporate specifically what was formerly incorporated only by reference. This can involve real tactical difficulties, and even raise new substantive issues, requiring full-blown collateral policy decisions just as serious as the decisions involved in carrying out the main thrust.

Consider a fairly simple example—a bill to repeal the "earnings test" under the social security program. That test reduces or eliminates the benefits to which an individual is otherwise "entitled" if that individual still works and earns more than a specified amount. The earnings test occupies only a single subsection in the law (section 203(b) of the Social Security Act), and it takes only two lines to repeal it.

But cleaning up the debris resulting from the elimination of that one subsection requires many pages of technical and conforming amendments—about 40 in all in the typical version of the bill (which, incidentally, is introduced in virtually the same form a few hundred times each Congress). Most of these amendments are purely technical (eliminating provisions that exist only for the administration of the earnings test, redesignating to close gaps, and striking old cross-references), but some have substantive policy overtones:

1. Two of them repeal the "noncovered employment" test for individuals working outside the United States. This test is the overseas counterpart of the domestic earnings test, and its repeal is generally regarded as a purely conforming amendment. But the considerations and mechanics involved are quite different, and some sponsors might want it left alone (or rewritten, possibly with modifications, as an independent provision).

2. One of them writes into the SSI law—another law altogether—a detailed definition of the critical term "wages", now handled in that law simply by a cross-reference to the definition that applies to the earnings test provision. This is just a matter of replacing the cross-reference with the verbatim language from the stricken provision; but that language (which is long and complicated, and contains some controversial items) will now become highly visible and attract attention, and the sponsor (or anyone else who notices it) may have second thoughts.

3. Two of them involve provisions in the social security law (sections 202(w) and 223) that are substantively unrelated to the earnings test but depend for their effectiveness on the way that test (whose critical levels change annually under a cost-of-living formula) applies to the individual involved. Assuming that sponsors do not want to change the effect of those provisions, drafters have usually substituted for the present cross-references to section 203(b) a new concept: The way in which the earnings test *would* have applied to the individual if it had not been repealed. This is cumbersome, and would require difficult hypothetical calculations; it is done in desperation, and a better approach would have to be found if such a bill ever began to move through the legislative process.

4. And one of them repeals the corresponding earnings test under the Railroad Retirement Act, which does not spell it out but just picks up and applies the social security earnings test by a cross-reference. There is probably no other way to get the ball rolling (and you can't simply

ignore the effect of the bill on the railroad retirement test), but the substantive and jurisdictional problems are obvious.

The lesson to be learned is that if you tamper with existing statutory language, expressly or impliedly, you will probably need technical and conforming amendments. And some of these amendments may themselves present substantive and tactical problems.

Technical and conforming amendments are discussed further in 12.10, which deals primarily with their proper placement in a bill. The author discusses these amendments here only to emphasize that, although most of them are purely mechanical (and can be handled as afterthoughts in the late stages of the project), those that are not deserve to be treated as a part of the policy development process. If you can identify the collateral questions early your job will be much easier from start to finish.

▶ **5.5**   **Finding aids**

Even if you become expert at sensing collateral questions, some will still escape your attention; they seem to hide in unexpected places. But if the provision that raises a particular collateral question actually cites the provision with which you are involved—and it will do that as often as not—there is hope.

The United States Code (in both its positive-law and nonpositive-law titles) routinely includes, immediately after each section, a note listing all the other provisions of the Code in which that section is explicitly referred to.

And in many fields there are published tables of cross-references to provisions of the major laws. If there is such a table in your field, or if you have made one of your own (see 3.6), it will refer you to all the places in the covered statutes where the provision you are working on is expressly cited, thereby identifying nearly all of the purely technical and conforming amendments you must make and most of the other collateral questions you need to address as well.

The value of the Code notes and the cross-reference tables is not limited to the quest for collateral questions, of course, but is greatest when they are used for that purpose. They will lead you to problems the existence of which neither you nor anyone else working with you has suspected, and their use will enhance your reputation for omniscience.

6

Organizing
the Bill

▶ **6.1   In general**

The basic principle governing the arrangement of a bill can be stated very simply (paraphrasing *HOLC,* pages 1-2): Every bill should be consciously organized, usually the most important thoughts should come first, and the organization should help convey the sponsor's message.

Hirsch (page 21) says pretty much the same thing, in an equally down-to-earth fashion:

> Divide your bill into bite-size chunks, and arrange those chunks in some digestible way, [with the aim of creating] a framework that others can readily understand, remember, and retrace and that future draftsmen can conveniently amend.

In most cases, you should organize the bill in a hierarchical arrangement so that the location of the various items shows their interrelationships and relative importance. But there are situations in which somewhat different considerations may apply:

1. In a bill involving a sequence of actions and reactions between the administrators and the persons covered by the bill, a temporal arrangement—describing the relevant events in the exact order in which they are to occur—will

sometimes make the connections clearer than a hierarchical arrangement.

2. In some amendatory bills, following the arrangement of the law being amended rather than the hierarchical principle will serve the reader better. This is discussed in detail in 17.1.

▶ **6.2**   **Organizing a bill substantively**

The drafter's principal objective in organizing a bill is to assure that the final product will be as clear and accurate as possible, with the relationship between the main and subordinate ideas made readily apparent, and that the subjects to be covered are arranged so that they can be found, understood, and referred to with the least possible effort.

No one arrangement is ideal; what is best in one situation may not be the best in another. You should of course keep the bill's structure as simple as possible, arrange its elements in a logical sequence, and follow the principle of "modular construction" (see 6.5); but you must also make sure that you are presenting the ideas in a way that effectively reaches the intended audience.

Provisions relating primarily to the conduct, rights, privileges, or duties of the persons substantively affected by the bill should be arranged from the viewpoint of those persons; while provisions relating primarily to administration should be arranged from the viewpoint of the prospective administrators. You should always identify the audience in your own mind before you start drafting.

A number of legislative drafting manuals specify an optimum arrangement of sections that a drafter should normally follow in structuring a bill, based on the nature, importance, and permanence of the sections that might typically be included. This approach can be moderately instructive and serve as a useful guide in your early discussions with the policymaker (see 4.6 for some examples of the kinds of questions it might lead you to ask). But it should be taken with a grain of salt and used as a safe starting point only, since different bills impose different demands.

Hirsch (page 23), for example, suggests the following as a possible model for most freestanding bills:

1. Short title.

2. Findings and purpose.

3. Definitions.

4. Principal operating provisions (which also define the bill's scope).

5. Subordinate operating provisions.

6. Prohibited acts and major exclusions.

7. Sanctions.

8. General administrative and procedural rules.

9. Jurisdiction of courts.

10. Relationship to other statutes.

11. Reports to Congress.

12. Appropriations authorization.

13. Savings provisions.

14. Effective dates.

HOLC (page 20) reaches a somewhat similar result from a somewhat different direction, stating that the following arrangement is appropriate for most bills and should be tried before choosing any other:

1. *General rule.* State the main message—that is, set forth the provisions necessary to carry out the bill's central purpose.

2. *Exceptions.* Describe the persons or things to which the main message does not apply.

3. *Special rules.* Describe the persons or things—

   A. to which the main message applies in a different way, or

   B. for which there is a different message.

4. *Transitional rules.* State the rules which are only temporary or transitional but which are important or will have effect for a relatively long period of time.

5. *Other provisions.* Add whatever administrative provisions, technical and conforming amendments, and collateral provisions may be necessary or appropriate to clean up any debris brought about by implementing the main message.

6. *Definitions.*

7. *Effective date* (if necessary).

Dickerson (pages 63-64) adds several helpful rules of thumb:

1. A bill's key operating provisions normally come first.

2. General provisions normally come before special provisions.

3. More important provisions normally come before less important provisions.

4. More frequently used provisions normally come before less frequently used provisions.

5. Permanent provisions normally come before temporary provisions.

6. Technical and "housekeeping" provisions normally come at the end.

There are of course many cases in which one or more of these rules of thumb should be ignored; common sense is your best guide. If the bill has a short title or table of contents, or contains a statement of findings and purpose, that provision will normally appear at the very beginning of the bill (ahead of the key operating provisions). And if the bill includes a separate section containing definitions of terms, that section (or a highly visible cross-reference to it) will also appear at the beginning.

In addition, the category into which a particular type of provision falls may not always be the same; an authorization of appropriations, for example, is treated as a "housekeeping" provision in most bills (since it simply provides funding and otherwise has no substantive content), but would have the flavor of a key operating provision (and should appear up front) in a grant-in-aid bill whose main purpose is to make funds available to meet a particular need and then allocate them among applicants who qualify.

All three of the cited sources emphasize the need to subordinate the less important provisions. If those provisions are isolated and minor, of course, there is no architectural problem; they can be woven into the main body of the key operating provisions as separate sentences or parenthetical phrases. Even when they are major, if there are only a few of them (one or two short exceptions to the general rule, for example), they can often be handled the same way.

Regardless of the nature of the subordinate provisions, however, if there are many of them they will usually be easier to handle if they are collected in separate sections or subsections, after the key operating provisions (with appropriate headings if stylistic considerations permit). So long as the relationship between the key operating provisions and the subordinate provisions is made clear, placing the subordinate provisions in a separate section also promotes readability, especially if they are long or complicated.

There is only one architectural rule that is always applicable: Give prominence to the more important thoughts, and downplay the others, but keep their relationship clear.

▶ **6.3**   **Structuring a bill stylistically**

When you are drafting a straightforward bill of limited scope, structuring it stylistically is not a problem. It will consist of a relatively few numbered sections, appropriately subdivided when necessary, and the correct arrangement will be obvious. (Chapter 20 discusses how to structure a bill at the Federal level; States have different requirements, of course, but you can always find a system to follow.)

If you are drafting a bill which contains provisions that are logically separate or which addresses several different subjects, however, you need to make some choices and do some advance planning. Should the bill be divided into titles, parts, or chapters in order to provide logical places for different subjects or for related groups of provisions? Is it long or complicated enough to justify dividing those titles, parts, or chapters into subtitles, subparts, or subchapters (for the same reason)? Are there political or tactical reasons for keeping some of the matters involved totally separated from the others?

Again, there is no single correct answer. Your objective should be to use a stylistic arrangement (as well as specific stylistic devices such as section headings) to help readers find and distinguish the substantive provisions they are interested in, just as your substantive organization (discussed in 6.2) is designed to help readers understand the content and relationship of those provisions once they are found. Whatever stylistic structure will best accomplish that result is the one to use.

▶ **6.4**   **A look at structural problems generally**

Dickerson (pages 57-63)—crisscrossing the line between substantive and stylistic structure—divides the problems that a drafter faces in organizing a bill into three kinds—division, classification, and sequence. Each of these raises its own set of questions:

1. *Problems of division.* Into what main segments or parts should the bill be divided? Should this division be based on relative importance, chronology of events, or other considerations? Should the bill simply consist of sections, or should it be broken down into titles and then further broken down (into subtitles or parts and then sections, or just into sections alone)?

And a subsidiary breakdown of the same kind may be needed in some or all of the main segments of the bill (depending on the breadth of the categories represented by those segments). A section of a bill is broken down into subsections and paragraphs for the same reasons and subject to the same logical considerations as those that apply in breaking down the bill as a whole into titles, subtitles, parts, and sections.

Thus, if a section's central theme is most readily understood when analyzed into its component themes, it should be divided into subsections, each developing a single idea that is readily distinguishable from (and ordinarily not logically subordinate to) the ideas developed in the other subsections; and subsections can be further subdivided in the same fashion.

2. *Problems of classification.* Once you've decided how to divide the bill, you must decide which pieces will go in each of the segments resulting from that division. For the most part this is easy—the nature of the segment will normally determine its contents. But in some cases (where the divisions are very broad or involve subjects that fall partly under one heading and partly under another, or where there are recurring situations that differ just enough to prevent their treatment at a single point in the bill) your ingenuity may be taxed.

3. *Problems of sequence.* The remaining problem is to arrange the segments or elements of the bill (at every level) in the most logical sequence. In general, the sequence should enable a reader to understand the bill by reading its provisions consecutively, like chapters in a novel. But there is no one right way to do it; as stressed earlier, the way that most effectively communicates the sponsor's message is always the best way.

▶ **6.5**   **Modular construction**

Good drafting calls for "modular construction" (*Hirsch's* term, pages 11-13), which means that each component and subdivision of the bill should be dedicated to a single subject and contain (or at least refer to) all of the substantive provisions that readers will need to understand that subject. Reasonable drafters might differ about the precise modules into which any particular bill should be divided, but in the interest of both clarity and readability and for tactical reasons as well (see below) the modular principle should always be at the center of your architectural planning.

The basic division of any statute is of course the numbered section. Ideally, each section should be devoted to a topic that is conceptually distinct from the topic of any other section; and it should always be possible for the reader to tell which sections deal with which subjects. In order to achieve this objective you should have a logical plan for allocating material among sections and be consistent in applying it.

Normally you should strive to create sections each of which deals comprehensively with a single idea or topic, making it possible for the reader to find within that section not only the basic idea but also every rule that is logically subordinate to it.

It is acceptable, however, to create sections that contain ideas or topics logically subordinate to those contained in other sections, so long as the logical hierarchy of those ideas or topics (or the relationship of the sections involved) is clear; remember that, if two integral ideas are not combined, there is always a risk that one of them when read alone will imply that the other doesn't exist. Again, it must always be possible for the reader to identify what each section does and to understand its relationship to the rest of the bill.

Theoretically your efforts to get the sponsor's message across clearly to the intended audience will be best served by following two basic principles:

1. For coherence, combine any ideas that are closely related or integral to each other, and

2. For clarity, separate any ideas that are inherently distinct.

Unfortunately, the two principles often push the drafter in opposite directions, sometimes with strange results. Many existing statutes embody a mixture of both principles that can only be explained by the drafter's lack of time for planning and organization (or by the fact that different drafters, at different times, resolve the problem in different ways).

But knowing when to separate ideas and when to combine them in a single section involves the balancing of intangibles in ways that no rules can cover. Suffice it to say that many times a set of related provisions could sensibly be combined in a single section or could just as sensibly be placed in separate sections. You can only rely on your experience and best judgment in determining which is best.

In addition to promoting understanding, modular construction has definite tactical advantages. It aids a bill's consideration in committee or subcommittee, because bills are normally read for amendment section-by-section and the Members and staff who are considering a bill are bound to have difficulty following (and dealing with) a single concept that is spread among widely scattered provisions. And it simplifies your task if and when the committee or subcommittee chooses to reject some of the bill's provisions, since the removal of one module from a bill does not usually require much redrafting of the remainder.

In any case, grouping the provisions of a bill by subject (however you choose to define "subject") is essential. It makes their purpose clear, helps to distinguish the main ideas from the subordinate, and promotes reader comprehension.

▶ 6.6   Split provisions and split amendments

A common violation of some of these rules is the so-called "split provision" or "split amendment", which is a provision or amendment that in effect has two parts. One section makes an apparently unequivocal statement (that is, it appears on its face to be unconditionally effective), but another section (as the reader discovers much later in the bill) conditions the effectiveness of that statement on satisfying some previously undisclosed requirement.

The inspiration for a split provision is usually the drafter's desire to avoid cluttering up the key operating provisions of a bill with exceptions and special rules that may be distracting to the reader (a subject discussed in detail in 12.3). But in avoiding this clutter the drafter risks misleading the reader, since the key operating provisions themselves then paint only a partial picture.

You should always include a specific cross-reference to the later provision in the earlier one in order to avoid this confusion, if possible, unless the context makes the situation clear without one. But there is at least one common type of split provision that does *not* call for a cross-reference; it involves effective dates and deserves special mention.

Several commentators have bitterly attacked the practice of placing the effective dates in amendatory bills outside of the substantive provisions to which they relate; they feel that this conceals important information from future readers of those provisions, and that every substantive provision in the law should reveal on its face exactly when and how it originally became effective. This is nonsense.

In the first place, most major laws are amended frequently, and provisions that are now merely hard to read would become incomprehensible if they contained a statement of when each of the various pieces became effective. Section 210(a) of the Social Security Act, which consists of a single 40-page sentence with over 100 tabulated subdivisions, was enacted in 1950 and is now largely the product of the several hundred separate amendments that have been made to it since then; a 40-page sentence that is only barely comprehensible is bad enough, but if it had to include 300 different effective date provisions (many of which are far from simple) it would become a 500-page sentence largely composed of deadwood, making the present provision look like something from *McGuffey's Reader.*

In the second place, most effective date provisions become immaterial to anyone but an historian shortly after the substantive provisions to which they relate go into operation. If an individual is an historian, or is involved in one of those relatively rare cases where the effective date of an old law actually retains its significance, it is not unreasonable to ask that individual to do a little research.

And finally, although most major laws set forth their effective dates explicitly, some do it without mentioning any specific date ("This Act shall take effect 60 days after its enactment", for example), and some do not contain any explicit effective date provision at all (relying on the "default" effective date— see chapter 26). It is hard to imagine how the critics would propose to handle this.

Effective-date split amendments are one case where balancing avoidance of clutter against full information to subsequent readers is easy, especially in major bills that contain numerous effective dates and involve laws that are frequently amended; avoiding clutter wins. Keeping substantive provisions free of effective date language that will quickly become executed (and of cross-references to effective date provisions as well) is one of the best ways—and sometimes the only way—to keep them both clear and readable.

▶ **6.7**   **The virtues and self-evidence of good architecture**

In closing this chapter the author concedes some overkill in the preceding text. For relatively short and simple bills you can usually solve the organizational problems in your head; a bill that does just one specific thing and is not part of a broader legislative tapestry can often be written as a single section, requiring at most a few technical or conforming amendments and perhaps an explicit effective date. And for long and complicated bills, such as omnibus and "reform" bills and bills establishing broad new programs, the right organization will almost force itself upon you.

Most of the bills that you are likely to face in your everyday work, however, fall somewhere between the two extremes, and it is for them that this chapter is written. They are of relatively limited scope (like the first category), but are sufficiently complex or multifaceted (like the modular segments of broader bills in the second) to require that you give conscious thought to their architecture.

As stressed earlier, good organization and arrangement (though it may appear on the surface to be primarily a technical or mechanical matter) can produce real substantive benefits. And it will enable your reader (whether a judge interpreting the law or a high-school civics student on assignment) to understand clearly and quickly what the bill does and the relative importance of its various provisions.

But its most tangible contribution may well lie in what it will do to ease your mechanical burdens as you work your way through the writing process. A concrete plan of organization and arrangement made in advance is indispensable when the bill is complicated or massive. It forces you to think your problems through, and allows you to subdivide the project into smaller and more manageable parts that can be worked on separately. It is one of the most important devices for easing the drafter's burden; and if it is done early it also saves time, since readjustments in basic arrangement become more difficult later and the risk of error increases.

In many ways the organization of a bill is like the organization of a novel; if the reader can get into the context early and follow the plot through to the end, it is a success. Remember that your main objective in organizing a bill is to promote clarity, accuracy, and comprehension. If the bill presents no apparent structural problems, don't try to invent any, but always stop and think about it first. And if that leads you to believe that there may be organizational questions after all, don't proceed until you have taken steps to resolve them.

Part III

Writing the Bill: Preliminary Considerations

The Mechanics of Good Writing

▶ **7.1   In general**

When you have learned all that you need to know about the sponsor's problem and its intended solution and have decided how to handle it—matters that were dealt with in part II—all that remains is to convert the intended solution into legislative language that will do the job effectively.

Many of the tools that you will need for this purpose are specialized tools, in that they are unique to legislative writing; but the most basic among them is not specialized at all—it is simply the ability to write clearly and effectively, without regard to the kind of writing involved. And it goes without saying that good legislative language, like all good writing, should be mechanically sound in grammar, punctuation, and word usage—subjects discussed fully in chapters 21 and 22.

Good writing in and of itself promotes the fundamental virtues of clarity and readability, of course; but it has another important legislative virtue as well. The drafter's audience will always include at least a few people who really care about the finer points of good prose composition—the technicalities of proper punctuation, grammar, word usage, sentence structure, and conceptual arrangement—and those people will be bothered if they find anything that does not measure up. Nothing threatens your credibility as much as the appearance of illiteracy, and this has very little to do with how well you accomplish your legal and substantive objectives.

Thousands of books and articles have been published on the subject of good writing, and more come out each month. They range from simple grammar textbooks to profound philosophical inquiries about human communication. Most of what they have to say is as valid for legislative drafting as it is for other forms of writing. H. W. Fowler, long considered a leading authority on English usage, might have been addressing today's legislative drafters some 65 years ago, for example, when he offered what recent commentators have described as his five basic commandments—prefer the familiar word to the farfetched, the concrete to the abstract, the simple word to the circumlocution, the short word to the long, and the Saxon word to the Romance—and then added that circumstances may sometime justify exceptions.[1]

Many of these books and articles, however, give advice not appropriate for legislative drafters. They devote an inordinate amount of attention to such things as "how to vary sentence structure for emphasis and variety", "how to amuse and arouse curiosity", and "how to bring the reader up short"— bits of advice that may be useful in fiction but not in legislative drafting. There is certainly nothing wrong with emphasis and even occasional amusement in statutes; but from a drafter's point of view variety is incompatible with consistency (see 4.4), and language that arouses curiosity or results in sudden surprises for the reader strongly implies either lack of clarity or poor organization, or both.

This book emphasizes the part that the principles of good writing play in good legislative drafting and in the development of good drafting habits; and it assumes that you know the fundamentals. But before rushing headlong into the subject of legislative form and style, it may be useful to look at a few of these principles from the drafter's point of view.

▶　7.2　　**Using 20th-century English**

Since any law is intended to communicate a message to its readers, it ought to be written in language familiar to those readers. It is not always possible to write a bill in a way that will be readily understood by everyone—complicated ideas and highly technical concepts cannot easily be expressed in language that the average person can grasp quickly—but you should always make the effort. You should use everyday 20th-

---

[1] Paraphrased from *A Dictionary of Modern English Usage* (Oxford at the Clarendon Press), London: Humphrey Milford (1927).

century English (American style) whenever you can.

Drafters generally agree in theory that conversational language is best, and that there is no legitimate reason why the structure of sentences in statutes should be any different from the structure of everyday speech. This makes sense, but only so long as the sentence involved is equal to the task of expressing its idea with the clarity and precision required for legislative purposes.

And individual words, like sentences, should ideally be part of everyone's everyday vocabulary; you should generally choose the simpler word over a synonym that is unfamiliar, awkward, or less well understood. But do so with caution, since many words that are usually thought of as synonyms are not or (because of their derivation or past usage) convey a different shade of meaning. Choose *dog* over *canine,* but only if you want to exclude foxes and wolves; choose *cat* over *feline,* and if you want to exclude lions and tigers add the adjective *domestic* (although even then you may be covering an occasional pet ocelot). Choose the word that is most accurate. Use the dictionary, and get feedback from colleagues; what a word means to you in a particular context may not be what it means to someone else.

Old laws were usually written in an obscure, stilted, ponderous, and even pompous style, but what was right for Benjamin Franklin or Alexander Hamilton is not necessarily appropriate today (indeed, a few visionaries—notably Thomas Jefferson—did not think it was appropriate then). Most people 200 years ago could not read or write at all, and one popular school of thought today suggests that the people who could always spoke and wrote ponderously (even to their family and friends) simply to demonstrate their superiority.

It is undoubtedly true (as *Hirsch* said in 1980 (page 1)) that since the time of Franklin and Hamilton "the draftsman's passion for the turgid and redundant has somewhat abated", but archaic forms are still with us, especially among lawyers, and every drafter should be forever on guard against them.

The determination of when and how to back away from archaic forms is not altogether clear-cut, however. Most of them are totally gratuitous. They conjure up images of medieval England and are unnecessarily intimidating; you would never use them in everyday speech, and should never use them in legislation either. Others (although you might not use them in everyday speech) have redeeming virtues because they represent a form of verbal shorthand that aids readability, and the need for them (or their less archaic equivalent) actually arises frequently. In the middle are a number of forms that you should avoid most of the time but which you should feel free to use selectively when special circumstances exist. Chapter 22 attempts to sort them out.

In addition to specific terms and expressions, there are archaic usages of all kinds to watch out for. Their fault lies mainly in their verbosity; old writers of legislation seemed to be constant participants in a contest to see who could use the most words to express a simple idea. Even as recently as 1950 Federal laws would still typically vest a function in an official by saying that the official "is hereby granted authority, and is hereby directed, to [take some specified action]"; today, no drafter should even consider saying anything but that the official "shall [take that action]".

And you should avoid Latin terms and expressions except when it is necessary to use them in referring to a document, judicial procedure, or legal concept that is known primarily by its Latin name. *HOLC* (page 3) observes that "[even] those few people who have had Latin in school can't agree on pronunciation".

To sum up, use a modern term or expression if at all possible. But if an archaic form suits your purpose exactly and doesn't sound stilted or awkward to you, use it without apology. Remember that achieving the desired substantive result is always more important than stylistic perfection.

▶ 7.3   **Short sentences, pro and con**

It is a well-known principle of good writing (and good legislative drafting) that long sentences should be avoided. Using two or three sentences to make a point is better English (other things being equal) than using one long and possibly convoluted one.

In declaring that most compound sentences should be broken down into two or more separate sentences, *HOLC* (page 2) claims to have discovered that "the median listener [or reader] tunes out after the 12th word", and that the offending sentence often conceals one or more unresolved policy issues or contains both a general rule and one or more exceptions or special rules that would be better handled separately.

For the most part the author agrees, and unless the context makes it impossible your sentences should be as short and crisp as you can make them without unduly jerking the reader about or interfering with the flow of your thoughts.

But tight compression of language in separated compartments does not always promote the supreme objective of maximum clarity, and *HOLC's* median listener may not be part of your intended audience; conciseness does not ensure clarity, and sometimes prevents it. You should condense your sentences only to clarify the meaning and help your reader's understanding. Ambiguity may often be reduced and both clarity and readability increased by using a longer compound sentence instead of two or three short sentences when the relationship of the ideas involved is particularly elusive or complex, and might be more readily grasped by a reader or a court if those ideas are contained within a single sentence where each "and", "or", "except that", and "subject to" can be expressed rather than only implied.

Consider for example the following hypothetical (and deliberately simplified) provision:

> The individual shall be paid a benefit computed under subsection (c). If he is over 55 years of age the benefit shall be computed under subsection (d) instead. The benefit shall be reduced by 20 percent if the individual is not enrolled in an approved rehabilitation program. No benefit shall be paid while the individual is outside the United States.

The four short sentences do paint the picture, but only when read together—three of them would be incorrect or at least misleading if taken out of context. Since it is a single concept (benefit entitlement) that is being expressed, a single sentence approach might be better—no less readable and definitely clearer, especially if the provision were surrounded by other (unrelated) sentences:

> The individual shall be paid a benefit computed under subsection (c) (or under subsection (d) if he is over 55 years of age); except that the benefit so computed shall be reduced by 20 percent if the individual is not enrolled in an approved rehabilitation program, and no benefit shall be paid while the individual is outside the United States.

(See chapter 23 for some special ways of handling unavoidably long sentences, and 9.5 for an example that indicates some of the considerations pro and con.)

Note that the same principles apply to subsections and

paragraphs, each of which ideally should also be short and limited in scope but some of which (especially in amendatory cases) may need to be longer and more compound in order to fit properly within the bill, or within existing law, at the place where the sense of that bill or law requires it. Any drafter writing an amendment to section 210(a) of the Social Security Act (the 40-page sentence cited in chapter 6 as an example of nonstop writing) really has no choice but to perpetuate the flaws and make the situation even worse, simply because it is unavoidable mechanically.

The basic rule is to keep each of the various elements of your bill as short, simple, and readable as you can. But you should not carry it to such an extreme that you run the risk of missing your substantive target; clarity and precision are more important.

▶ 7.4   **Directness and economy of expression**

Novelists strive for tone, mood, and flavor in their writing, and use as many words as may be necessary to achieve them; after all, their primary aim is to involve the emotions of the reader. The drafter's primary interest is very different (although of course he does not object at all to the right tone, mood, and flavor); his aim is to produce language that will achieve the prescribed statutory objective fully and accurately while avoiding language that may involve the emotions and consequently have different flavors for different readers.

Flamboyance and wordiness may serve the novelist's purposes well, but directness and economy of expression are the hallmarks of good legislative writing. A few briefly stated principles should suffice to illustrate the point (which will be discussed in more detail later):

> 1. Always try to express your ideas positively rather than negatively, use the active rather than the passive voice, and avoid unnecessary modifying adjectives or explanatory phrases. An approach that is direct and untrammeled by editorial comment not only has more "punch"—it is less ambiguous.

> 2. Always go straight to the point. And after you have made that point, leave it alone; once is enough. Circumlocution too often suggests that a point intended to be unequivocal is in fact subject to qualifications or exceptions; while redundancy, instead of emphasizing a point, usually diminishes its force.

3. When you have found the right word to express a particular idea or concept in a bill, use that word and only that word every time you express the idea or concept again, even at the cost of drabness in style. As *HOLC* (page 3) puts it, "your English teacher may be disappointed, but the courts and others who are straining to find your meaning will bless you".

The use of synonyms to express the same idea or concept within the same provision—a practice known as "elegant variation" [2]—should be avoided. If you want to display your erudition you should find some other document (such as a descriptive summary of the bill) in which to do it. As indicated earlier, there are almost always small differences in meaning or flavor between words that are thought of as being synonymous, and courts are very fond of treating those differences as indicators of some obscure legislative objective and using them to reach results that were not intended. And when a particular word has two different meanings and is used both ways in the same provision—a practice known as "utraquistic subterfuge" [3]—it is even worse, since the ambiguity is actually built into the words themselves.

▶ **7.5**   **Organization that gets the message across**

It is not necessary in writing legislative language to "capture the attention of the reader", since no one reads statutes for recreational purposes. But it is necessary to get the substantive message across, and to organize the legislative product in such a way as to make that message clear and help ensure that all readers will extract it in the same way.

Chapter 6 addressed this point in detail in connection with the overall organization and arrangement of a bill and its component parts. It is mentioned again here only to emphasize that these considerations are a particularly important part of good legislative writing. The thoughts you express must flow in the same rational way for all readers.

Thus, if concept A is dependent on concept B or doesn't make sense without a prior awareness of concept B, the reader cannot be expected to understand it if it appears in the text before concept B has been addressed. This can cause problems when concept A is more fundamental and should

2. Fowler, p. 130.

3. Charles K. Ogden and Ivor A. Richards, *The Meaning of Meaning* (4th Ed.), (New York: Harcourt Brace, 1936), p. 134.

logically be addressed first; but the legislative drafter (unlike the novelist) can easily handle them by simply including language in concept A that warns the reader of concept B and directs attention to it—for example, "(as described in section ____ [the place where concept B appears])", "(subject to section ____)", or "(unless section ____ applies)". The use of cross-references for this purpose is more fully discussed in 22.4.

▶ **7.6   Stylistic consensus and consistency**

The importance of stylistic consensus. Unfortunately (see *HOLC*, page 18), good legislative drafting cannot be reduced to a cookbook-style process in which items from lists of standard ingredients are combined to produce a bill. To believe otherwise creates a false sense of security, because the diversity of individual drafters makes a complete consensus on structure and style impossible.

Although you should use the drafting conventions described in this book as extensively as possible, you should not feel compelled to do so in circumstances where (because of the lack of stylistic consensus among the various drafters working on the project) insistence on the use of a particular convention would interfere with the drafting process or lead to an inconsistent legislative product.

Nevertheless, a general agreement on as many of these conventions as possible is one of your most valuable assets as a drafter simply because (even when the consensus is not complete) it makes the all-important quality of consistency easier to achieve.

The importance of stylistic consistency. The importance of substantive consistency in your drafting has already been stressed and will be mentioned again; but the specific virtues of stylistic consistency as an aid to the everyday drafter deserve special mention. (The following discussion paraphrases *HOLC*'s treatment of the subject (at pages 7-8)).

The consideration and enactment of legislation occurs in the midst of constantly changing circumstances and demands, indeed often in the midst of chaos. Style (despite variations from one legislative setting to another) should be one of the steady, predictable elements that drafters can use to reduce that chaos to order, and not one of the fluctuating factors that contribute to it.

A well-defined and uniformly applied style will make life

easier in many ways for the drafter, for the legislators who will have to deal with the legislative language, and for subsequent administrators and interpreters of that language. *HOLC* (pages 7-8) tells why:

1. Stylistic consistency provides a stable framework for analyzing the legal and other problems of a legislative proposal and for organizing and expressing the proposal rationally, and thereby promotes consistency of substantive expression.

2. It permits the best use of the drafter's time by permitting two or more drafters working on the same job to concentrate on substantive matters rather than on conforming style, and by permitting one drafter to substitute for another (or draft from another's work product) without stylistic complications.

3. It helps to communicate the sponsor's message by enabling the reader to concentrate on that message without being distracted by mere stylistic differences, particularly where they might be thought to have legal significance (under the doctrine that variations within a law are designed to have substantive meaning).

4. And it satisfies people's need for (or expectation of) orderliness in the expression of ideas.

Courts pay close attention to the stylistic aspects of a law in their quest for its true meaning; but very few of them seem to understand a fundamental feature of the legislative process—the fact that stylistic inconsistencies in a law result from time pressures, tactical limitations, and the participation of different drafters much more often than they do from congressional intent or just plain bad drafting.

But a bill that contains noticeable variations in structure or style, whatever the reason, cannot be called an example of good legislative writing even if it meets every other test. Such variations not only interfere with the communication of the sponsor's message; they give aid and comfort to people who are looking for grounds to misinterpret the language or to criticize the product or process involved.

The importance of having a list of rules. In any form of writing there are often two or more correct ways of expressing an idea or relationship. In most forms they can be used interchangeably, but in legislative drafting the need for internal consistency requires that one of them be routinely favored.

For this reason, every drafter ought to have a list of specific stylistic rules—stylistic "dos and don'ts"—on his desk and in the back of his mind. Part VI (chapters 19 through 28) is intended to provide this list.

Very few of the items on that list are unequivocal mandates or prohibitions—most of them merely express with varying degrees of forcefulness a preference for one usage or form over another. However, you are urged to take the list seriously, both because it incorporates what the author (along with most other professional drafters) would consider the best choices and because its uniform application will help you avoid the unpleasant necessity of making stylistic decisions on a case-by-case basis as you draft.

The Roman Rule

▶ 8.1   The rule defined

The Roman rule ("When in Rome, do as the Romans do") is just a way of saying that every drafter working in a particular setting should use the traditional form and style of that setting—the form and style which is most familiar and acceptable to the people who will be reading, considering, and acting on his legislative product as well as to those who will have to live with it after its enactment.

It is only a rule of thumb, of course, and subject to many exceptions, but it is one of the most basic of all legislative drafting principles.

This book lays down a multitude of rules and principles governing legislative form and style, and urges their adoption because they promote clarity or have other identifiable virtues; but there is in fact no single legislative form or style that is universally correct. A drafter for whom one form or style is second nature will often feel like a stranger in a foreign land when faced with another, and the Roman rule reminds him that (in such a situation) he had better learn the language. Doing so will almost always expedite his work, since it guarantees that the legislators, staffs, and administrators involved will pay no attention to how the bill is drafted and can proceed without distraction to what it does.

The fundamental thought that the Roman rule expresses is that a bill which amends an existing law, or is intended to become a part of the existing body of laws in any statutory field, should fit within that law or that field—it should look like it belongs there. After all, the whole purpose of the bill is to implant something new in the permanent law, and the consistency of the permanent law (once the bill is enacted) is far more important than the transitory vehicle—the bill itself—by which the implantation is effected.

Thus, for a bill making changes in the crop-subsidy laws, the Roman rule might be paraphrased to read "When drafting a bill to amend a crop-subsidy law, do as the drafters of the existing crop-subsidy laws have done".

Note, however, that there are two subrules to the Roman rule—one for the setting in which the drafter's product will be considered and enacted and one for the setting in which it will be carried out and administered. They might be paraphrased (in the example just given) to read "When drafting a crop-subsidy bill, do as the Committee on Agriculture does" and "When drafting a crop-subsidy bill, do as the Department of Agriculture and the farmers do", respectively. These two subrules would not usually conflict, since the Committee, the Department, and the farmers have long been coparticipants in the crop-subsidy-law process and are likely to look at these matters in the same way.

If the two subrules were to come into conflict, of course, you would normally give special weight to the first simply because it is the one that matters most to the people with whom (and for whom) you are working. But you should not forget the needs (and prejudices) of the people who will have to deal with your language at later stages in the legislative process or administer the bill after it is enacted.

The arguments in favor of applying the Roman rule and its subrules seem straightforward and convincing, but its application is obviously not a matter of absolute legal necessity. And there would be no occasion for a Roman rule if all legislative forms and styles were the same or were equally good. The application of the rule becomes an issue only when you are convinced that one form and style is significantly better for the purposes involved than the one the rule asks you to adopt.

You can of course apply the Roman rule selectively. Even when you feel that you simply must perpetuate an old law's unusual style of section designation, for example, you can almost always avoid using the archaic "wherefores", "abovementioneds", and "hereinbefores" since they serve no purpose and nobody is likely to miss them.

All of these things are matters of subjective judgment, about which reasonable drafters can differ. The author believes that there should be a strong presumption in favor of the rule in every case, but there are many professional drafters who would not go this far. In any event, the degree to which you should feel compelled to apply the Roman rule whether you like it or not will vary from situation to situation; and 8.2-8.4 are largely devoted to a discussion of these variations.

▶ **8.2   Form and style in amendatory bills**

The strict application of the Roman rule is most strongly indicated in the case of amendatory bills, because everything significant that you do in one of those bills is done within the actual text of an existing law. Every law has its own distinct form and style, and any formal or stylistic aberrations in amendatory language will be immediately apparent—and jarring—to even the most casual reader. Amendments that directly involve existing statutory language should always comply with the Roman rule.

On the other hand, amendments adding new and distinctly separate pieces to an existing law may give you more leeway. If you are adding a totally new title at the end of a law, for example, particularly if it deals with a new and separate subject, you might conceivably be forgiven if you write it in a form and style that differs from the form and style embodied in the rest of that law. Many professional drafters take this position (although the author personally would not).

One final point. You should always keep in mind that an amendatory bill is only a vehicle for making amendments to existing law. Every amendatory provision may be thought of as having two parts—the vehicular part (the introductory language, "outside the quotes"), which makes the amendments but has no other substantive significance, and the amendments themselves. The Roman rule applies to both parts, but the Romans involved in the two cases are often quite different. For the amendments themselves, the rule requires that you follow the traditional form and style of the law being amended; for the vehicular part it requires that you follow the traditional form and style of the legislative forum in which you are working.

Thus in drafting a bill to revise a major existing law, the amendments themselves (the parts "within the quotes") should be written in the traditional form and style of that law, but the vehicular part would normally be written in the form and style most acceptable to the House and Senate in general and to the committees involved in particular. The form and style indicated by one subrule is usually the same as the form and style indicated by the other, but if it is not there is nothing wrong with using both of them so long as each is limited to its own part of the bill.

This would produce stylistic inconsistency, it is true—one of the few kinds of stylistic inconsistency that are permissible in a bill—but it has the virtue of satisfying two divergent constituencies. In addition, it is an excellent entering wedge for bringing about broader stylistic improvements in the law (see 8.5).

▶ **8.3**   **Form and style in freestanding bills**

The presumption in favor of the Roman rule is not as strong in freestanding bills. Since a direct comparison of forms and styles is harder to make in this case than in the case of amendatory bills, the use of a nontraditional form or style is not as jarring; and you should feel freer to use the form or style you prefer if you think it is demonstrably better than the traditional approach in the field involved (so long as you can prevent it from becoming a major distraction).

The presumption still exists, however. Nearly every major substantive field is governed by a tapestry of laws, and a new law in any field, even if it is freestanding, will become a part of that tapestry as soon as it is enacted. The people who administer those laws or are affected by them will tend to read them all together, as part of a larger whole; and those people may be uncomfortable working with the new law if it looks strange or seems inconsistent with the others.

In his own drafting experience the author has been known to decide these questions in different ways at different times. It always involves balancing the advantages of the Roman rule against the advantages of other forms or styles; and if you can successfully do that you are as qualified as the author would be to determine which way to go in any given situation.

▶ **8.4**   **Broader considerations**

The most obvious case for the literal application of the Roman rule, in freestanding as well as amendatory bills, involves such specific things as headings, typography, the names and order of subdivisions, and the designations by which subdivisions are identified (in terms of Arabic or Roman numerals, uppercase or lowercase letters, or other devices). All of these have to do with the stylistic framework within which particular legislative ideas are presented.

Another obvious case involves out-of-the-ordinary definitions and usages of key words and phrases, especially where the odd definition or usage (in the jurisdiction or setting concerned) is not limited to just the particular statute with which the drafter is working.

But there are broader cases in which the rule—though it cannot be applied literally—may still have something to say. These cases usually involve the overall flavor that the drafter's approach will give to the relevant statutory law if the bill is enacted. They might include such things as the organization and arrangement of provisions, the extent to which particular drafting devices (such as definitions and tabulation) are employed, or the way in which verb forms are used.

There are no standards for dealing with these cases. If a future reader of the law that results from your bill's enactment (because of your approach or the flavor of your language) would be able to detect which of its provisions had been added or revised by someone other than its original drafter, there is at least a slight presumption that a modified Roman rule should have been applied; and you might want to reconsider whether the benefits of your improvements are really sufficient to outweigh the benefits of the rule.

▶ 8.5   **Sidestepping the rule with discretion**

Professional drafters apply the Roman rule routinely in most cases, without ever thinking about it or giving it a name, simply because it is good drafting practice; every bill should fit comfortably within its context. However, it must be admitted that the rule does perpetuate bad drafting practices.

To the extent that professional drafters disagree about the subject, their arguments usually concern cases where (although they may agree that applying the rule would perpetuate a bad drafting practice) they differ on the question of just how bad the practice needs to be before a violation of the rule is justified or on the question of whether the structural situation involved makes it acceptable. Their answers to these questions, as indicated earlier, are largely based on personal preferences and other subjective considerations.

There are a number of professional drafters, however, who may feel that some isolated drafting practice is sufficiently bad to warrant an all-out attack on it. They might be willing to apply the Roman rule in most cases, but they would never use that particular practice (and might even try to eliminate any existing instances of it they encounter).

And there are others with an even broader ax to grind. They suffer real anguish at the multiplicity of inferior drafting forms and styles that are in use; they feel that there is one approach to form or style that is demonstrably better (for one or more legitimate reasons) than any other; and they believe that one of the overriding objectives of the drafting fraternity should be to improve all drafting by bringing about the universal adoption of that approach.

In both cases the dissenters are often right in principle about the virtues of what they are trying to do (although of course different factions may be promoting altogether different styles); but their efforts usually fail because of practical considerations—most often because they have no way of preventing the stylistic inconsistency that would result from the input of other drafters (over whom they have no control). In addition, any head-on assault upon the Roman rule as a whole is hard to sell; even the House Legislative Counsel's Office, which is normally the final arbiter in the House on such matters, had to break off its long-term crusade to have all bills written in "revenue style" and content itself with merely recommending the adoption and use of that style (or a modified version) in all situations where it would cause no tactical or public-relations problems.

To what extent should you be willing to conduct a crusade for changes in form or style? Obviously there is no single answer. If you are certain that the changes you would like to see adopted are good ones, you ought to feel reasonably free to take a few liberties with the Roman rule. But don't do it if you are not in a position to carry the crusade through consistently, both in the bill you are currently working on and in future bills in the same field, or if you sense that it would evoke a hostile response from your sponsor or from anyone else whose appreciation of your product is important.

So long as the drafting world remains imperfect you must never forget, no matter how filled with crusading zeal you may be, that there will always be cases (especially those involving amendatory bills) where you have no choice but to follow the Roman rule. If it is likely that your work will be edited by another drafter somewhere along the line, you should keep in mind that the liberties you take with the rule may eventually tarnish your image as a drafter.

Readability

▶ **9.1   In general**

Producing legislative language that can easily be read and comprehended by any literate person is of course one of the drafter's major objectives. After all, when a bill becomes law it not only creates rights, liabilities, and obligations but must also inform the intended audience about them in a way that can be understood, so that the affected persons will know where they stand and the future administrators will know what is expected of them.

Thus the way in which you use words and structure sentences is just as important in the interest of readability as it is in the interest of clarity and precision. Unless it is absolutely necessary for the accurate expression of an unusual or complex idea, any language that could confuse or bewilder the reader is suspect even though it may be technically correct, and you should seek an acceptable alternative. The best drafting expresses its ideas in as easy and natural a way as the subject matter allows.

And of course simplicity and readability do tend to promote clarity in turn; they are much to be desired whenever it is possible to achieve them. The avoidance of unnecessary complexity will help readers grasp the intended meaning; and in addition it will help the drafter ensure that he is not the only person in the world who is capable of following the threads, so that later drafters of reasonable skill can easily adjust his words to fit changing circumstances.

Make no mistake about it. Every drafter should consciously strive to produce language that makes it possible for any serious reader to extract the message without undue effort. However, this is sometimes easier said than done; and the rest of this chapter addresses the reasons why.

▶ 9.2   Archaic usages

One barrier to readability in the law, of course, is the widespread use of archaic or excessively legalistic terminology, style, and form (see also 7.2 and chapter 22)—largely a bequest from earlier times but still quite prevalent among lawyers and (regrettably) among drafters. Except in the relatively few cases where a particular archaic usage still has demonstrable value, you should always try to avoid it.

Unfortunately, many archaic practices have become so imbedded in existing statutes that the drafter of an amendment may simply have to perpetuate at least some of the old forms and structural anomalies in order to maintain internal consistency and satisfy the Roman rule.

The only real way around this problem is to rewrite the old law entirely, eliminating the archaic forms and obsolete provisions first and then amending it. This is not normally a viable option, however. It would necessitate the restatement and reenactment of provisions that have nothing to do with the sponsor's proposal, and would not only obscure the sponsor's policy but also almost certainly cause legal and practical problems by gratuitously opening old wounds.

As an aside, it should be noted that the process of rewriting old laws to eliminate archaic forms and obsolete provisions on a broad scale—known as "codification" or "code revision"—has long been under way in many States as well as at the Federal level. However, it is not an easy task, or one that can be done quickly. Maryland and Virginia, for example, have been working at it for decades and are barely half finished. The head of the Maryland code revision project has estimated that it may continue well into the next century, adding that "there is some hideous work ahead" [1]. And Congress has been continuously revising the United States Code for many years with the objective of enacting the

---

[1] F. Carvel Payne, the director of the Maryland Department of Legislative Reference (which oversees the project), as quoted in the *Washington Post,* August 26, 1989.

revisions into positive law, title by title; but the job is less than a third done and most of the more difficult titles have not even been touched (see 29.4).

If a particular usage or form sounds outdated and is one that you wouldn't use in everyday speech or ordinary prose composition, it is suspect. But an occasional lapse doesn't diminish readability much, and there are many borderline cases along with a number of uniquely legislative practices that look out-of-date but are quite legitimate. All you can really do as a practical matter is scrupulously avoid any usage or form that is clearly an outmoded relic of an earlier age and make your judgment on a case-by-case basis in all doubtful situations.

▶ 9.3   **Complexity**

In spite of your efforts to write clear and simple 20th-century English and avoid archaic usages and forms, there is a more basic barrier to reader comprehension in many cases—complexity. The growing impenetrability of legislation is not wholly, or even primarily, the fault of its drafters; in the words of *Hirsch* (page 1), it simply—

> mirrors the increasingly complicated ways in which government intervenes in both private and public activity; . . . [A]s statutes grow longer, the main impediment to their intelligibility is the poorly organized, convoluted, or otherwise slovenly treatment [by the policymakers themselves] of concepts that demand precision.

Laws are more complex because life itself and the legislative policies necessary to deal with it have become increasingly complicated. Any policy that treats everyone exactly alike, without any qualifications, conditions, or exceptions, can always be written simply and readably, but it will almost certainly result in unfairness, because people's circumstances differ; it is the qualifications, conditions, and exceptions—not the basic objectives—that produce the complexity. If the policy of the social security program, for example, had been simply to pay a fixed benefit to everyone at age 65, the law would be only a few pages long, but the actual policy decreed that the benefits should be work-related rather than fixed, that dependents, survivors, and disabled people should be covered (under separate formulas), that eligibility must be proved, and so forth—which accounts for the several hundred additional pages and almost all of the complexity.

Faced with these problems in the real drafting world, readability must frequently take a back seat to more important objectives. Remember that readability is not the same thing as clarity. For proposals that are highly complex or technical or are addressed primarily to specialists, or the basic thrust of which is determined largely by long-established judicial pronouncements, readability may actually be incompatible with clarity, and it may hardly be worth the drafter's time to seek it. In the words of one practical and experienced drafter (*Hirsch,* page 43), the style of legislative prose "is cousin to that of the assembly instructions included with children's swing sets; it must take special pains to be precise, regardless of the cost to other literary values".

When readability and clarity are incompatible, it is invariably because there is a fundamental difference between the nature and purpose of legislative language on the one hand and the nature and purpose of ordinary communication between human beings on the other.

Everyday conversations between ordinary people are full of generalizations and imprecise terminology, but it usually doesn't matter. If one person speaking to another uses a word that describes 95 percent of what it is supposed to describe or makes a statement that would be true 95 percent of the time, and can reasonably assume that the listener understands in general what he is trying to say, any further effort to spell out the special conditions, qualifications, and circumstances that might define the 5-percent exception would be regarded by both of them as unnecessarily pompous and inappropriate. The speaker can express himself in simple everyday terms, without dotting each "i" and crossing each "t", and the listener will get the message.

In a statute, however, every contingency must be covered. If the language used would get the wrong result (or would simply not apply) in 5 percent of the situations which it was intended to address, the drafter has committed an unforgivable sin. And if covering every contingency means using unfamiliar or technical words, or adding a string of conditions, qualifications, exceptions, and special rules, the drafter must give up his quest for simplicity and easy reading, or at least make it secondary to his quest for precision.

Experienced drafters use the tricks of the trade discussed in chapter 23 every chance they get, not only because those devices promote clarity but because, although they may make the statutory language less readable than everyday prose, they make it significantly more readable than if they were not used (see 9.4).

There are many types of bills and fields of law that are relatively simple in their scope and content, of course, and a drafter working on such a bill or in such a field has a fighting chance to keep the product readable. There are probably just as many, however, that are not simple at all, and cannot be made simple.

No bill amending the Internal Revenue Code or the Social Security Act, for example, is likely to be simple and readable, even if the basic policy is completely straightforward. Given their inherent complexity and the endless interrelationships of their provisions, the drafter should not waste too much time seeking a simple and readable way to amend them, since the straightforward basic policy still has to be woven into the existing tapestry and in the process will become unavoidably hard to follow for anyone but a specialist.

Even James Craig Peacock—a well-known commentator on legislative drafting who is hardly an ardent admirer of modern-day drafting practices—admits that

> legislation dealing with technical subject matter cannot be couched in the ordinary language of the street. Neither is there ordinarily any occasion . . . to direct either phraseology or other phases of a draft to maximum comprehensibility at that level.[2]

He does go on to say (correctly) that

> [this] does not mean that a draftsman should ever relax his efforts to put his draft into the most convenient and intelligible form which is possible under all the circumstances. For judges and lawyers and administrators are human, and even though as a group they may have become more experienced in . . . legislation their work should not for that reason be made any more difficult than is absolutely necessary.

A final consideration (addressed more fully elsewhere) is that as laws become more complicated and technical, they are simply not intended to be read by the casual public at all. When this book says that good drafting should result in statutory language that can be comprehended by anyone (as it

---

[2] Peacock, *Notes on Legislative Drafting* (REC Foundation, Inc. (1961), page 7.)

does frequently), the word "anyone" should be read as meaning "anyone who is a member of the intended audience, or who is interested enough to expend the effort needed to become familiar with legislative language in general and with the concepts in the field involved in particular". It makes no more sense to expect a casual reader to grasp all the implications of a complicated law (no matter how hard the drafter works) than it would to expect a casual viewer of soap operas to understand how the television set manages to produce its picture.

For members of specialized audiences and serious students of legislation, legislative language is readable only if it is clear, accurate, and precise.

▶ **9.4**   **Maximizing readability in the face of adversity**

That a statute is hard to read and understand is not necessarily a compelling criticism of the drafter. What the drafter should be ashamed of is needlessly making a statute hard to read and understand. And there are ways of approaching difficult drafting assignments that can eliminate many unnecessary complexities.

You can achieve a respectable level of readability in most cases, and learn how to recognize (and forgive yourself for) the cases in which you can't, if you follow the precepts laid down in this book (particularly chapter 6 and part VI), even in bills that are inherently quite complicated. Nearly all of the drafting rules and principles recommended in this book have the effect of promoting readability even if that is not their primary purpose.

Admittedly, there are circumstances in which it may not be possible to achieve the degree of readability you would like. These circumstances generally involve cases in which the application of all the book's precepts would be impossible, undesirable, or at least impractical because—

1. the Roman rule or the underlying structure of the statute being amended does not permit it;

2. the overriding objective of maximum clarity unavoidably calls for a more technical (and less readable) approach; or

3. the substantive problems involved are so complex or esoteric that nothing could make their solution readable.

If you ever find yourself in one of these situations, resign yourself to it—you can't go on fruitlessly looking for some ideal that doesn't exist. But you usually can apply at least some of the precepts, and you should always try to improve readability by applying as many of them as you can. Partial readability is better than none at all. Give special attention to the techniques for handling complexity that are recommended in chapter 23. These techniques intimidate many people, probably because they often make the provisions involved look a bit like exercises in arithmetic or geometry, but once mastered they are anything but intimidating.

Columnar tables are actually quite easy to read and follow, if the headings and relationships of the columns are clear and adequately descriptive. And a good table, like a computer spreadsheet, can say with complete precision in half a page what it would take 10 convoluted pages to say in words.

Tabulated sentences sometimes do have a frightening appearance, but their only real drawback is that they have to be read slowly and with extra care, with special attention to the conjunctions and punctuation—not that they are actually hard to follow.

And incorporations by reference can be made more understandable by including "relating to" clauses—brief parenthetical descriptions of what the referred-to provisions do; for example, ". . . under section 216(i)(3) (relating to insured status for disability benefit purposes)", or ". . . in part IX (relating to expenses not deductible)". Such clauses are regularly used in the tax laws, and ought to be used more widely by drafters in every field.

In any event, when the intended audience is a specialized one the problem tends to go away—specialists in any field quickly learn to use these devices in their everyday work, simply because it makes the work easier. You should always remember that you are not comparing the readability of statutory language that includes these devices to the readability of a gothic novel—you are comparing it to the readability of statutory language that does not use them at all, which is a very different proposition.

As a drafter, you simply cannot ignore the virtues of these devices just because they have a superficial appearance of complexity. To the contrary, they eliminate complexity, they shorten a bill by removing mountains of convoluted language, and they make it easier for everyone—you, your co-workers, and your eventual readers—to talk about, analyze, and remember the ideas and concepts involved. With a little effort they can quickly become second nature; and the result will be statutory language which (in addition to being clearer and more precise) may astonish you by turning out to be simpler and more readable as well.

You should make that effort, and you should not hesitate to ask your readers to make it too.

▶ **9.5**   **Short sentences versus tabulation—a case study**

Hirsch (page 52), in gently chiding *HOLC* for its insistence on short sentences in legislation, uses as an example a provision from the (now-repealed) Medicare Catastrophic Coverage Act of 1988, which consisted primarily of one long tabulated sentence (and which, as it happens, was written in the very office that produced *HOLC*). It may be instructive to repeat that example here.

The provision as enacted read as follows:

(A) IN GENERAL.—Except as provided in subparagraph (B), for drugs dispensed in—

(i) 1990 or 1991, the administrative allowance under this paragraph is—

(I) $4.50 for drugs dispensed by a participating pharmacy, or

(II) $2.50 for drugs dispensed by another pharmacy; or

(ii) a subsequent year, the administrative allowance under this paragraph is the administrative allowance under this paragraph for the preceding year increased by the percentage increase (if any) in the implicit price deflator for gross national product (as published by the Department of Commerce in its *Survey of Current Business*) over the 12-month period ending with August of such preceding year.

Any allowance determined under clause (ii) which is not a multiple of 1 cent shall be rounded to the nearest multiple of 1 cent.

Hirsch's experimental rewrite of the provision in the short-sentence mode was as follows:

(A) IN GENERAL.—For 1990 or 1991, the administrative allowance under this paragraph is $4.50 for drugs dispensed by a participating pharmacy. It is $2.50 for drugs dispensed by another pharmacy. For a year subsequent to 1991, the administrative allowance for drugs dispensed under this paragraph is the preceding year's administrative allowance under this paragraph, adjusted. Make that adjustment as follows. Compute the increase, if any, in the implicit price deflator for gross national product over the 12 months ending with August of such preceding year. Then raise the preceding year's allowance by that increase. Finally, round the allowance to the nearest multiple of 1 cent. For purposes of the computation, use the gross national product established by the Department of Commerce in its *Survey of Current Business.*

None of the 8 sentences in the rewritten version is longer than 25 words and most are considerably shorter, as compared to the 100 or so words in the first sentence of the original. And each of its sentences is certainly more "readable" than the corresponding piece of the original. But the rewritten version as a whole is slightly longer than the original, the apparent moral (depending on your point of view) being either that length has nothing to do with simplicity or that too many sentences garble the message.

You must be your own judge, of course, about which version is more "readable" as a whole. The original (tabulated) version, however, has several advantages over the short-sentence version:

1. Because its various components are tabulated and have specific alphanumeric designations—for example "(i) 1990 or 1991" and "(ii) a subsequent year", or "(I) $4.50" and "(II) $2.50"—they can be more easily cross-referred to at other points in the statute.

2. For the same reason, its components can be more easily and intelligibly amended—for example, by breaking down the formula into 3 or 4 levels instead of just two—if that should become necessary later.

3. And its structure makes both drafting and statutory construction easier. The "except" clause at the beginning, for example, warns the reader that the allowances established by the provision may not actually apply in all cases (a warning which is relatively trivial in this case but could be quite important in slightly different circumstances),

while the many sentences used in the rewritten version do not lend themselves to the use of a single qualifying clause.

The example given is not intended as an attack on the short-sentence principle, which in most cases is the right way to go, or as a definitive demonstration of readability; and the differences described in the preceding paragraph are not always important. But it explains, at least in part, why drafters so often use long sentences—even drafters who tell us we must use short ones.

Part IV

Writing the Provisions
of a Prototypical Bill

General Considerations

▶ **10.1   Organization**

The organization of a bill—the determination of which provisions need to be included and the way they should be arranged—is a matter that you would normally decide upon before the actual writing begins. This subject was discussed in some detail in chapter 6, but it may be worthwhile to revisit it briefly.

All bills do not present the same organizational problems, of course. In very simple bills organization is not even a factor, and in more complicated bills it may have to be treated as tentative (and subject to modification as the work progresses). For the most part the succeeding chapters will assume that you are working on a midsized bill, of moderate substance and manageable proportions; but no matter what kind of bill is involved you shouldn't bother to sharpen your pencil until you are sure that you have some kind of overall framework into which your words can be fitted.

HOLC's general principle—that the most important thoughts should come first—is a good starting point. And *Dickerson*'s rules of thumb—that the key operating provisions come first, the general provisions precede the specific, the more important provisions precede the less important, the more frequently used provisions precede the less frequently used, the permanent provisions precede the temporary, and the "housekeeping" provisions come last—are worth keeping in mind as you work.

The order of a bill's "typical" provisions recommended by some legislative drafting manuals (see 6.2) can be moderately helpful, but it can mislead the unwary drafter since no two bills are identical and no one arrangement fits all situations; the organization of a bill in real life is never quite that straightforward. Most bills of any substance, for example, contain introductory provisions which should normally be placed ahead of the key operating provisions, superficially violating several of the general rules. And in addition the category into which a particular type of provision falls is not always the same, but may depend upon the nature and scope of the bill in which it appears.

However, the underlying thread in all cases is very simple: Give prominence to the more important thoughts and down-play the others, but keep their interrelationship clear.

This part does not pretend to tell you how you should organize and write any particular bill. It does list and discuss the various types of provisions that might be included, taking them in the order in which they would most often appear and indicating some of the considerations involved in writing them. But you will seldom encounter a drafting assignment in which all of these provisions would be included, or in which all of the recommended organizational rules would make sense; and in connection with any particular assignment you should just ignore the ones that don't.

▶ **10.2**   **Stylistic considerations**

Like the overall organization of the bill you are working on, the statutory format you will use in actually writing its various provisions should be clear in your mind before you start. Neither is something to be worked out as you write.

In this context the term "statutory format" describes only the external appearance of your provisions—the mechanical framework within which your thoughts are presented—and has nothing to do with the way in which the provisions themselves are phrased or what they should contain. (The term "drafting style" as used generally in this book—see especially chapter 31—is broader, including both statutory format and the internal phrasing of provisions.)

Statutory format involves such things as: How will you break down the bill into its various components? What system will you use for designating them? What system (if any) will you use for indenting inferior subdivisions? Will any or all of the bill's components have headings, and if so how and where will they be set on the page?

Every jurisdiction has one or more accepted statutory formats. The Federal Government has several, which coexist more or less amicably and which are discussed and evaluated in chapter 31; if you haven't read that chapter yet (and are working at the Federal level) you might be well advised to do so out of order, since the style and format you use often shapes the decisions you make. And sometimes, even within the same jurisdiction, the accepted statutory format in one field is different from the accepted format in another.

It is your obligation as a good drafter to know the accepted statutory format of the jurisdiction in which you are working (and in the field in which you are working if it makes a difference). If you work regularly in that jurisdiction (and field) it should be second nature to you, so that you never have to stop and think about it at all. In any other case you should do whatever is necessary to become familiar with it before starting to work, using some properly drafted bills or existing laws of the jurisdiction as models or consulting a manual if one is available.

▶ **10.3   Parliamentary considerations**

In every jurisdiction there are parliamentary rules and precedents that impose restrictions at various points in the legislative process.

Most of these restrictions are purely procedural and involve the way in which (or the stage at which) a bill may be considered after it has been introduced; they do not directly concern the initial drafter of the bill. But some of them actually limit what a bill may do, how it may do it, or what it may contain; and needless to say these concern the drafter at any stage.

Because there are so many parliamentary variations in different legislative settings, any detailed enumeration of parliamentary restrictions is beyond the scope of this book. But you should remain alert to the possibility of their existence, and should do what you can to identify at least the most obvious ones. Drafters working at the Federal level should pay special attention to chapter 32 (which deals specifically with the subject).

▶ **10.4   Using models**

In general.   There is no limit to the variety of bills you could conceivably be called upon to draft. Some are very short and to the point (which doesn't necessarily mean they are insubstantial—a two-line bill simply changing a date can affect millions of people in important ways). At the other extreme, a few are so demanding in terms of their size, scope, and complexity (or the number of different subjects involved) that they would intimidate any drafter. Most bills fall somewhere in the middle, being substantial enough to require serious attention to structure and form without posing insurmountable problems.

You as a drafter must often approach your subject head-on, straightforwardly saying what needs to be said and not worrying about whether some previous drafter may have said it differently. But many bills, and many provisions within bills, occur frequently or fall into recognizable categories—some bills are introduced literally hundreds of times each Congress, by Members who want to get onto some bandwagon or other, with little or no variation in form or substance.

You should take advantage of this and categorize the provisions you are working on whenever you can. You'll be able to treat already introduced bills or previously enacted statutes containing similar provisions (or isolated pieces of such bills or laws) as models. Using existing examples in this way can get you started when you are otherwise at a loss as to how to proceed, by helping you decide upon the approach you should take and by reassuring you that you have not forgotten to address any of the topics that need to be dealt with. Experienced drafters are constantly on the lookout for this kind of help.

Boilerplate. In addition to the more generalized models, there are many provisions that appear over and over again in the laws of any jurisdiction. Some of them are always exactly the same (for example, the limitation on attorneys' fees that is required under congressional rules for all private relief bills making cash awards); these are colloquially known as "boilerplate" forms. Others are always similar and have the same overall structure but the operative terms, dates, dollar amounts, and other specifics may differ (for example, bills creating study commissions, most of which are structured in more or less the same way and differ from each other only in such areas as the description of the problem to be studied and the membership of the commission); these may be viewed simply as boilerplate forms with a few blanks to be filled in.

Boilerplate forms are such good models that they hardly constitute models at all. In fact, they can often be inserted into a draft verbatim, without the painstaking modification that accompanies the use of models in other cases.

As you become aware of the boilerplate forms that recur in the field or fields in which you work, you should preserve them in a file, keep it handy, and use it regularly. Such a file will be a great time-saver; and it will promote accuracy as well if you are careful, since the use of language that has stood the test of time in similar situations avoids the inadvertent creation of new problems and furthers uniformity in the law.

Particular provisions.   The complexity of a provision, in and of itself, is usually not what creates the need for help in the form of a model—it is the fact that the provision involves a specialized area of law in which you are not a specialist, or a subject with which you are unfamiliar.

Thus in writing the opening provisions of a bill (discussed in chapter 11), you will not normally derive any benefit from the use of a model; the provisions are usually simple, the ground to be covered is clear, and even when one of them (such as a definition section) is complex the complications are likely to be related to the substantive area in which you are working (and with which you may be presumed to be reasonably familiar) rather than to the specific type of provision it is. The same thing is true of provisions authorizing appropriations, which are more central but seldom present difficulties.

But in writing most of the other provisions of the bill—the central or operating provisions (discussed in chapter 12) and the closing provisions (chapter 13)—you would frequently be well advised to cast about for a suitable model, either because those provisions are specialized (as in the case of administrative, judicial review, and penalty provisions, which can often be treated as just boilerplate forms with blanks to be filled in) or because they are unusual enough to be outside your everyday drafting arsenal (as in the case of savings provisions and separability clauses). Being knowledgeable in the substantive field in which you are working is not enough; collateral issues of this kind will often present you with your most difficult drafting problems.

If you need to include any of these provisions in your bill, the corresponding provision in an existing law or a previously drafted bill can be of help as a model even if the subject matter of that law or bill is totally different from yours. It could not be copied into your bill verbatim, of course—the difference in subject matter would make that impossible—but the specialized approach is what you are looking for, and that approach (along with its format) would usually be the same or at least quite similar.

Program models. All that has been said so far has had to do with specific types of provisions that might appear in any bill. But there is a much broader approach that experienced drafters often take in easing their task through the use of models.

When you are asked to draft a bill to establish a new program you may be able to find (and you should usually try to find) one or more existing laws or previously drafted bills that establish similar programs—not necessarily similar in terms of their specific purpose but in terms of their scope, the nature of the benefits they confer, and the kind of administrative structure they use to accomplish it.

Most loan programs, for example, require many of the same kinds of provisions—those relating to eligibility, application, amount, terms and conditions, funding, and monitoring—regardless of the different classes or types of recipients and the different purposes for which the loans involved are to be made. The same is true of most grant programs, most benefit programs, and most construction programs, as well as of most bills establishing new agencies or new entities within existing agencies. And most regulatory laws possess the same general set of specialized provisions. Usable models are available everywhere.

State plan programs. If a bill is intended to establish an assistance program that could appropriately be administered by the States with Federal funding (instead of being wholly federally run), you might use a State plan approach. The author proposes to address this approach in slightly more detail, using the AFDC program (title IV-A of the Social Security Act) as the model, because—

1. a State plan program is a very specialized form of legislation with the details of which most drafters will be unfamiliar, but which lends itself well to the modeling approach we have been discussing;

2. although it almost always involves substantive complications, it is quite straightforward from the drafting point of view; and

3. it exemplifies a number of the points made above.

In essence, a provision establishing a State plan program

simply says (not necessarily in this order) that any State which has an approved State plan will be entitled to Federal funds to carry out the program, that the plan must contain certain specified provisions in order to be approved, that the Federal share of the costs will be determined in a specified way, and that appropriations to pay this share are authorized.

Title IV-A of the Social Security Act contains four basic sections (reflecting the four items that any State plan provision must contain, as indicated in the preceding paragraph), followed by a number of miscellaneous sections which (however constructive) are not part of the main thrust and were not originally included. The four basic sections are as follows:

Section 401 (titled "Appropriation") says that, for the purpose of aiding dependent children and their families, an annual appropriation of whatever sums may be necessary is authorized, and that the amounts appropriated are to be used for making payments to States which have approved State plans. A drafter using this program as a model would only have to change the purpose clause. Section 401 itself is less than half a page long, and the purpose clause occupies most of it.

Section 402 (titled "State Plans . . .") lists in subsection (a) the things that a State plan must include in order to be approved, and then provides in subsection (b) that the Secretary (of Health and Human Services) must approve any plan that includes those things. Subsection (a) consists of 45 convoluted and further-subdivided paragraphs, most of which are unique to the AFDC program and would be ignored or replaced by the model-seeking drafter, but a number of which (such as those dealing with administrative structure, State financial participation, fair hearings, reports, privacy, and fraud) could be picked up and used anywhere. Subsection (b) contains a few exceptions to the automatic approval requirement, but they too are unique to AFDC and would be ignored or replaced. The overall structure of the section would be appropriate in any State plan program.

Section 403 (titled "Payment to States") directs the Secretary to pay quarterly to each State having an approved plan an amount determined in accordance with a specified formula. The section is very long and the formula impossibly complicated, but it's the thought that counts—the whole thing could have been done in 6 lines if the policy had been simple enough.

Section 404 (titled "Operation of State Plans") contains sanctions against States for imposing prohibited requirements or failing to comply with their approved State plans. These are not the usual civil or criminal penalties—they simply provide a system for withholding Federal funds when there is a substantial State violation—but they would be appropriate and usable in any State plan program.

These sections—along with the dozen or so sections that follow—do contain additional matter, but it is extraneous to the purpose of the example and could be ignored (or added to) in another State plan program.

Hirsch (page 33) asserts that "State plan provisions give Federal statutes a bad name", citing the 8,000 words and multiple subdivisions of the single sentence that comprises section 402(a) in the AFDC law (neglecting to mention the State plan provisions of the medicaid law, compared to which the AFDC provisions are a model of brevity and simplicity). But State plan provisions usually start off fairly simply and become complicated later because of two things—the need to accommodate the Federal law to the divergent situations in 50 States (a need whose specifics only gradually become apparent after the program gets under way) and the inevitable recognition of initial omissions in the list of requirements that any State plan should contain.

Companion bills.   When the same bill is introduced in both the House and the Senate—printed from the same type, as it were, and usually done that way because the proponents in the two bodies wish to present a united front—the two are said to be *companion* bills. A companion bill is cousin to a good model, but it is not a model—it is the exact duplicate of the document you need. This can be very helpful when you can't locate a copy of a bill that you need; its companion (if it has one) will serve your purposes equally well in most cases.

And when a particular bill is separately introduced by two or more Members in the same body the same considerations may apply, although the bills are not called companions since the introducers are less likely to have acted in concert.

In either case you must exercise caution, however, because many bills that are publicly touted as companion bills are not—they have minor differences that may be unimportant to most people but could be critical for a drafter.

A warning.   The use of models is one of the drafter's most valuable devices when the models are good ones and they are selected correctly and relied upon with discretion, but it is one of the most dangerous when they are not. Some of the worst horror stories in legislative drafting history involve cases where the drafter selected an inappropriate model or used it carelessly. What is right for one policy may be totally wrong for another, even though they may seem to call for similar structural approaches.

Every experienced drafter is familiar with requests for bills creating programs that are "exactly like the ABC program except...". Almost invariably the exceptions multiply as the project receives further thought, until it becomes obvious that what is really wanted is a different animal altogether.

And a simple substitution of one term or concept for another is almost never the answer. One of the most fun-filled afternoons in the author's professional drafting career was spent trying to explain to the staff of the select committee that eventually produced the NASA Act just how ludicrous it would be to start from the Atomic Energy Act and simply substitute "space" for "nuclear energy" wherever it appeared (which was the staff's preferred approach at the time).

However, models can serve you well if you keep the possible pitfalls in mind. And perhaps most important of all, the use of a model can get you started when you don't know which way to turn at the beginning of a drafting job that involves unfamiliar territory. Even if your more deliberate consideration of the similarities between the model and your project leads you to the conclusion that the model can't actually contribute much, you are ahead of the game and you have a picture of what needs to be done that you wouldn't otherwise have had at such an early stage.

▶ 10.5   **When and how should the writing begin?**

Although it should be evident by now that in most drafting assignments a good deal of work has to be done before the actual writing begins, you can't postpone the evil moment forever. Unfortunately, there is no objective rule for identifying that moment. It depends in any case upon the particular circumstances in which you are working: Is the policy completely clear? Do you have all the information you need? Are there time pressures? Will the sponsor leave you alone while you work, or keep looking over your shoulder until you finish?

There are some general principles that may help you determine when the time is ripe for picking up your pen, and the most basic among them is this: Having faithfully served the sponsor's needs in the process of determining what to write, you should now serve your own (to the extent possible) in determining when and how to do it.

The sponsor's initial policy statement to the drafter represents a set of legislative specifications to be carried out; and you must ask yourself at every stage whether you understand those specifications well enough to draft from them:

1. Are they clear? Can you understand each specification well enough to convert it into a legal requirement?

2. Are they complete? Does the set of specifications include an instruction on every item that needs to be included in the bill?

3. Are they administratively feasible? On a mechanical level, will the bill work? If you were the future administrator at the operating level, would you know how to carry out the bill's directives?

As a practical matter you will normally begin working on some of the specifications as soon as you receive them, but you may have to seek further guidance on others. In extreme cases the specifications may be so incomplete or ambiguous as to be unusable; most of the time, though, they will be sufficient to enable you, after clarifying a handful of issues, to write a first draft that contains at least something on every item with which they deal. Experienced drafters tend to develop a fairly reliable sense of what unresolved questions they should initially try to answer for themselves.

Needless to say, dividing the drafting process into discrete steps or stages (as described in 3.2 and 3.3) is an oversimplification in the real world. Unless the basic thrust of the policy is totally unclear or involves a subject about which you have no prior knowledge, you will almost always begin writing before all of the preliminary questions have been resolved. Preparing a rough working draft as soon as possible saves time in the long run, helps unearth some of the important questions that you may have overlooked, and is often the best way to smoke out the problems and stimulate the policymaker to face them.

Many experienced drafters prefer to begin writing immediately upon receiving a reasonably concrete drafting request, simply guessing at obscurities, arguing that the best test of whether they understand an idea is whether they can write a provision expressing it. After all, during the writing itself you can expect to discover gaps and ambiguities even in policies that at first seemed complete and clear.

This approach may seem at odds with what has been said earlier about the care that should be taken in carrying out the sponsor's policy exactly. And, admittedly, it might be more efficient to remove all uncertainties before beginning to draft. But a draft bill—even one that is incomplete or in very rough form—is a marvelous instrument for concentrating the policy-maker's mind; it usually precipitates changes in the sponsor's policy (especially the subsidiary and collateral policies) that might not be thought of otherwise. Policy in its early stages is typically fluid, and today's decisions hastily made are tomorrow's decisions hastily reversed.

It is usually the time spent on perfecting a first draft that is actually the time wasted, and time is the drafter's most precious commodity. In addition, policymakers are an impatient breed; they ordinarily prefer to review an imperfect draft bill rather than put up with the delays that are sure to attend the drafter's effort to resolve all policy issues before writing anything.

And it is sad but true that the time reserved for the drafter has often been eroded by the sponsor's delays in reaching final decisions on the policy issues. Sometimes the waffling on questions of policy would not end at all except that over the horizon there comes into view some event—a presidential message, a committee meeting, or a major political event—that forces meditation to yield to action.

But when the time has arrived to pick up your pen, how and where do you start? As a general rule it makes no difference—the various sections of your working draft can be written in whatever order is most convenient and assembled in the proper order later.

If the bill will be massive and complicated, however, you may face a dilemma. On the one hand, the bill's main provisions (which are likely to take the most time) will almost certainly require policy review by the sponsor; ideally the initial draft of those provisions should be done first, to allow adequate time both for the sponsor's review and for the redrafting that will inevitably result from it. On the other hand (as *Hirsch* puts it (page 8)), "when one confronts a hungry lion one throws to it whatever meat is handy". Boilerplate and routine administrative provisions are often voluminous but nevertheless easy to write quickly; and if the sponsor is screaming for something on paper you may be well advised to dash off these provisions first, creating the appearance of great efficiency and at the same time giving yourself an opportunity to draft the really important provisions at your comparative leisure.

If the policy is obscure on a very basic aspect of the proposal (such as the main thrust itself), however, especially if it would be unusually time-consuming or otherwise hard to draft, you should generally seek more guidance before writing anything at all. And in any other case what you do should depend upon the time you have available, your feeling for what the sponsor is most likely to want, and the sponsor's accessibility.

In the last analysis, there is no one best way that fits all cases. You should pick up your pen when you think you are ready; and where you should begin is up to you. Unless a particular approach is absolutely required (or strongly indicated) because of external circumstances, whatever will make the overall operation easiest for you and assure the most efficient use of your energies, while keeping the sponsor happy, is the right way.

The Introductory Provisions

11.1 *Long titles*

11.2 *Enacting and resolving clauses*

11.3 *First sections*

11.4 *Short titles*

11.5 *Tables of contents*

11.6 *Statements of findings and purpose; whereas clauses*

11.7 *Definitions*

▶ **11.1   Long titles**

The "long title" of a bill is the general description of what it does. It appears on the first page, just after the heading "A BILL" (or the corresponding heading in the case of a resolution) and just before the enacting or resolving clause. Every bill has one.

Some States have specific requirements for what the title of a bill must contain; these differ widely—a few States even require that the title contain an explicit reference to every single item in the bill, however insignificant—and are beyond the scope of this book. What follows relates to titles at the Federal level, where there are a number of precedents but few if any hard-and-fast requirements.

A long title should be accurate and relatively brief (although that is often easier said than done, of course). In theory at least, it should not read like a press release—that is, it should not describe the reasons for the bill or set forth any of the sponsor's arguments, and it should not contain extraneous material or bombast.

It should always describe the bill's main thrust, of course, and if there are other miscellaneous, minor, or unrelated items in the bill they are usually handled by simply adding ", and for other purposes" just before the period at the end of the title.

If the bill contains several major ideas or components, it is appropriate either to mention them specifically in the long title or to leave the title quite general, stating the broad objective of the bill without specifically addressing any of its components. Thus the title of a bill designed to eliminate fraud and abuse in the medicare program might read:

> To amend title XVIII of the Social Security Act to eliminate fraud and abuse in the medicare program by improving accounting procedures, penalizing persons who file fraudulent applications for benefits, and requiring periodic reviews of eligibility in long-stay cases, and for other purposes.

or it might simply read:

> To eliminate fraud and abuse in the medicare program.

or even:

> To improve the administration and cut the costs of the medicare program.

There are no specific requirements of any kind, and (although you should always strive to make your titles both accurate and informative and to emphasize the sponsor's main objective) it really doesn't matter much what a bill's long title contains.

In the first place, laws today are almost never cited or referred to by their long titles, which for the most part are ignored after their enactment. In the second place, parliamentary maneuvering sometimes results in bills whose long titles bear little or no relationship to the substantive provisions they contain—the 63-page Balanced Budget and Emergency Deficit Control Act of 1985 (the Gramm-Rudman-Hollings law) was tacked onto the end of a 6-line joint resolution "Increasing the statutory limit on the public debt", and was enacted that way.

And finally, long titles (at the Federal level at least) have no legal significance; in theory they could be used by courts as interpretive aids, but the author knows of no case where this has happened.

Technically, the long title of a law is not even subject to change by subsequent amendatory legislation, no matter how obsolete or misleading it has become with the passage of time, because it precedes the enacting clause and thus was not actually a part of what was "enacted".

Long titles are written in a "hanging style" (first line flush, remaining lines indented). All of them start with "To" and proceed with whatever descriptive statement the drafter (or the sponsor) wants to make, like the examples given earlier—except in a few specific cases:

1. In an amendatory bill that consists primarily of amendments to a single law, the title should normally begin "To amend [that law] to provide for . . ." instead of just "To provide for. . .".

2. In a joint resolution (or any other resolution), the title should normally begin with a gerund—"Providing for. . ." instead of "To provide for. . .".

3. In a private relief bill, the title should read simply "For the relief of John Doe".

A bill's heading (which is often read as if it were a part of the long title) changes from "A BILL" to "AN ACT" as soon as one House passes it; but this is an arbitrary stylistic change that affects the heading only—the measure remains a bill from the drafter's point of view until the President signs it.

▶ **11.2   Enacting and resolving clauses**

Every bill in Congress begins (after the long title) with an enacting clause, or (in the case of a resolution) with a resolving clause. Chapter 2 of title 1 of the United States Code prescribes the form of these clauses.

An enacting clause, always set in italic type, reads:

> *Be it enacted by the Senate and House of Representatives of the United States of America in Congress assembled,*

and a resolving clause in a joint resolution uses the single word *"Resolved"* in place of *"Be it enacted"*. The resolving clauses in concurrent and simple resolutions (which do not become law because the President doesn't sign them) are somewhat different—see chapter 30 for examples.

In the case of a joint resolution proposing a constitutional amendment (which requires a two-thirds majority in both Houses), the words "(*two-thirds of each House concurring therein*)" are inserted before the final comma.

Note that a bill or joint resolution is "enacted" when the President signs it or takes no action within a specified period (or when it is passed over his veto). A simple resolution is "adopted" when it is agreed to by the House involved; and a concurrent resolution is "adopted" or "agreed to" when both Houses have acted affirmatively.

The drafter does not actually have to write the enacting or resolving clause in most cases. All printed forms for bills and resolutions already contain the appropriate clauses (except in the constitutional amendment case). In addition, if a draft bill is presented for introduction ("dropped into the hopper") without an enacting clause, the official who receives the bill will automatically supply one. It is probably a good idea, however, to at least indicate the enacting clause in any draft so that disoriented readers will know what kind of document it is; many experienced drafters start out every rough draft with a condensed version of the clause—"*Be it enacted, etc.*"—for this reason.

▶ **11.3 First sections**

In the early days of the Republic, the text of a bill was considered a continuation of the enacting clause, so it was thought necessary to give every section of the bill its own separate enacting clause, followed immediately by "That...". The sections were not numbered. This practice gradually disappeared, and today title 1 of the United States Code provides that "no enacting or resolving clause shall be used in any section of an Act or resolution of Congress except the first". As a result, a bill has only the one enacting clause; and all sections are given section numbers except in two cases, both involving the very first section of the bill.

Unless the first section has a heading (or will be separated from the enacting clause by one or more other headings), it may still properly begin with the word "That" (run in at the end of the enacting clause, on the same line) instead of being paragraphed and having a number (and beginning on the following line)—

1. If the so-called "classic" or "traditional" drafting style is being used (see chapter 31), or

2. If the bill has only the one section (regardless of the drafting style being used).

In these two cases the beginning of a bill would look like this:

Be it enacted by the Senate and House of Represen-

tatives of the United States of America in Congress assembled, That this Act may be cited as . . .;

although (in case (1)) the succeeding sections would be paragraphed and have numbers, beginning with "Sᴇᴄ. 2.". If neither case (1) nor case (2) applies, the first thing after "*in Congress assembled,*" (despite the fact that it results in an apparent discontinuity in the text) is either the section number or a heading, on a new line.

Even in case (1) (where the traditional style is the one being used), you should designate the first section as section 1 whenever possible, since it promotes internal consistency, permits the use of a heading, and facilitates citation and cross-reference. If you feel that you simply must use the classic ("That . . .") style for the section, subsequent references to it must be made to "the first section of this Act" rather than to "section 1".

And in case (2) the single section should never be divided into subsections—subsequent references to them would be awkward or even confusing. If there is a need for separate subdivisions, convert at least one of them into a separate section.

Note that section 1 of a bill is the only place where the section designation itself is spelled out; you say "Sᴇᴄᴛɪᴏɴ 1.", but you abbreviate the word and use the form "Sᴇᴄ. ___." at the beginning of all succeeding sections. (When used in a statutory cross-reference to any section, of course, the word "section" is never abbreviated and never capitalized except when it is the first word of a sentence.)

▶ 11.4   Short titles

Major statutes need names by which they can be easily cited and referred to—their long titles are much too cumbersome for this purpose, and their public law numbers are too uninformative—so they are typically given "short titles". If the sponsor of a major bill has forgotten to ask for a short title, the drafter can quite appropriately suggest that one be included. You should not invent your own, however, since a short title has public relations consequences that are better left to the sponsor, except in those rare cases where the right short title is altogether obvious.

Narrower bills, designed to deal with particular problems or to meet particular needs, are seldom given short titles. Proud sponsors occasionally want to see short titles in relatively insignificant bills, but the drafter would do well to discourage them, as gently and diplomatically as possible; the committee to which the bill is referred will almost certainly regard a short title as inappropriate.

A bill's short title customarily appears in the first section of the bill, immediately after the enacting clause (although in a few substantive fields it is traditionally placed at the end of the bill instead). Its basic form is simple:

SECTION 1. This Act may be cited as the "ABC Act".

Note that the word "the" is not a part of the short title, and should not be included within the quotes.

Variations in this form do occur. If the bill is one of a series of comprehensive revisions of existing law that are enacted every year or two in the substantive field involved, the short title should reflect the bill's place in the series by mentioning the year of its enactment; the text of the section containing the short title should read "This Act may be cited as the 'ABC Act of [1992]' ". (Note, however, that you should not normally include the year of expected enactment in the short title when it is not necessary to distinguish among a series of laws; having to remember and restate that year will be a nuisance to everyone who has to cite the law.)

And if the bill consists primarily of amendments to one or more existing statutes, it is appropriate (but not necessary) to substitute "Amendments" for "Act" in the short title; thus ". . . the 'ABC Amendments [of 1992]' ".

There is a growing tendency to provide separate short titles for some or all of the principal components of a major bill, even though the bill itself has a more comprehensive short title. This practice should generally be avoided; for citation and cross-reference purposes "title II of the ABC Act" is just as convenient as a separate short title for the component involved, and is much less confusing.

However, a separate short title for an individual component of a major statute that has its own comprehensive short title may be both appropriate and desirable—

1. where that component is unrelated to the rest of the statute, so that the statute's comprehensive short title would completely misrepresent it (or would at least be misleading as applied to it); and

2. in the case of an omnibus bill (such as a budget

reconciliation bill) that consists of unrelated proposals which would otherwise constitute individual pieces of legislation.

The Congressional Budget and Impoundment Control Act of 1974 has separate short titles for its two major components— the "Congressional Budget Act of 1974" for the first 9 titles of the Act (which relate to the congressional budget process) and the "Impoundment Control Act of 1974" for title X (which relates to Presidential impoundments).

One final comment. A short title should be short—it loses its value as a convenient handle if it is not. It should simply describe the field that the bill covers rather than going into detail about what the bill does. The Social Security Act, the National Housing Act, and the Internal Revenue Code of 1986 meet the test. The Balanced Budget and Emergency Deficit Control Act of 1986, on the other hand, seems a bit too cumbersome. And some short titles are real stylistic horrors— consider for example the Mental Retardation Facilities and Community Mental Health Centers Construction Act of 1963 (Public Law 88-164), and the Augustus F. Hawkins-Robert T. Stafford Elementary and Secondary School Improvement Amendments of 1988 (Public Law 100-297).

The last example given is bad on another count. You should resist naming the sponsor in the short title; leave it to posterity to give the sponsor the recognition he or she desires (and may even deserve). Note that the colloquial sponsor-related names often given to laws after their enactment, for easy reference, like the "Robinson-Patman Act" and the "Gramm-Rudman-Hollings Act", are both convenient and proper even though they cannot be used in statutory citations (except parenthetically, in an explanatory way).

Needless to say, if the sponsor has a pet short title you have no choice but to include it. And if a short title is actually taken up and considered in committee or on the floor, and has to satisfy all of the legislators' conflicting public relations needs, almost anything can happen; and you just have to live with it.

If you can't come up with a short title that is short, simple, and easy to say, at least try to come up with one that has a pronounceable acronym (but always watch out for short titles whose acronyms, when read or pronounced, might seem derisive, suggestive, or otherwise inappropriate).

It helps if the short title is one that can intelligibly be shortened for conversational purposes. The Congressional

Budget and Impoundment Control Act of 1974 is usually called simply the "Congressional Budget Act" (even though, as indicated earlier, it consists of two parts that have manageable short titles of their own), while any law whose short title specifies the year of its enactment can be conversationally referred to as "the [1987] Act" when the context is clear. Note that the various administrative procedure provisions of title 5 of the United States Code are still commonly referred to (collectively) as "the Administrative Procedure Act" even though the latter Act was repealed and replaced by the title 5 provisions many years ago.

▶ **11.5   Tables of contents**

If a lengthy bill has internal headings and is broken down into a large number of separate sections, particularly if it deals with several subjects and is also broken down into major components such as titles, subtitles, chapters, or parts, it should have a table of contents listing the headings of the sections and major components. And if the major components are lengthy, a subsidiary table of contents at the beginning of each of them should also be considered. This will greatly assist readers in finding their way through the morass (and will also serve as a working outline for the drafter while the bill is being developed).

Conversely, if a bill consists simply of a relatively few numbered sections—say sections 1 through 9—there is normally no good reason for a table of contents at all.

The table of contents should be located in the first section of the bill, immediately after the short title if there is one. Its style and form are not important, although there is a more or less standard form that should be followed in many jurisdictions; the Government Printing Office prints all tables of contents in what it regards as the standard Federal form (no matter what form was used in the raw copy) except when the variant form is clearly marked. (Note that although published compilations invariably contain tables of contents of the laws involved, these tables are often supplied by the compilers, and you cannot assume they are included in the laws themselves.)

If the bill contains a provision adding a number of new sections to an existing law (such as a completely new title or chapter), it may be useful to show those sections in the table of contents along with the vehicular provision, adopting a format (such as indenting the items referring to those sections and surrounding them with quotation marks) that will distinguish them from the sections of the bill itself. See 16.5 for an example.

One word of caution. Section numbers are often changed, and headings are often revised, during the course of the drafting process; and the drafter should remember to conform the table of contents whenever that happens. Waiting until the bill is finished and then proofreading the table of contents against the numbers and headings of the bill's provisions (though a desirable final double check) isn't good enough, because there is too often no time to do it (or it is just plain forgotten) in the final rush.

▶ **11.6** **Statements of findings and purpose; whereas clauses**

The practice of preceding the substantive portion of a bill with a statement of legislative findings and purpose or a statement of legislative policy, or both, is becoming increasingly popular. Sponsors seem to like the approach because it gives them a way to make their arguments and speeches right there in the legislation. In a few rather extreme recent cases, bills have actually been enacted with nothing in them except a dozen or so pages of findings, purpose, and policy, followed by a six-line substantive provision simply directing the designated official, in effect, to "carry out the purpose of this Act".

You should diplomatically discourage this practice. In most cases statements of findings and purpose are without legal significance; and in addition they are matters that are more appropriately (and more safely) dealt with in the various committee reports that will accompany the bill. The proper function of a bill—whatever the sponsor's reasons for it—is to do what the sponsor wants to do.

Note that there is no set form for statements of findings and purpose in a bill.

"Whereas clauses"—technically called the "preamble"—are used in resolutions to do what statements of findings and purpose do in bills. They appear before the resolving clause (and are therefore not part of the resolution proper) and are written in a "hanging" style rather than being paragraphed like normal bill provisions. They are punctuated as a list or series in the regular way (see chapter 21) and lead into the resolving clause with ": Now therefore be it" in place of a final period. For example:

Whereas serious problems have recently arisen in the ABC program;

Whereas something ought to be done about them; and

Whereas time is of the essence: Now therefore be it

Resolved, That [the designated official] should take immediate action to . . .

If the sponsor insists on including a statement of findings, purpose, or policy in a bill, or a series of whereas clauses in a resolution, you should ask the sponsor to submit a draft of it. Explain that you are not a mind reader or an expert in politics, economics, or public relations, and that you will of course be happy to edit whatever you are given and put it in the proper form.

But there is one case where a statement of findings and purpose may be appropriate and even desirable. Courts frequently do give weight to legislative findings when construing regulatory laws and other laws affecting commerce in cases where the constitutional basis for the Federal action may be open to question. For example, when drafting a bill to govern the intrastate manufacture and distribution of a particular article you should be amenable to a congressional finding that the manufacture and distribution of that article "affects" and is a "burden" on interstate commerce (and therefore is subject to regulation under the commerce clause of the Constitution).

▶ **11.7   Definitions**

In general.   Whenever a bill repeatedly uses a term that may be unfamiliar, unclear, or ambiguous (even if only when taken out of context), or uses a term in a sense that differs from its dictionary meaning, you should define it in the bill. A formal declaration that "as used in this Act [or section], the term 'A' means 'XX' " effectively dispels all doubt about the term's meaning.

The corollary is that a definition should never recite the obvious. A term that is familiar, clear, and used in its dictionary sense should never be formally defined (unless there are special circumstances that call for reassurance to the reader)—it would be unnecessary and might create doubts about the meaning of other familiar words in the bill. For example, the term "State" should be defined if you want to include the District of Columbia or Puerto Rico, but not if you mean to include only the 50 States.

The proper use of definitions in a bill does more than simply clarify the meaning of its crucial terms, however. It promotes internal consistency by assuring that those terms are given the same meaning regardless of their context, it avoids clutter, and it promotes readability and drafting economy by making the bill shorter and its language less cumbersome. In short, the purpose of definitions is to achieve clarity and consistency without burdensome repetition.

Of equal importance is the fact that definitions can reduce complexity by allowing the bill's key operating provisions to be stated simply, even when the concepts they involve are extremely complicated. Dealing with those concepts in a separate definition section does not actually eliminate the complications, of course, but it segregates them from the operating provisions and makes them easier to handle (see 23.2). It must be admitted, however, that the intensive use of definitions in this way usually entails putting at least some of the substantive rules in the definitions—a practice that has powerful enemies (and about which the author's views may not reflect the majority position among drafting commentators). See the discussion of definitions containing substantive rules ("stuffed definitions") below.

Placement of definitions.   In general, definitions should be placed where they can be most easily found, and where they will be most helpful to the reader. Thus the definition of a term used in only one section of a bill should always be included in that section, while the definitions of terms used throughout the bill should always be grouped in a separate section (usually headed simply "Definitions") which normally appears early in the bill. The individual definitions in such a section are usually arranged in descending order of importance, although sometimes they are arranged alphabetically. (The problem with alphabetizing is that the addition of a new definition will require the redesignation of all the paragraphs appearing after the point where the new definition is inserted, often with extensive conforming changes elsewhere.)

Admittedly, definitions stacked at the beginning of a bill can be tedious and will delay the reader in coming to the bill's operative provisions. But their placement up front serves an important purpose: It gives the reader an early warning of any terms that may be obscure or technical or that are to be used in ways that differ from their dictionary definitions, and it ultimately makes the bill's operative provisions easier to comprehend.

If you do not want to confront the reader with a series of long and complicated definitions at the outset and prefer to place them instead in a later section of the bill—*HOLC* (page 25) takes the position that definitions should never precede the main message unless there are "strong organizational or tactical reasons" for it—you should at least include an unmistakable early cross-reference to that section. For example:

> ( ) Definitions.—For definitions of terms [or "the principal terms"] used in this Act, see section ____.

Sometimes the defined terms in a bill include one or two basic terms along with a number of others that are less important. In such cases it is appropriate to define each of the important ones in a separate section (headed "XX Defined") and the others in another section (headed "Other Definitions").

Whether or not the bill contains a separate section or subsection devoted exclusively to definitions, if there is a recurring term (for example, an organizational name or title such as "Agency" or "Secretary") that could use a short definition, it is quite proper (despite the apparent violation of the rules given above) to simply insert the definition parenthetically after the first mention of that term. Thus:

> Sec. 2.(a) The Secretary of Housing and Urban Development (in this [Act, section, or other provision] referred to as the "Secretary") shall. . .

And if a defined term is used ahead of the definition and it is particularly important in the context to warn the reader that the term has a specially prescribed meaning, a specific (though technically unnecessary) parenthetical warning— "(as defined in section ____)"—can be inserted immediately after the term where it is first used.

Forms of definitions.   Except as noted later under this heading, the basic form for every definition is as follows:

> ( ) As used in this Act [or section], the term "A" means . . .;

or, in a section or subsection containing a list of definitions (see part VI for more about punctuation and style):

> Sec. ____. For purposes of this Act [or section]—
>
> > (1) the term "A" means . . . ; and
> >
> > (2) the term "B" means . . . ;

The lead-in language of any definition may properly take either of the forms used in the models just given, or may drop the "As used" and the "For purposes of" and simply say "In this [provision]. . .". These three forms are interchangeable for all practical purposes, although the one that begins "For purposes of" may be slightly broader; in theory at least it could conceivably get a different result when two interrelated laws with different definitions are involved (and it works better when it precedes a list that includes both definitions and other things).

You should always include the modifying phrase "the term" in any definition. This avoids possible confusion over initial capitalization of the defined term, and in addition permits the later use of the construction ", except that such term does not include. . .".

If it is inevitable that the defined term will sometimes be used in the bill in a different sense, it is permissible to add the phrase "(unless the context requires otherwise)" after "As used in this Act". Examples include definitions of terms like "Secretary" or "Commissioner"—referring to the Federal official who will administer the bill—in cases where other officials with the same word in their title will be mentioned as well. It is usually better, however, to avoid the phrase, and to state the exceptions (by cross-reference) within the definition itself, unless they are too numerous. As a practical matter, if you spell out the full titles of the other officials each place they are mentioned, and never refer to any of them as just "the Secretary" or "the Commissioner", the problem solves itself.

If a defined term contains two or more terms that are themselves defined but are used only in the compound term, the definitions of those terms should be made subsets of whatever provision defines the compound term.

"Means" and "includes". In definitions, the word "means" is used to establish the complete meaning of a term, and the word "includes" is used when the purpose is to make it clear that the term encompasses some specific matter. To put it in a slightly different way, one thing means another when the two are identical or synonymous, and one thing includes another when the second is a part of the first.

The word "means" is seldom misused, but the word "includes" is frequently found where it should not be or is accompanied by language that prevents it from playing its part as the dictionary intended (see 22.5 and 22.15, which address some common instances of the latter).

Invented words. If there is no right word to describe a concept or relationship frequently referred to in a bill, or if the available words carry with them too much baggage, you should feel free to invent a word or term and then define it. Most cases of this kind involve complex concepts or relationships for which a short, simple, and fully descriptive term—at least one that is free of emotional content and partisan disadvantage—simply does not exist in the English language.

The point is that if you are going to have to refer frequently to a complicated concept or relationship, you need to give it a manageable name; and if one is not otherwise available you may have to make one up. It need not be clever or imaginative; consider the defined terms "section 38 property" and "section 306 stock", and the term "S corporations" (for businesses that are covered by subchapter S), in the Internal Revenue Code of 1986 (which even invents and defines "C corporations" to refer to businesses that are not covered by subchapter S). Or consider the defined terms "outyear" (for a fiscal year after the current one), "target" (for a prescribed spending limit), "breach" (for spending beyond the applicable limit), and "look-back" (to describe a retrospective search for breaches) in the Emergency Deficit Control Act.

Or consider how the drafters of the medicare law, unable to come up with a descriptive name for the key period of time against which medicare entitlement is calculated, finally settled for "spell of illness" despite the fact that the period's main component is a spell of non-illness, apparently on the theory that the term is so folksy that no one could expect it to be accurately descriptive.

In all fairness it should be noted that some commentators have reservations about using invented words, as a matter of principle. *Hirsch* (page 44) claims that "innovation in devising new meanings for words is a flaw, not an asset, in a draftsman", and goes on to say that "certainty of meaning largely depends on the draftsman's unbendingly conservative use of language".

If you do invent a term, just be sure that it points in the right direction and won't look silly in your bill, and then define it to mean exactly what you want it to mean.

Partial definitions. In many cases it is best to assume the dictionary meaning of a term and merely clarify its penumbra. For example, if you want to include osteopaths in a grant program on the same basis as physicians (the latter being a term that is reasonably clear on its face), you need not redefine "physician"—you can simply provide that "the term 'physician' includes an osteopathic practitioner as determined under the law of the State in which he is practicing".

To take another example, there is a world of difference between "The term 'State' means the District of Columbia" on the one hand and "The term 'State' includes the District of Columbia" on the other. The former (which is ridiculous on its face) is a true definition in every sense; while the latter (which is thoroughly rational) is considered a definition only because it is convenient to do so.

The use of the word "includes" in this sort of construction normally indicates that something which is not really within the defined term is to be treated as though it were; it is a "partial definition", and assumes that what is within the defined term is clear enough to need no definition. So long as this is so the use of "includes" is quite proper and even desirable—it saves having to restate (in the previous example) the self-evident fact that the 50 States are really "States" before going on to say that the District of Columbia should be treated as though it were a State too. But in any other situation "includes" should be avoided.

Definitions containing substantive rules. Sometimes a general term that occurs frequently in a long bill will be used in a slightly different way in particular circumstances or will have a slightly different application in particular types of cases. In this situation, building the necessary exceptions, exclusions, conditions, and even expansions into the definition of the general term instead of into the operating provisions themselves (in effect stating the substantive rules in the definition) is often the best and easiest way to accomplish what would otherwise require a whole series of "special rule" provisions throughout the bill. For example:

( ) As used in this Act, the term "A" means XX; except that—

(1) when used in sections ____ and ____, it means YY, and

(2) whenever used to describe [a particular kind of relationship], it also includes ZZ.

As indicated earlier, many professional drafters frown upon this practice as a matter of principle. *Dickerson* (pages 109-111) uses the term "stuffed definitions" to describe definitions that include substantive rules, and describes them as not only inartistic but dangerous; he feels that the practice, which the author approves primarily because it simplifies key operating provisions, in fact has quite the opposite effect because it makes it harder for the reader to fit the pieces of the puzzle together and makes the key operating provisions themselves unclear. He suggests that a good working test of whether a substantive rule and its accompanying definitions are properly stated is whether the reader can get a generally accurate and complete impression of the substantive rule without referring to the definitions at all.

And *Hirsch* (page 31) points out that the practice

> may mislead one who reads only the bill's substantive sections, which have thereby been rendered deceptively simple. The reader may believe that he has grasped the bill's essential rules, when unknown to him a body of them is elsewhere.

He cites as an example the definition of "new animal drugs" under the Federal Food, Drug, and Cosmetic Act, which regulates new animal drugs but authorizes the Secretary of Health and Human Services to exempt any such drug from regulation if the Secretary finds that it is generally recognized as safe, effective, and pure; unfortunately, this exemption authority is included in the definition itself instead of being stated as a substantive provision, so that the provision containing the Secretary's authority to regulate the drugs paints an incomplete picture.

The author concedes the point, within limits, because a reader would not instinctively expect to encounter substantive rules in definitions; and it is one of the drafter's objectives to help the reader find all the pieces. In a rational world all definitions would be sterile and totally devoid of substance; and you should normally keep your substantive rules in the operating provisions where they belong.

But placing substantive rules within a definition is often the fastest and easiest way to dispose of them, which makes the practice a valuable one for drafters facing time pressures. In addition, the most important objective is to keep the key operating provisions of the bill free of unnecessary clutter and complexity; and if burying some of the substantive complications in a definition section will promote that objective the practice will as often as not promote clarity as well as readability. See 23.2 for a further discussion, along with some examples.

Artificial definitions.   Defining the term "State" to include the District of Columbia and the possessions for purposes of some Federal program does create a fiction, but it is a rational way (and usually the best way) of saying that the District and those possessions should be treated the same as States under that program. After all, they are governmental entities like States, and possess many of the attributes of States; and in addition the practice avoids the need to repeat throughout the bill a litany of entities such as "a State, the District of Columbia, the Commonwealth of Puerto Rico, Guam, the Virgin Islands, American Samoa, and the Commonwealth of the Northern Mariana Islands". The convenience of the practice quite properly overcomes the reservations of the purists.

On the other hand, if a term is given a meaning that is too different from its dictionary meaning or from common understanding, the drag of its original meaning may lay a trap for the reader and even the drafter, who may have difficulty later in remembering the artificial usage (especially in a lengthy bill). *Dickerson* claims that "legal definitions are in disrepute . . . because so many pervert normal terminology. . . . Give an established word a special meaning and, Janus-like, it will show first one face and then the other"; and he goes on to say (page 103):

> Even a legislature is powerless to repeal the psychological law on which this is based. Like ghosts returning to a haunted house, established connotations return to haunt the user who attempts to banish them . . . [When a fiction is actually necessary] the draftsman should continue to use his words in their normal senses and label the fiction plainly by using "as if" [for example, by saying "X shall be treated as if it were Y" instead of "the term 'X' means (or includes) Y"].

As an example of the practice at its worst he cites a series of bills (in the 1950s) that defined "September 16, 1940" to mean "June 27, 1950" in a shorthand effort to apply some of the World War II rules to military personnel engaged in the Korean conflict. And *Hirsch* cites the case of a bill (which actually passed Congress twice) that defined "poultry" to include domesticated rabbits and "feathers" to include their pelts; this one is described more fully later.

Definitions of this kind, which *Hirsch* calls "definitional roulette" and *Dickerson* calls "Pickwickian" or "Humpty-Dumpty" definitions (the latter in reference to Mr. Dumpty's assertion of his freedom to make words stand for whatever he pleased), are unnecessarily artificial and completely irrational. They might be technically effective (in theory at least) but they guarantee confusion and invite massive administrative problems.

The author would not agree that terms should never be defined in ways that conflict with normal understanding—properly used the practice is too often the best way to solve a difficult problem—but he does agree with much of what these commentators have said. Extremely artificial definitions should always be avoided, and even moderately artificial ones should be used with special care. Some slight stretching of a term's meaning is often acceptable, especially when there is a reasonable relationship between the content of the term as defined and its content in normal usage, but if you stray too far from reality your sponsor may have to pay the price.

Across-the-board statutory definitions. In identifying the terms that need defining in a bill and in developing the definitions, you should be aware of any definitions and other rules regarding terminology that may be contained in the permanent law of the jurisdiction involved. Such definitions and rules (which are found in both Federal and State law) are often written so as to apply to all of the laws of that jurisdiction.

Most of the across-the-board Federal instances are found in chapter 1 of title 1 of the United States Code; these include definitions of such terms as "person", "officer", "writing", "county", "vessel", and "vehicle", along with various rules of construction (such as that the singular includes the plural and vice versa, the masculine includes the feminine, and the present tense includes the future). The pertinent part of the text of chapter 1 is set forth in 19.5.

But others appear elsewhere—the Congressional Budget Act of 1974, for example, included a Government-wide definition of the term "fiscal year", so that it is now correct to say simply "fiscal year [1990]" instead of "the fiscal year [ending September 30, 1990]" (see also 22.8). (Note however that the definition of the term "agency" in title 5 of the Code, which is often assumed to apply across-the-board, literally applies only to title 5.)

The existence of across-the-board statutory definitions may

render unnecessary (or require modifications in) some of the definitions that you would otherwise have to include in a bill. A word of caution, however. A later Congress can override, even by implication, what an earlier Congress has done, and if you think your bill (because of its special characteristics) might be judicially determined to have overridden one of these definitions, you might consider including an explicit citation to the definition involved to make your meaning absolutely clear.

The Central
Provisions

▶ 12.1   Preliminary comments

This chapter lists and briefly discusses the various provisions
or types of provisions that you might reasonably expect to
encounter in the central part of any bill—the part that actually
carries out the sponsor's basic policy. First, though, a few
comments are in order:

> 1. No two bills are the same. And only a very massive bill is
> likely to contain all of the provisions discussed in this
> chapter. However, the list in this chapter should not be
> considered exhaustive either; many bills will require addi-
> tional central provisions to serve some special purpose.

> 2. The majority of introduced bills, and nearly all amend-
> ments offered to bills, are "one-shot" in nature. The former
> typically consist of "key operating provisions" only (with
> perhaps one or two other "central" provisions to make

them work), while the latter (which typically attack or append a single item or element in the bill under consideration) are likely to be even narrower.

3. Any of the provisions discussed in this chapter can be either freestanding or amendatory. Part V discusses the two forms, along with the reasons you might have for selecting one form over the other.

4. Although all of the provisions discussed in this chapter after 12.2 are treated as independent "supportive" provisions only, they are often written as a part of (that is, integrated into) the key operating provisions rather than being stated separately; and in special-purpose bills of various kinds they may actually be the key operating provisions.

Please note that the order in which the various "central" provisions are presented should be regarded as no more than a rough approximation of the order in which they normally appear in a bill. Different bills use different systems of arrangement, and all are acceptable so long as the principles laid down in chapter 6 are observed.

▶ **12.2　The key operating provisions**

The key operating provisions of a bill are the provisions that carry out the bill's principal objective; they state the basic policy or main thrust, and might include most of the subsidiary and collateral policies as well. These provisions can take many forms because what they do and how they do it will depend upon the nature and scope of the bill's principal objective and upon the kinds of things that have to be done in order to achieve it.

They may be the only purely substantive part of the bill, with any supportive provisions being integrated into them (as would often be the case when the supportive provisions are short, simple, and few in number). Or they may constitute no more than a statement of the main thrust in its broad affirmative outlines, leaving some or all of the necessary supportive provisions to be handled separately in later sections. (Note that exceptions and special rules of the type discussed in 12.3 should always be thought of as part of the key operating provisions even when they are set forth separately.) And sometimes, when the focus of the sponsor's objective is narrow enough, the key operating provisions may constitute the entire bill.

In a bill intended to improve the everyday operation of some existing program, the key operating provisions may consist entirely of administrative provisions (which in most bills would be supportive only—see 12.8), or structural provisions (see 12.4). And in a bill designed to improve enforcement under an existing program they may consist entirely of criminal provisions or other sanctions (see 12.9). Indeed, any of the supportive provisions discussed in this chapter can turn out to be key operating provisions instead.

The key operating provisions of a bill are its centerpiece, of course—they are highly visible, always substantive, and frequently bulky—but they can be short and simple even in a major bill. The National Aeronautics and Space Act of 1958 (even before it became laden with extraneous subprograms) was anything but short and simple—it took a lot of words to create NASA and to deal with the many novel space-related problems—but its basic key operating provision occupied only a few lines:

> (a) The Administration, in order to carry out the purpose of this Act, shall—
>
> > (1) plan, direct, and conduct aeronautical and space activities;

The statement of the Act's purpose (which took a few pages) and the definition of "aeronautical and space activities" (which took about half a page) completed the picture; they were located elsewhere, of course. (Note that here, as in the similar cases mentioned in 11.6, the meat of the bill is not contained in the operating provisions at all; this approach may occasionally work, but you should try to avoid it.)

Needless to say, no matter how many of the supportive provisions you feel free to develop on your own, close collaboration with the sponsor on the key operating provisions is a must.

▶ **12.3   Exceptions and special rules**

The key operating provisions of a bill incorporate what drafters call the "general rule"—the sponsor's main thrust or primary purpose—but there are almost always persons or things to which the general rule does not apply ("exceptions") and there are often persons or things to which it applies but in a different way ("special rules").

In one sense the broadest exceptions are usually incorporated into the general rule—sometimes in the form of exceptions (clauses beginning with "except that" or "unless") but often simply in the form of descriptive language (characterizing the rights and duties involved) that has the effect of "excepting" anyone who doesn't fit the description.

It would be possible, of course, in the case of a bill that is to apply only to citizens of the United States, to phrase the general rule so that it applies to everyone in the universe, and then add a specific exception for anyone who is not a resident of planet Earth and a citizen of the United States. But it is easier (and better) to begin the general rule with "Every citizen of the United States shall ...", thereby excluding nonterrestrials and other aliens at the outset. (This is not quite as farfetched as it may sound; in the 1950s the Railroad Retirement Board, in an attempt to do something about the growing number of bereaved spouses who were concealing the deaths of their husbands in order to continue cashing the latter's benefit checks, seriously proposed legislation creating a rebuttable presumption that every beneficiary had died at the end of each month.)

In a similar but slightly more realistic vein, a provision designed to impose a special reporting requirement on people who claim trade or business expense deductions on their income tax returns should obviously begin "Any individual who claims a deduction for the taxable year under section 162 [of the Internal Revenue Code of 1986] shall file a report...". It should not impose the requirement generally and then add a special exception for people who don't claim such a deduction.

Even narrower exceptions and limitations can be written into the general rule instead of being separately stated. Thus (in the example just given), if the sponsor wants to exempt smaller businesses from the reporting requirement, one way to do it would be simply to insert the words "of more than $25,000" immediately after "deduction" in the general rule.

All of this should be self-evident. The point is, of course, that narrowing the scope of the bill by identifying at the outset the persons or things to whom it applies helps the reader, so long as the necessary language is not so lengthy and cumbersome that its inclusion makes the general rule harder rather than easier to read. And you can usually invent a term that fits the main target and then define that term at the appropriate place in the bill, including the limitations or exceptions within the definition; the language of the example given might then simply read "Every small-business taxpayer (as defined in section ____) shall file a report. . .".

But exceptions and special rules are often too long and complicated to be appropriately included within the general rule itself, or too obviously substantive to be included in a definition without incurring the wrath of the purists. It then becomes necessary to put them in a provision of their own, couched in language that clearly indicates just what it is they are exceptions to.

This also should be self-evident, and needs no detailed discussion here. If you feel compelled to create a separate provision for exceptions or special rules, there are only two questions that need to be addressed:

1. Where in the bill should the exceptions or special rules be placed?

2. To what extent should you include explicit cross-references to indicate the relationship between the general rule and the exceptions or special rules?

The answer to question (1) is clear. Exceptions and special rules are just as substantive as general rules even though somewhat narrower in scope, and they often constitute an extremely important part of the sponsor's basic policy. They should accordingly be treated as a part of the key operating provisions of the bill, and should usually appear immediately after the general rule—either in a separate subsection of the section in which the general rule appears or in a separate section immediately following that section.

The answer to question (2) is more difficult, and (assuming that your exceptions and special rules are clearly recognizable as such) you have a choice.

Assume, for example, that you are working on section 2 of a bill to require that visitors to national parks pay admission fees (or higher admission fees) with full knowledge that section 16 of the bill will exempt senior citizens or reduce the fees on legal holidays. Section 16 will clearly be effective in any case—by every standard of statutory interpretation it would be read as providing an exception to the general rule, so there is no actual need for any cross-reference at all. But an express acknowledgment of the relationship between the two sections (by a simple cross-reference in section 2 or even in section 16) might help the reader get the whole picture.

The considerations that might be involved in making this kind of choice are discussed in 22.4, but a few passing comments may be in order here.

On the one hand, maximum clarity would be served by including explicit cross-references at every opportunity, both in the general rule and in the exceptions and special rules. After all, if they were included within the general rule itself their relationship to that rule would be explicitly indicated by prepositional or conjunctive phrases such as "except that the individual may not . . .", "unless the individual is . . .", or "but any action taken under this section shall not apply to . . ."; and there seems no valid reason to be less explicit simply because the provisions involved are separated.

On the other hand, multiple cross-references do tend to interfere with readability, at least for people who are not used to statutory language. In addition, if the exceptions and special rules are carefully written, they will not only be readily recognizable as such but will also apply correctly, and reach the intended result, whether or not they show on their face the designation of the general-rule provision they affect. One of the accepted principles of statutory construction, when two provisions in a law are inconsistent on their face, is that the more specific will be given effect (as an exception, so to speak) over the more general.

Basing its position on this principle, *HOLC* recommends against explicit cross-references to exceptions and special rules in most cases. It stresses that in most bills of any substance there are many interrelationships between provisions, ranging from blatant inconsistencies to the subliminal, and expresses the view that if you decide to include explicit cross-references for the important ones but not for the others you may have trouble deciding where to draw the line.

The author has no strong feelings one way or the other, but he does like the relationship between a bill's provisions to be apparent to its readers. If the general rule and the exceptions are placed so that they can be read more or less as a unit—in successive subsections or successive sections—and especially if your drafting style permits the use of headings (so that the provision containing the exceptions can be clearly labeled "Exceptions"), you should feel free to omit the cross-references. In all other cases you ought to include them if you think it might help the reader.

▶ **12.4   Institutional structure**

In a significant number of bills the sponsor's basic policy cannot be properly effectuated without making changes in the structure, personnel, or procedures of the administering agency, or in its relationship to other agencies or programs. Sometimes it is even necessary to create a totally new office or agency. And other times the sponsor's basic policy involves no new substantive functions at all, but is simply designed to improve the administration of an existing program through changes in institutional structure or procedures or through a reallocation of existing functions. (In the latter case, of course, the institutional changes are the key operating provisions.)

Structural changes in an existing agency, and changes in existing functions and procedures, must usually be made through amendments to the existing law. But the creation of a new office or agency can often be done by either a freestanding or amendatory bill. If the basic policy plows totally new ground, the provision creating it would normally be freestanding (unless the entire bill is amendatory), but if it will operate in a field that is already covered by comprehensive legislation the provision likely would amend that legislation.

Drafting structural provisions is normally quite straightforward. Such provisions usually are boilerplate; after all, every agency must have a name, a staff, some functions, a fairly standard collection of powers, a fairly standard collection of administrative procedures, a source of funds, and various other attributes that are common to all organizations (along with whatever unique attributes may be appropriate for that particular agency in light of its mission).

Your best approach is to seek out one or two examples of existing laws that create Federal agencies of similar scope or provide for their operation, and to pattern most of your structural provisions on the corresponding provisions in those laws—always remembering that your project will be different enough to require modifications in many of the provisions of those laws before you can use them as models.

Note that if your bill creates a new agency that replaces an existing one in whole or in part, or provides for the exercise of existing functions by a new or different agency, an explicit transfer of the existing functions may be required. The transfer of the principal substantive functions is often inherent in the key operating provisions, with the transfer of any administrative and other supporting functions along with related property and personnel being accomplished in a separate section (titled "Transfer of Functions") toward the end of the bill.

▶ **12.5   Funding**

It would be hard to imagine a law that costs no money at all. Even laws that involve no identifiable expenditures (for example, a law simply honoring some individual or group, or a private law permitting a named alien to remain in the country) will eventually require the use of some pens and paper clips, some printing, and the expenditure of some time by salaried employees. Most laws, of course, indicate their cost in a way that is much more obvious. And in almost all cases the necessary funds are obtained through appropriations.

Every appropriation must be authorized in advance, but the authorization may be either express or implied. If an explicit authorization provision is required it will seldom involve any drafting difficulties; 13.1 discusses the factors you should consider and lists the forms you should follow.

In most cases the authorization of appropriations simply provides the funding necessary to carry out the key operating provisions—it is substantive in that it determines the size of the program but has no other substantive content. For this reason it normally appears at the end of the bill (for the detailed discussion of the subject see 13.1). Sometimes, though, it is a key operating provision itself; in a program that accomplishes its objective by creating a supply of money and then allocating it among designated recipients, like the AFDC program, the authorization of appropriations is not only a key operating provision but is often the first one set forth.

There are ways of funding Federal programs, in theory at least, without the authorization of appropriations; and a few words about some of them follow.

For many years major programs were often funded by simply permitting the administering agencies to issue bonds and then directing the Secretary of the Treasury to purchase them. This device was called "Treasury borrowing" or (less charitably) "backdoor financing", and it enabled the legislative committees of Congress to control the size of the programs over which they had jurisdiction, to the exclusion of the appropriations committees (which might have whittled down the funding). But the turf battle between the two types of committees was long ago resolved in favor of the appropriations process. Under current congressional rules and precedents, funds can still be obtained by an agency through Treasury borrowing, but such funds can only be spent to the extent approved, in advance, in an appropriation act.

As another example, the administrators of some of the older Federal trust funds were permitted to spend money from those funds without limit for their designated purposes, regardless of how that money got there. Under the current practice, money appropriated into a trust fund can still be spent that way; but money from any other source must be appropriated out of the trust fund before it can be spent.

And programs that generate revenues of their own (such as license or admission fees, or receipts from loan repayments) almost always have specific statutory limits on the extent to which those revenues can be retained and used for operating purposes.

Thus the old familiar ways of obtaining funds from sources outside the direct appropriation process are still available, but they have lost their luster, since they can no longer be used to avoid the ordeal of "selling" a program twice—once to the legislative committees and once to the appropriations committees. As a practical matter, the appropriation process cannot be circumvented; and it is no longer realistic for sponsors to seek ways of doing it.

For this reason, drafters seldom have occasion to even consider any funding mechanism other than the straightforward authorization of appropriations.

▶ **12.6   Entitlements**

Every drafter needs to understand what "entitlement" means, because sponsors are increasingly asking that their proposed programs be written as entitlement programs.

The true entitlement program is one in which the designated beneficiary (which may be a State or other public entity as well as an individual or other private entity) is legally entitled to a statutorily determined amount of assistance, whether or not the necessary funds are appropriated. In other words, the size of the appropriation does not govern the size of the program, since Congress is legally obligated (under the full faith and credit clause of the Constitution) to appropriate all the funds that are necessary.

You will sometimes hear "entitlement" inaccurately applied

to a program under which the designated beneficiaries are legally entitled to a statutorily determined *share* of the program's appropriations. But such a program does not actually create any entitlement in the current budgetary sense; Congress remains free to vary the appropriation from year to year as it pleases, and the designated beneficiary (though technically entitled to something) may in fact wind up with little or nothing when funds for the program are reduced or withheld. No matter what the specified share is, it equals zero if the amount appropriated is zero.

The significance of all this for the drafter is twofold. If the sponsor seeks to establish an entitlement program:

1. The authorization of appropriations, if there is one, should be for an indefinite amount and should not be limited to any particular fiscal year or years. An example is the first section of the AFDC law (title IV-A of the Social Security Act)—discussed at some length in 10.4—which authorizes the appropriation "for each fiscal year" of "a sum sufficient to carry out the purposes of [the program]".

2. There must be language in the bill that clearly establishes the entitlement. This is not difficult—it requires only the use of everyday English words in their everyday sense. The phrase "Every [designated beneficiary] shall be entitled to receive a monthly payment in the amount of . . ." or its equivalent will do the job. Do not add "from appropriations made therefor" or anything like it; that would create only the pseudo-entitlement mentioned earlier. And be careful—the common phrase "The Secretary shall pay to every [designated beneficiary] . . .", being addressed to the administering official rather than to the beneficiary, should not be regarded as creating an entitlement.

Entitlement language that governs an isolated situation within a nonentitlement program occasionally creates a narrowly limited entitlement, but more often it creates a pseudo-entitlement at best because of its context.

Most sponsors like the idea of true entitlement, because it guarantees that the beneficiaries of their bills will actually receive the intended assistance. But be aware (and warn the sponsor) that the Congressional Budget Act of 1974 imposes several parliamentary barriers, and prohibits Congress from even considering entitlement proposals under some circumstances (see chapter 32).

A full explanation of Federal budgetary concepts is beyond the scope of this book, but you need a good grounding in them if you are to properly translate the sponsor's decisions not only on entitlements but also on such esoterica as "budget authority", "obligations", "outlays", "spending authority", "advance funding", "extended availability", and "credit authority". You should always have access to the most current Budget and should pay particular attention to the part dealing with "The Budget Systems and Concepts"; looking at the definitions in section 3 (and section 401) of the Congressional Budget Act of 1974 may also be helpful.

▶ 12.7   Reports

It is common to require officials to make periodic reports (usually annually) on the functions or programs they are responsible for. A provision requiring such a report is usually quite straightforward and might look something like this:

> SEC. _____. The [Secretary] shall make an annual report to Congress on the program under this Act. Each such report shall include [specified items], shall indicate the progress that has been made during the preceding year toward achieving the objectives of this Act, and shall set forth in detail the [Secretary's] plans for carrying out the program during the ensuing year.

The items required by the report are often spelled out in considerably more detail, but this is a matter for the sponsor. Your concern with the additional details is very much like your concern with the specific declarations to be included in a statement of findings or purpose (see 11.6)—unless you have a model you can use without significant modification, simply take what the sponsor gives you and recast it in the proper form.

There are several other items worth noting and perhaps mentioning to your sponsor:

1. It may be desirable to include a specific reporting date in order to ensure that each report will be made in time to be taken into consideration in the annual budget process or will otherwise fit properly into existing procedures. The provision might then begin "On or before January 1 of each year, the [Secretary] shall make a report . . ." instead of just "The [Secretary] shall make an annual report. . .".

2. All department and agency heads are required by law to

make annual reports to Congress on the activities and programs under their jurisdiction. If the administering official in your bill is subject to that requirement, a special report requirement may be unnecessary. And if your administering official is a subordinate officer within a department or agency, you might want to require that the report be made to the head of that department or agency (for inclusion in the regular annual report) instead of directly to the Congress.

3. In many fields it is customary to require that annual reports from program administrators be made both to the President and to the Congress. There is nothing wrong with this practice, although the Department of Justice takes a dim view of it, and in any event it is probably unnecessary (since the President has his own sources of information).

Note that reports to Congress should be addressed to Congress—that is, your reporting provision should require that they be made "to Congress" or "to the Senate and House of Representatives", and not to the particular committees having jurisdiction over the matters involved. Requiring that the reports be made directly to the committees is unnecessary, since the presiding officers of both Houses will automatically re-refer the reports to them anyway; and it will antagonize the leadership officials of both Houses (who feel very strongly that it is their right and duty to receive and refer all executive communications), to the probable detriment of the sponsor.

▶ **12.8   Administrative and judicial review provisions**

Every program has to be administered by someone. And as a drafter you have a special responsibility to ensure that, mechanically at least, the bill's directives can be followed. There are plenty of horror stories involving beautifully written statutory provisions that for purely administrative reasons could not be given effect.

And if you care how it will be administered you had better think about the inclusion of some "administrative" provisions in your bill to make sure it is done the way the sponsor wants it.

Many things contribute to the administrative climate in which your bill will operate—the particular official or agency you choose to run the show, the institutional structure you create, and the nature and scope of the program itself, for example, as well as the extent of the administrative discretion which the sponsor wishes to allow.

You can prescribe whatever rules and procedures you like, of course, but unless you are an incorrigible innovator or an accredited expert on administrative law you will probably do what most drafters do—leave the details to the so-called Administrative Procedure Act (APA) (now spread over several chapters of title 5 of the United States Code). Every drafter needs to become well-grounded in that Act, which is too lengthy and complicated to be addressed in detail here, but there are several potential troublespots you should know about.

Rulemaking. If you are silent on the question of rulemaking (unless you are amending a statute that provides its own rulemaking procedures), any agency action under your bill will be subject to the informal rulemaking procedures set forth in section 553 of title 5. At a minimum, the public will have to be given an opportunity to present written views before a rule is adopted; and the issuance of regulations will in most cases require several stages—notice of intent to propose regulations, receipt of public comments, public hearings, notice of proposed rulemaking (with opportunities for more public comment), and final publication.

Judicial review of this process will be available, and the courts will set aside any agency action that is "arbitrary, capricious, an abuse of discretion, or otherwise not in accordance with law".

Sponsors frequently want to make it clear in the bill that interested persons will have an opportunity for a hearing. You can make this mandatory, without otherwise affecting the process; but if you do it by providing that the rule involved is to be "made on the record after opportunity for an agency hearing" you will have subjected it to the APA's formal rulemaking process, which involves a trial-type hearing (section 557) and invokes the substantial evidence rule upon judicial review.

Note that the APA's rulemaking provisions do not apply to matters involving loans, grants, or benefit payments (although some agencies—the Department of Health and Human Services and the Department of Energy, for example—have waived this exemption).

Adjudication.   Unless your bill provides otherwise, or provides for a de novo judicial hearing, the adjudication of any claims or disputes that may arise under the bill will be a formal process, and subject to the substantial evidence test upon judicial review. Thus if it seems more desirable to give an agency (or a State, in the case of a State grant program) the flexibility to design its own adjudicative procedures, based on program experience, than to reassure beneficiaries of their rights by extending them specific statutory protection, you must say so explicitly.

This point is most important in the case of a State grant program. The APA does not extend hearing rights to the beneficiaries of such a program, so any such rights must come either from the Federal assistance statute or from State law.

Authority to issue rules. Presumably you always want to be sure, when you vest a function in some Federal agency, that the agency head has the necessary authority to issue whatever rules and regulations may be required to carry out the duties of that office under the bill. If your concern is merely with the agency head's power to govern the conduct of agency affairs in implementing the new statute, section 301 of title 5 already authorizes it; and the power to interpret the new statute is inherent in the statute's mandate that the agency head administer it. You need not do anything in the bill.

But if you want to give the agency head substantive rulemaking authority—the power to issue a regulation imposing penalties, for example, or to issue any other regulation that would have the effect of law—you must say so explicitly in your bill. And the best way to do it is to express the desired power directly ("The Secretary may prescribe fines ..."); doing it indirectly by granting "substantive rulemaking authority", or authority to issue regulations "for the efficient enforcement of this Act", may be too obscure to withstand a court challenge.

▶ 12.9   Sanctions

When drafting a bill that provides benefits for persons who can qualify for them (like the social security and railroad retirement programs), imposes duties on specified classes of persons (like the Federal Food, Drug, and Cosmetic Act and most other regulatory programs), or requires States to meet specified conditions in order to receive Federal funds (like the AFDC program and most other formula grant statutes), where the likelihood of attempts at evasion is relatively great, you should at least consider the inclusion of explicit sanctions to promote compliance and assist in enforcement.

There are several kinds of sanctions that are frequently used in Federal legislation; which one is right for you in a particular case will largely depend on the nature of the activity or program you are establishing. Some of the more common sanctions are briefly discussed below.

Criminal penalties. Any criminal provision usually contains the following basic elements:

1. The persons subject to the provision,

2. the actions made unlawful,

3. the associated penalties (fine, imprisonment, or both), and

4. the malefactor's state of mind (if it matters).

Note that the persons subject to the provision need not be specifically described if anyone who engages in the prohibited actions is covered—most criminal statutes begin simply "Whoever . . ." or "Any person who. . .".

The first three elements are relatively straightforward, and sponsors understand them perfectly well; but most sponsors tend to overlook or underestimate the intricacies of the fourth. You should always direct the sponsor's attention to the question of the malefactor's state of mind. Is it to be an element of the offense, and (if so) how is it to be characterized? There are three main choices:

1. An offense may be established without any criminal intent, so that lack of any intention to commit the prohibited act (or even of any knowledge that it was being committed) is no defense. This is called "strict [or absolute] criminal liability", and is most common in regulatory laws such as the Federal Food, Drug, and Cosmetic Act. The typical way to draft a strict liability provision is to simply say that "Any person who violates [this Act or section, or a specified regulation] shall be [punished . . .]".

2. An offense may require a "generalized" criminal intent, which merely means that the individual must have actually intended to commit the prohibited act and was personally involved in it in some way. This kind of intent is usually signaled by characterizing the prohibited conduct as action that is performed "willfully" or "knowingly".

3. An offense may require a specific criminal intent, so that

the individual must not only have intended to commit the prohibited act but must have done it for a specific unlawful purpose. For example, when trying an individual under section 1107 of the Social Security Act, which punishes anyone who makes a false representation "with the intent to defraud any person", the prosecutor must prove beyond a reasonable doubt both the false representation and the fraudulent purpose.

Ignorance of the law is usually not a defense. If you intend to impose a penalty on an individual for specified conduct only if the individual knows that it is prohibited, you should say so.

Title 18 of the United States Code (which is positive law) is the general repository of Federal criminal provisions. If you propose to include such a provision in your bill, you should ideally do it through an amendment to title 18. But there are many criminal provisions that remain outside of that title, and if yours is narrow enough and unique to your particular proposal you can probably get away with writing it as a freestanding provision of your bill. Note that the House and Senate Judiciary Committees (which have jurisdiction over crimes in general and title 18 in particular) can claim jurisdiction, and have your bill referred to them for consideration, whichever way you do it.

In any event, before you write any criminal provision you should look at title 18 to see whether there is already a provision that covers your case; title 18 contains a number of provisions that punish such things as fraud and misrepresentation in any Federal program.

Note that in drafting a criminal penalty you should avoid the intermediate word "punished" (as in ". . . shall be punished [by a fine or imprisonment]"; it is unnecessary. Go straight to the point and say ". . . shall be fined . . . or imprisoned. . .".

Civil penalties. Civil penalties—fines imposed by agency heads for violations of program requirements—are less common. They are usually found only in regulatory statutes and often can be freely used in place of criminal provisions. But (as stressed elsewhere) the statute must clearly state that a civil penalty is what is intended. With civil penalties the offense need be proven only by "a preponderance of the evidence" instead of by the stricter "beyond a reasonable doubt" test that applies in criminal cases.

Imposing civil penalties is tricky—they raise more questions and involve more uncertainties than criminal penalties do.

And since they are much less common than criminal penalties the available models are fewer and less standardized. Questions about jury trial and double jeopardy rights remain unresolved, and there is even a possibility that civil penalties may be treated as criminal penalties if they are "too punitive". If you must impose a civil penalty, seek expert counsel.

Termination or withholding of funds.   In formula grant programs the preferred sanction for violations of program requirements is the termination or reduction of Federal assistance.

Under the AFDC program, for example, if a State's plan is changed so as to impose a prohibited requirement or the State fails to comply with a required State plan provision, the Secretary of Health and Human Services can withhold all funds otherwise payable to the State under the plan (or all funds ticketed for the affected portion of the State program) until the violation ceases. (As a practical matter this sanction is almost never applied even for flagrant State noncompliance since it entails the termination of aid to vast numbers of needy children; but the threat of its use has led to spectacular longrunning battles between Federal and State officials.)

These provisions are complicated but largely boilerplate. If you need to draft a program of this kind, you might use the AFDC or medicaid sanctions (section 404 or 1904 of the Social Security Act) as a model.

Note that no special provision is needed to recover amounts spent by a State for purposes outside the scope of the program (since such expenditures are simply not subject to Federal financial participation), and that a court may compel a State to comply with its plan conditions as long as it remains in the program.

▶ 12.10 Technical and conforming amendments

More often than not, especially when a bill does something that directly affects or is affected by existing law, the enactment of the key operating provisions (whether freestanding or amendatory) leaves some technical debris in its wake. And even the subordinate provisions can have that effect.

The amendments required to clean up the debris, universally referred to as "technical and conforming amendments", were discussed in chapter 5 in connection with the treatment of collateral policy questions. As indicated in that chapter, they are usually just mechanical—simply correcting, eliminating, or adding cross-references in other provisions of law to reflect what the key operating provisions have done—although sometimes they can raise serious substantive or tactical questions of their own.

The technical and conforming amendments in your bill should always be given a place of their own. Either put all of them in a separate section toward the end of the bill, or put those that relate to any particular substantive section in a separate subsection toward the end of that section. The former is most appropriate when the number of amendments is large; but the latter is usually preferable when the number is small or when they can be readily divided according to the substantive provisions involved (since it keeps them within their own "modules" and facilitates committee and floor amendments). In either case the amendments to any particular existing law should generally be grouped together, arranged within each group in the order of the provisions amended, and identified by appropriate headings whenever possible.

As an alternative, you can group technical and conforming amendments to other provisions of the law to which the associated substantive amendment was made (or which is otherwise most directly affected by the associated substantive provision) with the substantive provision, and use a separate section (titled "Other Technical and Conforming Amendments") for all of the technical and conforming amendments to other laws.

One final word of caution. There is often a gray area between substantive provisions on the one hand and technical or conforming amendments on the other. Be careful not to characterize any amendment as "technical or conforming" if it could have substantive significance.

If your sponsor insists on calling a provision "technical" when you know it isn't, you have an ethical problem to solve in your own way. At a minimum, be sure the sponsor understands that you do not regard the provision as technical, and that you would have to say so to anyone who requests your professional opinion under circumstances in which you can legitimately respond (but never challenge the sponsor publicly and always observe the applicable requirements of confidentiality (see 2.5)). Of course, if some other legislator or staff member erroneously characterizes a substantive provision as "technical" in your presence you do not have the same problem, although you may still have a diplomatic one.

As the drafter you are traditionally regarded as the expert in distinguishing between the substantive and the technical—legislators and committees will usually take your word for it and often won't even look at amendments that you characterize as purely technical or conforming. Nothing harms your credibility as much as being caught in the act of slipping in a substantive provision among the technical and conforming amendments.

▶ **12.11 Substantive amendments to other laws**

Substantive provisions in a bill that bear no relationship to the bill's main message are comparatively rare. They can be included in the introduced bill if the sponsor so desires—a tax reform bill, for example, could include military construction, crop subsidy provisions, or low-income housing—but they would cause parliamentary problems (especially in the area of committee referrals) and their presence would be likely to offend the committee having primary jurisdiction. (They cannot be added later by amendment in committee or on the floor, since they would not be "germane".) If unrelated substantive provisions are included they should be kept altogether separate and placed as far back in the bill as possible.

It is quite common, though, for a bill dealing primarily with one subject and extensively amending one law to include substantive amendments to other laws when an appropriate relationship exists.

The social security program, for example, is closely related to the SSI program (in the administrative area), to the railroad retirement program (in the benefit computation area), and to the medicare program (in the eligibility area); and the medicare program is closely related to the medicaid program. It would not be irrational to include amendments to all of them in a comprehensive social security bill; such amendments would in many cases be almost (but not quite) like technical and conforming amendments, and the parliamentary complications would be less troublesome because the several committees involved are accustomed to working with each other.

Related substantive amendments to other laws should be appropriately grouped by subject or target law and clearly identified, especially when their inclusion would vest concurrent or consecutive jurisdiction in other committees. They are usually placed just before the technical and conforming amendments; but they can be located earlier in the bill if they constitute a sufficiently important part of it. Many of the recent laws making comprehensive amendments to the social security program have included the corresponding SSI amendment—when there is one—in the same section as the social security amendment that it resembles.

Needless to say, in an omnibus bill, or any other bill with multiple main messages, the treatment and arrangement of the major elements is a matter for the policymakers and tacticians rather than the drafter, because it involves judgments about the relative importance of those elements. Their order of precedence in the bill becomes in effect a basic policy question.

▶ **12.12 Appropriation bills and riders**

Bills and amendments in general. Most drafters seldom get a chance to work on an appropriation bill as such. The big annual appropriation bills are not even introduced—they are written in the Appropriations Committee and make their first public appearance when they are reported in the House. They have a form and style of their own, and often bear little resemblance to anything that is discussed in this book.

However, sponsors do quite often ask for amendments that they can offer to appropriation bills (and drafters in executive agencies and lobbying organizations spend a good deal of time developing language to be submitted to the Appropriations Committees). These usually pose no special problem for the drafter; the typical amendment to an appropriation bill simply changes a dollar figure, adds or eliminates a specific appropriation, or earmarks funds, and is just like any other amendment (see part V). If its purpose is to limit the uses to which an appropriation may be put, however, there are complications (see the discussion of appropriations riders here and in 32.6).

And sponsors do occasionally introduce special-purpose appropriation bills, seeking funds (or additional funds) for particular programs in which they are interested, although these seldom go anywhere. The text of such a bill should read like the first sentence of the form for authorizing appropriations set forth in 13.1, but with the words "authorized to be" omitted.

If you must draft a bill to make an appropriation or amend such a bill, and the job turns out to be more difficult than the preceding discussion indicates, try the following:

Get a copy of a recently enacted annual appropriation act that includes the substantive area in which you are interested and find an appropriation that resembles the one you are proposing to make in both its purpose and scope; then pattern your language after that appropriation. But if you are drafting a separate bill rather than an amendment, you must be sure to specify the fiscal year for which the appropriation is being made. The provision you are using as a model will not do that, since by definition all of the appropriations in an annual appropriation act are for the upcoming fiscal year and that year is specified only in the act's general introductory language.

And always remember that no appropriation can be made unless it has previously been authorized (see 13.1 and 32.5).

Finally, a word may be in order about "continuing resolutions", the desperation method of funding the Government that Congress uses when it is deadlocked on one or more of the regular annual appropriation bills. The stated purpose of such a resolution is simply to continue the current level of appropriations until the new appropriation bills are passed (although in practice such resolutions tend to become primarily "Christmas trees" full of substantive goodies). It is substantially the same sort of vehicle as an appropriation bill from the drafter's point of view except for two things: You will never be called upon to write one, and such resolutions are usually adopted in an atmosphere of great haste so that there are far fewer opportunities to offer amendments.

Appropriations riders.   Neither an appropriation bill nor an amendment to an appropriation bill can include "legislation"—that is, it cannot include any language that would have the effect of changing existing law. But before leaving the subject of appropriations, it should be mentioned that a great deal of substantive legislation does originate in appropriation bills, and is enacted in appropriation acts and continuing resolutions, notwithstanding the rules which forbid it. The parliamentary difficulties are considerable (they are discussed in detail in chapter 32); but if your sponsor proposes to seek the stated objective through an "appropriations rider"—a legislative amendment to an appropriation bill or a continuing resolution—you should know a bit about it.

As *Hirsch* (page 40) puts it—

For an ... individual Member, the single most potent legislative tool—the device with the largest return for the lowest investment in time and energy—is the appropriations rider. . . [I]f an appropriations subcommittee accepts it, the rider is almost certain to be accepted also by the parent committee and passed by the House to which it is reported. [And] whatever may be the fate of other bills, the enactment of an appropriations bill, or a continuing resolution embracing its text, can be relied upon.

If the parliamentary prohibition were absolute, and were uniformly applied, appropriations riders could hardly exist. In fact, however, legislating through appropriations riders has long been a common practice, based largely on the so-called principle of "limitation", which provides in essence that, since Congress is not obliged to appropriate anything just because there is an authorization on the books, it is permissible for Congress to limit the use of any appropriation it does make to selected purposes. It is not as easy as it used to be to legislate this way, but it is still being done.

The more detailed discussion of appropriations riders will be reserved for chapter 32, since their special problems are all parliamentary in nature. They are mentioned here because they are really just freestanding legislative provisions couched in appropriations terminology, and because they often offer the sponsor (for the reasons given by *Hirsch*) the best chance to achieve a legislative objective.

Every drafter should learn how to write appropriations riders that will stand up against parliamentary challenges, and should know enough to advise sponsors on whether that approach in a particular case would or would not be feasible (32.6 deals explicitly with the subject).

▶ **12.13** **Provisions involving congressional procedures**

Provisions that call upon Congress to perform specified functions in connection with the operation of a statute are becoming increasingly common, and they often include changes in congressional procedures in order to ensure that the functions involved can be effectively carried out. The procedural changes are sometimes accomplished by direct amendments to the rules of the House and Senate; but more often the provisions are freestanding, with the changes being either directly stated or merely implied as matters of necessity.

When the specified congressional function is the adoption of a resolution approving or disapproving some impending executive action, or setting forth a finding to serve as a trigger for some executive action or process, the provision usually attempts to expedite the performance by Congress of the specified function by eliminating at least some of the omnipresent procedural obstacles to quick congressional action. Section 254 of the Emergency Deficit Control Act, which provides for the adoption by Congress of a joint resolution suspending various provisions of that Act in the event of a recession, is a good example. And section 274(f) of that Act, which calls for the adoption of a joint resolution establishing a new system for triggering the sequestration process if the old one is found to be unconstitutional, picked up the expedited procedures from section 254 with a number of interesting variations. (In fact, the Supreme Court did strike down the old system, and the new one then went into effect.)

Or such a provision may be necessary because the existing House and Senate rules and procedures would actually prevent or seriously inhibit the performance of the specified function. The Atomic Energy Act of 1954 established the Joint Congressional Committee on Atomic Energy primarily because the existing rules on committee structure and jurisdiction got in the way of effective congressional oversight in what was then a relatively uncharted area.

Or it may be simply that the congressional presence is unavoidably involved in everything the statute aims to do, so that a massive procedural facelift is necessary. Both the Congressional Budget Act and the Emergency Deficit Control Act consist almost entirely of provisions requiring congressional participation.

There is nothing wrong with changing congressional rules and procedures by statute, and the changes made are perfectly valid as long as they are in effect; but they exist on shaky ground because they can remain in effect only as long as both the House and Senate want them to. Section 5 of Article I of the Constitution provides that "Each House may determine the rules of its proceedings", and no mere statute can take away that constitutional right. Thus, either House can unilaterally revoke such changes at any time (insofar as that House is concerned) in spite of the fact that they were duly enacted into law. (The House eventually withdrew from the Joint Committee on Atomic Energy, and that committee continued to operate with only Senate members for quite some time.)

If you are faced with the necessity of drafting this kind of provision, there are three things you should do:

1. Make sure the sponsor knows that the provision can fail if either House becomes disenchanted.

2. Follow the Roman rule religiously—it applies with a vengeance in these cases—by adopting the form, style, and terminology of the congressional rules regardless of the form and style in which the rest of the bill is being written.

3. Consider the inclusion of an explicit statement recognizing that the provision represents a statutory usurpation of the constitutionally protected congressional rulemaking powers. Such a statement is pure boilerplate, and should read like this:

( ) The provisions of this [title or section] [other than . . .] are enacted by the Congress—

(1) as an exercise of the rulemaking power of the House of Representatives and the Senate, respectively, and as such they shall be considered as part of the rules of each House, respectively, or of that House to which they specifically apply, and such rules shall supersede other rules only to the extent that they are inconsistent with them; and

(2) with full recognition of the constitutional right of either House to change such rules (insofar as they relate to that House) at any time, in the same manner and to the same extent as in the case of any other rule of that House.

The preceding language is viewed by some as nothing more than an attempt to be honest with the reader, since the result (being constitutionally required) would be the same without it; but it is important to include it when the procedural changes involved are accomplished by simply overriding the existing rules rather than explicitly amending them.

A different sort of statutory provision involving congressional participation in the administration of laws is the so-called "committee veto". Since about 1960, a number of congressional committees (especially the House Committees on Science and Armed Services) have been experimenting with ways to prevent the executive branch from initiating and carrying out projects for which funds are legally available but which the committees have not specifically considered (or to which they may simply be opposed).

The early committee-veto provisions required the executive official involved to notify the relevant committees of Congress before initiating any project of the specified type, and then either (1) flatly forbade that official from initiating the project unless those committees approved, or (2) gave those committees a set period (usually 30 days) in which to veto it. Constitutional rumblings were heard, however, and eventually the true committee-veto provision disappeared. It is now clear that such provisions are unconstitutional.

The current replacement for the committee veto simply requires the executive official to notify the relevant committees of Congress and then wait 30 days before undertaking the project, the theory being that if the committees wish to prevent it they will have enough time to introduce, report, and secure the enactment of legislation to do so. This approach is almost certainly constitutional (although a few legal scholars would still disagree) because the veto, if exercised at all, is exercised through a duly enacted statute rather than just by action of one or two legislative committees.

Such a provision is largely boilerplate, and normally reads something like the following (from a recent enactment authorizing NASA to transfer earmarked funds and use them for unspecified projects—without waiting for the next regular authorization act—when sudden changes in the needs of the national space program occur):

> No such funds may be transferred or obligated until a period of 30 days has passed after the Administrator has transmitted to the Committee on Science, Space, and Technology of the House and the Committee on Commerce, Science, and Transportation of the Senate a written report describing the nature of the construction, its cost, and the reasons therefor.

If you are asked to include such a provision (or any similar provision) in a bill, make sure the sponsor understands that you both are walking on the edge of a constitutional precipice. You are probably on safe ground if you use the form just given, but you should never feel totally comfortable with any provision that allows the legislative branch (without enacting a new statute) to second-guess the executive on the everyday administration of the laws after the authority has been granted and the funding has been made available.

The Caboose

▶ **13.1   Authorizations of appropriations**

Provisions authorizing appropriations were mentioned briefly in chapter 12 because of their relationship to a bill's key operating provisions, but in most bills they appear at the end (just before the effective date provision if there is one) because they simply provide funding and are not actually part of what the bill does substantively. People who are accustomed to reading legislation will expect to find them at the end of the bill, and you should not vary this placement without good reason.

At the Federal level, before any appropriation can be made it must be authorized in a "legislative" provision—that is, in a law that came through the legislative committees of Congress rather than through the appropriations committees and is totally separate from (and enacted before) the law actually making the appropriation.

But an explicit statutory authorization of the appropriation is not required unless it is desired to limit that appropriation in some way. It is well established that the enactment of legislation providing for the performance of a function or for the establishment or expansion of an agency or program, or authorizing or directing any other action or thing that requires money to accomplish, is in and of itself an authorization of whatever appropriations may be necessary for that purpose—without limitation as to amount or time. (See 32.5.)

Thus the only legitimate purpose of a provision authorizing appropriations is to place a ceiling on their amount, or to limit the period for which they may be made or within which the money appropriated may be spent.

Although a provision authorizing the appropriation of "such sums as may be necessary" is almost always unnecessary, some legislators feel uneasy when they can't see the authorization of appropriations in a bill. You should make it your practice to avoid unnecessary "such sums" authorization language, which promotes inconsistency and possible confusion; but if your sponsor is unhappy without it, go ahead and put it in—it won't do any real damage.

There is one case in which a "such sums" authorization is needed. When a bill intends to authorize the appropriation of a definite amount for one or more specified fiscal years and an indefinite amount thereafter, it should say so. Otherwise there is a strong implication that nothing is authorized after the period for which the definite appropriations are authorized.

For example, a provision simply reading "There is authorized to be appropriated $1,000,000 for fiscal year 1990." is inadequate if the sponsor wants a three-year program with no maximum appropriation during the last two years. The provision should include the phrase ", and such sums as may be necessary for each of the two succeeding fiscal years" just before the final period.

The authorization of an appropriation customarily states the purpose of the appropriation, the agency or official to receive the appropriation, the amount, the fiscal year or years involved, and any restrictions that may apply. All else being equal, these items should be stated in the order given. For example:

> ( ) For grants under section _____, there is authorized to be appropriated to the Secretary the sum of $1,000,000 for the fiscal year 1992. Of the amount appropriated pursuant to this subsection, the Secretary shall obligate . . .

If it is desired that the amount appropriated be available indefinitely (that is, until it is used up), you may omit the reference to fiscal year 1992 or replace it with the phrase "to be available without fiscal year limitation" (the so-called "no-year money"). But you should be aware that the law actually making the appropriation will almost certainly override your provision, since the appropriations committees like to keep control by limiting the availability of appropriations to a specified amount (which may or may not be the amount the legislative committees wanted), and to a single fiscal year, regardless of what the legislative committees have said.

(Note that the legislative committees are increasingly asserting their right to control expenditures too, by requiring annual authorizations for continuing programs, although the appropriations committees still have the last word.)

▶ **13.2   Effective date provisions**

An "effective date provision" is a provision in a bill—it may be a section, subsection, paragraph, sentence, or clause—that specifies exactly when and how the bill or the substantive provision involved is to go initially into effect.

If the bill is to go into effect immediately upon its enactment, there is usually no need for an explicit effective date provision at all; but there is a need for such a provision where—

1. the sponsor wants the bill or any part of it to become effective at a time other than the time the bill is enacted; or

2. the effectiveness of the bill (or any of the substantive provisions involved) cannot be stated in terms of time alone, or left unstated, but instead must be tied to one or more specific events to which it will relate.

Occasionally an effective date provision can pose a real challenge—in a massive bill requiring interrelated effective dates for different provisions it can become very complicated, and often turns out to be the most controversial provision in the entire bill—but most effective date provisions are relatively simple, consisting largely of boilerplate.

Chapter 26 deals in detail with the specifics of the subject—when explicit effective date provisions are needed, the forms they should take in different situations, and some of the collateral considerations that may be involved—but a few more general comments are in order here.

The question of when and how a bill is to go into effect upon its enactment sounds technical and nonsubstantive, but it is often one of the most troublesome policy questions you will face. The effective date determines the universe of cases to which the bill will apply, and often determines its cost and budgetary impact as well.

It is certainly true that in most cases the effective date of a bill has nothing to do with the sponsor's substantive policy decisions, and can safely be dealt with at the last minute. It is also true that sometimes the effective date is such an integral part of the sponsor's final tactical decisions that it *must* be left until the last minute. But in a significant number of cases the substantive policy and the effective date are part of the same package, in that early decisions made about either one will affect the other; and you must always be alert to this possibility as you plan your work.

Although the decision on what effective date to adopt is ultimately the sponsor's, the date that should be chosen will often be obvious to the drafter. In such a case you may feel quite safe about making the decision yourself if you have heard nothing from the sponsor, but you must always remember that it is a policy decision you are making on the sponsor's behalf, and when there is any doubt you should always inform the sponsor about what you propose to do.

And you should be aware that many bills contain special provisions indirectly or selectively involving their effective dates, the most common being transitional provisions, savings clauses, and sunset provisions. These are dealt with in the rest of the chapter.

▶ **13.3   Transitional provisions**

Sometimes the abrupt substitution of new law for old causes hardship or creates inequities for some or all of those affected, but the sponsor does not wish to exempt anyone altogether by including one or more explicit exceptions (or by using a savings provision—see 13.4).

"Transitional provisions" are the means used to make the changeover more gradual and give time for adjustment, while not unduly postponing the effective date of the new law as a whole; in theory at least that is all they do (although there is regrettably much substantive abuse in practice). They can apply to everyone covered by the new law, or (like savings clauses) they can apply only to classes of people for whom the adjustment would be particularly difficult. But they always differ from savings clauses in one significant respect—after the transitional period is over the new law will apply to everyone according to its terms.

Thus if the sponsor of a bill raising specified rates or charges by 30 percent wants to phase in the increase over a three-year period in order to ease the adjustment, the drafter (instead of putting the whole thing in the key operating provisions) might impose the full 30-percent increase effective immediately but then add language somewhere else (usually toward the end of the bill) that partially overrides the effective date by limiting the increase (in some or all cases) to 10 percent in the first year and 20 percent in the second.

A different sort of example (and invariably a more complicated one) might be a regulatory bill that imposes a series of new requirements effective immediately, but includes a provision waiving or softening (during a specified transitional period) the ones that require the most time to prepare for, or waiving or reducing (during that period) the penalties imposed for noncompliance.

Most transitional provisions can be placed either inside or outside of the particular substantive provisions to which they relate, depending upon their length and complexity and to some extent upon past practice in the field involved.

In tax bills (where they are most frequently used), and in regulatory bills, transitional provisions are invariably complicated and are almost always placed after the operating provisions. They are sometimes the most difficult and controversial provisions in the entire bill (usually because the bill could not pass if the Members' constituents were required to face the new burdens "cold turkey"). In areas that are relatively uncomplicated, however, they are more likely to be found within the affected substantive provision itself. Thus in the first example given above the temporary 10-percent and 20-percent rates could very well be prescribed along with the final 30-percent rate in the substantive provision, although in drafters' parlance they would then be "transitional" in the dictionary sense only, since they would be part of the basic rate structure and no one would think of them as part of a transitional "provision".

A transitional provision placed within the substantive provision itself has the disadvantage of complicating the permanent law with material that will soon become obsolete, while placing it elsewhere results in a "split" provision that may cause confusion (see 6.6)—each case must be decided on its own merits. The new "decoupled" benefit formula established by the 1977 amendments to the Social Security Act (which resulted in smaller benefits at all levels) included a 5-

year transitional period; its drafter felt that the unusually long duration of that period (for large numbers of beneficiaries) justified the complexity involved in integrating the transitional provision into the underlying statute. (*Hirsch* (page 39)) suggests that anyone who thinks this solved the split amendment problem should look at the result in section 215 of the Social Security Act, a section "that looks like the drafter's version of *Finnegan's Wake*".)

Unless a transitional provision is clearly straightforward (like the rate increase example), it should be treated as though it were a separate piece of legislation with all of the policy problems and collateral issues that are involved in drafting a stand-alone bill from scratch.

▶ **13.4   Savings clauses**

Regulatory statutes and other statutes that impose burdens on the affected persons often create a perceived need to "save" the rights that some of those persons had under prior law, either permanently or for a longer period than a transitional provision would normally allow. Meeting this need in a bill calls for the inclusion of a "savings clause", which is not a clause at all but is usually a full-scale section or subsection, and which in theory at least (like the typical transitional provision) is nothing more than an effort to be fair. Savings clauses are sometimes called "grandfather clauses", after the post-Civil War practice in some States of extending the right to vote only to individuals whose grandfathers had been eligible to vote.

A savings clause allows specified persons or groups already operating in the area covered by the bill to continue their established operations as though the bill had not been enacted, or addresses particular problems that those persons or groups might face in adapting to the new rules. Like transitional provisions, savings clauses can be placed either within the substantive provisions involved—sometimes a straightforward exception or special rule (or even a simple qualifying phrase) is really a savings clause in disguise—or in separate provisions of their own after the operating provisions. For example, if you are imposing new requirements on interstate carriers, but wish to exempt existing carriers whose long-established infrastructure would be unduly disrupted by those requirements, you might say (in the substantive provision) that "Every interstate carrier, other than a carrier which has been continuously operating as such for at least 10 years on the date of enactment of this Act, shall be required ...”; or you might simply say “Every interstate carrier shall be required ...” and then add a formal savings clause toward the end of the bill:

Sec. ____. The requirements imposed by section ____ shall not apply to an interstate carrier which has been continuously operating as such for at least 10 years on the date of enactment of this Act.

As with transitional provisions, the former has the disadvantage of complicating the statute with material that will soon become obsolete, while the latter results in a “split” provision that may cause confusion. Again, you must decide. The longer and more complicated savings clauses are almost always placed in separate provisions of their own (as would be the case in the example just given, for instance, if the exemption were to be available only upon the carrier’s satisfying specified alternative requirements). In a major bill requiring a number of savings provisions they are customarily collected in a single section toward the end of the bill.

A special kind of savings clause is occasionally called for to deal with the thorny question of Federal preemption. In some fields (the regulation of commerce, for example) the courts are increasingly finding a presumption that the enactment of a valid Federal law in a particular substantive area “preempts” that area—it becomes the sole governing law in the area, nullifying preexisting State law even on points that the Federal law doesn’t address. If you want to be sure that your bill won’t have that effect, you should at least consider the inclusion of specific language to the effect that it will not supersede State law unless the two are inconsistent.

Savings clauses are generally thought of as exceptions to effective date provisions, though they are more substantive than that. They have elements of boilerplate in them, but every case is different and there is no standard form. You should try to acquire a feeling for what a typical savings clause looks like—it will help you decide upon your approach—but when you are ready to proceed you will be faced with the same kinds of problems you would face if you were drafting a separate bill.

▶ **13.5   Sunset provisions**

A "sunset provision" is a provision in a law—usually at the end—that terminates all authority to carry out that law (or to spend money under that law) at some specified future time. The idea is not to repeal the law automatically, but to suspend its operation after a suitable period so as to enable Congress to review it to determine whether it is still needed and whether it is being overfunded or underfunded. The expectation is that Congress will in effect reenact the law with whatever changes may be needed based on that review.

There is nothing complicated about writing a sunset provision—anything that will effectively bring the law to a halt at the desired time (without actually repealing it) is sufficient. It might read:

> SEC. _____. The Secretary may not make any loan under this Act [take any action to carry out this Act] [enter into any contract or obligation under this Act] after September 30, 1992.

or

> SEC. _____. The Secretary may not obligate budget authority under this Act for any fiscal year beginning after fiscal year 1992.

Sunset provisions are becoming increasingly popular, and Congress has periodically considered bills to subject a broad range of government programs (or even all government programs) to sunset review. But they still do not appear in most bills, chiefly because there are more traditional ways for Congress to retain control.

To begin with, Congress can always review and amend an existing law, no matter what that law says. And in any event the same result can be achieved on the face of a bill without a separate sunset provision. The operating cutoff date can be expressed internally, as a part of the bill's substantive provisions (instead of using the first type of sunset provision shown above). And the funding cutoff can be accomplished by limiting the authorization of appropriations to the desired period (instead of using the second type).

In one situation, however, there may be a difference. A subsequent "continuing resolution" (see 12.12) would preserve the law and its funding beyond the termination date if the cutoff were accomplished simply by limiting the authorization of appropriations, but would not do so if it were accomplished by a sunset provision (or by an internal cutoff); and this could be significant because of the increasing use of continuing resolutions by Congress.

▶ 13.6   Severability clauses

A severability (or separability) clause is a provision declaring that if any part of the statute in which it appears is found to be unconstitutional, the rest of that statute is not to be affected. Severability clauses are always unnecessary and usually undesirable; it is debatable whether such a clause can affect the outcome of a judicial determination, or indeed (in most cases) whether you would want it to.

The court that invalidates a particular provision of a law is in a better position than anyone else to say what should happen to the remaining provisions of that law. It is foolish to suppose that the legislature—which after all cannot usually predict exactly what part of its product might be invalidated or on what grounds the invalidation might be based—really intends that everything not specifically struck down will be automatically preserved however interrelated the provisions may be, or that all of the statute's collateral provisions will remain active after the key operating provisions are gone.

In any case, the courts will always have the last word regardless of what the legislature says. As *Hirsch* (page 37) puts it:

> If a court finds some part of a statute unconstitutional, it may be expected to leave the rest of the statute untouched, even without the clause, unless its decision has left the statute in tatters, [in which case] one would expect the court to strike down the entire statute, notwithstanding a severability clause. If a court finds the application of a provision unconstitutional, it may ordinarily be expected to narrow the provision to valid applications without the clause's help.

And the Supreme Court has made it clear that invalid portions of statutes are to be severed (and the remaining portions left alone) "unless it is evident that the Legislature would not have enacted those provisions which are within its powers independently of [those provisions] which are not" (*INS v. Chadha*, 462 U.S. 919, 931 (1983); *Buckley v. Valeo*, 424 U.S. 1, 108 (1976)).

A typical severability clause is pure boilerplate. It should be placed as near the end of the bill as possible—just before the general effective date provision if there is one—and in its basic form it reads as follows:

> SEC. ____. If any provision of this Act (or the application of that provision to particular persons or circumstances) is held invalid [or found to be unconstitutional], the remainder of this Act (or the application of that provision to other persons or circumstances) shall not be affected.

But if you must include such a clause in a bill, try to modify this language so as to provide in detail which provisions are to fall, and which are not to fall, if a specified provision is held invalid. (Note, however, that the question of whether courts would feel compelled to honor a severability clause so modified—a few "reverse" severability clauses have been tried in recent years—is still up in the air.)

The only good thing about a severability clause is that (if it is relatively specific) it could conceivably help the Court in one of those relatively rare cases where legislative intent is a crucial constitutional factor.

Part V

Writing Amendatory Provisions

General Considerations

▶ **14.1 Freestanding and amendatory bills compared**

Much of the time this book deals with matters of form and style as though all bills were entirely freestanding. Many are, of course. But most bills that are taken seriously and progress beyond the introduction stage are amendatory in nature.

A substantial part of all Federal statutes (nearly half of the active titles of the U. S. Code) has been codified and enacted into positive law; and in most States the law is entirely codified. If the subject matter of the sponsor's proposal falls into a statutory field already covered by a positive-law title of the Code there is seldom any choice; the bill must amend that title of the Code, which after all was enacted for the express purpose of putting in one place the entire body of Federal law in the field.

And most major statutory fields not yet covered by positive-law titles of the Code are already blanketed by comprehensive laws into which nearly anything on the subject involved could appropriately be put. When a drafting project falls in such a field, the sponsor's objective can almost always be rationally accomplished either by a bill amending the existing law or by a freestanding bill. You have a choice, and there is no difference in legal effect between the two approaches. But if a place can be found in the existing law where the proposal would logically fit, it is usually better to amend that law rather than to draft a freestanding bill, for at least two reasons.

First, the amendatory approach places the sponsor's proposal in the midst of its relatives, where it naturally belongs and where future researchers would normally expect to find it, and avoids the all-too-common occurrence of separate laws that have to be somehow fitted together and read as a unit in order to get the full picture.

And second, many of the structural, administrative, and procedural provisions that may be required to make the sponsor's proposal work will already be contained in the existing law and will automatically apply to any newly added piece of that law, enabling you to keep your bill shorter and simpler. (Note, however, that if the sponsor's proposal is one that requires structural, administrative, or procedural provisions substantially different from those that are generally applicable in the law being amended, you would have to add special exceptions and conditions, possibly making the amendatory approach longer and more complicated instead.)

Drafting an amendatory bill is not fundamentally different from drafting a freestanding bill. All of the steps that precede the actual writing are the same, and the organizational principles set forth in chapter 6 will normally apply. And nearly all of the drafting rules and principles set forth in parts IV and VI will apply in the same way.

There are, however, a number of drafting rules and principles that are especially or uniquely applicable to amendatory bills. Some of them simply involve special application of the general rules and principles discussed elsewhere; others are totally different. Because, as previously mentioned, the drafting of amendatory provisions is probably the most important single aspect of any drafter's work, these rules and principles deserve special attention; and they are examined in depth in this part.

▶ **14.2   Hybrid bills**

For purposes of this book a bill is considered amendatory if it uses amendments to existing law to accomplish its basic objective and freestanding if it does not. But many bills in fact are neither entirely freestanding nor entirely amendatory. Indeed, most bills of any consequence that are essentially freestanding contain at least a few substantive amendments to existing laws, and almost all of them contain technical and conforming amendments. These bills might be called hybrid, or partially amendatory.

The rules and principles set forth in this part will normally apply to the amendatory portions of hybrid bills the same as they do to bills that are wholly amendatory.

▶ 14.3   Vehicular language

Every amendatory provision has two parts—the one that serves as the vehicle by which the amendment is made and the one that comprises the amendment itself.

If a section of a bill reads

> SEC. 12. The ABC Act is amended by adding at the end the following new section:
>
> "SEC. 4. . . . ,

the new section 4 is the amendment itself, while everything that precedes it (that is, the language by which it is added to the ABC Act) is purely "vehicular"; section 12 is a provision of the bill, and has no relationship (other than vehicular) to that Act.

When the bill is enacted, the amendment itself—the part that is "within the quotes" or is otherwise identified as material to be added to or stricken from the law being amended—becomes a part of the permanent law. The vehicular language does not; since it is a part of the bill only, it is completely executed once the bill is enacted. It does its job—striking or inserting, or both—and then disappears.

▶ 14.4   Interaction of amendments

There are two principles of modular construction that apply uniquely to amendatory bills. They are best combined and thought of as parts of a single amendatory principle, which might be stated as follows:

Early amendments should not anticipate later ones; but later amendments should assume the enactment of earlier ones.

Assume, for example, that section 2 of a bill you are working on makes an amendment to section 123(a) of the ABC Act, and that section 15 of your bill makes another (quite different) amendment to section 123(a). Section 2 of the bill should ignore what section 15 does, and should address section 123(a) of the ABC Act as though no other change in it were anticipated, while section 15 should address section 123(a) as though it already contained the amendment made by section 2. If the two amendments involve the same language in section 123(a) or are otherwise related, however, section 15 should indicate parenthetically that it is the revised version of section 123(a)—the version that would result from the enactment of section 2—that is being addressed.

Thus if section 123(a) contains three numbered paragraphs, and section 2 of your bill inserts a new one after the existing paragraph (1) while section 15 inserts another new one after the existing paragraph (2), section 2 should read:

> SEC. 2. Section 123(a) of the ABC Act is amended by redesignating paragraphs (2) and (3) as paragraphs (3) and (4), respectively, and by inserting after paragraph (1) the following new paragraph:
>
> "(2) . . . ;

and section 15 should read:

> SEC. 15. Section 123(a) of the ABC Act (as amended by section 2 of this Act) is further amended by redesignating paragraph (4) as paragraph (5), and by inserting after paragraph (3) the following new paragraph:
>
> "(4) . . . .

The point is that anyone interested in the amendatory bill will normally read it from the beginning, will understand an amendment that refers to what has come before, but may be quite mystified by an amendment that assumes something not yet seen. If sections 2 and 15 had made unrelated amendments to totally different parts of section 123(a), you would not need to acknowledge in section 15 the earlier amendment (by including the parenthetical reference to section 2), but you should do so if there is the slightest chance of confusion.

And needless to say, in those relatively rare cases where organizational or tactical considerations require a reversal of the amendatory principle stated earlier (so that the earlier section has to assume the enactment of the later), you must give the reader adequate warning; in the example given, since section 15 would then be treated as having been enacted first, section 2 (the earlier section) would have to contain the phrase "(as amended by section 15 of this Act)".

▶ 14.5   Problems for the occasional drafter

Aside from the mechanical differences that are discussed later in this part, the chief difference between the freestanding and the amendatory approach from the drafter's point of view is that the amendatory approach involves one additional step— fitting the pieces properly into an existing statute. Since under either approach the drafter's words must coexist rationally with the words already contained in the relevant law, this is largely a mechanical step; but it can be a very difficult one if the statute is massive and complex, and it can pose a serious problem for the occasional drafter.

There is seldom any practical way for a drafter not intimately familiar with the operation of a complex law to acquire the competence to draft amendments to it in the time available. There are a number of things you can do to help yourself, however, and they are all variations on one simple theme: First, actually read the law or laws involved, and if that isn't possible, or doesn't work because you find yourself confronted with a 700-page monster, then consult an expert to direct you to the most relevant provisions and possibly even to the specific provisions you will need to amend. (*Hirsch* points out that your main problem may be not in eliciting an expert's cooperation but in preventing the expert from trying to draft the bill for you.)

And whether or not this resolves your initial drafting problems, you should always have some knowledgeable person waiting in the wings to review your draft, if possible, when it is finished.

▶ **14.6   Amending a bill in Congress**

A brief digression may be in order here to consider the drafting of amendments to be offered to bills in committee or on the floor, while they are still in the legislative mill, before proceeding to the main business of this part (the drafting of amendments—*in* bills—to laws that have already been enacted).

The considerations involved in amending a bill are important, because the number of amendments to bills that a typical legislator offers is usually much greater than the number of bills the same legislator introduces, and the chances of having an amendment actually adopted are much greater than the chances of having an introduced bill passed.

Amendments to bills are usually easier to write than amendments to provisions of existing law. They are most often short and present no major technical problems; and since they are usually addressed to a single proposition, many of the more complicated drafting problems (such as those involving modular construction) do not normally arise.

There are, however, two principal differences in form and style that you should keep in mind:

1. The vehicular language is always written in the imperative mood in an amendment to a bill, rather than in the indicative mood as in an amendment to existing law. And in essence that language is merely an instruction to the legislative clerk who will enroll the bill, indicating how the bill is to be changed, so (as discussed more fully later) you can sometimes take liberties with it; if the clerk understands what you mean it is sufficient.

2. The place where the amendment is to go is usually identified simply by a page-and-line reference in an amendment to a bill, rather than by a descriptive reference to the target provision (by its section number or otherwise) as in an amendment to existing law.

Thus an amendment to a bill might simply read "On page 3, line 6, strike 'XX' and insert 'YY' ", while an amendment to existing law doing the same thing in a bill would read "Section 123(a) of the ABC Act is amended by striking 'XX' and inserting 'YY' ". For a fuller discussion see 30.7, which also gives examples of the proper form.

The Basic
Amendatory Tools

▶ 15.1 In general

Every amendment to existing law does one of three things—it eliminates something old, it adds something new, or it does both. If it does both, what it adds is most often simply a changed version of what it eliminates (as in the case of an increase in a dollar figure or a change in a date).

It can be accomplished either by a "cut-and-bite" approach (addressing only the specific language that is to be stricken, added, or changed), or by a "restatement" or "substitute" approach (striking the entire provision in which that language appears or will appear and substituting a revised version with all changes shown in place).

And it is always stated in the indicative mood, since amendatory bills are drafted on the assumption that their amendments are self-executing and do not require intervening action by anyone else.

These concepts, and the other terms, concepts, forms, and usages involved in drafting amendments to provisions of existing law are defined and discussed later in this chapter and in chapters 16, 17, and 18.

▶ 15.2 Cut-and-bite amendments

A cut-and-bite amendment is an amendment that achieves its purpose by attacking specific language—eliminating, adding, or changing that language by direct reference to it—in the text of the provision of law affected.

The key word for eliminating something is "striking", and the key word for adding something is "inserting" (unless the addition occurs at the very end of the provision affected, in which case it would be "adding"). As more fully discussed later, a "repeal" has the same legal significance as a "strike", but should generally be reserved for the elimination of whole sections or larger units.

The following are examples of all of the basic cut-and-bite amendment forms you will ever be likely to need:

( ) Section 101 of the ABC Act is amended by striking "XX".

( ) Section 101 of the ABC Act is amended by striking "XX" and inserting "YY" [or by striking "XX" and inserting the following: "YY"].

( ) Section 101 of the ABC Act is amended by inserting "XX" before/after "YY" [or by inserting before/after "YY" the following: "XX"].

( ) Section 101 of the ABC Act is amended by adding at the end the following: "XX".

( ) Section 101 of the ABC Act is repealed.

Note that in these examples the terms "XX" and "YY" could represent anything from a single word or figure to a full subsection, and that in the first three examples the addition of the words "each place it appears" would permit the single cut-and-bite amendment to make multiple changes (when the term involved appears repeatedly in the section).

The last example could of course have read "Title I of the ABC Act is amended by striking section 101" instead of just repealing the section. At the Federal level at least, there are considerations both pro and con. Amending a larger component of a bill than is necessary just to strike a piece of it (which is what you would be doing if you amend title I of the ABC Act to strike section 101) sometimes creates parliamentary problems, at least in a reported bill (see 16.1 and chapters 30 and 32). But it often promotes clarity, and in addition it enables you to use serial amendments (see 17.2) in cases where striking that piece is only one of several changes that have to be made in the larger component. For example:

( ) Title I of the ABC Act is amended—

(1) by striking sections 101 and 103;

(2) by striking the fourth sentence of section 107(b); and

(3) by adding at the end of section 111(c) the following new paragraph:

"(5) . . .".

Cut-and-bite amendments are most often used when the changes to be made are relatively few and can easily be isolated. They have both advantages and disadvantages.

On the one hand, they highlight the particular changes being made so that the reader can identify and focus on them (unless the number or complexity of the changes is so great that it would be overwhelming). And they avoid the risks that might be created by including unchanged language; only the changes themselves are opened up to public view. (There may be highly controversial language in the unchanged portions of the provision involved, but anyone who is looking for an opportunity to challenge that language must look elsewhere—the amendments themselves will not serve as a reminder.)

On the other hand, in many cases cut-and-bite amendments (on their face) tell the reader absolutely nothing about what they are trying to accomplish or how they propose to accomplish it. A side-by-side comparison of the amendments and the provisions of law affected is required in order for the reader to understand their effect.

One useful technique for making a cut-and-bite amendment more understandable is to strike (and then reinsert) a few more words than necessary, and you should always consider this approach whenever the additional words would help provide a context.

For example, if existing law provides that a specified official "shall pay a benefit to individuals who qualify under section 6" and your sponsor wants to make that benefit available also to individuals who qualify under section 7, an amendment simply inserting "or 7" after "6" would be legally sufficient but probably meaningless to the reader. Striking "section 6" and inserting "section 6 or 7" instead would be an improvement—at least it would tell the reader that the numbers involved are section numbers—and striking four additional words and inserting "individuals who qualify under section 6 or 7" would be better yet; but striking the whole phrase and inserting "shall pay a benefit to individuals who qualify under section 6 or 7" (though going this far would not be necessary in most cases) would be most informative of all.

▶ 15.3　Amendment by restatement

An amendment made by restatement sets forth the entire section, subsection, paragraph, or sentence in which you want to make changes, with those changes incorporated into its text but without any specific indication of what they are.

The classic form for an amendment by restatement is as follows:

    ( ) Section 123 [or title I, or the fourth sentence of section 201(a)(4)] of the ABC Act is amended to read as follows:

Note that a cut-and-bite amendment that strikes an entire section, subsection, paragraph, or sentence and inserts a revised version of it is in effect an amendment by restatement (of that section, subsection, paragraph, or sentence), and will be so treated in this part. The second example set forth in 15.2 ("Section 101 of the ABC Act is amended by striking 'XX' and inserting the following: 'YY' ") would be one of these if XX were a complete subsection.

Amendments by restatement are most often used when there are multiple changes to be made in the provision affected; obviously restating a whole three-page section to reflect the insertion of a single word (or even a single new sentence) would make no sense. But the restatement form might be appropriate even though only a single substantive change has to be made, if it necessitates conforming changes in areas such as indentation and paragraph designation; the alternative might be a couple of dozen cut-and-bite amendments to effectuate the single substantive change, and that makes no sense either.

Amendments by restatement also have both advantages and disadvantages—the exact opposites of the advantages and disadvantages of cut-and-bite amendments.

On the one hand, since an amendment by restatement shows the sponsor's changes already firmly fixed in their proper places, it gives the reader a clear picture of what the revised provision as a whole will look like and aids in understanding its effect.

On the other, it tells the reader absolutely nothing about what specific changes have been made (so that a side-by-side comparison of the amendment and the existing provisions of the law affected is still required in order for the reader to locate those changes). In addition, it results in the unchanged portions of the affected provision appearing in the bill, which is often tactically unacceptable, has the legal effect of reenacting the unchanged language, and invites further amendments to that language. If there are people ready to bleed and die about language that is contained in the unchanged portions of the provision involved, the amendment will gratuitously invite them to the fray.

Note that the restatement form (both versions) should be reserved for cases in which the amendment will produce a revised version of the original. It should not be used when the intent is to repeal one provision and insert a totally unrelated provision in its place; if that is what you want to do, you should strike the old provision and insert the new in two distinct steps, using the cut-and-bite approach. Using the classic restatement form would strongly imply a nonexistent relationship between the two provisions, and might cause confusion at best and judicial misinterpretation at worst. Ideally you should strike or repeal the old provision at one place in the bill and insert the new provision at a later place; but if you must do the whole job at once at least modify the basic strike-and-insert form so as to make it clear that two unrelated steps are involved. For example,

( ) Title I of the ABC Act is amended by striking section 123, and by inserting after section 122 the following new section:

instead of using either of the two more usual forms.

▶ 15.4 Is there a better way?

As a drafter, when confronted with the necessity of drafting an amendment or series of amendments on the borderline between cut-and-bite and restatement, you can only balance the advantages and disadvantages of each and use your best judgment.

Is there an approach that combines the best qualities of each? Indeed there is, but it has serious drawbacks and as a practical matter is not usable at all at the Federal level (although it has been suggested on several occasions).

A number of States have adopted a requirement that a bill amending the text of an existing provision of law must first make the amendments in a cut-and-bite fashion and then restate the text of that provision in its entirety, showing the amendments in place.

As an example, assume that the text of section 10 of the ABC Act provides (in its entirety) that "Benefits under this Act shall be payable only to a child, and only for periods beginning on or after January 1, 1994.", and that your sponsor (before 1994) wants a bill covering disabled people as well as children but delaying the key date for a year. In a State that requires that the amendment be shown both ways, the operative section of the bill would read something like this:

> Sec. _____. Section 10 of the ABC Act is amended by inserting "or a disabled individual" after "child", and by striking "1994" and inserting "1995", so that the section will read as follows:
>
> "Sec. 10. Benefits under this Act shall be payable only to a child or a disabled individual, and only for periods beginning on or after January 1, 1995.".

The changes are shown both by cut-and-bite amendments and by restatement.

This approach embodies all of the virtues of both amendment forms, and its only vice is the inclusion of unchanged language. It works very well in an isolated case that is short and simple like the example given. But it becomes a potential horror when the changes are numerous or the affected provisions are long. One two-word change in a provision that is three pages long—the kind of amendment normally made by a simple five-line cut-and-bite amendment—would take over three pages of text in the sponsor's bill.

And the typical bill making major revisions in a broad field of Federal law (such as taxes, housing, welfare, education, or defense) contains hundreds of separate amendments and involves existing provisions which tend to be lengthy to begin with; the use of the combined approach would result in a bill that could hardly be lifted from the table, let alone read through. Even worse, nearly every page would consist primarily of unchanged language, with all the hazards that entails.

The only way to make the combined approach workable would be to sharply limit the number and scope of the amendments that can be included in a single bill, which is presumably what is done by rule or law in the States that use it (but which is obviously not within the drafter's power to do in most legislative settings). Without such a limitation, the increased clarity that might result from the combined approach would be more than offset by the sheer bulk and surface complexity that would tend to hide the sponsor's changes and obscure their effect, much more than either of the two basic amendatory techniques.

▶ 15.5   Repealers

As indicated in 15.2, the "repeal" of a provision accomplishes the same result as "striking" it, and has the same legal significance, but is usually reserved for the elimination of entire sections or larger statutory units. Thus you would "repeal" a section, chapter, or title of a bill if you wanted to get rid of it, but you should "strike" a subsection or paragraph; in other words, say "Section 6 of the ABC Act is repealed" but say "Section 6 of the ABC Act is amended by striking subsection (c)".

This seems quite straightforward, and need not be discussed further. But since repealers are the device of choice for disposing of programs that have expired, are no longer being funded, or are being superseded, it may be worthwhile to mention some of the collateral points that you should keep in mind when you are deciding whether or how to remove an old law from the books:

1. An existing law can be effectively eliminated without actually repealing it, by simply adding to it a provision terminating its key operations.

2. An existing law can be repealed for some purposes but not for others. When the old State-plan welfare programs for the aged, blind, and disabled were replaced by the SSI program in the 1960s, they were expressly repealed; but another provision of the law repealing them made the repeal inapplicable in Puerto Rico, Guam, and the Virgin Islands, which continued to operate under the old law. (There are still two title XVI's in the Social Security Act, although only the one containing the SSI program can be found in most compilations.)

3. The repeal of an existing law does not wipe out or disturb any of the continuing legal obligations or liabilities that were incurred under it (unless the repealer expressly so provides). This rule is stated in section 109 of title 1 of the United States Code.

4. When the law to be eliminated is one that has been extensively amended over the years and under which there may be continuing obligations and liabilities, it is often better to insert a termination provision and leave the law

on the books than to repeal it. The law in its most recent pretermination form then remains available in the Code and in compilations, so that anyone who is affected by those obligations and liabilities can find the relevant provisions.

5. The repeal of a law that itself repealed a predecessor law does not revive the predecessor law; a repealer is "executed" upon its enactment, and its work is still not undone when it is itself wiped from the books. This rule is stated in section 108 of title 1 of the Code.

A repealer should always be specific—you should never say that "all laws in conflict with [or inconsistent with] this [provision] are repealed". If you do not have the time to identify the particular provisions of law that need to be eliminated, you are better off relying on the established rules of statutory construction (see 19.5) to achieve the intended result.

Amendatory Form
and Style

▶ **16.1   Amendatory terminology**

Most of the stylistic rules and principles set forth in the other
parts of this book apply equally to freestanding and amendatory bills, but there are a number of rules that are uniquely
applicable to amendatory drafting. You should think of these
rules (some of which have already been mentioned in a more
general way) as just adding a few specialized extras in the
amendatory area; but following them will help both you and
your readers by eliminating archaic usages and surplusage
and by promoting consistency. They are the subject of this
part; and 16.1 begins the discussion with a concentrated look
at the terminology of amendatory drafting.

Striking and inserting.   Material is eliminated by simply
"striking" it. Do not use "striking out" (the "out" is surplusage). And do not use the archaic "deleting" unless you are
drafting for a State legislature that still uses it.

Material is "inserted" when it is being placed within the text
of an existing provision, and "added" when it is being placed
at the end of the provision. Do not use the archaic "inserting
in lieu thereof" when replacing existing matter (the "in lieu
thereof" is surplusage if the insertion is being made at the
place where the striking occurred).

Hirsch recommends using "instead" in place of "in lieu
thereof"; and a few commentators have even pointed out that
the words "strike" and "insert" are themselves somewhat
archaic (deriving as they do from the lingo of old typesetters

and scribes), urging the use of more up-to-date terms. The author has no objection in principle to any of these—he personally likes *Hirsch*'s "instead"—but fear of the stylistic inconsistency that might result in bills with input from multiple sources has kept them from being widely adopted. Simply omitting the "out" and the "in lieu thereof" is better.

A more basic caveat is in order, however. "Striking out" and "inserting in lieu thereof" have been the standard amendatory form for 200 years, and they are only now beginning to die out; most drafters still use them instinctively. When what you are drafting will be a part of a larger product that has input from other sources and you cannot control its final form and style (either by persuading the other contributors or by editing the draft at the last minute), you should try to make your style consistent with the prevailing style of the bill. And if you think the others will be using the old form, you should too. As the old saying goes, "if you can't beat 'em, join 'em".

Narrowing the target.   Any amendment to an existing law should be addressed to the smallest possible subdivision of that law. If it is desired to strike a word in the fourth sentence of section 5(b) of a lengthy law, it would be legally sufficient to do it by saying "The ABC Act is amended by striking 'XX' " (at least if the word does not appear anywhere else in that Act); but a reader would find it nearly impossible to locate the offending word and there might be parliamentary complications resulting from the overly broad approach (see chapter 32).

Addressing the amendment directly to section 5 would be better, addressing it to section 5(b) would be better still, and addressing it to the fourth sentence of section 5(b) would be best of all. It ought to read "The fourth sentence of section 5(b) of the ABC Act is amended by striking 'XX' ".

Note that addressing the amendment to a broader component than is necessary and then limiting it later in the same sentence—by saying "Section 5(b) of the ABC Act is amended by striking 'XX' in the fourth sentence", for example—is a permissible compromise if the chosen component is not too much broader than is necessary. This form resembles the one used in making "serial" amendments (see 17.2), but of course the choice of the broader component in that case is a matter of necessity.

It can also be a matter of necessity when the words to be stricken are not located in a part of the section that can easily be referred to by its alphanumeric designation. Thus if section 5(b) consists of a single tabulated sentence beginning with a few lines of "lead-in" language and followed by 20 indented numbered paragraphs and then by a few unindented valedictory lines (a fairly common format), and the words to be stricken are located in the lead-in or valedictory language rather than in one of the numbered paragraphs, the amendment should indicate that location. It ought to read "Section 5(b) of the ABC Act is amended by striking 'XX' in the matter preceding paragraph (1) [or in the matter following paragraph (20)].".

Descriptive characterizations. Any descriptive characterization of material that is to be stricken, added, or changed (such as "the word . . .", "the number . . .", or "the phrase . . ."), and which is only part of a sentence, is surplusage and should be omitted if the material itself is set forth. Say simply "Section 5(b) is amended by striking 'eligible on that date' "; do not say ". . . is amended by striking the phrase 'eligible on that date' ".

But when striking an entire statutory unit (such as a title, section, subsection, paragraph, or sentence), or amending it by restatement, the existing text should never be set forth in the amendment; it should simply be referred to by its proper name—". . . by striking section 301", ". . . by striking subsection (b)", or ". . . by striking the fourth sentence".

And when inserting or adding an entire new statutory unit, the preferred form would be ". . . is amended by inserting after 'XX' the following new [title, section, subsection, paragraph, sentence]:". However, all of the language after "following" and before the colon is actually unnecessary; and many professional drafters choose to omit it. (Note that you should always omit it if what you are inserting or adding is less than a full sentence.) Some drafters adopt the preferred form in substance, but omit the word "new" on the grounds that it is surplusage (which it is).

Headings and designations. The heading of a section or other subdivision (if it has one), and its designation ("Sec. 3." in the case of a section or "(a)", "(3)", or "(B)" in the case of an inferior subdivision), are parts of that section or subdivision. Thus if you amend a section "to read as follows" and fail to reinsert its heading, you have repealed the heading; you can avoid the problem, of course, by amending only the "text" of the section.

But you should remember that the designation of a section is not a part of any of its subsections. Thus if you amend section 3(a) "to read as follows" you must of course reinsert the designation "(a)", but you must not insert the designation "SEC. 3." (even though the two designations appear together on the page); if you do you will have two "SEC. 3."s.

Adding new material after cut-in paragraphs. If you want to add a new and separate sentence at the end of a section or subsection that contains nothing but some lead-in language followed by several indented ("cut-in") paragraphs, you need to make sure that using the usual form—simply saying that the provision involved "is amended by adding at the end the following new sentence:"—will not result in the new sentence appearing in the last cut-in paragraph instead of after it.

Use the expanded phrase "is amended by adding at the end (after and below paragraph (6)) the following new sentence:". And start the new sentence on the next line—not right after the colon—being careful to indent it properly; give it the same indentation as the lead-in language, not the indentation of the cut-in paragraphs.

"Place" rather than "time". The word "place" has to do with location, and the word "time" with chronology. Thus when changing a word or phrase that appears more than once in a provision, "place" is better than "time" as a way of referring to its various locations. For example, say "Section 10 is amended by striking 'XX' each place it appears [or the first and third places it appears if you want to leave it alone at its other locations] and inserting 'YY' ". ("Wherever" can be substituted for "each place" if you prefer the sound of it.)

If you think it is clearer to be explicit that "YY" is to be inserted each place "XX" is stricken (since literally the phrase "each place it appears" or "wherever it appears" modifies only "by striking 'XX' "), it is permissible (though unnecessary) to add the words "in each instance" before the final period.

"Such Act". The first time an act, a section, or any other designated subdivision is amended in a section of a bill, it is always cited by its full name—"the ABC Act", "section 5(b) of the ABC Act", or "paragraph (3)(C) of section 5(b)". If that same act, section, or subdivision is subsequently amended one or more times in the same section of the bill (without any intervening provisions that refer to some other act, section, or paragraph), the customary practice is to cite it as "such Act", "such section", or "such paragraph". (See also 24.11.)

"Immediately". Avoid the use of "immediately" in conjunction with "after" or "before" to identify the place at which new language is to be located; the intended meaning is invariably clear without it. Say that the provision involved is amended "by inserting 'XX' after 'YY' ", not that it is amended "by inserting 'XX' immediately after 'YY' ".

"Thereof". The use of "thereof" in the description of the matter being amended is redundant. Say that the provision involved is amended "by adding at the end [or after subsection (d)] the following:", not that it is amended "by adding at the end [or after subsection (d)] thereof the following:".

Consolidated reference convention. In a lengthy bill consisting mostly or entirely of amendments to one particular law, having to refer to that law by name over and over again (in the process of amending it) can be an irritation to both drafter and reader. One good way of avoiding these repetitive references is to use the following convention (placing it at or near the beginning of the bill):

( ) [Except as otherwise specifically provided,] whenever in this Act [or title] a section or other provision is amended or repealed, such amendment or repeal shall be considered to be made to that section or provision of the ABC Act.

Using this convention eliminates the necessity of specifying, each time an amendment is made, the act in which the provision being amended is located. The drafter can say "Section 5(b) is amended..."—anywhere in the bill—instead of "Section 5(b) of the ABC Act [or of such Act] is amended"; and the reader will know that the law being affected is the ABC Act since the convention would not be used if the bill also contained amendments to other laws. (See also 24.10.)

Actually, a few scattered amendments to other laws in the bill would not prevent the use of the convention—those laws would of course be cited by their full names in the usual manner, and the "except" clause in the suggested language (as stated above) would take care of them. But if there are more than a few the reader might become confused, and the convention should not be used. (*Hirsch*'s alternative is simply to use "the Act" throughout the bill to identify the law in which the provisions being amended are located, after first defining the term to mean that law [for example, "References to 'the Act' in this Act [or title] are to the ABC Act"]).

▶ **16.2   Amendatory punctuation**

Quotation marks in general. It goes without saying that when a bill adds language to an existing law, or specifies language in an existing law for the purpose of defining the location of an amendment, that language appears in regular quotation marks ("double quotes"). The same is true when the bill strikes language from an existing law if that language is expressly set forth. When the quoted language being added or stricken itself includes quoted material, the marks surrounding that material are converted to "single quotes".

There is only one possible exception to these rules. When the material being added or "amended to read as follows" is very lengthy (such as a complete new title) and constitutes substantially all of the bill, it is permissible and often desirable to show it without quotation marks. In a case of this kind the possibility of confusing the reader (by omitting the quotes) is minor, and the omission of the quotes will save a lot of work, promote readability, and minimize errors in drafting and in the bill's enrollment and printing.

"Following"; Colons. A cut-and-bite amendment inserting language can be stated in either of two ways—". . . is amended by striking 'XX' and inserting 'YY' ", or ". . . is amended by striking 'XX' and inserting the following: 'YY' ". The former approach is best when the material being inserted is short and can be run in without indentation, while the latter should always be used when the material is long or a particular indentation is required.

An amendment by restatement always includes the words ". . . is amended to read as follows:" or ". . . and by inserting the following:".

And in a tabulated list (such as a provision making serial amendments—see 17.2), if the numbered paragraphs are to end with periods (instead of with commas or semicolons as they would in a true tabulated sentence—see 23.5), the lead-in language usually winds up with ". . . is amended as follows:" or ". . . shall include the following [things]:".

Whenever "as follows" or "the following" appears this way (in lead-in language), use a colon, not a dash or some other device. And for the sake of clarity keep those terms as close to the colon as possible—say that the provision involved is amended "by adding after 'XX' [or at the end] the following:", not that it is amended "by adding the following after 'XX' [or at the end]:".

Periods and quotation marks.   Never include any part of the vehicular punctuation inside the quotes along with the language of the amendment.

When inserting, adding, or striking quoted material, any punctuation that is to be included at the end of (and as a part of) the quoted material must appear within the quotes, and any final punctuation that is a part of the vehicular sentence (and not a part of the quoted material itself) must appear after the closing quotation marks. (This will be stressed again in chapter 21.)

Most journalists can get away with placing the final punctuation mark of a sentence or clause before a closing quotation mark—editors generally endorse this practice, as does the Government Printing Office in everything except bills (and it took several years of struggle to make them stop doing it in bills)—but a legislative drafter cannot. There must be no confusion in a bill about whether or not a final punctuation mark was meant to be part of the quoted material.

The material inside the quotes is being inserted into an existing statute, after all; and if the vehicular sentence's own final period is placed within the quotes, as is customary in expository writing, that period will also wind up in the statute—where it doesn't belong—even though you merely used it in a vehicular way. And the reader of your words will often have no way (short of doing a comparative check of the statute being amended, and sometimes not even then) of knowing what you intended. Leave the vehicular period outside the quotes, where it can do its job properly.

And if the quoted material does end with a period (and the amending sentence goes no further), there should be another period after the closing quotation marks to serve as the final punctuation mark of the amending sentence itself. Letting the period within the quotes serve also as the final period of the amending sentence would leave the reader and the courts totally in the dark about your meaning (just as it would in the reverse case mentioned in the preceding paragraph). Admittedly, a sentence that appears to end with a double period, one outside the closing quotation mark and the other just inside it, will strike many people as strange-looking (21.6 gives an example); but the device is critically important in the interest of clarity and precision. It would be unforgivable to hide your punctuational intent.

In either case, if the result is contrary to the conventional editorial rules for final punctuation in sentences containing quoted material there is a good reason for it: Those rules do not penalize lack of precision the way legislative drafting rules do.

Needless to say, these considerations also apply when the quoted material is in the middle of a sentence and is followed by a comma or semicolon rather than by a period.

Punctuation marks by themselves. A punctuation mark all by itself within quotes (such as ",", ";", or ".") is confusing and can easily be misread. Always call it by its name rather than quoting it. Thus do not say ". . . is amended by striking ',' and inserting ';' "—say instead ". . . is amended by striking the comma and inserting a semicolon". And in a similar vein, do not say ". . . by inserting 'X' before ','—say instead ". . . by inserting 'X' before the comma".

▶ 16.3   Being literal

There is one requirement of amendatory form that is so obvious that it should need no mention, but in practice is so often ignored that it deserves special emphasis. It might be called the "amendatory Roman rule".

When drafting an amendment that actually shows (in quotes) the matter being inserted or added, that matter must be shown exactly as it should appear in the law upon its enactment. This goes beyond merely designating it properly and writing it in the proper style, and addresses its external parameters—how it will look on the page in the statute.

If it should be paragraphed in the permanent law, it must be paragraphed in exactly the same way in the bill. If it should be indented in the permanent law, it must be indented the same way in the bill. And any capitalization or punctuation that you want to see in the permanent law must appear in the bill.

Too many drafters seem to assume that somewhere along the line someone—the enrolling clerk, the printer of the bill, or the publisher of the Statutes at Large—will somehow convert the external parameters of their provisions into the correct form. But enrolling clerks, printers, and publishers cannot and will not do this—they are not qualified to judge the drafter's intent, and anyway they are bound by law to follow the provision's words and arrangement literally. Don't make this mistake.

▶ **16.4**   **Special forms**

"Metes and bounds" references to long material. When faced with the necessity of removing large chunks of language, especially when showing all of it would not aid the reader in understanding what the bill is doing or would be tactically unacceptable, you can delineate the language to be removed by simply identifying its beginning and ending. (The beginning or ending of the language can be implicit if it coincides with the beginning or ending of the unit being amended.)

The following are examples of "metes and bounds" references:

    ( ) Section 101 of the ABC Act is amended by striking "XX" and all that follows through "YY".

    ( ) Section 101 of the ABC Act is amended by striking "XX" and all that follows, and inserting a period.

    ( ) The first sentence of section 101 of the ABC Act is amended by striking all that precedes "XX" and inserting "YY" [or by striking all that precedes "XX" and inserting the following: "YY"].

    ( ) So much of section 101 of the ABC Act as appears after "XX" and before "YY" is amended to read as follows: "ZZ".

Note that the first example given uses the phrase "all that follows through 'YY' "—a fairly common string of words in amendatory language. For many years it was customary in this situation to say "all that follows down through 'Y' "; the word "down" is pure surplusage, although many drafters still use it. You should not.

A word of caution. Remember that when you strike part but not all of a sentence and do not substitute anything for the part stricken, you must repair the damage. Thus if the part stricken includes the beginning of the sentence, you must go one step further and capitalize the first remaining word (which has now become the first word of the sentence); and if the part stricken includes the end of the sentence you must reinsert the period (see the second example given above).

Margin and alignment amendments. The traditional method for converting an unsubdivided, unindented subsection (or other provision) into an indented paragraph solely to make it possible to add an additional (indented) paragraph, or for correcting the margin or indentation of the provision, is simply to replace the existing provision with a new provision containing the same words but written in the proper form, with the desired new margins, indentations, and designations.

This can take take the form of a cut-and-bite amendment (striking the existing provision and reinserting it in the desired form, including the new paragraph) or an amendment by restatement (amending the existing provision "to read as follows:"). Either one does the job; but each of them displays the entire unchanged text of the provision on the face of the bill, with all of the tactical hazards mentioned earlier.

In recent years efforts have been made at the Federal level to address this kind of problem without repeating the text of the provision involved; and a number of them have actually been enacted into law. An example is section 2661(m) of Public Law 98-369:

> (m) Subparagraph (B) of section 223(c)(1) of such Act is amended by moving clause (iii) two ems to the left, and by moving the preceding provisions of such subparagraph two ems to the right, so that the left margin of such subparagraph and its clauses is indented four ems and is aligned with the margin of subparagraph (A) of such section.

This type of provision—full of printers' jargon—would obviously be very hard for most people to follow and understand; but no one except the drafter and an occasional technician pays any attention to it, and it works. However, no two cases are the same, and no standard approach has been developed. If you are in a position where you need to use it, you should seek out and study two or three examples of the approach and then try to write a similar provision that will fit the facts of your particular situation. But be careful—it's tricky and still regarded as somewhat radical.

Moving provisions around.   Occasionally it becomes necessary to move a provision of existing law from one location to another, with or without substantive changes. There is no reason why you can't do this, and it does not require complicated or esoteric language. A typical provision of this kind might read:

> ( ) Title I of the ABC Act is amended by moving subsec-

tion (b) of section 123 to the end of section 124 and redesignating it as subsection (g) [and by appropriately redesignating the remaining subsections of section 123].

But remember that when you change the location or designation of the provision involved you must watch for any cross-references to it that may need to be conformed, and you must be sure you are aware of any more general provisions that may become automatically applicable to it in its new location.

▶ **16.5**   **Specific usages that vary from the freestanding**

There are several specific provisions that may appear in bills of any kind but that are handled in a slightly different fashion when they appear in amendatory bills. Most of them have been mentioned elsewhere, but it may be worthwhile to repeat them in the present context.

Long titles. When a bill's primary purpose is to make changes in a particular existing law, the long title should begin "[A BILL] To amend the ABC Act so as to provide . . .", instead of simply beginning "[A BILL] To provide . . ." as it would in a freestanding bill.

Short titles. When a bill's primary purpose is to make changes in an existing law and it is broad enough to warrant a short title at all, it is appropriate (and probably desirable) for the short title to read "ABC Amendments [of 1992]" instead of "ABC Act [of 1992]" as it would if it were freestanding.

Tables of contents. When a bill contains a section or other provision adding a number of consecutive new sections to an existing law (such as a new title or chapter), it may be useful to show those sections in the bill's table of contents if it has one.

Thus if section 2 of a bill adds a new title to the ABC Act or broadly revises one of that Act's existing titles, the table of contents for the bill would show the heading of section 2 in the usual manner but might follow it with a table of contents for the new or revised title. The latter should be artificially indented (to distinguish its elements from the elements of the bill itself), and should be surrounded by quotation marks (to indicate that its elements do not refer to subdivisions of the bill itself but rather to something added by the bill). For example:

SEC. 2. Revision of title IV of the Public Health Service Act.

"TITLE IV—NATIONAL RESEARCH INSTITUTES

"Part A—National Institutes of Health

"S<small>EC</small>. 401. Organization of the Institutes.

"S<small>EC</small>. 402. Appointment and authority of Director.

"S<small>EC</small>. 403. Report of Director."

S<small>EC</small>. 3. Technical and conforming amendments.

Amendments to tables.   The elements of a table of contents, or any other table, are generally referred to as "items" for amendatory (or cross-reference) purposes.

Note that whenever you add a new major component (such as a title, chapter, or section) to an existing law that has a table of contents, you must make a conforming change to that table of contents. (But be careful if you are working from a compilation; many compilers of major statutes that have no table of contents add their own tables of contents as a convenience to readers, and since these do not actually appear in the law they should of course not be conformed.)

Effective dates.   If a bill makes amendments to existing law and an explicit effective date is required for those amendments, it should be stated in terms of the amendments rather than in terms of the bill itself.

Thus, if sections 4 and 6 of a 10-section bill consist of amendments to existing law that require explicit effective dates, the bill's effective date provision should say that "the amendments made by sections 4 and 6 shall take effect ...", adding that "the remaining provisions of this Act shall take effect ..." if those provisions also require explicit effective dates. Relying on the traditional effective date provision ("This Act shall take effect ...") is often unclear in its application to amendments, and relying on it is chancy.

Organization of Amendments

▶ **17.1   Sequence of amendments**

How should an amendatory bill be structured? As indicated in chapter 6, the basic organizational rule is that all bills should set forth their provisions in the relative order of their importance or at least in some rational arrangement of subject matter, whether they are freestanding or amendatory. The key operating provisions should come first, housekeeping provisions last, and so forth.

However, serving the objective of orderly arrangement is often not as clear-cut in the case of an amendatory bill as it is in the case of a freestanding bill, since you may feel somewhat limited by the preexisting arrangement of the law you are amending. If, for example, the basic operating provisions of that law are to be found after its housekeeping provisions for some reason, you may be tempted to follow the same approach in your (amendatory) bill and make any necessary housekeeping amendments first.

In most cases you should firmly resist this temptation. You should group your amendments by subject ("modular construction"), and arrange the subjects as you would if you were writing a freestanding bill. You should normally acquaint the reader with any changes in the existing law's key operating provisions first, and then with any changes that may be needed in its definitions, before going on to deal with collateral matters. Any imperfections in the arrangement of the existing law you are amending will be perpetuated—you will rarely have the opportunity of totally overhauling that law's organization—but your bill (the vehicle by which the amendments are being made) will have internal coherence.

This approach will avoid unnecessary confusion, facilitate the bill's consideration as it goes through the legislative mill, and simplify the redrafting process if some but not all of the amendments are rejected. Your primary aim should be to place the various amendments in the sequence that makes their substantive impact most understandable, even when the provisions being amended are not in that sequence.

But it is only fair to point out that there are certain areas in which the recommended sequencing approach is not followed. In some fields of Federal law which are governed by positive-law titles of the United States Code or by one or two comprehensive statutes and which are routinely subject to periodic reauthorizations or comprehensive revision—such as the military construction laws (which are revised annually) and the education laws (which are written on a six-year cycle)—the amendatory bills customarily make their changes in the exact order of the provisions of the law being amended, without regard to whether or not that results in a rational arrangement for the amendatory bill itself.

And some very respected commentators strongly favor following the exact order of the law being amended, as a matter of course, whenever that law is massive and the amendments cover many topics (so that they are not all part of a single theme), especially when those topics would be regarded by most of the players as approximately equal in importance. They regard it as foolish, for example, in a comprehensive reauthorization bill for educational programs, to deal with the title IV student aid programs before the title I provisions just because the title IV provisions carry the "main message"; and they feel that following the order of the law being amended helps the reader to find items of interest and avoids having to deal with conflicting ideas about which provisions are "more important".

And there are sometimes mechanical considerations (not present in a freestanding bill) that are inescapable. For example, when you must redesignate some of the numbered paragraphs in a list in order to create a space at the proper point in the list for a new paragraph (3), you should do it before you add that paragraph even though it is a trivial detail; if you insert the new paragraph first you are risking ambiguity and confusion, because you will (temporarily) have two paragraph (3)'s, and when you do get around to redesignating the remaining paragraphs the reader may not be able to tell which of the two is to become paragraph (4).

One final word. Everything that has been said here has addressed the subject of sequence in terms of amendatory bills taken as a whole; but the same considerations apply, in exactly the same way, if all of the amendments involved are made in separate subdivisions of a single section instead of being made in separate sections of the bill.

▶ 17.2 Serial amendments

If you want to make several cut-and-bite amendments to the same provision of law, and they are of approximately equal importance or are interrelated, you can put them in a single subdivision of your bill (a section, subsection, or paragraph) instead of putting them in separate subdivisions, one for each amendment.

This format sets forth the amendments as a series, with a separately numbered cut-in paragraph for each of them, and is an example of the basic form of "tabulated list". The lead-in language is followed by a dash rather than a colon, and is read as a part of each numbered paragraph. Each paragraph begins with a lower-case letter and ends with a semicolon (except the next-to-last paragraph, which ends with "; and", and the last paragraph, which of course ends with a period). This may sound complicated but it is not; it will actually be easier for most readers to wade through and understand than stating the amendments in separate provisions. You should read 23.4 and 23.5 to make sure you understand the mechanical details.

As a simplified example, assume that you want to make several amendments to section 123(a) of the ABC Act. If you use the serial approach, your amendatory provision might look something like this:

( ) Section 123(a) of the ABC Act is amended—

(1) by striking "XX" and inserting "YY" in paragraphs (1) and (2);

(2) by inserting "PP" after "QQ" in paragraph (3);

(3) by adding at the end of paragraph (7) the following new sentence: "_____."; and

(4) by adding after paragraph (8) the following new paragraph:

"(9) The preceding provisions of this subsection shall apply. . .".

You have made five separate amendments in a single sentence. (Note that the word "by" is repeated in each of the numbered paragraphs rather than being stated only once just before the dash; see 23.4.)

A close relative involves lead-in language that ends with a colon instead of a dash (and represents the second kind of tabulated list described in 23.4); it is not actually an example of the true serial amendment format but might be called a modified serial approach. Each of the numbered cut-in paragraphs begins with a capital letter, ends with a period, and consists of one or more sentences.

If it were drafted in the modified serial format, the example given above would read like this:

( ) Section 123(a) of the ABC Act is amended as follows:

(1) Paragraphs (1) and (2) are each amended by striking "XX" and inserting "YY".

(2) Paragraph (3) is amended by inserting "PP" after "QQ".

(3) Paragraph (7) is amended by adding at the end the following new sentence: "_____.".

(4) The following new paragraph is added after paragraph (8):

"(9) The preceding provisions of this subsection shall apply. . .".

Some drafters prefer this approach because each numbered paragraph is a self-contained unit (that is, the subject of the sentence need not be imported from the lead-in language), and because it is easier to make subsequent additions to or deletions from the list (since there would be no punctuational complications).

Either serial approach has the advantage of gathering together in one place all of the amendments that involve the subject under consideration and are related to the particular provision of existing law that is being amended, clearly indicating that relationship to the reader.

Note that under both approaches the new language in quotes is shown in exactly the form in which it is to appear in the law being amended (as it must be—see 16.3), with the correct paragraphing and indentation, even though it may make the amendatory provision itself look strange or untidy. The new paragraph (9) which is added by paragraph (4), for example, seems to be out of alignment with the rest of the provision, but there is a reason for it; it is indented less than the four amendatory paragraphs because that is how it will appear in the law being amended.

As with any drafting device, the serial format should be used with discretion. You can legitimately use it many times in the same bill, but you should make sure each time that the amendments involved are reasonably localized. A set of serial amendments that begins "The ABC Act is amended—" or "Title 28 of the United States Code is amended—" would be too broad; the individual amendments would be too scattered, too hard to find, and too likely to produce parliamentary problems.

▶ **17.3   Cumulative amendments**

When amendments are made at several different places in a bill to the same provision of existing law, especially when those amendments add new paragraphs or subdivisions sequentially, the amendatory language for each of the later amendments must take account of what the earlier amendments have done, and should embody one of the following formulations:

( ) Title I of the ABC Act is amended by adding after section 123 (as added by section 5 of this Act) the following new section:

"Sec. 124 . . .

( ) Section 123 of the ABC Act (as amended by sections 6 and 7 of this Act) is further amended by striking [quoted language including part or all of the language previously inserted by sections 6 and 7] and inserting the following: [new quoted language]

( ) Section 123(a) of the ABC Act (as amended by the preceding provisions of this Act) is further amended [this assumes that the preceding provisions added new paragraphs (12), (13), and (14), for example]—

(1) by striking "and" after the semicolon at the end of paragraph (13),

(2) by striking the period at the end of paragraph (14) and inserting "; and", and

(3) by adding after paragraph (14) the following new paragraph:

"(15) . . .

In the case of cumulative amendments of this kind the earlier amendments should never anticipate the later ones—it would be unforgivably confusing to the reader. But (as you will note in each of the examples just given) the later amendments assume that the earlier (preceding) amendments have been executed. And remember, when the amendment adds a new paragraph at the end of a tabulated series of paragraphs, you must clean up the punctuation; the third example given above illustrates this.

Cumulative amendments would not be necessary in a rational world. But the various amendments to the single provision involved are usually designed to accomplish quite different objectives; and they are often offered and adopted at different times and at different stages of the legislative process. Even if it were possible from a political and tactical point of view, the drafter seldom has the opportunity to combine them.

▶ **17.4   Organizing amendments to support legislative strategy**

When organizing a group of provisions to amend an existing law, your primary aim is to place them in the sequence that makes their purpose the clearest; the order you put them in will not usually alter their legal effect. Sometimes, however, the order of your amendments, or how you organize them, may have tactical implications bearing on their enactment.

As a general rule, proposed changes that depend on each other should be combined in a single section or other subdivision of the bill, so that they can be considered together; if one of them falls they will probably all fall, but that is as it should be. And amendments that are not interrelated should usually be kept separate enough so that if one is rejected the others will not be affected. Amendments should normally be arranged so as to facilitate their consideration by the legislative body involved.

But there are times when unrelated amendments should be combined, and made to appear as interdependent as possible, usually to serve tactical needs. This would be the case, for example, when one of them is strong enough or popular enough to provide coattails upon which the less popular ones can ride to enactment. (This is very similar to the practice of attaching riders to appropriation bills or unrelated amendments to bills increasing the debt limit, which are much prized by Members of Congress as vehicles for their unpromising proposals because they are absolutely sure to pass in some form—see 12.12.)

As a drafter, you are not expected to be a parliamentarian or a political tactician—these are matters for the sponsor exclusively. You should organize your amendments in the recommended manner unless there is an obvious reason to do otherwise—the sponsor (or some other person who is wise in political or tactical matters) will let you know if some other course is indicated.

Amendatory Cautions

▶ **18.1   Redesignations**

It is desirable when adding or repealing provisions of an existing law to make certain that the existing law will appear (and function) as it would if the amendments had been incorporated into the law as originally enacted. In other words, any new provisions should be where they logically belong, consecutively numbered or otherwise designated; the scheme of the law should remain rational and consistent; and there should be no gaps between sections or other subdivisions.

Ideally, the reader of the amended law should not be able to tell (except possibly by their subject matter) which provisions were a part of its original factory equipment and which are optional extras that were added later.

One way to accomplish this objective is by appropriately redesignating any of the provisions of the existing law which (if left with their prior designations) would prevent it, so as to create a slot for new provisions and close gaps resulting from the elimination of old ones. This involves simply changing the alphanumeric designations of the provisions involved, without making any other change in them.

To take a simple example, when a new definition is being inserted in a section of existing law that already contains a list of 20 consecutively numbered definitions in strictly alphabetical order, you would normally insert the new definition where it belongs alphabetically and renumber the succeeding paragraphs to create an opening for it. If the new term begins with the letter "p" and would be the 16th term in the alphabetical listing, you might say

> ( ) Section _____ of the ABC Act is amended by redesignating paragraphs (16) through (20) as paragraphs (17) through (21), respectively, and by inserting after paragraph (15) the following new paragraph:
>
> "(16) . . .".

Or, when subsection (d) of a section already containing five subsections is being stricken in its entirety, you would normally close the resulting gap by saying

> ( ) Section _____ of the ABC Act is amended by striking subsection (d), and by redesignating subsection (e) as subsection (d).

In either case you must of course be careful to correct any cross-references that may be rendered erroneous by the redesignation. If any other existing provision of law refers explicitly to paragraph (16), (17), (18), (19), or (20) in the first example, or to either subsection (d) or (e) in the second, you would have to make a conforming change in that other provision as well.

If internal amendments have to be made in any of the existing paragraphs that appear after the point where the new paragraph is to be inserted and that consequently will have to be redesignated, it is often desirable (when it wouldn't interfere with the flow of the bill) to make those amendments before inserting the new paragraph and making the redesignations. This approach avoids awkwardness—otherwise each of those amendments would have to indicate specifically that the designation given for the paragraph being amended is its new one ("Paragraph (7) of such subsection, as redesignated by paragraph (1) of this subsection, is amended . . .", for example). It also makes it easier for readers to execute the amendments to the law they have in front of them, especially when the bill will contain a number of cumulative ("piggyback") amendments of the type discussed in 17.3.

A word of caution, however. A provision whose section number or other designation has become inextricably linked to its substance in the public eye should never be redesignated. If that section number or other designation alone is widely used as its name, by the public or in nonstatutory literature, redesignating it would result in more confusion than benefit. Section 126 of the Internal Revenue Code of 1954 (relating to trade and business expense deductions) is a frequently cited example of a provision that should never be redesignated.

And if there would be too many redesignations (and cross-reference corrections) to deal with in the time available, you should not hesitate to forget about some or all of them. In the first example given above you could just place the new definition nonalphabetically at the end of the section (or call it "paragraph (16A)"), and in the second you could just leave the gap. Failure to make desirable redesignations produces no adverse legal effects—it only results in an untidy law.

You should never, in desperation, use the old scatter-gun approach—specifically redesignating a section or subsection and then providing that "all cross-references thereto" are amended "accordingly"—just to save time. It leads to chaos and confusion.

It may be noted in passing that redesignation has long been a favorite target of writers on the subject of legislative drafting, who complain about the "burdens" that redesignation places upon users of the statute and of other materials making reference to the statute, and the undue demands that are consequently placed upon their time, with resulting great possibility of error. James Craig Peacock[1] called redesignation an "abominable practice ... contributing to [the law's] so unnecessary complexities", and stated flatly that it "should be totally scrapped as a legislative drafting technique".

These complaints fail to recognize the very real virtues of keeping the permanent law tidy, and ignore the realities of the drafter's situation. In addition, although it is true that a recent redesignation may make the provision involved a wee bit harder for a student or practicing lawyer to locate, there are always clues to what has happened. And the primary burden on users of the statute (which the complainants don't mention at all) arises from recent substantive changes that alter what the amended provision does.

In major statutory areas that are subject to frequent broad revision, frequent redesignation is an absolute necessity. If nothing had ever been redesignated in the Social Security Act, for example, that Act would today be many thousands of

---

[1] *Notes on Legislative Drafting* (REC Foundation, Inc. (1961), pages 37 and 44).

pages long, with 90 percent of it consisting of gaps with "repealed" notations and most of the rest consisting of intermediate designations from "(aaa)" to "(zzz)" and beyond—and even that would be better than the hodgepodge that would have resulted if no effort had been made at all to keep its provisions in some logical order. In statutory areas of this kind, redesignation is absolutely essential to keep the law reasonably usable.

In taking the middle ground (as every drafter should, at least in theory), *Hirsch* (page 16) stresses on the one hand "the desirability of having a bill's provisions in the sequence that best ensures their being found and understood, and having their designations logically reflect that sequence"; but he recognizes on the other that the renumbering or relettering of provisions of existing law can cause confusion and sometimes mislead readers—especially readers of other laws that contain cross-references to the redesignated provisions, pointing out that if a redesignated provision is referred to in other laws the drafter who fails to correct those references will invariably mislead the users of those laws. (Needless to say, if you don't have time to identify and correct all relevant cross-references or to assure yourself that there are none, you should never redesignate.)

As you will have noted, the author is not at all reluctant to approve sensible redesignations; but he agrees that the practice should not be used promiscuously.

▶ **18.2** **Amendments in substance but not in form**

A special word of warning may be in order about implied and hidden amendments, chiefly to remind you that they are very common and very real while stressing that they don't actually belong in this part. They are mentioned here (although they are not cast in amendatory form) in the hope that a better understanding of what they are and what they do may help you recognize the problems they create, and encourage you whenever possible to eliminate or solve those problems by using express amendments instead.

Inconsistent enactments. It is a well-established rule of statutory construction that when two legislative enactments are inconsistent, the later enactment governs because it constitutes an "implied amendment" to the earlier one.

Thus if law A says that "every citizen of the United States shall be entitled to [some specific monetary benefit]", and law B as subsequently enacted says that "no person convicted of an offense under this section may receive any payment from the United States", law B has amended law A (by implication)—unless of course it specifically provides otherwise—as surely as if it had amended it expressly by inserting "(other than a person convicted of an offense under law B)" after "every citizen of the United States". (Note that if law B had been enacted first, however, the situation would not be quite so clear.)

It is also well established that when two simultaneously enacted provisions are inconsistent (but not totally inconsistent), the more specific will be read as an implied exception to the more general unless that is impossible in the circumstances or there is a strong indication that some other result was intended.

Thus if the two provisions cited in the example just given had been contained in sections 3 and 7 of a single law instead of in two separate laws, the result would be the same: Section 7 would simply be read as an exception to section 3.

Inconsistencies between provisions of law are usually partial rather than total, of course, and it is usually possible to reconcile them (as in the example given). In addition, there are many cases in which it is unclear whether or not two provisions are actually inconsistent at all.

But the main problem is not really the necessity of interpreting their interrelationship in order to eliminate the inconsistency; it is rather that their interrelationship has to be implied because it doesn't show on the face of either of the provisions involved.

Hirsch cites the provisions for determining the maximum interest rate on FHA-insured home mortgages. Section 203(b)(5) of the National Housing Act—the basic law on the subject since 1935 and the place where any intelligent person seeking to learn that rate would look for it—has for years fixed the rate unambiguously at 6 percent. But memorizing that section in its entirety would not tell you that Public Law 90-301 (an obscure statute originally introduced in 1968 to amend the veterans' home loan program) contains a section directing the Secretary of Housing and Urban Development to fix the maximum rate at whatever the mortgage market requires; and as any homebuyer knows, the rate has not been 6 percent for some time.

The point is that if the drafter (in any of the examples given) had taken the trouble to make an express amendment—even a simple cross-reference in one or both of the affected provisions—the problem would not exist.

Hidden extras. One law may expand or restrict the scope of another "from a distance"—without expressly amending it, and without doing anything that would objectively qualify as an "inconsistency"—by simply providing (for example) that the affected law shall include a new function or be administered in a new way. The difference between this case and the "inconsistency" case is that here there is no problem of interpreting what the laws (taken together) will do—the result is perfectly clear, at least to anyone who is aware of both laws, and the problem is simply finding them.

Hirsch (page 17) cites a spectacular example. In the late 1970s Congress undertook to require the inspection of domesticated rabbits slaughtered for human food, and in the process "enacted (twice) what is surely one of the most peculiar bills ever vetoed (twice) by an American President". The drafter used the Poultry Products Inspection Act, but didn't amend it, use it as a model, or repeat its provisions. The drafter simply wrote a short freestanding bill stating in effect that the Poultry Act applies to rabbits, and that all poultry-related terms (when used in that Act) are "deemed" to refer to rabbits as well as poultry, even going so far as to deem domesticated birds to be domesticated rabbits, and feathers to be pelts.

Extremely artificial usages of this kind are always undesirable (see 11.7) even when they work, but the least of the bill's sins was the quaintness of its definitions. Far more serious was its failure to amend the statute expressly. Had the bill actually become law there would be no whisper of a suggestion in the Poultry Act to warn the reader that its scope had been expanded to include rabbits.

The moral is that some amendatory techniques—particularly the use of implied and hidden amendments—can make it very difficult for anyone to understand exactly how the affected statute would operate. And the operation of the Poultry Act (even with the inclusion of invisible rabbits) is comparatively straightforward; techniques of this kind are most commonly used in the more complicated statutory fields, where they make the situation far less penetrable.

When you are drafting any bill you should constantly be aware that your provisions may impliedly amend other laws—indeed the possible effect of your words on other laws (and vice versa) is one of the most frequently occurring "collateral questions" discussed in chapter 5.

Other things being equal, it is almost always better to use an express amendment—one making an appropriate cross-reference at the very least—if there is an inconsistency that is both clear and significant or if there is a hidden extra, simply because that makes it easier for a person who may be subject to the affected law to understand and cope with the situation.

"Notwithstanding" clauses.   Another questionable type of provision is one that begins with the words "Notwithstanding any other provision of law, . . .". When taken with care this approach can be moderately useful (even though it is almost always unnecessary, since the result would be the same without it); it can serve as a warning to the reader that there may be conflicting provisions somewhere and (if indeed there are any) as an indication of how to resolve the conflict.

But what it really says is that the drafter was unable (perhaps from lack of time or the exigencies of the political process) to integrate the bill with whatever other statutes might be relevant. *Hirsch* (page 18) says that this drafter "is a little like the hunter who fires at anything that moves and then checks to see what he has killed, [and] who uses an intangible bullet and thus leaves no visible wound on his victim as evidence to others of his marksmanship".

Use the "Notwithstanding any other provision" clause if you like when you believe the warning would help the reader, but do not delude yourself—it has no value other than that.

Note that making the clause more specific is somewhat better, but does not solve the problem. Saying "Notwithstanding section 123 of the ABC Act" puts the explicit provision in the wrong place; the implied amendment is still only implied or at least hidden, unless of course you also indicate the interrelationship by a cross-reference in section 123.

▶ **18.3**   **Amendments to amendments**

There is almost never any reason to amend a provision of existing law that was itself an amendatory provision, because an amendatory provision (being only a vehicle for making changes, with no substantive content of its own) is fully executed and becomes surplusage for most purposes—it does its job and then melts away—as soon as its amendments become effective. It remains on the books but is of historic interest only; the amendments that it made to the permanent law, on the other hand, are fully operative in accordance with their terms. Subsequently repealing it may remove it from the face of the law, but does not invalidate those amendments.

You should always amend a provision of permanent law directly, not by addressing the amendatory provision that added it to the permanent law.

However, there are a few exceptions to this rule, usually involving the vehicular portion of newly enacted amendatory provisions rather than the amendments themselves.

One such exception involves a previously enacted provision with a delayed effective date that has not yet arrived. The most common reason for wanting to amend such a provision is a desire to further delay its effectiveness, and the easiest way to do that is to go back to the amendatory provision and simply change its original effective date—for example, by striking "Effective one year after the date of enactment of this Act, the ABC Act is amended . . ." and inserting "Effective two years after [that date] . . .". Obviously this could not be done (or at least could not be done without causing serious problems— see 26.4) if the provision were already effective.

If you want to make a substantive amendment to a provision of law after it is enacted but before it has become effective you should do so directly—by amending the provision itself and not by going back to the law that added it—since it is in fact an existing statute despite its delayed effective date. But you must always make it completely clear whether or not you want the amendatory law's own effective date to apply to your changes.

And you must always remember that administrative and other actions may already have been taken in reliance on the provision in its original form even though the provision is not yet effective, and you might have to undo those actions or deal with their consequences—a task that is always thorny and sometimes impossible.

Another type of exception occurs when the previous amendatory provision, through inadvertence or typographical error, added a new sentence or other undesignated new language to the wrong subdivision of the law—to subsection (e) of some section, for example, when it should have been to subsection (b). The necessary correction can be most easily made, whether the substantive provision has already become effective or not (at least if its enactment was fairly recent), by going back to the vehicular language of the amendatory provision, striking "is amended by adding at the end of subsection (e)", and substituting "is amended by adding at the end of subsection (b)"—with the correct effective date, of course.

Most readers will never have to face challenges of this kind. If your problem concerns the substantive content of the changes made by the amendatory provision (or concerns the erroneous placement of a designated subdivision such as a subsection or numbered paragraph), and the changes made by that provision have become effective as a part of the permanent law, you should ignore the amendatory provision altogether and address the problem directly by amending that law.

In an erroneous placement case, for example, you might say something like this:

> ( ) Subsection (f) of section 123 of the ABC Act, as added by section 456 of the XYZ Act, is redesignated as subsection (e).

The exact form would depend on whether the erroneous placement resulted in a gap (as in the example just given) or in a duplication (in which case you might have to rearrange some of the other provisions as well).

▶ **18.4   Amending the wrong law**

As indicated earlier, when the sponsor's subject matter falls within a Federal statutory field that is already covered by a positive-law title of the U.S. Code, your bill must be amendatory in nature and must amend that title. But the converse is equally important; when the statutory field involved is not yet covered by a positive-law title (and you decide that your bill should be amendatory in nature), you must amend the underlying statute and not the nonpositive-law title of the Code in which that statute is codified.

That a nonpositive-law title of the Code can never be directly amended should be abundantly clear (see chapters 24 and 29), but it deserves special emphasis because inexperienced drafters (and regrettably even some experienced ones) regularly overlook the point and try to amend the wrong thing. Don't do it.

▶ **18.5   Annual authorization amendments and other quantitative changes**

A relatively minor but occasionally perplexing drafting problem involves the question of how to draft an amendment to a provision of existing law that authorizes annual appropriations for a particular program or specifies other periodically changing quantitative values. If an authorization provision already authorizes specific amounts for one or more prior fiscal years, for example, and you are asked to draft an amendment providing an authorization for the upcoming fiscal year, do you simply add your new authorization at the end of the existing list or do you replace the existing authorizations with your new one?

Assume that you are asked to draft a provision authorizing appropriations of $40,000,000 for fiscal year 1992 to carry out the ABC Act, and that section 123(d) of that Act (the authorization section) presently reads as follows:

> (d) For the purpose of carrying out this Act, there is authorized to be appropriated—
>
>> (1) $10,000,000 for fiscal year 1989,
>>
>> (2) $20,000,000 for fiscal year 1990, and
>>
>> (3) $30,000,000 for fiscal year 1991.

You could strike everything after "authorized to be appropriated" and insert "$40,000,000 for fiscal year 1992.", on the theory that paragraphs (1), (2), and (3) are executed and thus no longer necessary; or you could simply add a new paragraph (4) (with conforming punctuational changes) setting forth your 1992 authorization, on the theory that the retention of the previous years' authorizations has historical value as a description of the program's scope and growth.

And the same sort of question—when successive quantitative values are involved, do you save the old ones and add to them or do you replace them with the new?—arises in areas other than just annual authorizations.

Under the social security program, for example, the "earnings base"—which is the maximum amount of a worker's earnings that is covered each year for both tax and benefit purposes—was increased by statute from $3,600 to $13,200 in eight separate steps between 1950 and 1975 (when automatic annual adjustments took over). Most of the social security coverage provisions are the same in both the tax provisions and the benefit provisions, but with the earnings base they differ; every time the earnings base was increased to a new dollar amount the tax provisions were amended to eliminate the old figure and substitute the new (since tax changes are prospective only), while the benefit provisions added the new dollar amount prospectively and retained the old ones (since benefit levels are based on the worker's lifetime covered earnings and the earnings for past periods therefore remain relevant).

If you have no guidance at all on a question of this kind the choice is yours. But you should consider what approach the institutional establishment might prefer; in the annual authorization example, the fact that the existing section 123 contains three different prior-year authorizations suggests that someone in the past has appreciated their historical value (especially if the 1990 and 1991 authorizations were added after the original enactment of the section) and that you should probably keep those authorizations in the law. You would not have that clue to guide you, however, if the section contained only a single prior-year authorization.

And you should always consider the possibility, before eliminating the existing values, that (as in the social security earnings base example) there may be a rational reason for retaining them.

Part VI

Style, Form, and Usage Generally

General Considerations

▶ 19.1   Using this part

Part VI is primarily intended as a reference document for use by drafters during the writing process. It represents an effort to bring together and discuss, in one place, substantially all of the drafting rules relating to style, form, and usage that have not already been discussed in detail.

When the author does find it necessary to address a point that has already been treated in depth in one of the previous chapters, he will attempt to minimize the repetition by keeping it brief and referring you to the earlier chapter for the more detailed discussion.

And part VII will add some basic stylistic information for those of you working at the Federal level. Chapter 31 describes in detail the specific drafting styles you might use and the other chapters in that part discuss the legislative context in which you will be using them.

▶ 19.2   Common complaints

By and large, people who are not particularly familiar with legislation have one general complaint about it (in addition to their dislike of specific substantive policies, of course): Laws are too complicated, and too hard to read and understand. Up to a point they are right, but for the most part (as emphasized earlier) they just do not understand the kinds of problems that both drafters and policymakers face.

Many writers and commentators who are familiar with legislation also complain about complexity and lack of readability, but they add a variety of more specific complaints about the drafting techniques and practices that they believe produce those undesirable characteristics. Most of their complaints fall into several recurring categories:

1. *Long sentences.* One writer calls them "statutory prose in search of a period". [1]

2. *Excessive subdivision.* Several commentators have actually taken the trouble to count the number of different statutory subdivisions—subsections, paragraphs, subparagraphs, clauses, and the like—that are contained within selected sections of carefully chosen statutes, recoiling in horror when they manage to find one in which the number seems excessively high.

3. *Legalese.* This includes such things as provisos, archaic words, stilted usages, Latin expressions, cross-references, and interlocking definitions.

4. *Overcomplicated construction.* This includes the high incidence of exceptions and qualifications, the use of "broken verbs" (that is, sentences whose subjects and predicates are interrupted by substantive matter that ought to have been placed elsewhere), and sentences laden with parentheses and commas.

5. *Bureaucratic words.* Among the most frequent targets are "effectuate", "institute", "finalize", "facilitate", "coordinate", and "input".

6. *General failure to use conversational language.* The reader of this book will have long since realized that in some cases the author's view of the matters involved is diametrically opposed to the sentiments expressed in these complaints, while in other cases he is sympathetic in principle but not always in practice.

Thus he agrees that long sentences should generally be avoided but considers them necessary (and even desirable) in many situations. He agrees that intensive subdivision looks intimidating but considers it one of the drafter's most valu-

---

[1] John A. Bell, *Prose of Law: Congress as a Stylist of Statutory English* (The Paper Tiger, Ellicott City, Md. (1981), page 29).

able tools in dealing with complicated ideas. He completely agrees that legalese and bureaucratic terminology should be avoided, but he regards such things as multiple exceptions, broken verbs, and the intensive use of parenthetical expressions and commas as highly valuable parts of the drafter's arsenal. And he considers the quest for language that resembles conversational speech, though a worthy objective in theory, to be fruitless and even inappropriate in many cases.

The substantive aspects of these complaints (and the reasons for the author's opinions on them) were dealt with more fully in parts II and III (see especially chapter 9); and the stylistic considerations that bear upon the matters complained of are given special attention in this part.

▶ **19.3 Consistency**

The need for consistency in drafting has been mentioned many times earlier, but it is so essential that it deserves to be reemphasized here.

The style and arrangement of your bill should never vary internally, and should be as consistent as possible—or at least be capable of comfortably coexisting—with the style and arrangement of other laws in the same field.

The way you break down the bill and its major components into lesser subdivisions, your paragraphing, your indentation, your sentence structure, your typography, and the particular drafting style you adopt—whether or not it is one of the recognized Federal drafting styles—should be uniform throughout the bill.

The words you use to express a particular idea or concept should always be the same regardless of the number of times it appears, and regardless of the availability of words that might otherwise be regarded as synonyms in everyday speech.

And the words you use to express a particular idea or concept should never be used to express any other idea or concept. As *Hirsch* (page 43) puts it:

> It is an elegant bit of poetry for Shakespeare's Berowne to declaim, "Light, seeking light, doth light of light beguile", but it is an inelegant model for the legislative drafter.

Failure to observe these rules does more than make your end product look untidy. A bill that contains unwanted or inadvertent variations in style cannot be called an example of good legislative writing, whatever its other virtues. Such variations not only interfere with the communication of ideas and concepts to the intended audience; they almost guarantee that your bill will contain substantive ambiguities, they give aid and comfort to people who are looking for grounds to misinterpret the language or to criticize the product or process involved, and they invite both courts and administrators to get the wrong result in close cases.

▶ **19.4   Ambiguity, vagueness, and generality**

Dickerson (pages 22-33) describes ambiguity, overvagueness or overprecision, overgenerality or undergenerality, and obesity (that is, prolixity, circumlocution, avoidable redundancy, and other unnecessary verbiage) as "the major diseases of [legislative] language". He and a number of other writers have devoted considerable attention to the apparently widespread confusion between them.

A term is ambiguous if it is capable of more than one legitimate interpretation. Ambiguity is the bane of legislative language, and the use of an ambiguous term is always bad (unless, of course, the sponsor affirmatively wants ambiguity for tactical reasons). Many of the stylistic rules and principles discussed in this part serve primarily as weapons in the battle against ambiguity.

A term is vague if it is "uncertain in its application to a number of particulars", and is general if its application is not limited to entities that are specifically identifiable. The use of a vague or general term is good if it reaches the result the drafter is seeking, and bad otherwise. A drafter may seek a degree of vagueness because of the sponsor's policy or for the express purpose of giving the administering agency room to exercise judgment consistent with the sponsor's objective; but precision and specificity are highly desirable in most cases and a drafter must never be vague inadvertently.

The use of undefined modifying adjectives, though as essential to drafting as it is to other forms of writing, risks creating either ambiguity or vagueness or both and can cause endless legal difficulties if done carelessly (see 22.5). *Hirsch* (page 44) points out that every modifier used in a bill will eventually call for some sort of administrative judgment, and expresses the view that, other things being equal, the fewer the modifiers the better the bill.

Readers with a scholarly bent may wish to dig into these matters more deeply; others should simply avoid ambiguous terms and obesity to the extent possible, and make sure that their choice of words helps achieve, with minimal difficulty, the sponsor's objective.

▶ 19.5   Rules of statutory construction

Statutes do not exist in a vacuum, and legislative language does from time to time have to be interpreted. To meet this need there has developed over the years a substantial body of rules of statutory construction—rules of thumb that courts (and administrators) can apply in determining legislative intent and attributing meaning to legislative expressions that might otherwise be unclear.

Many of these rules were developed by the courts for their own use, and constitute in effect a part of the common law. None of them are absolute; they can always be ignored by a court when there is external evidence that a different result was intended. Some of them are almost always followed, such as the rule that a later enactment overrides an inconsistent earlier one (to the extent of the inconsistency). Some are not quite so obvious but are still of frequent importance to the drafter, such as the rule that the specific overrides the general (or is treated as an exception to it).

Many others are found scattered through the Federal statutory law itself, where they usually read like definitions. Some are specifically intended for application only to the law in which they appear, while others apply across the board to all Federal statutes. The most important of the latter is chapter 1 of title 1 of the United States Code, the very first section of which (for example) provides in part that "In determining the meaning of any Act of Congress, unless the context indicates otherwise—

> words importing the singular include and apply to several persons, parties, or things;
>
> words importing the plural include the singular;
>
> words importing the masculine gender include the feminine as well;
>
> words used in the present tense include the future as well as the present; . . .
>
> the words "person" and "whoever" include corporations, companies, associations, firms, partnerships, societies, and joint stock companies, as well as individuals; . . .

It should be obvious that one or more of these rules will significantly affect nearly every bill you ever write.

A fundamental but potentially troublesome rule of construction is the one that requires a court to do everything within its power to reconcile two provisions that appear to be inconsistent before decreeing that one of them must be treated as overriding the other in whole or in part. What this means to you as a drafter is that if you do not make yourself absolutely clear about the intended relationship between two provisions you are inviting the courts to decree a relationship that may be quite unintended.

Major textbooks have been written on statutory construction. The subject is well beyond the scope of this book, of course; but you must be aware that there are accepted rules of statutory construction that will be used in determining the effect of your words, and you should become thoroughly familiar with the ones that come into play most frequently in your particular field.

▶ **19.6   Contributing to the legislative history**

Many of the most important judicially prescribed rules of statutory construction have to do with the use by courts of a statute's "legislative history"—the full array of all the things that happened to it while it was still just a bill making its way through the legislative process, along with all the things that were said about it in the accompanying legislative documents.

Most courts (both Federal and State) give considerable weight to a statute's legislative history when they feel that the "plain language" of one of its provisions leaves the meaning, intent, or effect of that provision in doubt (even though some judges, on the theory that every statutory provision has a "plain meaning" which can be unearthed with a little effort, claim that they never use it). And the Federal agency that has to administer a law always pays close attention to the relevant committee reports and other aspects of its legislative history in trying to determine just what Congress intended.

No drafter can control a bill's legislative history, of course. But if you are strategically placed you can often make a contribution to some of its more important parts, specifically the committee reports that accompany the bill when it is being sent to the floor in the House and Senate and the statement of managers that accompanies the conference report when the bill is approaching final passage.

A committee report or statement of managers is the vehicle by which the standing committee or committee of conference that considered the bill explains what has been done, why it was done, and what is expected to occur as a result. A large part of it typically consists of language designed to clear up ambiguities and to specify what is supposed to happen under the bill in particular cases; and much of that language might otherwise have been included in the bill itself.

Every committee understands full well that it has choices of this kind, and (since it knows that the administering agency will treat the directions contained in the committee report or statement of managers almost as though they were contained in the law) it will seldom hesitate to move legislative language out of the bill and into the report or statement when tactical, political, or other considerations indicate that that would be expedient. Many heated arguments about controversial amendments are amicably settled by a simple agreement to "handle the problem in the committee report (or the statement of managers)".

When this happens, the strategically placed drafter is often called upon to assist the committee staff in the writing of the report or statement since the language involved, being intended to achieve a legislative result, needs the same kind of careful attention to soundness and detail that it would receive if it were part of the bill itself.

Note that a committee report or statement of managers lends itself to use by courts in decisions based on legislative history because it is a required step in the legislative process—a formal document with an officially assigned number. A subcommittee report is not such a document—it can normally take any form or even be bypassed altogether—and therefore it is not as likely to be so used; but the same considerations would apply insofar as the drafter is concerned.

Breakdown, Designation, and Headings of Subdivisions

▶ **20.1   General considerations**

A rational system of subdivisions and subdivision designation in a bill, uniformly followed, not only helps the drafter in his work and promotes clarity and precision—it also aids in orienting the reader and makes legislation easier to follow and understand.

Every jurisdiction has its own established system for breaking down a bill into subdivisions and designating them. The Roman rule usually governs what you should do, because there are few jurisdictions, outside of those States whose statutory law is completely codified, in which the established system is applied universally and without exception.

This book does not address the breakdown and designation systems that are used in the several States—there are too many of them, and they differ too widely. And since Federal statutes are still being written in several different formats (see chapter 31), it might appear that no general statements about breakdown and designation can be made in the Federal area either; but fortunately this is not so. As indicated in 10.2, the various Federal formats manage to coexist more or less amicably, largely because their breakdown and numbering systems are nearly identical. The differences between them lie almost entirely in the external characteristics of the individual subdivisions—the headings, the placement of designations, the indentation, and the typography.

It is important to remember that the way in which a bill is broken down into subdivisions has nothing to do, directly at least, with the contents of the bill's subdivisions or the style in which they are written. It is only the external format of the subdivisions that varies according to the drafting style being used.

The reader is warned that when this chapter describes the mechanical and typographical attributes of the various subdivisions of a bill, it employs many of the technical and colloquial terms that both drafters and printers use in their everyday work, such as "full measure" in contrast to "cut-in", "flush" in contrast to "paragraphed", and "paragraphed" in contrast to "run in". All of these terms are defined and discussed fully in chapter 28; if you have any trouble with them you should consult that chapter before reading this one. And most of what is said in this chapter will obviously be repeated, and expanded upon, in chapter 31.

In any event, when reading what follows you should keep in mind that this chapter is narrowly focused, and (except for 20.5, which deals specifically with headings) concerns itself only with two things: How a bill is broken down into its component pieces and what those pieces are called.

▶ **20.2   The basic section**

The fundamental division of all statutes—Federal and State— is the numbered section. Some simple bills have no other divisions of any kind, while bills that are more complicated invariably include both broader divisions—the "senior components", of which the numbered sections are a part—and narrower ("inferior") subdivisions into which the sections themselves are broken down. Most bills have at least some of the narrower subdivisions.

A section is always a self-sufficient unit, in that its text (after the heading if any and the designation) starts with a capital letter, ends with a period (no matter how many sentences or inferior subdivisions it contains), and is grammatically complete without any help from what precedes or follows it. Every section is designated by an arabic numeral (not enclosed in parentheses), and its text always appears on the page as a "full-measure" paragraphed subdivision.

In a bill without any senior components, the sections are numbered consecutively beginning with section 1. In a bill divided into titles, however—

1. the sections in each title are numbered consecutively beginning with section 101 in the case of title I, section 201 in the case of title II, and so forth (so that the first digit

in any section number reflects the number of the title in which it appears); except that

2. if a particular title is further subdivided into subtitles, chapters, or parts, appropriate gaps are normally left in the numbering of the sections so as to leave space for the future addition of new sections—if title II of a bill were divided into parts A, B, and C, for example, the sections in part A might be numbered consecutively beginning with section 201, those in part B with section 211, and those in part C with section 221.

▶ **20.3   The inferior subdivisions**

In Federal statutes—regardless of the style in which they are written—sections that need to be subdivided are always broken down successively into—

1. subsections (starting with subsection (a)),

2. paragraphs (starting with paragraph (1)),

3. subparagraphs (starting with subparagraph (A)),

4. clauses (starting with clause (i)), and

5. subclauses (starting with subclause (I)).

Each subdivision is always referred to by its proper name and alphanumeric designation—for example, a subdivision designated "(a)" is always called "subsection (a)", and a paragraphed subdivision designated "(1)" is always called "paragraph (1)" whether it is a self-sufficient unit or just an element in a tabulated sentence or series.

But there is one case where it is not necessary to mention the name of the subdivision to which you are referring at all—it arises when more than one level of subdivision has to be specified in order to identify the target subdivision. For example, the second subdivision in paragraph (4) of subsection (c) (in any given section) could properly be referred to as "subparagraph (B) of paragraph (4) of subsection (c)", since it is a subparagraph, of course, but it could also be properly referred to as "paragraph (4)(B) of subsection (c)" or as "subsection (c)(4)(B)"; the more compact form is usually preferred if the location of the reference permits it. For further guidance in cases like this, see the discussion of "multiple breakdown" or "composite" references in 24.8.

A subsection, like a section, is always a self-sufficient unit in that its text (after the designation) starts with a capital letter, ends with a period (no matter how many sentences or inferior subdivisions it contains), is grammatically complete without any help from what precedes or follows it, and always appears on the page as a "full-measure" paragraphed subdivision.

Paragraphs, subparagraphs, clauses, and even subclauses can also be self-sufficient in this sense, but they are just as often used as grammatically incomplete parts of a tabulated list or series, or a tabulated sentence, separated by commas or semicolons rather than periods. In the latter case, there is a temptation to call them all by the generic name "clauses". Some drafters yield to this temptation, but you should not. The virtue of having a consistently designated hierarchy of inferior subdivisions greatly outweighs any momentary confusion that the occasional use of one of them in a slightly different way might cause.

There is one important exception to this hierarchy, however. Since subsections must always be self-sufficient and full measure, they can never be parts of an indented list or series that depends on lead-in language for its completeness. Thus if a section that is not divided into subsections contains lead-in language followed by a list or series of designated items (such as a definition section that begins "For purposes of this Act—"), those items become numbered paragraphs just as they would be if they were part of a subsection, and the subsection stage of division is simply omitted.

And finally, here are a few things to watch out for:

1. If a section or other statutory unit contains subdivisions of any kind, it should never contain subdivisions of any other kind unless they are parts of one of those subdivisions. Thus if a subsection has to contain two separate lists of items (which ought to be numbered in the same way since they occupy the same level of subdivision, but which obviously cannot both be numbered starting with "(1)"), you should not number one of them starting with "(1)" and the other starting with "(A)"; you must find a way to give each list its own paragraph designation (that is, create lists "(1)" and "(2)") and then designate the items on each list—which will now be located in its own separate statutory unit—as subparagraphs starting with "(A)".

2. You should create all the subdivisions you need in order to separate your ideas and indicate their hierarchy, of course, but you should not carry the technique to ex-

tremes. Peacock is quite correct when he says that excessive subdivision (regularly going below the subparagraph level, for example) can be "an imposition upon the captive public [which] is indefensible".[1]

3. Never use undesignated subdivisions above the sentence level. Every paragraphed subdivision of a bill must be given its own alphanumeric designation, in accordance with the system you are using. Failure to do this makes it impossible to refer to the provision later in a sensible way.

A good example of the horrors created by the undesignated subdivision can be found in section 209 of the Social Security Act (the definition of "wages" for OASDI purposes), which is a stylistic mess in many other respects as well. It consists of some lead-in language followed by paragraphs (a) through (s) (which should of course have been numbered rather than lettered), and these paragraphs are followed in turn by about a dozen undesignated paragraphs; so that if you wanted to refer to the provision containing the statutory rule on coverage of tips the best you could do is call it "the fourth undesignated paragraph following paragraph (s)".

▶ **20.4   The senior components**

If the bill you are working on deals with two or more separate major topics, or is so massive that it must be broken up somehow in order to be manageable, you will have to consider dividing it into pieces that are broader than mere sections.

Each drafting style has its own rules for doing this, of course. Just to get the ball rolling, here is the way you might conceivably divide and subdivide a monumentally large and complicated bill into senior components (at the Federal level) if you are using "revenue" style:

1. Divide the bill into titles (beginning with title I).

2. If any title needs to be further broken down into senior components, divide it into subtitles (beginning with subtitle A).

3. If any subtitle needs to be further broken down, divide it into chapters (beginning with chapter 1).

4. If any chapter needs to be further broken down, divide it into subchapters (beginning with subchapter A).

[1] *Notes on Legislative Drafting* (REC Foundation, Inc. (1961), page 15.)

5. If any subchapter needs to be further broken down, divide it into parts (beginning with part I).

6. If any part needs to be further broken down, divide it into subparts (beginning with subpart A).

7. And finally, divide each subpart (or the lowest senior component you wound up with) into the individual sections you were aiming for in the first place. A senior component is always divided at least into sections.

This is the way the Internal Revenue Code of 1986 is structured (except that it treats itself as a single title and begins the subdividing process with step (2))—the author knows of no other Federal statute that actually has so many levels of senior components. (The nonrevenue drafting styles prescribe similar but not identical forms for the hierarchy of senior components—see 31.6.)

The trouble with all this is that only the first operation—the division of the bill into titles—is universally used. Every bill that is divided into senior components at all is divided into titles, whether or not it is further subdivided (and regardless of the drafting style being used). But if it is further subdivided all bets are off—in actual practice the next lower components may be subtitles, chapters, or parts. In most cases it seems to depend on how many levels of senior components are going to be required.

The United States Code—a special case—is itself divided into titles, and every title is divided into chapters (whether or not it is first divided into subtitles or parts). The chapters are always odd-numbered, in order to leave space for the future addition of new ones.

In most cases it is probably best to divide the titles into parts, thus omitting several steps, if two levels of senior components are all you will need—this is in fact the approach most often used in practice regardless of style—but divide the titles into subtitles and follow the sequence given above in any other case. (Needless to say, when amending an existing law you simply apply the Roman rule.)

One final comment. Sections, not senior components, are the vehicles that carry the substantive freight. From the drafter's point of view, titles and other senior components of a bill are nothing but defined spaces within which related sections can be grouped—they are empty receptacles for holding the substantive provisions. And except for their designations those provisions (the sections themselves) are written and structured in the way they would be written and structured even if the bill were not divided into senior components.

Thus when drafting a new section, giving it a heading and a number is only a trivial preliminary—the real work has barely begun—but when creating a new title the job is finished as soon as you have inserted its designation and heading at the appropriate place in the bill. As a consequence, the only stylistic decision you have to make in creating a title or other senior component involves its heading.

▶ **20.5   Headings**

For your own good as well as for the edification of your eventual readers, you should make maximum use of section and subsection headings. This rule applies whether or not the bill you are working on is divided into broader segments such as titles, chapters, and parts (which always have headings).

As a general rule, headings should be as short as possible, but informative enough to be of help to the reader—they need not (and indeed should not try to) exhaust the ideas expressed in the text. And they should be accurately descriptive—courts are increasingly taking headings into account when interpreting the law.

Chapter 31 sets forth literal examples of all of the types of headings that are used in the various Federal drafting styles.

Headings for sections and inferior subdivisions. Section and subsection headings are highly visible when flipping through the pages of a draft. They orient the readers, and help give an understanding of the overall organization of the bill as well as the purpose of each of its provisions.

In the early stages of a lengthy draft, headings can be particularly useful to you as a drafter. They give you an excellent road map of your product, enabling you to locate provisions quickly and saving you time and irritation; language hastily inserted while putting together a rough working draft is often hard to find later without them. Headings also help you plan the architecture of the bill, since they give you a built-in working outline and force you to provide logical places in advance for all the pieces.

At least as important is the fact that the necessity of inventing headings (especially when they are used for the lower-level subdivisions) makes you think about what you are doing. It is amazing how often your efforts to come up with an appropriate heading for a section, subsection, or paragraph will reveal to you for the first time that you have been guilty of trying to combine ideas that don't really go together, or of failing to combine ideas that do.

As a rule, the harder it is to come up with a heading that is both succinct and illuminating for a particular section, subsection, or paragraph, the more likely it is that some further thought is needed. The provision involved may cover too much territory (and need to be further divided), or the whole scheme of division for the bill (or for the part of the bill in which that provision appears) may need to be reconsidered.

When sections fall into logical groupings, it is sometimes helpful to give each section in a group a compound heading stating first the common idea and then the subject of the particular heading, with the parts separated by a colon. For example, in a bill dealing with traffic safety you might have a section headed "Speed of motor vehicles: passenger cars", followed by sections headed "Speed of motor vehicles: trucks and buses" and "Speed of motor vehicles: motorcycles".

And when you put several coordinate subjects in the same section you can quite properly use a compound heading with the parts separated by semicolons; for example, "Appointment of Commissioner; tenure; removal for cause".

Of course, whether or not a bill may properly include headings for its sections and subsections (and what kind of headings should be used) depends on the formal style in which it is being written. This is sometimes the drafter's choice, although it more often depends on the context in which the drafter is operating, and is normally governed by the Roman rule. But if headings are used at all in a bill for subdivisions of a particular kind—sections, subsections, paragraphs, or subparagraphs—then all subdivisions of that kind in the bill should have headings.

In most cases today a bill containing more than one section, written in any of the accepted drafting styles, will include section headings of one kind or another. The "traditional" or "classic" style permits headings for sections but does not require them, and generally does not use them at all for inferior subdivisions. "U.S. Code" style requires headings for sections but almost never uses them for inferior subdivisions. The "modified revenue" style requires both section and subsection headings, and recommends (but does not require) paragraph and subparagraph headings as well. And the full-blown "revenue" style requires headings at every level—sections, subsections, paragraphs, subparagraphs, and clauses.

In the traditional style the section heading (if there is one) is centered, and appears by itself on a separate line; the designation appears at the beginning of the text. In all the other styles the section's designation and heading are combined on the same line, just above the text, and are not centered. The heading for any lesser subdivision in both the revenue and modified revenue styles is "run-in"—it appears within the text, immediately after the designation.

Thus a section dealing with criminal penalties written in U.S. Code style would begin

§ 123. Criminal penalties

    (a) Any person who . . .

while in revenue or modified revenue style it would begin

SEC. 123. CRIMINAL PENALTIES.

    (a) IN GENERAL.—Any person who . . .

and in traditional style it would begin

CRIMINAL PENALTIES

    SEC. 123. (a) Any person who . . .

(The typographical details are spelled out in chapter 31.)

Headings for senior components.   All senior components have headings (called "superior" headings in this book), even when the sections and subsections they contain do not. As has been indicated, in one sense they consist of nothing but their headings. And all superior headings are "centered" on the page (in combination with the associated component designations) even when the bill has section and subsection headings that are "flush".

Each of the accepted Federal drafting styles has its standard rules for superior headings, but in practice (as in the case of the rules for subdividing a bill generally—see 20.4) they are not always followed. The only thing you can say with certainty is that a bill's superior headings should be prominent, consistent, and in accord with the Roman rule. Read 31.6 for guidance—it contains a tabular comparison of the rules prescribed for superior headings under the various drafting styles. But if you remain in doubt, just follow the best models you can find.

Grammatical Considerations

▶ **21.1   Preliminary comments**

Good legislative language must be mechanically sound in terms of grammar, punctuation, word usage, and arrangement. As indicated in chapter 7, this usually involves nothing more complicated than the application of the everyday rules governing good writing of any kind.

And of the differences that do exist between legislative writing and other forms of prose composition very few are actually clear-cut matters of right and wrong. Mostly they involve choices between alternative usages that are matters of personal preference or subjective judgment, where either usage would adequately serve a novelist's purposes but one is demonstrably better than the other for the drafter.

But it cannot be repeated too often that legislative language has an overriding need for clarity and precision; and you must always apply (or not apply) the established rules of grammar and punctuation in the way that will best meet that need. It is the purpose of this chapter to help you do it.

▶ **21.2   Number**

The clearest expression of an idea or concept uses singular rather than plural nouns, if for no other reason than that it cuts out one unnecessary layer of possible relationships; it avoids the question of whether the plural applies to each individual member of the class or only to the class as a whole. The phrase "Any employee who ..." works the same as "Employees who ...", but it eliminates the risk that a reader or a court will erroneously interpret the statement to mean that at least two employees must be involved before any employee is covered, or that it only applies to groups of employees as such.

In stressing that the use of the plural is a major source of ambiguity in legislative language, *Hirsch* (page 43) offers the following as a typical example of a provision that raises unnecessary questions:

( ) The Secretary shall not award grants, or enter into contracts, in excess of $25,000 without the approval of the National Advisory Committee.

Does the $25,000 restriction limit the aggregate amount of the grants that may be made or merely the size of each individual grant? Does it limit the aggregate amount of the contracts that may be made or merely the size of each individual contract? Or does it perhaps seek to limit the combined aggregate amount of both? Read literally, it seems to limit each of them separately, although that is clearly not what it intended. Simply substituting "a grant" for "grants", and "a contract" for "contracts", would remove all doubt (unless of course an aggregate limitation was intended, in which case that fact should be explicitly stated).

A statute speaks to each person who is subject to it, and should be drafted that way. The singular is not limiting. You should avoid the use of plural nouns in the interest of clarity; and if there is any reason in a particular case to think that a singular noun might be read as not applying to every person in the group you are trying to cover, use "each" or "every" instead of "a", "an", or "any".

(Note that where number is a matter of indifference, you can often avoid both the singular and the plural by using the generic, as in "Proof of hardship may be by affidavit".) And if you must begin a sentence by describing the individuals covered in the plural, remember that it is almost always possible to switch over to the singular in midstream—before you get to the part that requires precision—by saying (for example) "individuals who ..." and then starting a new sentence beginning "Any such individual". Or, in the case of the example given above, by simply inserting "(in the case of any recipient)" after "$25,000". But remember also that the reverse approach—describing the covered individuals in the singular and then switching to the plural when the situation demands it—would have been easier.

▶ **21.3   Tense**

Whenever possible, use the present tense rather than the past or future tense. As *HOLC* (page 2) puts it, a statute is a movable feast—that is, it speaks as of whatever time it is being read rather than as of the time when it was drafted, enacted, or put into effect. The use of verbs in the past or future tense may raise unnecessary (and misleading) questions about who or what is being covered.

It is true that, when expressing time relationships in a law, there may be cases in which it is appropriate to use the present tense for facts contemporary with the law's operation and then the past (or future) tense for facts that must precede (or follow) its operation. But even in those cases it is preferable whenever possible to keep the main verb in the present tense throughout and to express the temporal relationships explicitly. In this context phrases such as "An individual who is or has been a member of a subversive group is not eligible ..." and "If, having been convicted of a felony, an individual is found to be ..." are quite proper.

The use of the passive past participle when referring to past events can be particularly troublesome. The phrase "an individual who was married on January 1, 1986", for example, can be read as meaning either an individual who got married on that date or an individual who was a married person on that date (depending on whether the intended verb is "was" or "was married"). Unless the context clearly resolves the ambiguity, the phrase should be recast.

Note that the use of the auxiliary verb "shall" in the imperative mood—as in "The Secretary shall award a grant ..."—should not be regarded as a violation of the rule laid down here. And even if you agree with the view that the use of "shall be" in a phrase like "This Act shall be effective ..." constitutes a use of the purposive future tense (see 21.5), you should treat it as a permissible exception to the rule laid down here. In the author's opinion the use of "shall", like the use of "may", is completely compatible with that rule.

▶ 21.4   Voice

Use the active voice rather than the passive voice unless the actor cannot be identified or the statement is intended to be universal. It not only gives your language more "punch", it also identifies much more clearly who is to do what.

The use of the passive voice in a sentence invariably leaves one or more of its material elements unspecified. In a provision reading "Proceeds derived from such sale shall be used for [some specified purpose]", for example, it obscures whose proceeds are covered and quite possibly (depending on the context) leaves some doubt about whose responsibility it is to use them in the required way.

And in a sentence granting a power or privilege or imposing a duty, the use of the active voice helps to avoid vagueness by forcing the drafter to name, as the subject of the sentence, the person in whom the power or privilege is vested or upon whom the duty is imposed.

▶ 21.5   Mood

Any provision that is intended to make something happen or to force someone to take an action—a provision imposing a duty or requirement, for example, or a provision creating a function or establishing an agency—should be written in the imperative mood, with the auxiliary verb "shall" accompanying the main verb. The same principle applies (with the auxiliary verb "shall not", of course) when the provision is intended to prevent something from happening or to force someone to refrain from taking an action. If you mean to issue a command, you should write it as a command.

A provision that is intended to confer a right or privilege, or to describe a statutorily mandated state of affairs, can usually be written either in the imperative mood ("A qualified applicant shall be entitled to receive . . ." or "This Act shall be effective on [a specified date]") or in the indicative mood ("A qualified applicant is entitled to receive . . ." or "This Act is effective . . ."). Many experienced drafters prefer the indicative, because it seems less stilted and artificial, and because it better expresses the present-tense flavor; and a number of major Federal laws use it as a matter of course.

In a similar vein, *Dickerson* and others—contending that the use of "shall" and "shall not" merely to declare a legal result rather than to prescribe a rule of conduct (as in "A qualified applicant shall be entitled to receive . . .") constitutes a "false imperative"—feel that it is not only unnecessary but involves a circumlocution in thought, because the purpose of the provision is achieved by the very act of declaring the legal result; they recommend that the indicative rather than the imperative mood should always be used in any declaratory (that is, self-executing) provision.

The author understands their point but does not totally agree—he confesses to a tendency to follow his visceral instincts; he would never say "the term 'X' shall mean . . ." instead of "the term 'X' means . . .", for example, but he sees nothing wrong with "shall be effective" or "shall be entitled".

And he urges caution in flocking to the indicative banner because many statutory expressions in the indicative mood look suspiciously like mere descriptions of the existing state of affairs, without any apparent legal or substantive effect; in extreme cases they can look positively silly, and sometimes (in theory at least) they run the risk of being misinterpreted, especially when the imperative mood is used elsewhere in the law involved. But using the imperative mood for commands and in noncommand situations where the indicative just doesn't look right, while using the indicative mood in most noncommand situations, will inevitably produce a widespread and very obvious stylistic inconsistency in your bill, with all the potential problems that entails.

If you develop a preference for the indicative approach, go ahead and use it. But make sure that you have a rational criterion for distinguishing the situations in which you use it from the situations in which you don't, that you apply the criterion consistently, and that your readers will be able to understand the lines you have drawn.

▶ **21.6 Punctuation**

In legislative drafting even more than in other forms of writing, proper punctuation is critical, because of the tremendous contribution it can make to the drafter's twin objectives of clarity and readability.

Despite the medieval rule (not yet totally dead) that "punctuation is no part of a statute", courts do rely upon it in interpreting laws (as they should); and the right punctuation helps to ensure the right interpretation. Even those who still cling to the rule not only concede the efficacy of punctuation as a practical aid to readability—when sufficiently pressed they would have to admit that correct punctuation is often essential to clarity as well.

For the most part, the generally accepted rules of punctuation apply with equal force to punctuation in legislative language. The drafter should depart from the accepted rules only when maximum clarity demands it; and that does happen, of course, but only when those rules—

1. would result in language that is insufficiently precise to serve the special needs of legislation, or in language that makes it unnecessarily hard for the intended audience to extract and understand the message;

2. would be unequal to the task of handling a particularly complex concept within a confined space; or

3. would not adequately deal with a particular form or usage that is unique to statutory language.

As will soon become clear, the chief offender is the comma—an indispensable writing tool but unfortunately one that can easily produce ambiguity or otherwise mislead the reader if used carelessly.

It should not be necessary to belabor the subject further. As a drafter, you need to know the accepted rules of punctuation and religiously follow them in most cases, but you must also learn to recognize the situations in which a departure from (or special application of) those rules may be justified for one of the reasons just cited. For illustrative purposes (and at the risk of repeating things that have already been said) there are several specific punctuational points that arise frequently and deserve mention here.

Commas in series.   When setting forth a series of items in a sentence either in conjunctive or disjunctive form, the last two items in the series, like the earlier items, should always be separated by a comma; for example, "A, B, and [or] C"—never just "A, B and [or] C". The omission of the final comma in the series—a common practice in expository writing—sometimes invites the misreading that the last item is part of the preceding one (that is, that B and C, together or as alternatives, are a single item), and sometimes even suggests that the last item is not a part of the series at all but is rather a part of what follows it.

Commas used parenthetically.   Use commas to set off clauses that describe a subject already identified (as in "The Administrator, who shall be appointed as provided in section

103, may ...''), but not clauses that themselves identify the subject (as in "A disbursing officer who is responsible under section 507 may ..."). In the latter case the "who" clause is defining or restrictive while in the former it is not—the same distinction that is made between the relative pronouns "that" and "which" in 21.8.

Colons and dashes. When the words "as follows" or "the following" are used in making an amendment or as lead-in language for a list or description, or for any similar purpose, they should always be followed by a colon (with the first word after the colon capitalized)—never by a dash. Dashes should be reserved for language that could be read (with or without the punctuation) as a continuous sentence.

Lists. As will be discussed more fully in chapter 23, it is often necessary or desirable in a bill to set forth a list of items—definitions, rules, powers, functions, or just plain descriptive nouns—and the most practical all-purpose approach is to tabulate the list, with appropriate lead-in language and a separate indented paragraph for each item. There are two ways of doing this.

If the lead-in language ends with a dash—

1. each item should be paragraphed and its margin indented 5 spaces (with any further subdivision being indented an additional 5 spaces);

2. the first word in each item should begin with a lower-case letter (unless it is a proper noun);

3. each item other than the last item should end with a comma or semicolon; and

4. the conjunction "and" or "or", which determines whether the items on the list are collective or separate, should appear at the end of the next-to-last item only.

If the lead-in language ends with a colon, on the other hand, the following guidelines would apply:

1. Each item should be paragraphed and indented as though the lead-in language ended with a dash.

2. The first word in each item should be capitalized.

3. Each item should end with a period.

4. The collective or separate nature of the items is expressed in the lead-in language itself.

(It is hopefully unnecessary to point out that each of the two foregoing statements is written so as to embody the stylistic approach it describes. Additional examples can be found in 23.4.)

Periods and quotation marks in amendatory legislation.   When a sentence amends existing law, and sets forth the language being inserted or added (or literally repeats the language being stricken), any punctuation that is a part of that language must appear within the quotes; and the sentence's own punctuation that follows—whether a final period or an internal comma or semicolon—must be kept outside them.

Thus, if the language being inserted or added ends with a period, just put that period inside the quotes where it belongs and leave the amendatory sentence's final period outside the quotes where it belongs, despite the odd appearance of the double period. For example:

> (b) Section 123(a) of the ABC Act is amended by striking ", except that" and all that follows and inserting "but shall not include minors.".

These rules, which were addressed at some length in 16.2, are contrary to the accepted practice in expository writing; but they are important and should be followed consistently. You must never leave the reader (or the courts) in any doubt as to whether or not the punctuation within the quotes is really meant to be added to or taken away from the existing law.

Commas after dates.   The rule for punctuating a date such as "January 1, 1992", is the same in legislative drafting as it is in expository writing—add a comma after the year as well as after the day (unless of course the date is the last thing in the sentence and is followed by a period). The point is mentioned here only to provide a vehicle for two comments:

> 1. Commas after dates are an abomination to the drafter, and are placed there only to satisfy a completely arbitrary convention the reason for which is unknown to the author. A comma traditionally indicates a pause in the sentence, but dates are like single words and their final commas do not indicate pauses except when the date involved would be followed by a comma even if it were a single word. Placing a comma after a date not only brings the reader up short at a point where (in most cases) no pause is intended—it also promotes confusion and ambiguity in

many cases because the reader has no way of knowing whether or not the pause is intended (and the presence or absence of a pause can sometimes make a real substantive difference). Most drafters would love to see the general adoption of the military system of expressing dates—day, month, and year, totally unpunctuated, instead of month, day, and year with two commas.

2. In the author's opinion you should abide by the convention, but only because if you don't it would look like a typographical error to most people (so that they still would not know what you intended). And if the sentence is already complicated and you think that the arbitrary comma would cause undue damage to its clarity and readability, you will be forgiven (by the author at least) for any contortions you may have to go through in order to omit or relocate the date.

Hyphenated words.   The rules for determining whether or not you should hyphenate the two words making up a compound noun are clearly prescribed by dictionaries and style manuals, and you should normally follow those rules religiously. But when there would be the slightest doubt about whether the two words are a compound noun or about what their combination means, you should always hyphenate them regardless of what the authorities say. The term "cross-reference" means a reference that crosses subdivision lines, but if you omit the hyphen as many dictionaries recommend, it could just mean any reference that is made angrily; "cross-reference" is clearer.

▶ **21.7   Capitalization**

The accepted rules of capitalization in statutes vary from jurisdiction to jurisdiction, but there is a hard core that you can start from. In the first place, there are the basic rules of proper English composition that are observed everywhere; it is assumed that all readers of this book are familiar with them. In the second, every jurisdiction has a style manual for governmental documents (like GPO's *Government Style Manual*), which should be followed in legislation unless there is a compelling reason to do otherwise. Insofar as they involve capitalization, the conventions established by these rules and manuals are almost always completely consistent with good legislative drafting.

Once again, however, you must remember that legislation has

special needs. When these needs are not adequately served by the generally accepted stylistic rules (of capitalization, punctuation, or anything else), you should ignore them if you can get away with it or else use whatever devices may be available to circumvent them. (An everyday example of the latter is the inclusion of the modifying phrase "The term" in all definitions—see 11.7—to circumvent the requirement (which cannot be ignored) that the first word in a sentence must always start with a capital letter; beginning a definition with that phrase guarantees that the capitalization or noncapitalization of the term itself will be the same in the definition as it is in the text.)

Government style manuals differ in their specifics from jurisdiction to jurisdiction, of course, and you must become familiar with (and follow) the one that governs documentary writing in the particular jurisdiction in which you are working. In general, however, capitalization should be used sparingly. For those who work at the Federal level, here are a few rules of capitalization (from the *Government Style Manual*) that ought to be second nature but in fact are often violated by both occasional and experienced drafters:

1. The term "Federal" is always capitalized when used as an adjective, as is the term "Government" when used as a noun referring specifically to the national government as an institution. The term "federally" is not capitalized, nor is the term "government" when used as an adjective.

2. The term "State" is always capitalized (whether used as a noun or an adjective) when referring to one of the 50 States. (The term "possession" is never capitalized.)

3. The terms "Act" and "Public Law" are always capitalized when referring to a specific statute, but the term "public laws" when used generically is not.

4. Terms such as "title", "chapter", and "section" are never capitalized when referring to a subdivision or component of a statute (even though they are capitalized, initially or as a whole, when used as designations at the beginning of the provisions involved).

5. Official titles such as "President", "Secretary", "Administrator", and "Governor" are always capitalized.

6. The terms "Department" and "Agency" are capitalized when referring specifically to governmental entities whose

official names contain that term, but not when referring to a "department" or "agency" generically.

7. The first word following a colon is always capitalized, whether it is a single item on a list or the beginning of what would otherwise be a complete sentence in and of itself (unless, of course, it is an uncapitalized word in quoted matter).

▶ **21.8**   **The relative pronouns "that" and "which"**

A common grammatical question that drafters face involves the choice between the two relative pronouns "that" and "which". For example, should you say "a benefit under this section that is payable by reason of disability shall be reduced ...", or should you say "a benefit under this section which is payable by reason of disability shall be reduced..."? This choice presents itself to the drafter about once every half dozen lines of text, and consequently it deserves special mention.

Many people use the two interchangeably; but to grammatical purists there is a real distinction. When properly used the pronoun "that" is defining—it prefaces a relative clause that limits or restricts its antecedent (and is almost never preceded by a comma). The pronoun "which" on the other hand is nondefining—it prefaces a relative clause that explains or gives a reason, or adds a new fact, but does not limit or restrict the antecedent (and it is almost always preceded by a comma).

To put it another way, use "that" if the relative clause is needed to complete the thought being expressed, but use "which" if it is informative only and the thought would be complete without it.

Thus the answer to the question in the first paragraph depends on what you are trying to say. The first alternative (using "that") would be correct if the section involved provided benefits in nondisability as well as disability cases and you wanted to limit the proposed reduction to the latter. The second, with commas before "which" and after "disability", would be correct only if the section provided benefits in disability cases alone and you simply wanted to note that fact or to indicate the reason for the reduction.

Note, however, that the second alternative without the commas would be ambiguous on its face. Most likely it would be read as defining—that is, as though the "which" were a "that"—but you would be better off (other things being equal) if you used the terms properly and eliminated all doubt.

H. W. Fowler, after making a plaintive plea for proper use of the two relative pronouns, admitted that "It would be idle to pretend that [their proper use] is the practice either of most or of the best writers".[1] And he went on to acknowledge that there are sometimes legitimate practical reasons for choosing the less-preferred term:

1. The defining "that" must always be the first word of the relative clause, and if a preposition is needed it must often follow at quite a distance, while the nondefining "which" is easier to work with because it can be preceded by its governing preposition ("of which", "to which", or "from which"). Indeed, the use of "which" becomes a necessity when you are writing a series of terms and one or more of those terms has to be stated prepositionally (as in ". . . a benefit which is paid to a widow, and the amount of which is calculated . . .").

2. The defining "that" can often be omitted and still be operative ("the man you saw", for example, is equivalent to "the man that you saw"), while the nondefining "which" must always be expressed—it cannot be omitted without altering the sense of the sentence.

A few less scholarly observations may be in order. The use of the word "that" as a relative pronoun is clearly closer to everyday speech, but it has disadvantages to the drafter because it is also used in so many other senses—adverbially, adjectivally, and as a demonstrative pronoun or conjunction. The word "which" avoids most of these disadvantages.

And conversely, using both "which" and "that" (as relative pronouns), even within the same sentence, is sometimes the only practical way of avoiding the appearance of a series (despite the fact that it constitutes a form of elegant variation you would normally stay away from).

The best advice is to use the two relative pronouns in their proper grammatical senses as much as you can—reserving "that" for defining clauses and "which" for nondefining clauses—simply because that is the correct way to do it. But when the various "thats" begin to proliferate, or you have

[1] H. W. Fowler, *A Dictionary of Modern English Usage* (Oxford at the Clarendon Press, London: Humphrey Milford (1927)), p. 635.

special series-related needs, or you just think it would improve readability, follow your instincts and choose the pronoun that seems best in the circumstances. Fowler's rules may sometimes sound like they are written in stone, but he always recognized the need for flexibility in special circumstances, and the author believes that if he had been addressing legislative language specifically he would have agreed.

▶ 21.9 The relative pronouns "who" and "whose"

As a general rule, the relative pronouns "who" and "whose" are used to refer to particular individuals, while "that" is used to refer to individuals generically and "which" is reserved for things (or nonhuman "persons").

There is one case, however, in which the use of the relative possessive pronoun "whose" to refer to things is such a convenience (and so improves readability) that it has become acceptable even among grammatical purists and legislative drafters. When it is necessary to enumerate the attributes of a particular thing, it is permissible to substitute "whose" for "of which" if the alternative would be too awkward or cumbersome. Thus you can respectably say "an agency whose head is presidentially appointed and most of whose employees occupy professional positions", for example, instead of "an agency the head of which is presidentially appointed and most of the employees of which occupy professional positions".

And there is another case in which any pronoun chosen would be partially inappropriate. When the subject is a "person" in the broadly defined legal sense, you need "who" for situations where the person is an individual and "that" or "which" for situations where the person is a corporation or other nonhuman entity; but you can't have it both ways. The best advice is to use "that" unless the provision's impact on individuals is significantly greater and more obvious than its impact on nonhuman entities; but one pronoun is probably just as good as the other in any case.

▶ 21.10 The conjunctions "and" and "or"

Every third-grade student is well aware of the fact that the words "and" and "or" have totally different meanings, but it is amazing how often drafters use them carelessly. You should never forget that using the wrong conjunction (or using the right conjunction in the wrong way) can get a result that is diametrically opposed to the one you want.

As both *Dickerson* and *Hirsch* point out, simply distinguishing "and" from "or" is not the whole story; each of the two terms is itself semantically ambiguous, and can be used in two quite different senses.

The phrase "A and B" may mean A and B jointly and severally (so that the provision involved applies to either or both of them), or it may mean A and B jointly but not severally (so that the provision applies to both or not at all). And the phrase "A or B" may mean A or B or both (so that the provision involved can apply inclusively to either or both of them), or it may mean A or B but not both (so that the provision can apply only to one of them).

Thus the use of "and" between paragraphs (18) and (19) of a 19-paragraph list means one of two quite different things with respect to, say, paragraph (2) of that list—either that the section applies in every case described in the list and therefore always applies in the case described in paragraph (2), or that it applies in the case described in paragraph (2) only if it also applies to all of the cases described in the other 18 paragraphs. The use of "or" between paragraphs (18) and (19) also means one of two quite different things—either that the section applies in the case described in paragraph (2) without regard to any of the other paragraphs, or that it can apply in that case only if it does not apply in any of the others.

In each instance the effect of the conjunction depends upon the lead-in language of the list—often separated from the conjunction itself by many pages—which is one reason why it is so easy to be careless about it. Normally "and" is used in the joint and several senses and "or" is used inclusively, but if any doubt exists in a particular case you should deal with it explicitly in the lead-in language or in language placed immediately after the list. There is no set formula for doing this—any combination of words that makes your intent clear will serve. Do not fall back on the ancient "and/or" approach; it is a sloppy device and doesn't solve the problem in most cases.

A variant that is particularly important for the everyday drafter to understand is the relatively common case, involving the enumeration of two or more persons or entities, in which it may be unclear whether the linkage produced by the "and" or "or" is meant to apply to the enumerated persons or entities themselves or to their characteristics.

On its face, for example, the phrase "every husband and

father" could be read as meaning "every person who is either a husband or a father" or as meaning "every person who is both a husband and a father". And the phrase "every husband or father" could be read as meaning "every person who is either a husband or a father" or as meaning "every person who is a husband or a father or both".

In every such case—and this is the most important point in the whole discussion of "ands" and "ors"—the desired meaning can be unambiguously expressed by using either "and" or "or", without any difference in substance, by simply making it clear whether it is the persons or entities themselves or their characteristics to which the term applies. Whether you use "and" or "or" then depends upon whether you choose to identify the affected persons by enumerating the classes into which they fall or by defining them as a single class and then enumerating their qualifying characteristics. Thus a provision reading:

( ) A payment shall be made under this section to—

(1) each person who is 70 years of age or older, and

(2) each person who is physically disabled.

is the exact equivalent of a provision reading:

( ) A payment shall be made under this section to each person who—

(1) is 70 years of age or older, or

(2) is physically disabled.

The word "and" is necessary to the first version because it enumerates two separate classes of persons each of which must be included, whereas "or" is necessary to the second because it names a single class of persons by enumerating its two alternative qualifications for membership.

For you as a drafter, it need not be this complicated. Look hard at what it is that you are trying to do, and choose explicit clarity over compactness if there is the slightest doubt about what your "ands" and "ors" would accomplish.

▶ **21.11 Questionable practices that can help**

There are a number of grammatical practices which are condemned, or at least frowned upon, by the purists, but which nevertheless may often represent the easiest and most natural way to express a particular thought. A few of them deserve comment here.

What should the drafter's attitude be about such things as using split infinitives and ending sentences with prepositions? On the one hand these practices do not detract from clarity, and it is often hard to find an alternative that is not cumbersome or confusing; but on the other they are likely to be jarring for many readers.

Although most grammar textbooks frown upon these practices, many do not; and highly literate authors from time immemorial have engaged in them without apology. They are simple, direct, and forceful; they are never ambiguous; and the contortions a writer has to go through in order to avoid them often result in awkward sentences that border on the ludicrous.

H. W. Fowler said of split infinitives that, although they are not desirable in and of themselves, they are "preferable to . . . real ambiguity and to patent artificiality".[2] He described sentence-ending prepositions as "a valuable idiomatic resource [and] an important element in the flexibility of the English language", going on to say that "to shrink with horror from ending with a preposition is no more than foolish superstition".[3] (Fowler claimed that the only reason for the traditionalists' distrust of sentence-ending prepositions in English is that they were never used in Latin.) Winston Churchill once made the point somewhat more sarcastically, in responding to a noisy critic of the practice, by declaring that "the ending of a sentence with a preposition is a practice up with which I will not put". And Ruskin is said to have scrupulously removed all sentence-ending prepositions from his early writings, by proofreading each manuscript one last time for this express purpose, but to have restored them in later editions when he found that their removal had deprived his words of vigor and rendered his language "unnatural".

Another common practice of expository writers that is widely questioned by the textbooks is that of beginning sentences with conjunctions ("And", "Or", or "But"). They engage in the practice for one very simple reason—it is a useful way of indicating how successive thoughts are intended to fit together, without having to combine them into long sentences or to include cumbersome explanations of their relationship. In theory at least, this practice could obviously have value in

2. *Op cit,* pages 558 and 560.

3. *Op cit,* page 458.

legislative drafting for the same reason.

How should you as a drafter sort out all these considerations in your everyday work? There is of course a presumption that you should not use any practice that may be frowned upon by a substantial segment of your intended audience, since making it easy for that audience to read and understand your words without distraction is one of your primary objectives. But you should not risk distorting your language simply to follow convention either.

The best and most conservative advice is to follow the majority view (thereby offending the smallest number of readers), unless you think clarity and precision are compromised. The following guidelines may prove useful:

1. You should feel free to use a split infinitive whenever it seems natural and clear to you. The effort involved in making your sentence "correct" is seldom worth it, and the alternatives will make your sentence worse (from a drafting point of view) as often as they make it better. Reversing the order of the verb and the offending adverb, for example, will indeed eliminate the "split", but it usually results in an awkward or jerky sentence, and it sometimes leaves the reader in doubt about whether the adverb applies to that verb or to a later one. (See the discussion of "squinting modifiers" in 22.5.)

2. You should be willing to end a sentence with a preposition whenever the situation seems to call for it, but you should do it with caution. When a preposition strays very far from the verb to which it relates there is always a possibility of losing it in the shuffle, with resulting confusion or ambiguity.

3. You should avoid sentences that begin with conjunctions. There is usually a simple alternative (such as using "In addition," instead of "And") or some other easy way to make the relationship between sentences clear; and in many cases the sentences involved could be combined.

(The author has not avoided sentence-starting conjunctions in this book, as you will have noted, but has almost never used them in statutory language. You too should feel free to use them if you write a book; just don't put them in statutes.)

Fowler's general conclusion about sentence-ending prepositions is a good statement of principle for determining what the drafter's approach should ideally be to any grammatical practice:

> Follow no arbitrary rule, but remember that there are often two or more possible arrangements between which a choice should be consciously made; if the abnormal, or at least unorthodox, final preposition that has naturally presented itself sounds comfortable, keep it; if it does not sound comfortable, still keep it if it has compensating vigour, or when among awkward possibilities it is the least awkward.[4]

4. *Op cit,* page 459.

Word Usage
in General

▶ 22.1   Preliminary comments

Most of the commonly occurring usages and forms that legislative drafters need to know about are addressed elsewhere in this book—either along with the general subjects to which they primarily relate or in a special place set aside for usages and forms of the particular type involved. But there is a residual body of commonly occurring usages and forms—not set forth or adequately addressed anywhere else in this book—that may be worth your attention.

Many of these usages and forms are relatively trivial, and involve matters of preference rather than matters of right or wrong, but some (see for example 22.2) are fundamental. The purpose of this chapter (along with chapter 27) is to complete the picture by touching upon them briefly.

▶ **22.2   Use of "shall" and "may"**

In general.   When requiring that some action be taken, use "shall" rather than "is directed to" or "must"; and when permitting some action to be taken, or granting a right, privilege, power, or authority, use "may" rather than "is authorized [or empowered] to". To distinguish the case in which authority granted elsewhere is required to be exercised by the provision at hand, the provision can read "shall, under section ＿＿, take [the action involved]". (It would not actually be wrong to use "must" in place of "shall", but it is best to reserve that term for cases that require special emphasis.)

When denying a right, privilege, power, or authority, use "may not"; and when prohibiting the taking of a specific action, use "shall not". (Some commentators do not draw this line, and indeed the distinction is sometimes elusive, but consistently making the effort will help to avoid ambiguity in close cases.) Note that "shall not" and "may not" speak to the person subject to the prohibition and are silent as to whether an action taken by that person in violation of the prohibition is nevertheless valid, particularly as to an innocent third party; if that is of legal or political concern, the question of the effect of the action on others should be explicitly addressed.

The controversy over questions of mood—whether to use the imperative or indicative mood when granting or denying a right, privilege, power, or authority, and the undesirability of using the "false imperative" to simply declare a legal result—was addressed in 21.5 and will not be further discussed here.

Imposing duties.   The best way to impose a duty on an individual is through the use of a sentence, in the active voice, whose subject is that individual and whose main verb is accompanied by the auxiliary verb "shall"—for example,

"The Secretary shall pay to any qualified applicant ...", or "An applicant shall file with the Secretary...". This form should not be unnecessarily varied or embellished.

Note, however, that to state as a command what is intended only as a condition precedent often creates ambiguity. Thus "Any appointee shall be a citizen of the United States" might (in some contexts) be read as merely requiring an individual to become a citizen if he is appointed rather than as limiting the class of individuals eligible for appointment.

Conferring rights.   The best way to confer a right, privilege, power, or authority upon an individual is through the use of a sentence, in the active voice, whose subject is that individual and whose main verb is accompanied by the auxiliary verb "may"—for example, "Any individual who has attained age 65 may file an application...". This form should not be unnecessarily varied or embellished either.

But the granting of a right should not leave the reader in any doubt about who has the option. Sometimes a simple "shall"—as in "A member of the commissioned corps shall receive transportation"—could be viewed as requiring the individual involved to exercise the right, while a simple "may"—as in "A member of the commissioned corps may receive transportation"—could be viewed as leaving unclear whether the agency involved is obliged to provide it. Substituting "shall be entitled to" or "is entitled to" (for the naked "shall" or "may") will resolve the doubt.

If you fear in a particular case that the grant of a power to an official might be construed as imposing on him a duty to exercise that power, you can add a phrase such as "in his discretion" (after the "may"). But you should not do this indiscriminately, because such a phrase is implicit in the word "may" and the use of the phrase in one instance may cast doubt on the intended meaning of your other "mays", and also because the use of the phrase can have unintended consequences under the administrative procedure provisions of title 5 of the United States Code (see 12.8).

Imposing prohibitions.   *Hirsch* recommends that you always place a prohibition in the verb rather than in the subject, through a sentence, in the active voice, whose subject is that individual and whose main verb is accompanied by the auxiliary verb "may not"—for example, "An individual under the age of 18 may not use the facility" rather than "No individual under the age of 18 may use the facility".

Dickerson and *HOLC* disagree; their preference is the other way around. The author of this book has no strong feelings and has done it both ways.

But when you do choose to put the prohibition in the subject rather than in the verb, do not combine the negative subject with an affirmative "shall", as in "No individual under the age of 18 shall use the facility"; if the word "shall" is given its dictionary meaning ("is required to") the sentence would then mean that the individual, though not required to use the facility, could do so if he wished. Say "No individual under the age of 18 *may* . . .".

▶ **22.3   Use of "such"**

The use of "such" as a demonstrative adjective to mean "the previously mentioned" (as in "pay such benefit" or "within such agency") is frequently denounced by commentators and scoffed at by critics of legislative style. It is admittedly a somewhat archaic way of referring to an antecedent; many professional drafters flatly refuse to use it, and in most cases a more natural term ("the" or "that") will indeed sound better and work equally well.

But there are enough situations in which either of those alternatives would be confusing that the use of the more precise demonstrative "such" to refer to the antecedent is almost indispensable. Sometimes "the" would fail to identify the antecedent unambiguously; and sometimes "that" would be confusing or awkward because the provision involved already contains too many "thats" being used in other senses (compare the demonstrative pronoun dilemma described in 21.8). And the use of "such" in legislation is so common (partly for the reason just given and partly from sloth) that it cannot possibly constitute a jarring note for the reader.

The author would encourage you to use "the" or "that" in place of the demonstrative "such" as long as you can do so consistently and are satisfied that the meaning is clear. And in the process you can often use the word "involved"—as in "pay the benefit involved" or "within the agency involved"— to add a touch of specificity. But you should feel free to use "such" without apology if you are comfortable with it, and you should always use it when you suspect that the alternative would jeopardize the clarity and precision of your product.

(When used with an indefinite article as a synonym, as in "pay such a benefit" or "within such an agency", the word "such" has no similar problems—it is considered quite proper even in everyday speech. The author notes in passing, however, that Fowler regards both this and the demonstrative use of the word as "illiterate" although he concedes that both uses "have grammar on their side".)

And needless to say, you should always shun the extremely archaic expressions "said" (as in "the said agency") and "the same" (as in "calculate the benefit and pay the same to the beneficiary").

▶ **22.4   Use of explicit cross-references**

If you want to be open and above-board, on the face of the bill, about the relationship between two provisions, you should use an explicit cross-reference. In whichever one of the two provisions is most substantive (or in both), cite the other specifically.

Admittedly, multiple cross-references may make the bill seem hard to read for some people; but usually the lack of readability is caused not so much by the cross-references themselves as by the bulk and internal complexity of the subject matter that made them necessary. (The Internal Revenue Code, often cited as the worst offender in this area, couldn't exist without them.) And their use saves time, shortens the bill, and (most importantly) promotes clarity, precision, and internal consistency.

Cross-references may have direct substantive impact or be merely informative. They are usually used for one of several specific purposes:

1. To indicate that another provision of the bill, or a provision of existing law, is to apply also under the provision at hand. For example, "Section 123 applies [in this situation]", "The rules that apply under section 123 also apply [in this situation]", or "as defined in section 123" (where the definition involved would not otherwise apply). These are typical examples of incorporation by reference, a subject discussed in detail in 23.3.

2. To indicate that another provision is to be read as making an exception to or modification of the rules contained in the provision at hand. For example, "except as provided in section 123", "subject to section 123", or "as computed without regard to section 123". This type of cross-reference, which is not usually necessary but often desirable, was discussed in 12.3.

3. To simply describe and identify a concept or relationship that is established in another provision. For example, "benefits under section 123", "any action taken under section 123", or "the rates in effect under section 123".

4. To simply call attention to another provision or to its effect on the provision at hand. For example, "as defined in section 123" (where the definition involved would apply anyway), or "as described in section 123".

The use described in paragraph (1) is substantive; the use described in paragraph (2) can be either substantive or just informative (usually the latter); and the uses described in paragraphs (3) and (4) are primarily informative.

Except in cases in which the cross-reference has real substantive effect (as in the case of an incorporation by reference, where the only alternative is either to restate the other provision verbatim (which would be cumbersome, repetitious, and time-consuming) or to try and paraphrase it (which might be dangerous)), the drafter faces a choice: Should the other provision be acknowledged by an explicit cross-reference in the provision at hand, as an aid to readers, or should the drafter remain silent about it and simply let the bill operate according to its terms?

The broader aspects of the problem were discussed at length in 12.3 in connection with exceptions and special rules; the remainder of this subdivision focuses on the mechanics of making the choice—the things you need to take into account before deciding which way to jump.

As indicated earlier, many professional drafters avoid most cross-references as a matter of principle; they feel that, given the unavoidable interrelationships within most statutes, all laws of any substance would soon consist of nothing but "except that", "subject to", and "notwithstanding" clauses if they were allowed a foothold. Others use them liberally, without regard to the clutter, simply because they make those interrelationships clear.

In the author's view there is a sensible middle ground.

Isolated minor exceptions to (or qualifications of) a basic provision of a bill are to be expected, and everyone familiar with legislation knows this—they need not be flagged in advance. And many other purely informative cross-references actually provide little or no information that the readers would not otherwise have. Since cross-references in these cases contribute nothing substantively to the bill, and are almost never actually necessary, you should feel free to use them or not, as your best judgment indicates; but you should use them consistently if you use them at all, and you should not use them if their number is so great that the bill would look cluttered as a result.

In addition, when the basic provision is closely followed by exceptions or special rules and the format makes their relationship clear (as by the use of consecutive headings such as "General Rule", "Exceptions", and "Special Rules"), the use within the basic provision of internal cross-references to those exceptions or special rules would actually be redundant.

But there are situations in which the use of "except that", "subject to", and "notwithstanding" clauses is not only permissible but desirable in the interest of both clarity and readability. For example:

1. When an exception or modification is not minor, but actually changes the thrust of the bill, the drafter should always be up-front and explicit about the hierarchical interrelationship of the provisions involved if there could be the slightest doubt about it.

2. When there is a genuine question about whether or not one provision is an exception to or modification of another, or whether a definition would or would not apply, the relationship should always be made clear.

3. And when the other provision is contained in an existing law rather than in another section of your bill (and conversely when your bill does something that significantly affects a provision of existing law), the relationship should always be spelled out. In such a case the rule of construction that specific provisions are to be treated as exceptions to general provisions when they are inconsistent may be overridden by the rule of construction that later enactments are to be treated as modifying earlier enactments.

Case (3) is of course a subset of case (2), and (unlike the situation in which the two sections involved are contained within the same bill) it depicts a true "split provision".

Remember, however, that "except that" and "subject to" clauses placed in the bill's basic substantive provisions are considerably more useful than "notwithstanding" clauses in the collateral provisions. Being absolutely clear about the scope of the substantive provisions at the outset is more important to the reader than being reminded later that an exception is really an exception.

One final comment: Scattergun notwithstanding clauses ("Notwithstanding any other provision of law, . . .") should be avoided. If you strongly suspect when writing a bill that there are provisions in existing law that may importantly affect or be affected by what you are doing but you have no time to identify them, and you are willing to gamble by overriding them all without even knowing what they are (thus leaving their identification to the administrators and courts), there may on balance be some slight value in including such a clause as an obscure general warning to readers; but you should never do it routinely as a kind of automatic safety valve.

▶ 22.5   Modifiers and explanatory phrases

Adjectives, adverbs, and explanatory phrases enrich the meaning of nouns and verbs, and are as essential to legislative drafting as they are to other forms of writing. But in drafting they can cause endless legal difficulties when used carelessly, because a modifier typically ascribes to a noun or verb a characteristic that it does not precisely define.

Hirsch (pages 44-45) offers as an example the use of the term "serious physical injury" in a hypothetical definition of "domestic violence". He would tolerate the use of the term "physical" even though it is not altogether clear, but regards the term "serious" as

> so vague that it would add to the administrative burden of the agency and otherwise multiply the points of controversy between the agency and those that the statute affects. It would compel the agency to define the term . . . by regulation, open the agency to legal action to test that definition, and be a constant source of friction between the agency and those whose injuries the agency refuses to consider "serious" despite their seriousness to the victims.

And all of this without actually adding anything to the definition except a little flavor.

Consequences of this kind are often knowingly accepted by Congress and the administering agency for political or tactical reasons, or as the price of giving the agency the opportunity to exercise flexible judgment in the light of its experience.

Vagueness for reasons of policy is quite proper; vagueness resulting from the careless use of modifiers is not.

Other things being equal, the fewer the modifiers the easier the statute is to administer. Every modifier that you use in a bill is likely at some stage to require an administrative or judicial interpretation (which may or may not accurately reflect the true legislative intent), no matter how aptly it is used or how much it smoothes out the language. Most modifiers in practice are legally unnecessary and are intended only to add flavor; ideally they should be used only to add meaning. Use them, of course, but with discretion.

An inclusionary clause is a special form of modifier—usually parenthetical—that lists some of the more important things that the noun or verb involved is intended to include or affect. It is most often intended simply to indicate the principal targets of the legislation; but this is dangerous because it may strongly imply that anything not listed is not covered. Thus a statement about "domestic animals (including dogs, cats, and horses)"—even though problems involving dogs, cats, and horses may indeed have been the reason for the legislation—leaves the reader in some doubt about its effect on hamsters, canaries, and tropical fish. And the practice of saying "including but not limited to" is a bad solution in most cases for the reasons discussed in 22.15.

You should also avoid the use of modifiers that are merely redundant, like "real", "true", "actual", and "complete". They may seem useful for purposes of emphasis, but their occasional use in a bill casts doubt on every noun in the bill that is not similarly modified.

Finally, a word of caution. When you do use a modifier, make sure it is completely clear what it applies to. In a sentence that reads "The Secretary shall request the borrower promptly to submit a full report . . .", for example, the word "promptly" could be read as applying either backward or forward—that is, either to the Secretary's request or to the borrower's submission; this is called a "squinting modifier" by *Dickerson* (and is usually caused by the drafter's desire to avoid a split infinitive—see 21.11). And beware of modifiers that immediately precede or follow a series; in the phrase "corporations and partnerships that are exempt from taxation" it may be quite unclear, depending on the context, whether or not taxable corporations are included.

Some years ago a popular song titled "Purple People Eater"

was at the top of the nation's hit parade for many weeks. Most people instinctively thought of the title character as a purple being of some kind who ate people; it took a very careful study of the libretto to discover that he (or it) was simply a being of undetermined hue who ate purple people.

In any of these cases the solution is relatively simple, of course: Adjust the context so that the modifier is semantically incapable of modifying anything but the intended term, even if it takes a split infinitive to do it. (Note that the same kind of ambiguity, with the same simple solution, can result from the careless use of "because" or "since" clauses, or of juxtaposed prepositional phrases.)

▶ 22.6   Vesting functions in an agency

When you want a function to be exercised by or within a particular department or other Federal agency, vest that function in the head of the agency—not in the agency as such, and not in some subordinate official or branch of the agency even when you expect or intend that the function will be exercised on a day-to-day basis by that official or branch.

Everything that a Federal agency does is by law the responsibility of its head, and for many years it has been the firm policy of the Federal Government to reflect that fact in all statutory provisions conferring functions, powers, or duties upon any department or agency. This gives Congress a single high-level official who is accountable and cannot deny responsibility, and leaves subordinate officials in no doubt about who is in control.

The assumption is, of course, that the agency head will delegate the performance of any function vested in him to the appropriate subordinate official or branch of the agency.

Thus a bill changing the method of calculating social security benefits should say "The Secretary [of Health and Human Services] shall compute ...", and a bill providing for the construction of a new space station should say "The Administrator [of NASA] shall construct ...", even though the named agency head would hardly notice the statutory directive as it passed across his desk on its way to the appropriate operating officials.

There are a few areas in which modern statutory grants of authority appear to violate this rule (those involving relationships between the Secretary of Defense and the Secretaries of the Army, Navy, and Air Force, for example, or between the Secretary of the Treasury and the Commissioner of Internal Revenue), but most instances of this kind are relics from the remote past. If in doubt, you should take the trouble to check existing laws to see how things are done in the area involved.

If it is important from a political or tactical point of view that a particular subordinate official or branch of an agency be formally recognized as the day-to-day administrator of a proposal, there is nothing wrong with mentioning that official or branch in passing—for example, by saying "The Secretary (acting through the Assistant Secretary for Internal Affairs) shall carry out a program . . ."—so long as the function itself is clearly vested in the agency head.

And you can sometimes address subordinate officials or branches directly when the matters involved are purely administrative or otherwise clearly nonsubstantive, although even then it is better in most cases to apply the usual rule and address the agency head.

▶ **22.7   Use of "person" and "individual"**

Always use the term "individual" to refer to a person who is a living member of the human race. The term "person" is much broader than that, including corporations and governmental entities as well as other public and private entities of various kinds, under the common law as well as under title 1 of the United States Code and corresponding State statutes.

Use the term "person" only when you affirmatively mean to include more than just individuals; and if the other entities you want to include are not the same as those listed in the applicable statutory definition, define the term (for your purposes) to make the difference clear.

There is one situation in which it is convenient (and permissible) for a drafter to use the term "person" to refer to an individual. When you are describing one individual's relationship to another individual, it is often helpful to call the latter "another person", so as to facilitate subsequent references to "such individual" and "such person" and distinguish them clearly. But you should do this, of course, only when you are absolutely certain that the use of the broader term will not unintentionally expand the coverage of your provision by including corporate and other nonhuman entities along with individuals.

▶ **22.8   References to fiscal years**

The Congressional Budget Act of 1974, which changed the fiscal year of the Federal Government to its present form—the 12-month period beginning on October 1—also added to the law (section 1102 of title 31 of the United States Code) a definition of the term "fiscal year". As a consequence, in specifying a particular fiscal year in language authorizing appropriations or in any other context, you should simply call it "fiscal year [1992]"; it is no longer appropriate to say "the fiscal year ending [September 30, 1992]".

The only choice you have to make is a trivial one—do you say "the fiscal year 1992" or just "fiscal year 1992"? Experienced drafters divide on the question, although the latter form is now preferred (since the former is largely a relic from the days before the term was statutorily defined). Subject to the Roman rule, however, you can use either one.

▶ **22.9   Other references to times and time periods**

In general. The terms "before", "after", and "at the same time as" are all that you need to express the temporal relationship between events. You should avoid stilted terms like "prior to", "subsequent to", and "concurrent with".

When describing a period after some stated event, such as a period within which some action must be taken, you should say (for example) "within 30 days after [the event]", or "not later than 30 days after [the event]". Do not say "within 30 days of [the event]"; if it is read literally (and sometimes even if it is not) it creates uncertainty about whether the action is to precede or follow the event, or both. And do not say "within [a specified period]" at all unless you really mean it; if you mean "at any time before the end of [that period]" you should say so.

When describing a period by specific reference to its beginning and ending dates, you should make very clear just what those dates are. Do not say "from", "to", "until", or "by" a specified date—those terms create doubts about whether the date specified is included as part of the period; say instead (for example) "any action taken during the period beginning January 1, 1991, and ending March 31, 1992", or "any action taken after December 31, 1990, but before April 1, 1992".

Do not say "any action taken [during the period] between January 1, 1991, and March 31, 1992"; the effect of the term "between" is unclear in most people's minds, but read literally it excludes both of the specified dates.

(Note that a similar ambiguity can exist in describing individuals' ages. The phrase "less than 21 years old" is clear enough, but a phrase like "more than 21 years old" or "between 18 and 21 years of age" is ambiguous.)

The word "year" is normally understood to mean a calendar year, so the term "calendar" should be omitted unless the context requires it. If you mean to refer to a fiscal year the term "fiscal" should always be included, of course. If you mean to refer to any period of 12 consecutive months (regardless of the stage of the calendar year at which it begins) you should always say "12-month period", not "year". And if you mean to refer to one continuous period but the context might permit the aggregation of shorter periods, you should be explicit about the requirement of continuity—say "two years of continuous service" or "service for a two-year period", for example, rather than just "two years' service".

When used to fix the beginning or ending of a period, the word "time" can be read as referring to the exact time of day (or night) when the relevant event occurs. This can cause problems. If you intend (as you almost always would) that the period be measured in whole days, use "day" or "date" instead of "time", as in "90 days after the date on which. . .".

References to enactment dates. When referring to the date on which a statute is enacted—whether the reference is internal (like a reference in a bill to the date of its own enactment) or external (like a reference in a bill to the enactment of some existing law)—either "the date of enactment of this Act [or that law]" or "the date of the enactment of this Act [or that law]" is correct.

Experienced drafters divide more or less evenly on this question; some prefer the former (in which "date of enactment" is a single compound noun) because it is more to the point, while others prefer the latter (which keeps the two nouns "date" and "enactment" separate) because they think it reads better. Needless to say, if the reference is to an existing law the actual date of its enactment (being already known) can always be specified instead, although this may leave the reader unclear about the reason for selecting that date.

And a bill should never use terms like "now", "present", "already", "heretofore", and "hereafter" in relating events to the date on which it is enacted or takes effect. A law speaks continuously, as of the time it is being read or applied, and to prevent ambiguity you should relate those events involved to that date explicitly, using one of the forms mentioned in the preceding paragraph.

▶ **22.10 Indefinite articles**

Under the accepted rules of statutory construction (see 19.5), the indefinite articles "a" and "an" are equivalent in effect to the pronominal indefinite adjectives "any", "each", and "every"; accordingly, when referring to a person or thing generically you have a choice. However, the preferred style in most cases (because it is simpler and a bit freer of possible substantive implication) is to use "a" or "an"—for example, "a beneficiary" or "an agency".

The terms "any", "each", and "every" should ideally be reserved for expressions that require unusual emphasis, or for those cases where the use of "a" or "an" might permit the unintended interpretation that the obligation is to be discharged (or the privilege exhausted) by applying it to a single member of the class instead of to all of them. And when you feel the need for such emphasis, use "any" (or "no") with "may", and "each" or "every" with "shall".

▶ **22.11 Deeming, treating, and considering**

Deeming is nothing more than a device for claiming that something is so when it is not; it creates a legal fiction, and has many of the same problems as unduly artificial definitions (see 11.7). Treating something as being so when it is not also creates a legal fiction, although it is more flexible in the sense that it can be used to establish a rule of law as well as to create the fiction unadorned.

Thus the phrases "For purposes of this Act a tennis racquet is deemed a handgun" and "For purposes of this Act a tennis racquet shall be treated as a handgun" are equivalent; they both create a blatant legal fiction and do nothing more. But the phrase "For purposes of this Act the Attorney General shall treat a tennis racquet in the same way as a handgun" creates no fiction; it rather establishes a rule of law under which the designated official is to operate—an approach that is often useful and that avoids many of the problems of the artificial definition.

The term "consider" should be used only to indicate an exercise of judgment or discretion, as in the phrase "For purposes of this subsection an individual who satisfies subsection (b) shall be considered qualified even though . . ."; it should not be used to create a legal fiction.

Note that when you deem or consider something to be so when it is not, or treat something as being so when it is not, you are doing it only for a specific and limited purpose; and (unless the context makes it absolutely clear) that purpose should be explicitly indicated. Whether you say "For the purpose of . . .", "For the purposes of . . .", or just "For purposes of . . ." is immaterial (most experienced drafters seem to prefer the latter)—you can choose the one you like best, and you should use that one consistently.

▶ **22.12 Directness, informality, and positive expression**

In writing legislative language you should always try to express yourself directly and in a positive manner.

Dickerson (page 117) urges the drafter to use "live" words— "finite verbs instead of their corresponding participles, infinitives, gerunds, and other noun or adjective forms"— because they are less artificial and in most cases will reach the intended audience better. For example, use "consider" instead of "give consideration to", "applies" instead of "is applicable", "provide for" instead of "make provision for", and "pay" instead of "make payment to".

In a similar vein, a number of commentators have strongly recommended that you always use the simplest and most conversational word available as an aid to readability. For example, use "begin" or "start" instead of "commence" or "institute", "stop" instead of "cease", "before" instead of "prior to", "get" instead of "obtain", "tell" instead of "inform", and "ask" instead of "inquire". This is a good rule so long as it is not carried to extremes (which of course is a matter of subjective judgment); in the author's opinion the first three examples given in the preceding sentence are clearly desirable while the last three sound too conversational to be appropriate in legislation.

And when the same idea can be expressed either positively or negatively, you should do it positively unless what you are expressing is a mandatory prohibition. Say "This section applies only to individuals who have reached age 60", not "This section does not apply to individuals under age 60".

You obviously have a good deal of slack on all of these recommendations—there is nothing really wrong with using the more indirect, formal, or negative form when you think it

reads better or is more compatible with neighboring forms—
but by and large the advice is good on all counts.

▶ **22.13 Circumlocutions and redundancies**

In general, you should avoid using pairs of words that have
the same effect (such as "each and every", "final and conclu-
sive", "from and after", "full and complete", "force and
effect", "null and void", "over and above", and "unless and
until"); one of the pair is always unnecessary, and should
usually be dropped in the interest of brevity and simplicity.

And you should also avoid using pairs of words where one of
them includes the other (such as "any and all" and "means
and includes"); the broader term can carry the freight alone.

Many such expressions are nothing but relics from older
times. However, some of them can be useful for purposes of
emphasis. The author is a great believer in giving emphasis
where it is needed, and in proper cases would tolerate any of
the examples cited (except "means and includes"); but he is
constrained to admit that it is probably better to avoid them
since so many commentators find them offensive.

▶ **22.14 Order of thoughts in a sentence**

The view has frequently been expressed that the circumstances in which a rule is to apply should normally be stated
before the rule itself. For example, "Whenever the Secretary
finds it necessary in carrying out section 123, he shall . . .", or
"If, after having taken the steps described in section 123, the
Secretary determines that it is necessary to . . . , he may. . .".
And any exceptions that may be necessary should normally be
dealt with after the rule has been fully stated. The idea, of
course, is to avoid cluttering up the statement of the rule itself
with collateral matters of either kind.

If the circumstances in which the rule is to apply involve a
number of contingencies or conditions, however, it is usually
preferable to state the rule first (since otherwise it will be
buried too deeply in the middle of the sentence), and to
place any exceptions that can be stated briefly ahead of the
rule. For example, "Except as provided in section 4, the
Secretary shall . . . ; but he may do so only if. . .".

These recommendations are obviously aimed at the objective
of increasing readability, and they do make sense. But no two
cases will be exactly the same, so use your own judgment
about whether or not they will promote readability in your
particular case.

▶ **22.15 Use of "means" and "includes"**

One thing means another when the two are identical or synonymous, and includes another when the second is a part of the first. This rather obvious distinction has its most important application in the case of definitions, and was addressed in 11.7.

But "means", "includes", and their derivatives are much more than definitional concepts—they are regularly found in ordinary narrative sentences—and you should be careful to use them correctly. For example:

1. You should always avoid the phrase "means and includes". It is totally redundant, and its use at any point in a bill (in a misguided attempt to give emphasis, presumably) invites misinterpretations elsewhere.

2. And you should not shackle the word "includes" with language that changes (or appears to change) its meaning by adding phrases like "but is not limited to". Such phrases have unfortunately become popular in recent years (in a misguided fear that readers may not know what the word means, apparently). Since "includes" is not exhaustive, the additional words are unnecessary—they add nothing to the dictionary definition, and they too invite misinterpretation.

The latter practice can probably be tolerated when the purpose is to make absolutely certain that hostile administrators will not limit the application of the provision involved to just the named items, or when because of the context the word "include" might reasonably be read as meaning "consist of" (as in "The membership of the Commission shall include ..."). In any other case, however, it should be avoided unless it is consistently used in parts of the bill over which you have no control. And if you use it at all you should use it consistently throughout the bill, since there will otherwise be a strong implication that you do not want "includes" to have its dictionary meaning unless you say so.

▶ **22.16 Use of "insure", "ensure", and "assure"**

As synonyms for "make certain", the terms "insure", "ensure", and "assure" are largely interchangeable, but only the latter two should be used in that sense in legislation. And of their noun forms only the term "assurance" should be used when describing an ironclad and enforceable promise that makes something certain.

The term "insure" should be reserved for use in describing what happens under a commercial or government insurance policy, or for use (with "against") in describing generically a form of safeguard or protection that resembles an insurance policy—for example, "regulations to provide insurance against fraud and abuse in the program".

▶ **22.17   Use of "by", "under", and "pursuant to"**

In general, if the result being sought in a provision you are writing is to be achieved through the operation of that provision itself (without the necessity of some administrator taking a particular action), use "by"—as in "the reduction required by this section".

If the result is to occur through some action that is required or permitted by that provision, or that is required or permitted by some other cited provision, use "under"—as in "an adjustment made under this section [or under section 123]". This assumes that the provision to which you refer establishes reasonably clear rules for the taking of actions of the type involved.

If the provision to which you refer does not establish such rules, or the result is more remotely derived from the authority of the provision you are writing (as it would be if the cited provision is merely a very general authorization of some kind), "pursuant to" is an acceptable alternative—as in "The Secretary shall prescribe regulations pursuant to section 123 for the purpose of ..."—but you should normally avoid "pursuant to" when "under" would do the job.

▶ **22.18   Use of "if", "when", and "where"**

The terms "if", "when", and "where", when used as conjunctions to mean "in case it happens that" or otherwise to express a condition or supposition, are often treated in expository writing as more or less interchangeable. In legislative drafting there are subtle or not-so-subtle differences; and over a period of time you will achieve a net increase in clarity and precision if you recognize those differences and consistently reflect them in your writing.

"If" has the most universal application; and you will always be safe if you choose it to express a condition based on the existence or nonexistence of a fact or on the occurrence or nonoccurrence of an event. "When" expresses a condition as to time, and should normally be used only for that purpose. In all fairness it must be admitted, however, that in most cases these two terms can be used interchangeably—a fact that may be useful to you when you are trying to make a complex or difficult sentence readable. "Where" expresses a condition as to place, and should never be used for any other purpose. The concept of "place" can be stretched a bit, however, permitting "where" to be used as a synonym for "in which" in formulations such as "in any case where" or "in any situation where"; in a complicated sentence this can help.

The terms "whenever" and "wherever" are occasionally useful, in places where "when" or "where" would otherwise be used, to emphasize that the clause which they introduce applies no matter how many times the conditioned fact or event occurs.

▶ 22.19   "Hereby", "thereof", and their kin

There is a class of adjectives and adverbs each of which consists of "here", "there", or "where" in combination with an ordinary preposition. They can be quite useful in difficult drafting situations because they permit a three-word or four-word thought to be expressed clearly in a single word, but they have a definitely archaic or artificial flavor and constitute the kind of "legalese" that is subject to caricature.

What should your attitude be toward these words? Unfortunately there is no single answer; it depends on a balancing of the value of the word in the case at hand against the degree of artificiality it exhibits. Some are so regularly useful that you should use them without apology, some sound so archaic that you should never use them, and most fall somewhere in between. The following are random recommendations based on the author's own drafting experience and personal preferences, and should not be regarded as holy writ.

The words "hereunder", "thereby", "thereof", "thereunder", and "thereafter" should be part of every drafter's arsenal. They are highly useful, and the need for them arises with great frequency.

Words like "herein", "thereto", and "whereof" should be avoided, simply because their archaic sound outweighs their usefulness (and "herein" is almost always ambiguous). Words like "hereafter" and "heretofore" are undesirable when used to describe the location of a provision in a bill (see 22.21), and simply have no place in legislative language when used in a temporal sense. "Aforementioned" is beyond the pale.

And words like "therefor", "therein", "whereas", and "whereby" fall somewhere in the middle. In the last analysis, it's a matter for your own subjective judgment.

Note that the word "hereby"—as in "section 6 is hereby amended" or "the Secretary is hereby empowered"—is something of a special case. It is suitably descriptive but almost always redundant, and should be used only when necessary to make it clear in a doubtful case (usually arising out of the use of the indicative mood) that the language involved is actually meant to accomplish some result rather than simply to describe the preexisting situation.

▶ **22.20   "Respectively" and "as the case may be"**

When you want one provision or thing to apply in a particular case and one or more other provisions or things to apply in one or more other cases, and you have to accomplish it (or prefer to accomplish it) in one fell swoop, you can do it by saying "A, B, and C apply to X, Y, and Z, respectively". The word "respectively" means that A applies to X, B applies to Y, and C applies to Z. Note that the relationships are always concurrent, and the verb is always plural.

One very common example (discussed in part V) involves the redesignation of a series of numbered paragraphs; thus

( ) Section 123(a) of the ABC Act is amended by striking paragraph (6), and by redesignating paragraphs (7) through (10) as paragraphs (6) through (9), respectively.

When you want to say that if one thing should happen one particular provision or thing will apply and that if one or more other things should happen one or more other particular provisions or things will apply, you can do it by saying "If X, Y, or Z occurs, A, B, or C (as the case may be) applies". The phrase "(as the case may be)", which need not be but usually is parenthetical, means that if X occurs then A applies, or if Y occurs then B applies, or if Z occurs then C applies. Note that in this case the relationships are alternative rather than concurrent, and the verb is singular. (Note also that some experienced drafters consider the phrase too ambiguous, for untutored readers at least, and prefer to spell out the relationships individually.)

▶ **22.21   "Above", "below", and "hereafter"**

If it is worth taking the trouble to indicate the general direction in which the reader of your bill should turn in order to find a particular item or provision, it is worth going one step further and specifying the place where that item or provision is located.

Thus, unless the context makes the location obvious, you should not say "the individual described above [or below]", or "the [term] as hereafter defined"; say instead "the individual described in paragraph (2)" or "the [term] as defined in section 9".

▶ **22.22 Percentages**

In keeping with the earlier admonition to favor 20th-century English over Latin, when expressing a percentage you should always use "percent" rather than "per centum".

▶ **22.23 A few closing cautions**

There are one or two fairly common drafting mistakes that are quite easy to make, and that have not been mentioned earlier:

Wrong placement of negatives. Be careful to place your negatives where they belong. It should not be necessary to belabor this point; but many an innocuous-looking sentence reaches a result that is altogether different from what was intended simply because the word "not" was incorrectly located. For example, "The Secretary shall appoint not more than 10 assistants" is very different from "The Secretary shall not appoint more than 10 assistants". In the former case the Secretary is limited to no more than 10 assistants but must appoint some; in the latter the Secretary is not legally obligated to appoint any at all.

The undistributed middle. When you divide any thing, entity, or progression into two mutually exclusive parts, be careful not to leave a small piece in the middle that is not included in either of the two divisions.

Probably the most common example of a drafting error that leaves an "undistributed middle" has to do with dates. If you are drafting a provision that will establish one rule until a specified date (say May 1, 1991) and a different rule there-after, and you provide that the first rule is to be effective "before May 1, 1991" and the second "after May 1, 1991", you have left a 24-hour gap—there is no rule at all on May 1. You should have made the second rule effective either "on and after May 1, 1991" or "after April 30, 1991". Arriving at the correct result is easy, but unfortunately so is overlooking the problem.

As a slightly different example, if you want to divide all

employees into two classes and confer some benefit on one of them—say "any employee who is at least 65 years old or has at least 35 years of service"—but not on the other, you can't describe the second class by just substituting "less than" for each of the "at leasts" unless you remember to change the "or" to an "and" as well (see 21.10); the result would be to place a number of employees in both classes simultaneously (or in neither). An easier solution (after making sure you have described the members of the first class correctly) is simply to describe the members of the second class as "any other employee".

(Note that still another example involves the rounding of dollar figures for administrative convenience—see 27.5.)

Devices Especially Suited for Coping with Complexity

▶ **23.1 Preliminary comments**

The ideal way to handle complexity in a drafting project is of course to break the proposed bill down into as many short, simple subdivisions as may be necessary to cover all the different aspects of the problem, and then to arrange those subdivisions rationally so that their interrelationships will be clear. As has been indicated, that course may not always be available as a practical matter; but fortunately there are a number of special approaches and techniques that can help you get the job done in a way that is both clear and readable in spite of it all.

Some of these approaches and techniques are obvious and straightforward, some are not. Most of them have been touched upon earlier in this book, although their special utility in dealing with unusually complex drafting problems may not have been sufficiently stressed. It is the purpose of this chapter, by gathering them together and discussing them in one place, to emphasize both their existence and their special utility.

▶ **23.2 Definitions**

In many cases, a bill's complexity resides chiefly in the various concepts and terms that have to be used in expressing the drafter's thoughts rather than in the operating scheme itself. When everything that bears upon the meaning of those concepts and terms can be made clear in their definitions, the key operating provisions of the bill often turn out to be relatively simple. Definitions, like mathematical symbols, serve to make complex thoughts easier to express and to understand.

Consider, for example, the concept of "fully insured status" under the social security program. Since fully insured status is almost always a prerequisite of eligibility for benefits, the term "fully insured individual" appears about 200 times in title II of the Social Security Act; and the definition of that term (which is only moderately complicated on its face) takes up about half a page.

But that definition is based on "quarters of coverage" (which takes six pages to define) and also involves "periods of disability" (another six pages). The term "quarter of coverage" depends in turn upon the definitions of several other terms—"employment", "self-employment", "wages", "net earnings from self-employment", and "self-employment income"—which occupy 60 or 70 pages. With a few minor terms added in, the definitions needed for a clear understanding of fully insured status would come to nearly 100 pages of highly complicated language.

Keeping the complexities in the definitions, away from the key operating provisions, permits those provisions to make their point simply and in a straightforward manner. Thus:

> SEC. 202. (a) Every individual who . . . is a fully insured individual . . . shall be entitled to an old-age insurance benefit. . . .

The example given is admittedly an extreme one, but the principle would be the same if the relevant definitions were short and the term defined appeared only a few times in the bill.

The uses and forms of definitions generally (along with the widespread opposition from some sources to what the author is recommending here) have already been discussed in detail—see 11.7. Suffice it to say again that segregating as many of a bill's complexities as possible in its definition section is one of the first options you should explore when you find yourself wondering if you'll ever see daylight.

You should of course avoid the inclusion of substantive rules in the definitions if you can, as the critics urge, in cases where the reader would have no reason at all to look for them there. But most of the substantive rules that are found in definitions are in fact nothing but elaborations of the concepts and terms used in the operating provisions, and when this is the case you should not hesitate to include them as part of the definitions of those concepts and terms rather than in the operating provisions themselves. Matter in definitions is not hidden, after all—it can readily be found by anyone who needs to know the details, since the serious reader will always expect to encounter detailed definitions of key terms collected at an appropriate location in the bill. And if necessary a few judiciously placed cross-references can lead the way to any definitions that might otherwise be overlooked.

When you do it this way there is a good chance that your key operating provisions can be kept short, simple, and clear despite the complexities, and without concealing anything from the reader. The technique does not actually eliminate the complications, of course—it just puts them in a place where they can be studied one by one and keeps them from interfering with the expression of the message.

▶ **23.3   Incorporation by reference**

As indicated in 22.4, one of the main uses of cross-references is to incorporate the substance of one provision into another without having to repeat or paraphrase it. This device is of course particularly valuable when the material to be incorporated is long and complicated, but it simplifies the drafter's task even when it is not.

A good (though relatively trivial) example of what incorporation by reference can do to make a complicated concept short, easy to handle, and relatively readable is the last sentence of section 215(d)(5) of the Social Security Act, which reads (in its entirety) as follows:

> (5) This paragraph shall not apply in the case of any individual to whom subsection (a)(7) would not apply by reason of subparagraph (E) or the first sentence of subparagraph (D) thereof.

This is not exactly bedtime reading, but it separates the complications and produces a clear gain in readability. The subsection (a)(7) referred to comprises over 5 pages of convoluted technical language, and nearly all of it would have to be repeated in order to reach the desired result without cross-references. Why bother? Once is enough.

When the purpose is to achieve parallel results under two provisions—complete uniformity is very important when the same concept or situation repeats itself in a bill—incorporating the substance of one into the other by a simple cross-reference guarantees those results, while restating or trying to paraphrase the language in its entirety, in a totally new and different setting, risks creating unintended problems. And you can use the device even when the two provisions need not be exactly parallel or the two concepts or situations are not exactly the same, by adopting the borrowed language by cross-reference and then modifying it (at the place where the cross-reference appears) to the extent necessary to limit or expand its application at that place. It can still save time, minimize effort, and promote consistency.

Dickerson (page 96) distinguishes the case where substantive material is incorporated into a provision by reference to another provision of the same bill from the case where it is incorporated by reference to another law altogether. He simply urges reasonable caution in the former case, but expresses serious misgivings about the latter. His recommendation (in the latter case) is that you always make it clear that you are merely adopting the substance of the other law, and not in effect amending it to extend its coverage, by saying (for example) that an individual "has the same rights or duties" (under the bill) as those prescribed by the other law rather than by saying that the other law "applies" to that individual.

The advantages of incorporation by reference—uniformity, clarity, consistency, and the saving of space and time—do come at some risk, however. The chief danger is that the incorporated language may not exactly fit the case at hand. And this risk is increased because in all likelihood the very pressures that cause the drafter to use the device often preclude a thorough check to ensure that seemingly parallel situations or seemingly identical concepts are in fact so. You should not use the device unless you are absolutely certain that the incorporated material exactly fits your situation, even though screening the material for this purpose may take more time than you would like to give it.

In addition, incorporated language is less likely to be checked by the sponsor (or by anyone else for that matter), which increases the chances of mistake and even deception. More than one commentator has complained that the device of incorporation by reference is regularly used "in a cunning and devious manner" to obscure what is being done.

And you must always be aware that the incorporated material may not continue to fit your situation if there are future amendments to either of the two provisions involved. For example, if you are drafting a bill to establish a new program dealing with employees and you want the term "employee" to mean the same thing in that program as it means for social security purposes, you might include a provision like this:

( ) The term "employee" means an employee as defined by section 210(j) of the Social Security Act.

Such a provision will normally keep the coverage of your new program parallel with that of the social security program. But if the nature, scope, or coverage of either program is materially changed by a future law, the "fit" may disappear—the problem then falls into the lap of the drafter of that law, and you can only hope that that drafter will be able to recognize it.

Even if your sponsor believes (for political or tactical reasons, for example) that your program should parallel the social security program no matter what changes are made in the future, some court may very well come along and interpret your reference as a reference to section 210(j) only as it was in effect on the date your bill became law. To allow for this possibility you might add after "section 210(j) of the Social Security Act" the (usually unnecessary) phrase ", as that section may from time to time be amended".

But, if the sponsor believes that future amendments to section 210(j) might not be appropriate for your new program—there is no way of knowing what those amendments would be, of course—you might add instead ", as in effect on the date of enactment of this Act". This would require that those who are interested in the new program after its enactment keep a close eye on what happens to section 210(j) in the future.

These considerations are important because, although courts have tended to hold in the absence of words to the contrary that the incorporation of a specific provision picks up only current text while the incorporation of a broad body of law also includes future changes, the lines are often hard to draw; and in borderline cases it is safer to nail it down.

A further consideration for drafters who do not work at the Federal level is that a number of State constitutional provisions (expressly, by implication, or by judicial interpretation and with varying degrees of clarity) forbid or restrict incorporations by reference. The author has no idea why those provisions exist or how they work in practice, but a drafter in such a State is obviously stuck with them.

In summary, incorporations by reference when done correctly will promote accuracy and precision while easing the task of dealing with complex and interrelated concepts, but they must not be used carelessly. Since the cross-reference conceals the text of the substantive provision it invokes, it makes it harder for a reader (and for the drafter) to be certain that the desired result has actually been achieved, especially when revisions are made in the provision that contains it. Every cross-reference in a draft should be periodically checked and rechecked.

▶ **23.4   Tabulated lists**

Ordinary lists of things are as common and as useful in bills as they are in other kinds of written documents; but the list form has a special utility for the drafter who must deal with complicated concepts in legislative language and whose options are limited by the arrangement or structure of the bill he is working on.

When a bill contains a number of related elements—definitions, rules, powers, functions, limitations, restrictions, or other substantive concepts—that would otherwise have to be dealt with essay-style in separate subdivisions, their relationships to each other and their respective places in the overall scheme of the bill can often be clarified by presenting them as items on a single list instead.

In any event, whether the items involved are substantive concepts or simple descriptive nouns (or are serial amendments as described in 17.2) the listing process can be managed in any one of several ways.

When the items are few in number and each of them is short, they can be set forth as parts of a single unbroken sentence. Thus for example: "The prohibition contained in this section shall not apply to a minor, an alien, or a disabled individual.". (All three terms would of course have to be defined elsewhere.) This form does contain a list, but it is just a common everyday mode of expression and needs no special discussion.

When some of the items are longer and more complicated, however, or when it will be necessary to cross-refer to one or more of them at other points in the bill, the ideal approach would be to deal with each of them individually in a separate freestanding subsection or paragraph. But this is not always possible, especially when you are amending an existing law; space for the necessary subsections or paragraphs may be unavailable because of that law's arrangement, or other structural considerations may prevent it.

The most practical all-purpose approach is to tabulate the list, with appropriate lead-in language (ending with either a dash or a colon) and a separate indented paragraph for each item.

If the lead-in language ends with a dash (the "dashed" form), the whole thing is technically a single sentence and the example given above would appear as follows:

( ) The prohibition contained in this section shall not apply to—

    (1) a minor,

    (2) an alien, or

    (3) a disabled individual.

This has several advantages. It can accommodate items that are relatively long and complicated (although its items should end with semicolons rather than commas if that is the case). It can fit most anywhere, since it comprises a single sentence and can even be used as only a part of a larger sentence (in which case it would not begin with a capitalized word or end with a period, of course). And it gives each item its own designation (thus facilitating cross-references). It still requires that the terms be defined elsewhere, however.

If the lead-in language ends with a colon (the "colon" form), the provision can be viewed as consisting of several self-sufficient items or compound nouns listed separately and would look slightly different:

( ) The prohibition contained in this section shall not apply to any of the following:

    (1) A minor.

    (2) An alien.

    (3) A disabled individual.

The colon form is even better than the dashed form at handling lists including long and complicated items, because it allows any of the numbered items to be broken down into two or more sentences (as would be desirable, for example, if you wanted to include the relevant definitions within those items themselves). And it too gives each item its own designation. But it is less flexible than the dashed form, since its use of capitalized initial words and final periods in the indented paragraphs usually prevents its insertion into the middle of an existing provision.

In general, the dashed form should be used when the items on the list are relatively short (or when structural considerations make it necessary) while the colon form is better when the items are more substantial. In both forms proper punctuation is essential; the two examples given above indicate how the punctuation should be handled, and 21.6 sets forth the detailed specifications for doing it right.

In either form the items on the list should always be recognizable for the kind of things they are—that is, it should always be possible to tell (without reference to the lead-in language) whether the items represent verb-type calls for action, noun-type descriptions of things or functions, amendments to existing law, or something else. The dash or colon dividing the lead-in language from the items on the list should always be placed so as to achieve this result, either by making the items complete enough to be recognizable for what they are or by putting the "pause" where it belongs in the sense of the sentence.

In the colon form this result is almost automatic (since each item on the list is a self-contained unit); but in the dashed form you have a choice, and in every case but one you can use your own judgment about where the dash should go. The one exception involves the case of serial amendments (see 17.2) or any other case in which each item is introduced by a preposition ("by", "for", "to", "in", or "with"). In such a case the dash should be placed so that the preposition is repeated at the beginning of each item rather than being stated only once (just before the dash); this puts the pause where it will do the most to make the nature of the items clear even when they are quoted out of context.

Note that subsequently adding a new item to the end of a list will require three separate amendments if the list is in the dashed form (one to strike the "and" (or "or") at the end of the next-to-last existing item, one to strike the existing final period and insert "; and" (or "; or"), and one to actually add the new item), but can be done with a single stroke if the list is in the colon form. (Subsequently inserting a new item somewhere in the middle of the list is just as easy in the dashed form as in the colon form, since in either case the succeeding items have to be redesignated.)

Note also that the lead-in language must apply to all of the items on the list; and when using the dashed form each item must be a logical and grammatical continuation of the lead-in language so that the two can be read together, without regard to the rest of the provision, as a complete grammatical sentence or phrase.

Failure to observe this rule constitutes what *Dickerson* calls "the sin of bastard enumeration". The phrase "the several States, possessions, and the District of Columbia", for example, commits this sin, as becomes obvious when it is put in tabular form:

( ) [This section shall apply to] the several—

    (1) States,

    (2) possessions, and

    (3) the District of Columbia.

Paragraph (3) is unresponsive to the lead-in language, both because the word "several" does not belong with "the District of Columbia" and because of the two "the's". The sin is easily removed, however, by transferring "the several" to paragraphs (1) and (2) (possibly combining the two into a single paragraph). Actually the best solution in the untabulated version—in real life you would seldom bother to tabulate such a short sentence—is simply to eliminate the "several" (it is unnecessary anyway) and the second "the", or to substitute "and" for the first comma so that the phrase reads "the several States and possessions, and the District of Columbia".

And finally, it is not enough that each item on the tabulated list is a logical and grammatical continuation of the lead-in language—it should also be the same kind of continuation. Consider the following (which is a not uncommon example of what happens in hastily drafted provisions):

( ) In order to qualify for assistance under this Act, a State must demonstrate that it has—

    (1) met the eligibility requirements of section 2, and

    (2) a State plan approved under section 3.

Paragraphs (1) and (2) are both logical and grammatical continuations of the lead-in language, so there is no bastard enumeration in the strict Dickersonian sense. But the construction is nonetheless undesirable and can result in misinterpretations as a form of utraquistic subterfuge (see 7.4), since the key word "has" must be given two different meanings to make it work; for purposes of paragraph (1) it is a part of the past-tense verb "has met", while for purposes of paragraph (2) it stands alone as a present-tense verb equivalent to "possesses". A little fairly obvious shifting about of the words is all that it takes to repair the damage, of course—the only prerequisite is that you recognize the problem.

▶ **23.5   Tabulated sentences**

One of the most valuable tools for handling a complex concept or relationship within a confined space—that is, within a single subsection or paragraph (or even as a single sentence within a subsection or paragraph)—is the tabulated sentence, which is in fact nothing but an expanded version of the tabulated list described in 23.4. It includes one or more tabulated lists, and often sublists, just like its relative, but there is one important difference—it treats each of them as just one of its terms or grammatical elements, and does not stop when the listing process is completed.

The simple example given in 23.4 could be written as a tabulated sentence instead of as an ordinary sentence that just happens to contain a tabulated list. It would look like this:

( ) In the case of—

   (1) a minor,

   (2) an alien, or

   (3) a disabled individual,

the prohibition contained in this section shall not apply.

In this form it is indeed a tabulated sentence, because the sentence goes on after the list is finished. But it embodies such a simple policy that most drafters would not normally bother to tabulate either the list or the sentence, and real life is seldom that straightforward. Suppose that the sponsor (after listening to other people express their fears of possible abuse and evasion) decides to limit the provision to the most clearly deserving cases by imposing specific requirements that individuals in each of the three categories must meet in order to be covered, and to limit the total benefits which any such individual may receive as a result of the lifting of the prohibition.

Suppose also that the sponsor (after listening to other people express their astonishment at the omission of various alleg-edly deserving groups—this scenario is fairly typical of the way laws become complicated) decides to include military and diplomatic personnel as well, but only in times of crisis.

And suppose finally that, for logical or tactical reasons, the drafter cannot afford the luxury of using up a whole section or subsection with a series of individual subdivisions to present the message, but must write the provision as a single sentence in the middle of a single existing paragraph.

Now the tabulated sentence approach becomes the drafter's salvation. The provision, which has by now become a real monstrosity, could be written in any one of a number of ways, but it might look something like this (with the terms deliber-ately generalized—in actuality the provision would have to be longer and more technically precise):

The prohibition contained in this paragraph shall not apply in the case of—

(A) a minor who—

(i) is regularly attending school, or

(ii) is under age 12 and receiving AFDC benefits,

(B) an alien who—

(i) is legally within the United States, and

(ii) has no criminal record, or

(C) a disabled individual who—

(i) is eligible for medicare benefits,

(ii) has been under the same disability for at least 5 years, and

(iii) is participating in an approved rehabilita-tion program,

or, in time of war or national emergency, in the case of—

(D) a member of the armed services on active duty, or

(E) a member of the diplomatic corps serving overseas,

if such minor, alien, disabled individual, or member files a formal request for an exemption from the prohibition; ex-cept that no individual shall be entitled to a benefit by reason of this sentence for any month after he has received such benefits for a period of 12 months (or after the termi-nation of the war or national emergency involved, in the case of an individual described in subparagraph (D) or (E)).

Note that the indentation tells you exactly what the undesignated portions (beginning "or" and "if") apply to, and that the breakdown of the sentence into designated pieces (however intimidating it may otherwise look) actually helps you to follow the thread.

The drafter could theoretically have written the provision in the required single sentence without tabulation, but that would have eliminated any hope of achieving readability, clarity, or precision. Turning it into a tabulated sentence did not make it easy to read, but it did make it possible to read, and it allowed the drafter to achieve maximum clarity and precision. Careful attention to proper punctuation, meticulous distinction between "ands" and "ors", and progressively increasing indentations to indicate the subordination of ideas is what made it possible.

The example given is of course a pure invention, and a ridiculous one at that, but if you ran across it in an actual existing law (and are reasonably familiar with such things) you would not consider it unique or atypical in form.

▶ **23.6   Parenthetical expressions**

Grammatical purists and most expository writers seem to believe that parenthetical expressions in a sentence are only additive—that their sole function is explanatory—and that the contents of any parenthetical expression must be such that omitting it altogether would not detract from what the sentence says.

When confronted with the necessity of writing a complicated sentence in a bill, forget this. For the drafter, parenthetical expressions are the best available device for combining complicated ideas within a single sentence in a way that achieves clarity. Use them in an additive way when appropriate, of course, but don't hesitate to fill them with substance when the occasion arises.

Most parenthetical expressions could just as well be set off by commas instead, of course, and commas are generally better when the sentence involved is short and simple. A sentence that reads "The Secretary may terminate the contract, without giving any advance notice, if [a specified event] occurs" would satisfy anyone; and most drafters would not even think of converting the language between the commas into a parenthetical expression.

But parentheses are generally more reliable than commas in

setting off a phrase when there is possible uncertainty as to how the ideas that follow the phrase are linked to those that precede it. And a long sentence tends to be already full of phrases set off by commas, so that as new ones are added it is likely to become harder and harder for the reader to sort out the pieces. If the language within the quotes in the preceding paragraph had appeared in the middle of such a sentence (instead of constituting the entire sentence), any good drafter would instinctively consider using the parenthetical approach rather than the commas.

Substantive parenthetical matter, like parenthetical matter that is purely additive or explanatory, can be skipped over by the reader without making nonsense of the sentence. There is a big difference, however. If purely explanatory parenthetical matter is omitted the sentence still says what it set out to say, whereas the omission of substantive parenthetical matter detracts from the sentence by removing part of its message.

But it is this very fact—that substantive parenthetical expressions can be skipped over by a reader—that makes them so useful to the drafter. The first time through, an overwhelmed reader can ignore the parenthetical expressions and still get a good general picture of what the message is, and then mentally replace those expressions and evaluate them one by one, thereby getting the whole convoluted picture without having to wade through the entire thicket at the outset.

The point is quite straightforward, and it should not be necessary to belabor it. When a sentence is becoming long and complex, and you can't find a good way to solve the problem by breaking it down into several separate sentences, put some of the substantive ideas—preferably the less important ones—in parenthetical form. At minimal cost to readability, this approach will make it possible for you to pack a sentence with complex concepts and relationships without sacrificing clarity.

▶ **23.7   Tables, formulas, and other graphic aids**

Columnar tables.   Anyone who has ever done any bookkeeping knows that many complex relationships can be described better in columnar tables than in any other way. This is especially true of relationships between amounts that vary with time or with other factors. A good table can say with complete precision in half a page what it would take 10 pages of convoluted language to say in narrative form.

Adjusted Net Worth of a Business or Farm	
If the net worth of a business or farm is—	Then the adjusted net worth is—
Less than $1	$0
$1–$60,000....................................	40 percent of NW
$60,001–$180,000...........................	$24,000 plus 50 percent of NW over $60,000
$180,001–$300,000.........................	$84,000 plus 60 percent of NW over $180,000
$300,001 or more............................	$156,000 plus 100 percent of NW over $300,000

▶ **Figure 23.7 Table from the Higher Education Act of 1965**

Columnar tables are widely used in all legislation—Federal, State, and local. There is no standard form, since each table has to be custom designed to fit the particular situation being addressed, but they are almost always easy to construct and they are not intimidating to any reasonably well-informed reader.

The key to a good table lies in the headings of its columns, which should clearly identify each of the concepts whose interrelationships are the subject of the table. In many tables, the headings, when read from left to right across the top of the table, comprise a complete sentence that could have been placed verbatim before the table instead of in it.

The most familiar use of tables in the Federal law is in the basic income tax provisions, where hundreds of tax rates are shown by reference to the taxpayer's income level and number of family members. Another example is the pre-1978 social security benefit table, a seven-page table in which the nine column headings comprise a technical 75-word sentence. But most table heads are considerably shorter and simpler, and much more likely to be useful models for the average drafter. The table from the Higher Education Act of 1965 in Figure 23.7 is an example.

A columnar table guarantees clarity and precision, and (once the right structure and format have been worked out) it eases your task by providing a ready-made resting place for each of the quantities you will have to specify and for any modifications or adjustments you may subsequently have to make in those quantities.

In addition, it eliminates and replaces a great deal of legislative language that might otherwise be very tricky to handle, and makes the bill shorter and simpler. It does not eliminate or replace all of that language, of course—there will still have to be appropriate preliminary language to put the table in context, and the terms used in the headings may have to be defined elsewhere—but the main message is generally shorter, simpler, and more precise than it would be if it were expressed entirely in words. Every drafter should use columnar tables whenever the opportunity arises.

Formulas. Anyone who has made it through one or two years of high school knows that numerical relationships are most readily described through the use of mathematical formulas, which can be either verbal or algebraic. Verbal formulas are found everywhere in the law—whenever the amount of some rate, benefit, payment, or other numerical quantity has to be calculated—while algebraic formulas are much less common.

A verbal formula is just a specialized form of everyday writing. A statement that "an individual's weekly unemployment compensation benefit shall be equal to one-half of the weekly wage he was earning when last regularly employed" constitutes a formula, of course, although you might not think of it as such. The current procedure for computing social security benefits (which replaced the table discussed above in 1978), on the other hand, is recognizable as a formula by any test:

(A) The primary insurance amount of an individual shall (except as otherwise provided in this section) be equal to the sum of—

(i) 90 percent of the individual's average indexed monthly earnings (determined under subsection (b)) to the extent that such earnings do not exceed the amount established for purposes of this clause by subparagraph (B) [the first "bend point"],

(ii) 32 percent of the individual's average indexed monthly earnings to the extent that such earnings exceed the amount established for purposes of clause (i) but do not exceed the amount established for purposes of this clause by subparagraph (B) [the second "bend point"], and

(iii) 15 percent of the individual's average indexed monthly earnings to the extent that such earnings exceed the amount established for purposes of clause (ii), rounded, if not a multiple of $0.10, to the next lower multiple of $0.10, and thereafter increased as provided in subsection (i) [the annual cost-of-living adjustment].

You may regard this provision (which is a classic example of a properly used tabulated sentence) as unforgivably complicated, but it is actually about as simple as it could be made, given the policy; the real complications are elsewhere. Defining the crucial terms (average indexed monthly earnings, bend points, and cost-of-living adjustments) requires many pages of language that could cause nightmares.

Almost any verbal formula could also be stated algebraically, but the latter has two disadvantages: It entails an extra step—defining the algebraic symbols themselves—and it is intimidating to people who fear mathematics. However, in the right situation it can be clearer and more precise than the verbal form, and it makes the formula far easier to remember and restate (which is a real plus for the drafter while working on it). The formula "$E = mc^2$" is bandied about (and reasonably well understood) in high school science courses addressing the nature of the universe, but far fewer people would develop an interest in such things if Einstein's theories or the Lorentz transformation had to be discussed in verbal terms exclusively.

Several good examples of the algebraic approach can be found in the Railroad Unemployment Insurance Act, which uses the formulas

$$B = 600 \left(1 + \frac{A - 37,800}{56,700} \right) \text{ and } R = \left(\frac{A + 2C}{3} \right)$$

in the computation of an individual's "monthly compensation base" and the applicable "contribution rate", respectively. (In each case the meaning of the algebraic symbols is defined in the clause immediately following the formula.)

You shouldn't go out of your way to present your formulas in algebraic terms, or spend a lot of time looking for opportunities to do so; but if you are working on a policy that lends itself to that approach and the situation permits it you should at least consider the possibility.

One useful approach—a kind of compromise between the purely verbal formulas and the mathematical ones—is the so-called "cookbook" formula, which takes the reader step-by-step through the various determinations and calculations that have to be made, in more or less conversational language. For example:

( ) The Secretary shall determine the [quantity sought] as follows:

(1) He shall first determine A and B.

(2) He shall then determine the percentage of B that is equal to A.

(3) He shall then multiply C by that percentage.

* * * * * * * *

(8) He shall then subtract the larger of the two figures determined under paragraphs (6) and (7) from the figure determined under paragraph (3).

(9) The [quantity sought] is one-half of the amount determined under paragraph (8).

Note that *Hirsch's* experimental rewrite in the chapter dealing with readability (see 9.5), though not in tabulated form, is an example of the "cookbook formula" approach.

Other graphic aids. Devices such as graphs, diagrams, and odd charts are very common in supporting documents such as committee reports, but are relatively rare in legislative measures. A number of them, however, have actually been enacted into law (including at least one musical score).

A few jurisdictions actually forbid such things by rule or law; but in most cases the reluctance to use them results from considerations of precedent, or simply from the fact that they look strange to people who are not used to seeing such things in legislation and who want everything written in plain English.

Nevertheless, there are situations in which the use of unusual graphic devices might be the best possible way to achieve clarity and precision while reducing complexity; and you should feel free to give them a chance.

▶ **23.8   Summing it up**

It is important to understand that most of the approaches and devices described in this chapter—though their best and highest use may be in dealing with complexity—can always be used when appropriate. Even in a relatively short and simple bill, the crucial terms should be defined, and without cluttering up the main message. Cross-references are really the only way to clearly indicate the interrelationship of provisions. Any series of related ideas, things, or other items (for maximum clarity) should logically be set forth in a list of some kind. And the virtues of columnar tables are obvious in any bill dealing with variable numerical quantities.

The others—sentence tabulation and the intensive use of substantive parenthetical expressions—are usually reserved for situations involving both a high degree of complexity and a shortage of maneuvering room. And in those situations their virtues easily outweigh the sensibilities of the purists who are offended by them. But if you are an occasional drafter without much exposure to such things you ought not attempt tabulated sentences gratuitously—they can be tricky to write, and can create more problems than they solve if done incorrectly or carelessly. Use them when they will make your work significantly easier, of course, but always look for a good model to follow and make sure you understand how its construction can be adapted to serve your purposes.

References to
Statutory Provisions

▶ **24.1   Preliminary comments**

Any reference or citation to a provision of law has two main purposes—to identify that provision briefly and in an unambiguous manner, and to provide a finding aid for readers. The methods suggested in this chapter are consistent with those purposes; they are generally followed in the case of Federal laws, and should serve as useful guides (making allowances for differences in statutory structure and nomenclature) in the case of State and local laws as well.

In most cases, the reference mentions only the provision's alphanumeric designation ("section 123", "paragraph (7) of subsection (c)", or "part B of title III", for example), although it will often include a parenthetical citation to the corresponding provision of the United States Code as an aid to readers if it is not a reference to a positive-law title of the Code itself (see 24.4).

Most of the examples given in this chapter (and chapter 25) are taken from *HOLC* (pages 43-51).

▶ **24.2   References to positive-law provisions of the United States Code**

If the provision to which you wish to refer has been enacted into positive law as part of the United States Code, it should be cited by its Code designation, directly and without parentheses or abbreviations—for example, "section 1234 of title 34 of the United States Code".

In referring to some positive-law titles of the Code, however, the proper form is "section 1234 of title 34, United States Code" (substituting a comma for "of the"). And a few titles use still a slightly different form. (It is not necessary that you memorize the variant forms; a note at the beginning of each positive-law title will tell you which form should be used in citing it.)

When the provision making the reference is itself within a positive-law title of the Code, however, the words "United States Code" are unnecessary, and should be omitted, so that in the example given in the first paragraph the reference would read simply "section 1234 of title 34" (or "section 1234 of this title" if the two provisions are both in title 34).

Because you cannot cite a provision by its U.S. Code designation (except for purely informative purposes—see 24.6) unless it is in a positive-law title of the Code, you must know which titles of the Code are positive law and which are not (29.4 and 29.5 contain the information you will need to sort them out, including a complete list of the titles in each category). In addition, each title that has been enacted into positive law so states on its first page.

▶ **24.3   References to laws with short titles**

If the provision to which you wish to refer has not been enacted into positive law as a part of the United States Code, always cite the statute in which it is contained by its short title if it has one. Showing its Code citation parenthetically, for purely informative purposes, is not actually necessary but is usually a good idea; for example, "section 345 of the ABC Act (34 U.S.C. 1234)".

▶ **24.4   References to laws without short titles**

If the provision to which you wish to refer is contained in a law that does not have a short title (and is not within a positive-law title of the United States Code), there are several ways it can be cited:

By public law number.   If the law was enacted after 1956 (when the present system of public law designation went into effect), it should usually be cited by its public law number—for example, "section 1234 of Public Law 98-356". (The latter number simply means that the law was the 356th public law enacted in the 98th Congress.)

Pre-1957 laws also had numbers, of course, but their numbers did not reflect the particular Congresses in which they were enacted, so they are not usually cited by their public law numbers. If you do choose to use that method of citation, you must remember to specify the Congress—thus "section 1234 of Public Law 567 of the 79th Congress".

By long title.   If the long title of the law is not too long, particularly when that title's content would be helpful to the reader, you can refer to it as "the Act entitled 'An Act [to . . .]', approved [May 6, 1974].".

By enactment date.   If the law was enacted before 1957, it can be referred to simply by the date of its enactment, with a citation to the Statutes at Large—for example, "the Act of [January 5, 1945] (33 Stat. 3434)". Note that the parenthetical citation tells the reader where to find the law being referred to, but it gives only the first page of that law; if the reference is to a provision of the law that appears several pages later, it is usually desirable to expand the citation to indicate also the actual page on which the provision appears—thus "(33 Stat. 3434, 3451)". And whenever you cite the older Statutes at Large you should watch out for the relatively rare cases in which there are two Acts beginning on the same page. In such a case the parenthetical citation should be enlarged to include the chapter as well as the page—thus "(33 Stat. 3434; ch. 883)".

Citations to a law by its public law number or date of enactment are excellent candidates for "relating to" clauses aimed at aiding the reader, since the nature of the provision being cited will not be clear from the citation alone—for example, "section 123 of Public Law 91-456 (relating to admission fees in national parks)". And in the case of a law without a short title but with a generally known popular name, the popular name may be included in the parenthetical reference for the same purpose—for example, "section 343 of Public Law 91-353 (commonly known as the Chappell-Bell Act)".

Note that the use of parenthetical U.S. Code citations for

informative purposes (as a finding aid) is particularly important when referring to laws in any of the ways described here—each of the examples given should have included such a citation (which was omitted simply to avoid obscuring the points being made).

▶ **24.5**   **"As amended"**

The name of an Act invariably remains the same throughout its life, and it speaks as of the time it is being read or applied, no matter how many times it has been amended since its original enactment. It is therefore never necessary (and can be misleading) to attach the phrase ", as amended" when referring to an existing law; and the practice should be avoided. This rule always applies when the law involved is the United States Code or has a short title, and normally applies in any other case as well.

There are a few situations, however, in which a reference to a law by its long title or date of enactment may mislead the reader (because of some quirk in its amendatory history) unless you make it abundantly clear that it is the up-to-date amended version you are talking about. If you believe that you are in such a situation, go ahead and attach the phrase, but do it with regret; and if possible vary the phrase—say "as amended by section 15 of the ABC Act", for example, or "as most recently amended" so the reader will realize it is a special case. (The other side of the coin is, of course, that if for some reason you really do need to address the old unamended version of the law you must always explicitly say so.)

And there is one situation—superficially similar but actually quite different—in which a mention of a previous amendment is always proper. When you must refer to a provision that was amended so recently that the changes made have not had time to be reflected in the Code or in other published documents, it is appropriate to indicate that fact—not for the sake of accuracy but as a warning to readers who may not yet be aware of the changed version. Thus if you want to refer in a bill to section 10 of the ABC Act, which was extensively changed last month by section 234 of the XYZ Act, your citation might properly read "section 10 of the ABC Act (as [recently] amended by section 234 of the XYZ Act)".

▶ **24.6** **Code citations for purely informative purposes**

Most people who read a provision that you have drafted will not have ready access to the slip laws or the Statutes at Large, or to compilations of the laws referred to in that provision. Consequently, when referring to a provision which is not within a positive-law title of the United States Code and which is contained in a law that has no short title, you should always include a parenthetical Code citation after the basic reference—for example, "section 123 of Public Law 91-456 (42 U.S.C. 2983)", or "section 123 of the Act of January 5, 1945 (33 Stat. 3435; 42 U.S.C. 2983)". You owe this to your readers. (Note that in parenthetical Code citations of this kind "United States Code" is always abbreviated.)

The device is frequently (and properly) used even in cases where the law to which you are referring does have a short title, although it is less important in those cases since laws with short titles are easier for the reader to find (both in their literal form and in the Code).

Citations to appendices in titles of the United States Code should take the form "(50 U.S.C. App. 660)"; and citations to nonstatutory provisions that are included in the Code as notes (such as treaties and executive orders) should take the form "(5 U.S.C. 3301 note)".

Public laws beginning with the 94th Congress generally give the U.S. Code citations for all of their substantive provisions, and you can use those citations as soon as the laws involved are enacted. But if the law to which you want to refer was enacted too recently to be reflected in the volumes of the Code that are generally available, it is advisable to use the public law citation as well—thus "the XYZ Act of 1990 (Public Law 101-234; 42 U.S.C. 2983)".

Provisions that are temporary, obsolete, or executed do not appear in the Code at all, so you will have to cite them in the manner described in 24.3 or 24.4 without any accompanying Code citation.

▶ **24.7** **References within an Act or section**

When one section of an Act refers to another section of that Act, or one subdivision of a section refers to another subdivision of that section, it is unnecessary to specify the location of the section or subdivision being referred to. You do not have to say "section 123 of this Act" or "paragraph (6) of this subsection"—just "section 123" or "paragraph (6)" is enough. The reader will assume that both the subdivision containing the reference and the subdivision referred to have the same parent.

An exception may be appropriate, however, when there are also references to other Acts or subdivisions in the vicinity. If you think the shorter approach recommended in the preceding paragraph might be confusing to the reader because of the neighboring references, you should feel free to include the phrase "of this Act", "of this section", or "of this subsection" in the interest of clarity.

▶ **24.8   References to components of a section**

References based on alphanumeric designations. As indicated in 20.3, a section (to the extent that subdivision is necessary) is broken down into—

(1) subsections (starting with (a)),

(2) paragraphs (starting with (1)),

(3) subparagraphs (starting with (A)),

(4) clauses (starting with (i)), and

(5) subclauses (starting with (I)),

all of them paragraphed and the lesser ones often indented. (Remember that a provision is "paragraphed" when its first line is indented more than the remaining lines, whether or not the provision as a whole is indented.)

Paragraphed provisions are always referred to on the basis of their class designation—thus paragraphed provisions designated with lower case letters ((a), (b), (c)) should always be referred to as subsections, those designated with arabic numerals ((1), (2), (3)) as paragraphs, and so forth. However, if the provision is a designated part of a continuous run-in sentence and is not paragraphed, it is always referred to as a clause or subclause, whatever its letter- or number-designation.

Note that a few older laws have systems of designation that differ from the system just described—the Federal Food, Drug, and Cosmetic Act, for example, consistently refers to units beginning "(a)", "(b)", or "(c)" as paragraphs—and you should of course apply the Roman rule and follow those systems when amending or referring to those laws.

Composite references. For the sake of both clarity and brevity, a composite reference such as "section 503(b)(2)(A) of the XYZ Act" is preferred to a "strung-out" reference such as "subparagraph (A) of paragraph (2) of subsection (b) of section 503 of the XYZ Act", although the two are of course identical in effect—see 20.3.

There are, however, a few cases in which this rule should be varied:

(1) *In amendments.* When amending just one piece of what would otherwise call for a composite reference, that piece should be separated out and referred to specifically in order to make clear exactly what is being amended. Thus an amendment to section 503(b)(2)(A) should not use the composite reference but should be stated as an amendment to subparagraph (A) of section 503(b)(2). Experienced drafters always apply this rule when the amendment is being made by restatement (see 15.3), and most of them, including the author, apply it in the case of cut-and-bite amendments as well.

(2) *For later reference.* When it will be necessary at a later point in the bill (or in some other law) to refer specifically to just one piece of what would otherwise call for a composite reference, that piece should be separated out. For example, saying "subparagraph (A)(i) of section 503(b)(2)" instead of "section 503(b)(2)(A)(i)" will make it possible to say simply "such subparagraph" in the later reference. (See 27.7.)

(3) *Joint references.* When referring simultaneously to two or more pieces of what would otherwise call for a composite reference, those pieces should be separately stated. A reference to "clauses (i) and (ii) of section 503(b)(2)(A)" is easier to understand (and clearer) than a reference to "section 503(b)(2)(A)(i) and (ii)".

Note that a composite reference always uses the generic name of the senior unit involved. Thus if you want to refer to paragraph (1) of subsection (a) of section 5 and you choose (as you normally would) to do so by a composite reference, you should say "section 5(a)(1)" rather than "paragraph [or subsection] 5(a)(1)" even though it is the paragraph you are interested in.

▶ **24.9**   **References to senior components**

The senior components of a bill, like the individual sections and inferior subdivisions, should be referred to by their class designations—for example, "title II" or "part C".

The composite approach, however, should be reserved for references to sections and their subdivisions; it should not be used in referring to the senior components of a bill. Thus a reference to subtitle C of title III of a bill or law should read "subtitle C of title III"—not "title III-C". In a few areas there is a growing tendency to use composite references for senior components (part A of title IV of the Social Security Act—the AFDC program—has been referred to as "title IV-A" so often that the latter might be regarded today as an acceptable form); but it is still a bad practice and should be avoided.

And remember that the reader normally wants to know the particular sections to which the reference applies. If the senior component being referred to is a title of the bill or of a law the section numbers involved can be easily identified (since the section numbers in a title always begin with the same number as the title—see chapter 20), but if it is a subtitle, chapter, or part it cannot. In the latter case it may be helpful to include a parenthetical indication of the particular section numbers involved—for example, "part C of title I (sections 161 through 175)".

▶ 24.10 Consolidated reference convention

In a lengthy bill or title consisting primarily of amendments to a single law, the use of a consolidated reference convention of the type described in chapter 16 is often a desirable alternative to endless repetitions of the law's full citation. By indicating in an early section that all amendments are to that law unless otherwise specified, you can avoid the necessity of naming it every time you want to refer to one of its provisions; you can just say "Section 123(b) is amended . . .", for example, instead of "Section 123(b) of the ABC Act is amended. . .". The text of such a provision is set forth in 16.1.

▶ 24.11 Abbreviated references; use of "such"

Once a reference has been made in any section to another provision of your bill (or to a provision of some existing law), that provision should be referred to later in the same section simply as "such [provision]" rather than by repeating the full citation, unless a reference in that form would be unclear because of the distance between it and the original reference or because of the intervention of references to other provisions. (See 16.1.)

Thus, for example, the first time you refer in a section of your bill to section 123(a) of the ABC Act, you should give it its full name—"section 123(a) of the ABC Act"—but whenever you refer to that section or that Act later in the same section of your bill (unless it would be unclear for one of the reasons given in the preceding paragraph) you can just say "such section" or "such Act".

This practice can do wonders for the smoothness and readability of your prose in any bill where numerous references to other provisions are necessary. And if you are one of those drafters who—unlike the author—is opposed in principle to the use of "such" as a demonstrative adjective, you can in most cases use "that" or "the" instead (see 22.3).

References to
Nonstatutory Provisions

▶ 25.1   Executive orders

When making reference to a specific Executive order that appears as a notation (along with the provision of law involved) in the United States Code, include a parenthetical citation to the Code along with the order number. For example, "Executive Order 987 (5 U.S.C. 3301 note, relating to civil service rules)".

If the order does not appear as a notation in the Code, cite directly to the Federal Register instead (all Executive orders are printed in the Federal Register on the day they are issued)—thus "Executive Order 987 (19 Fed. Reg. 7521, relating to civil service rules)". And if by reason of amendment the order as currently in effect derives from more than one entry in the Federal Register, you should cite each of them: "Executive Order 987 (19 Fed. Reg. 7521 and 20 Fed. Reg. 648, relating to civil service rules)".

▶ 25.2   Regulations

In most cases, Federal regulations should simply be cited by their section and title number in the Code of Federal Regulations (CFR). For example, "section 73.658(j)(i) of title 47, Code of Federal Regulations (commonly known as the 'Network Syndication Rule')".

Occasionally a regulation carries with it an identifying name that has greater currency than its CFR section number. In such a case it is preferable to refer to it by that name, with only a parenthetical citation to the Code of Federal Regulations. For example, "Federal motor vehicle safety standard numbered 208 (49 CFR 571.208, relating to occupant crash protection)".

▶ 25.3 Treaties and other international agreements

A treaty or other international agreement should be referred to by its full name (including the names of the countries involved in the case of a bilateral or multilateral agreement), together with—

> (1) a reference either to the location and time of its signing or to the time at which it became applicable to the United States (whichever is more appropriate for the agreement and context), and

> (2) a finding aid consisting of either a citation to the "United States Treaties and Other International Agreements" (UST), which is comparable to a Statutes-at-Large citation, or a citation to the "Treaties and Other International Acts Series" (TIAS), which is comparable to a public law citation.

Examples of proper references to international agreements are "the Convention on the Territorial Sea and the Contiguous Zone, signed at Geneva on April 29, 1958 (TIAS 5639)" and "the Seabed Arms Control Treaty (entered into force with respect to the United States on May 18, 1972; 23 UST 701)".

A few important treaties that directly involve Federal statutes are printed in the United States Code. In such cases, it is helpful to include a Code citation—for example, "the Universal Copyright Convention (as revised at Paris on July 24, 1971; 25 UST 1341; 17 U.S.C. 104 note)".

▶ 25.4 Legislative rules

The rules of legislative bodies always have their own special systems of organization—their provisions are usually not broken down into sections, subsections, paragraphs, and so forth in the same way that statutes are. The Rules of the House of Representatives, for example, are broken down progressively into—

> (1) Rules (starting with Rule I (designation not in parentheses)),

> (2) clauses (starting with clause 1 (also without parentheses)),

(3) paragraphs (starting with (a)),

(4) subparagraphs (starting with (1)), and

(5) subdivisions (starting with (A)).

When amending or referring to provisions of these Rules, you should of course reflect this breakdown and system of designation.

▶ **25.5   Other public documents**

It will occasionally be necessary for you to refer to measures and documents from jurisdictions other than the one you are working in. A drafter in the Federal context, for example, may sometimes have to refer to a State statute or constitution or a local ordinance, or to a State or local rule, regulation, or other executive action, or to an interstate compact, or even to a private measure or document that is legislative in nature (such as a corporate charter or the records of a public-service organization).

Needless to say, there is no one rule that covers these things, since each jurisdiction and entity will have its own system for designating and referring to the items involved. The simple answer is to follow the Roman rule, of course, if you can find out what it is; but the necessary information about just how the Romans would do it in a particular case may not be available to you as a practical matter. In the absence of that information, all you can do is be as careful and descriptive as possible in making your reference, so that (whether or not it is in the right form) it will lead the reader and the courts to the intended destination.

Dealing with
Effective Dates

▶ **26.1   When an explicit effective-date provision is unnecessary; the "default" rule**

At the Federal level and in most States, every law takes effect on the day it is enacted—by default, so to speak—unless some other effective date is specifically provided for. (In general, a bill is "enacted" when the President signs it or fails to act on it within 10 days, or when Congress overrides his veto.) A few States have constitutional or statutory provisions making all laws effective (unless otherwise provided) only at the close of a specified period after their enactment or after the close of the legislative session in which they are enacted; the "default" effective date is different but the principle is the same.

As a consequence, it is not usually necessary to include an explicit effective-date provision in a bill that is simply intended to go into effect immediately upon its enactment. Except when an event-related approach is required (see 26.4) or other special factors are present, an effective-date provision should be used only to contravene the "default" rule stated in the preceding paragraph.

Under the old common law rule that "the law knoweth not parts of a day", making a bill effective "on the date of its enactment" is exactly the same thing as letting it become effective by default—in either case the bill will apply all day long on the day the President signs it. There is one exception, though; in a criminal bill (one creating a new crime or changing a criminal penalty) the old common law rule is overridden by the constitutional prohibition against *ex post facto* laws, and the bill may not become effective until the split second of its enactment (only after 2:17 p.m. eastern standard time, for example, if that is when the signing occurs) whichever approach is taken.

It does happen from time to time, of course, that a sponsor insists on including a totally unnecessary provision declaring that the bill is to take effect on the date of its enactment, probably just because other bills have it. If not having an explicit effective-date provision seems to worry the sponsor, go ahead and put one in; it causes no real harm, and you should save your energy for more important matters.

▶ 26.2   **Delayed effective dates**

One obvious example of a bill that *does* need an explicit effective-date provision is a bill whose sponsor wants it to become effective only after some time has elapsed following its enactment.

There are several possible reasons for wanting to postpone the effectiveness of a newly enacted statute. The officials who will have to administer it may need time to get the machinery in motion, or the persons who will be affected by it may need time to adjust. If it establishes a new or substantially revised government program, regulations may have to be written and published before that program can work effectively. Or there may be budgetary considerations; after all, a newly established program whose effectiveness is postponed for a two-year period won't cost as much (and can't cost anything during that period). These are matters for the sponsor; you would not usually volunteer a delayed effective date to take care of them (although if you recognize a possible need for delay you should of course point it out to the sponsor).

The most common cases in which delayed effective dates are used do not really involve intentional delays at all, but merely administrative necessity. There are many programs that operate on a monthly, annual, seasonal, or other periodic basis (social security, SSI, AFDC, Federal salaries, retirement annuities, and crop subsidies, to name a few), and bills affecting those programs should logically become effective at a time (usually the first day of the first month or another relevant period after enactment) that reflects this periodicity and is convenient for both the administrators and the public. If the field of law involved has an established tradition of briefly delaying effective dates for this kind of administrative reason (as many do), you should not hesitate to make the decision on your own.

And in any case it is important to remember that the specific changes to be made by the final version of the bill (whether its effective date is strictly time-related or is event-related as described in 26.4) typically remain fluid until the last stages of the House-Senate conference—only a few days before enactment and much too late for immediate implementation.

▶ 26.3   **Retroactive effective dates**

Delayed effective-date provisions are very common, and generally pose no special difficulties for the drafter. But retroactive effective-date provisions, though relatively rare, are full of problems that have to be dealt with if the job is to be done right.

On its face a retroactive effective-date provision is the same as a delayed effective-date provision except that it specifies a past date instead of a future one. The trouble is that during the period between the specified past date and the date of the bill's enactment a number of significant things may have happened.

The sponsor most likely wants retroactivity in order to ratify one or more past actions that were not strictly authorized at the time they were taken, or in order to confer past benefits on some deserving class of people. More often than not the proposal is intended to undo the past effect of regulations that the sponsor regards as ill-advised. Or the sponsor may simply have been fighting to get some statutory provision enacted for a long time and thinks (upon finally succeeding) that it should be effective back to the beginning of the fight as a matter of principle.

But remember that if a bill makes retroactive changes in existing law, it wipes out the changed provisions as they were in effect during the retroactive period and substitutes new ones. Benefits that were properly received under the law then in effect may now prove to have been improper (and repayable). Actions that were optional may now turn out to have been mandatory (and vice versa). And actions that were perfectly legal may now turn out to be illegal. Even worse, it is now probably far too late (without a time machine) for anyone to do anything about those benefits or those actions; and if anything could be done about them now it would probably be inequitable to insist on it.

What are you to do when confronted with a sponsor who wants a retroactive effective date? There are no rules that cover all cases, except that you should always look first to see what might have happened under the provisions that would be retroactively superseded. If you find for certain that nothing significant could have happened (which is quite possibly the case if the sponsor is acting rationally), you are home free, and can just write a regular effective-date provision with an odd-looking date in it.

If, though, you believe that significant actions may have been taken during the retroactive period in reliance on the then-existing law, you're on your own. All you can do is try to identify all of the undesirable consequences that might result from the retroactive feature, point them out to the sponsor, and suggest the kind of language (probably in the form of a savings clause—see 13.4) that might be added in order to deal with them.

▶ **26.4   Event-related effective dates**

There are a number of situations where the primary effective-date question is not the date on which a bill is to go into effect but rather the events (occurring on or after the chosen date) to which it is to apply.

The "events" involved might be particular months or pay periods, or might be benefits received, applications filed, grants made, or offenses committed on or after the chosen date. Occasionally an effective date is tied to the issuance of regulations implementing the statute. And bills involving programs of financial assistance are usually made effective with the beginning of a particular fiscal year or with respect to appropriations for a particular fiscal year.

For example, if a bill increasing monthly benefits under some public program were enacted on April 25 without any explicit effective-date provision, what would an individual's monthly benefit check for April look like? Should it be in the old amount or in the new increased amount? Unfortunately, neither would carry out the bill's mandate. What *would* happen, since the bill becomes effective (by default) in the middle of the month, is that the April check would have to be in a prorated amount equal to 24/30 of the benefit computed at the old rate plus 6/30 of the benefit computed at the new rate—an administrative nightmare that would satisfy no one.

Since the program operates on a monthly basis the bill should have included an explicit provision making it effective with respect to specified monthly events rather than simply at a specified time. The most logical provision would be one making the increase effective with respect to benefit payments, either for months beginning on or after the chosen date (which would in effect defer the increase until May 1 and keep the April checks at the old rate if the chosen date were the date of enactment) or for months ending on or after that date (if the sponsor prefers instead to apply the full increase to the April checks).

Note that simply making the increase effective on April 1 or May 1, or with respect to benefits paid on or after the chosen date (without any reference to the periods for which they were payable), would leave doubts about what is intended and might not get the right result in all cases.

The principle illustrated by this example—using events rather than just times to fix effective dates when the bill makes changes that fall in the middle of the very process that it seeks to affect—applies to many different kinds of bills; any quantitative change that affects an ongoing process is normally handled this way. Thus a bill changing income tax rates would be tied to specified taxable years; a bill changing admission fees at national parks would be tied to admissions occurring, or admission tickets purchased, on or after the chosen date; and a bill increasing Federal salaries would be tied to specified pay periods.

And a bill increasing criminal penalties is normally made applicable only to penalties imposed for crimes committed on or after its chosen date. If its effective-date provision specified only a date (which would always fall in the middle of the crime-indictment-trial-punishment process for at least a few people), the increased penalties would literally apply to individuals who have been charged but not yet brought to trial or convicted but not yet sentenced on that date as well as to those who commit the crimes thereafter, with resulting constitutional and other drawbacks.

It should be emphasized again that the chosen date in event-related cases need not be the date of the bill's enactment; indeed, delays in event-related cases (as in strictly time-related cases) are the rule rather than the exception.

▶ **26.5   Placement of effective-date provisions**

A general effective-date provision that applies to the bill as a whole or consists of separate effective dates for all of the bill's various substantive provisions should always be the last section of the bill.

If most but not all of the bill's substantive provisions are to have explicitly stated effective dates, it is still best to group those effective dates in a section at the end of the bill, where most readers would expect to find them. If you fear that readers might be mystified by your failure to mention some of the bill's substantive provisions in the effective-date section, you can fill in the gaps by adding a paragraph or sentence— which would otherwise be unnecessary—to remind them that "the remaining provisions of this Act shall be effective upon their enactment".

If some but not most of the bill's substantive provisions are to have explicitly stated effective dates, it is probably better to omit the general effective-date section at the end altogether, and to set forth the effective date for each of those provisions in a separate subsection, paragraph, or sentence at the end of the section (or a separate section at the end of the title) in which that provision appears.

And if only a few of the bill's substantive provisions are to have explicitly stated effective dates, or the bill does indeed have a general effective-date section at the end but some of its provisions require an explicitly stated effective date that is different from the one contained in that section, it is perfectly respectable to state each of the maverick effective dates within the text of the provision to which it relates. Normally the effective date in these cases would be placed in a separate subdivision at the end of the substantive provision, in the usual way; but it can just as easily be placed at the beginning—see 26.6.

Whenever you include special effective-date provisions in particular sections of a bill that also has a general effective-date provision, however, you must remember to begin the latter provision with the phrase "Except as otherwise specifically provided,".

It should be emphasized that a "substantive provision" for these purposes need not be an entire title or section; it can be a subsection, a paragraph, or any other subdivision of a bill. Even a single sentence can sometimes require its own unique effective date.

▶ **26.6   Form and style in effective-date provisions**

Except in those relatively rare cases with complications that require extensive improvisation on the part of the drafter, effective-date provisions are short, simple, and easy to write. Most of them are just different versions of the same boiler-plate sentence, of which the following might be regarded as the basic form:

> SEC. ____. This Act shall take effect on January 1, 1993.

All of the pieces of this form—the section designation, the subject, the verb, and the adverbial phrase at the end—may be freely varied to fit the circumstances involved and to reflect the kind of effective date that is being prescribed. (In the models that follow, the changed portions of the form are indicated by italics.)

For example, when the effective date applies only to one particular section rather than to the bill as a whole, it would normally be placed in a subsection at the end of that section rather than in a section at the end of the bill, and would read:

> *(d)* This *section* shall take effect on January 1, 1993.

Note that these examples depict only two of the many possible variations in the sentence's subject, which describes the substantive provision or provisions to which the effective date is being applied. In the examples just given, "This Act" became "This section"; but it could just as well have become "This paragraph", "Section 101", "Subsection (c)", "The second sentence of section 202(d)(4)", or "Sections 14, 37, and 355".

And if the bill is essentially just a "vehicle" for making amendments to some existing law, the effective-date provision should reflect that fact:

> SEC. ____. *The amendments made by* this Act shall take effect on January 1, 1993.

The italicized words are not strictly necessary, but including them makes things clearer. Remember, however, that this form technically allows the bill itself to become effective upon enactment (by default) while postponing the effectiveness of the amendments; and if there is anything in the bill that has possible significance other than the amendments themselves you may want to omit those words or use the form "*This Act and* the amendments made by this Act. . .".

Either "shall take effect" or "shall become effective" (or even "is effective" if you are a devotee of the indicative mood) is proper when the effectiveness of the substantive provision involved is being tied solely to a particular date—they are totally interchangeable. But you should substitute "shall apply to", "applies to", or "shall apply with respect to"—the author prefers the latter because it deals better with collateral matters—when the effectiveness of that provision is being tied to events. In this case the basic form would become:

> SEC. _____. This Act [or the amendments made by this Act] *shall apply with respect to [events of the relevant type] occurring* on or after January 1, 1993.

It should be noted that in all of the models presented in this subdivision the use of the indicative mood—"is effective" or "applies" instead of "shall be effective" or "shall apply"—would be equally correct. Many drafters prefer it, adhering to the rule that "shall" should be used only to impose a duty (see 21.5 and 22.2); the author, as you will have observed, regards effective dates as permissible exceptions to that rule.

And it should be mentioned that if the effective date is simply intended to tell when an official may begin to exercise some function that the substantive provision vests in him, or the substantive provision uses an amendment to some existing law to confer that function, it may be more convenient to weave the effective-date language into the text by placing it at the very beginning of the substantive provision instead of at the end (which would make it a first cousin to the "internal" effective dates discussed in 26.7). In the first case, the opening sentence of the substantive provision might then read "*On and after [or with respect to events of the relevant type occurring on or after] January 1, 1993,* the Secretary may. . . ."; and in the second it might read "*Effective January 1, 1993,* the XYZ Act is amended. . . .".

Before leaving the subject of effective-date form and style, there are several points that should be emphasized.

First, it is important to be precise, whatever form you are using. A provision that reads "This Act shall take effect six months after its enactment" invites confusion, especially if the bill will operate on a monthly or other periodic basis. It is always safest to tie a bill's effectiveness to a definite day; for example, "This Act shall take effect *180 days after the date of* its enactment", "This Act shall take effect upon the expiration of *six months after the month in which* it is enacted", or "This

Act shall take effect *on the first day of the sixth month beginning after* the date of its enactment".

Second, as indicated earlier, special effective dates for particular provisions in a bill (and internal effective dates) are always permissible even though the bill also has a general effective-date provision, if it seems desirable for any reason, so long as the general effective-date provision adequately warns the reader that there are exceptions.

Third, special effective dates at the beginning of the substantive provision involved (instead of at the end) are always appropriate when only a few sections of the bill need explicit effective dates—for example, "Effective January 1, 1993, any person who. . .". They are particularly useful in writing serial amendments (see 17.2); thus "Effective January 1, 1993, section 123 of the ABC Act is amended—". And they have a special value in cases where the provision involved amends an existing law to phase in a quantitative change (such as an increase in rates or dollar amounts) over a period of time.

In the latter case, for example, if a dollar figure in some existing formula is to be increased by $300 in three equal increments over a three-year period and the entire formula has to be rewritten each time an increment is added, you can simply write the three amendments in consecutive subsections and begin each of them with its own effective-date language; the first could begin "(a) Effective January 1, 1993, section ___ [the formula] is amended. . .", the second "(b) Effective January 1, 1994. . .", and the third "(c) Effective January 1, 1995. . .", so that each of the latter two, in effect, repeals the preceding one while enacting the new formula.

Fourth, an event-related effective date can always be tied either to events occurring "on or after [the key date]" or to events occurring "after [the day preceding that date]"—for example, either to "applications filed on or after May 1, 1993" or to "applications filed after April 30, 1993". The two forms are totally interchangeable. The only advantage of the "on or after" approach is that it does specify the key date, which may be helpful to the reader.

And finally, no matter what form you use, the adverbial phrase that indicates the time at which the provision or provisions involved will become effective (whether it is time-specific or event-related) need not actually specify a particular date at all. It is a very common practice, especially where the delay is intended simply to give time for adjusting to the new law, to measure the delay by the passage of time after enactment rather than by specifying a date. In such a case, the adverbial phrase in the basic form might read "shall take effect *30 days after the date of the enactment of this Act*" instead of "shall take effect on January 1, 1993".

▶ **26.7   Internal effective dates**

When it doesn't matter when the bill as a whole becomes effective, but it is thought desirable to postpone the exercise of some particular function for a while, it is a common practice to place the temporal limitation at the core of the relevant substantive section—not at the beginning or end of that section (or in a separate subsection or paragraph) but at the precise place where the function involved is being authorized. The section then has a built-in or "internal" effective date, without any effective-date "provision" to make it so.

For example, if the sponsor's policy is to make certain specified monthly benefits subject to new deductions, but only beginning with the benefits payable for some future month (say March 1993), the effective date might be handled either—

(1) externally, by stating the substantive rule without any temporal limitations—"there shall be deducted from any benefit. . . ."—and then including somewhere else, either at the beginning or end of the section involved or at the end of the bill, an explicit event-related effective-date provision declaring that "[the section involved] shall apply only with respect to benefits payable for months after February 1993"; or

(2) internally, by including the temporal limitation in the substantive provision itself, stating that "there shall be deducted from any benefit payable for a month after February 1993" instead of simply "there shall be deducted from any benefit".

The two approaches get the same result. Some drafters prefer the separate effective-date provision (option (1) above) be-cause it leaves the permanent substantive law uncluttered by dates that become history almost as soon as they are enacted, while others prefer the internal effective date (option (2)) because it eliminates any necessity for a separate effective-date provision or even because it does show the substantive provision's history on the face of the law. (See 6.6 for a more detailed discussion of the "split amendment" controversy.)

A somewhat different kind of internal effective-date provision involves bills that simply authorize or make appropriations for ongoing programs. Since the fiscal years for which the appropriations involved are being authorized or made are always specified—"There is authorized to be appropriated to the Secretary for fiscal year 1993. . .", for example—those bills too have built-in or "internal" effective dates.

Other Usages and Considerations

▶ **27.1 Numerals**

When expressing a cardinal number, use figures rather than words—that is, say "12", "36", or "1,375" rather than "twelve", "thirty-six", or "one thousand three hundred and seventy-five". It not only is clearer (and much less cumbersome when the number involved is large), but it also makes it easier for both drafter and reader to find key numbers in a bill. Figures stand out from words in the statutory text when the pages of the bill are rapidly scanned.

And when expressing a number in its ordinal form, do likewise—say "10th" or "150th" rather than "tenth" or "one hundred fiftieth"—for the same reason.

These rules, which apply to fractions as well as to whole numbers, should always be followed when the number involved (or either of the numbers involved, in the case of a fraction) is 10 or more. In the case of numbers below 10, you have some flexibility—most drafters begin using figures well below that level (partly for the reason given in the first paragraph above and partly because the Roman rule so often requires it)—but the safest approach is to spell them out.

HOLC recommends the use of figures for all numbers, including "1" and "1st", but you should not go this far unless you are amending the Internal Revenue Code or another statute that does it this way. Small figures in a sentence look peculiar on the page, and might be confusing because the cardinal "1" would often be just a synonym for "any" and the ordinals "1st", "2nd", and "3rd" are more relational than numerical.

Note the following possible exceptions regardless of the style you choose:

(1) If in a particular instance a number appears at the very beginning of a sentence, it is usually better to use a word (which can be capitalized) rather than a figure (which cannot).

(2) If the number appears in the middle of a provision that contains many section or paragraph references (which of course are numbers too) or a series of short, numbered clauses, it is sometimes confusing to add another figure to the pot, and it may be preferable to use a word instead.

(3) When two or more numbers are stated in a series or grouping that straddles your cut-off point, they should all be expressed in the same form. If you normally start using figures at "10", for example, either "8, 9, 10, or 11" or "eight, nine, ten, or eleven" would be correct—but not "eight, nine, 10, or 11".

One final word about numerals. Legal writers of old liked to express numbers by both words and figures, as in "sixty-five (65) years of age". This is nonsense; once is enough.

▶ **27.2 Provisos**

Provisos are ancient stylistic devices originally intended for use in expressing conditions in sentences. They are awkward and confusing as well as archaic, and you should avoid them like the plague.

For what it is worth, a true proviso is recognizable by the italicized term *"Provided", "Provided, however",* or *"Provided further",* which is always preceded by a colon and followed by the word "That" (always capitalized).

Provisos are commonly used by nondrafters and even by some experienced drafters to express simple exceptions and totally unrelated thoughts as well as conditions, probably because a proviso is an easy way to insert language without having to worry about its interrelationship with the surrounding words. But they make sentences long and cumbersome; and when a proviso is inserted in the middle of a sentence it is often impossible to determine where the proviso ends and the sentence proper resumes. And in addition they signal poor organization, and often suggest that the thought expressed was an afterthought which, for convenience, the drafter inserted in the wrong place. The Legislative Counsel's Offices in the House and Senate do not use them, and the Law Revision Counsel will not use them in the United States Code.

Anything that might be stated as a proviso would be better expressed in a clause beginning with "except that", "if", or "but", or in a separate sentence.

In all fairness, however, it must be admitted that there are one or two situations in which the use of a proviso may be permissible:

(1) When inserting new language into an existing provision that already contains a number of provisos (and there is no other place to put it), you should just grit your teeth and feel free to add another one.

(2) When the specific language you are inserting in a sentence of existing law will have to be cited or referred to in a later provision (and there is no other place to put it), using a proviso gives that language a designation by which it can be identified—the later provision might then say, for example, "subject to the proviso in the first sentence of section 123".

And when your sponsor wants to insert a legislative provision in an appropriation bill—a practice that is flatly forbidden by the Rules unless the provision constitutes a "permissible limitation" (see 12.12 and 32.6)—the use of a proviso is often the best way to do it. It suggests that the provision involved is indeed only a limitation, and thereby helps (if there is any doubt about whether the limitation is "permissible") to downplay its legislative nature.

Note that the use of "provided that" (lowercase and unitalicized) as a simple conjunction—as in "The Secretary may hold a hearing, provided that adequate public notice is given of the time and place"—does not constitute a true proviso, and might be permissible, although a plain old "if" or "after" would be better English.

▶ **27.3   Gender**

One of the most difficult challenges that you face as a drafter in your everyday work is the elimination of apparent gender bias in the language you use. This challenge may appear trivial in the sense that it is not substantive, but how you handle it can be highly important from a tactical standpoint.

The dilemma may be stated briefly.

As a practical matter, masculine pronouns in the law are always read as including the feminine (that is, "he", "him", and "his" are read as meaning "he or she", "him or her", and "his or her", respectively), except where the context requires otherwise. This rule is expressly set forth in the Federal law (title 1 of the United States Code) and in most State laws, and is universally applied by the courts.

The use of the masculine pronoun alone is therefore legally sufficient, and simplifies the drafter's task. But it reflects a historic gender bias and (other things being equal) is objectionable on that account; and all drafters should be on the lookout for ways to avoid the practice.

The problem is that no one has ever come up with a good way to do it. There are only two obvious choices (other than writing everything in the plural rather than the singular, which would foster ambiguity): One is to consistently use the feminine pronoun along with the masculine ("he or she", and "him or her"), and the other is to consistently repeat the antecedent noun instead of using a pronoun (for example, if a particular provision leads off with a reference to "an individual" or "a claimant", repeat "the individual" or "the claimant" every time a pronoun would normally be used). Either of these courses eliminates the apparent bias, but both of them too often result in a product that is awkward, cumbersome, and hard to read. *Hirsch* (page 44) expresses the view that conscious efforts in this direction often lead to "sentences so ludicrous as to suggest an ironic intent".

Most drafters would give their right arms for a singular pronoun that is gender-neutral. A few have even gone so far as to suggest keeping the classic rule that the masculine includes the feminine but adding a corollary rule that the feminine includes the masculine (except when the context requires otherwise, in either case), with each drafter having a free choice; obviously this would not be a satisfactory solution, since it would result in inconsistency and often in language that is uncomfortable to read, but it indicates how desperate they have become.

There will naturally be many provisions in which everything could be written in the plural, or in which (because of their brevity or the scarcity of pronominal situations) either of the two other courses described earlier could easily be followed without diminishing the quality of the prose at all. But good drafting requires stylistic consistency, and if that course (or any other stylistic device) is used anywhere in a bill or law it would have to be used every time the opportunity presents itself, even at the cost of awkwardness and reduced readability, because the use of "he or she" in some places and simply "he" in others would suggest that a substantive difference is intended.

Similar problems exist, of course, in words that use "man" or "men" as a prefix or suffix but are intended to designate people of either sex. Fortunately these problems are usually localized, and can be handled neutrally with relative ease.

You must make your own choices in the avoidance of apparent gender bias, subject to the sponsor's desires, of course. In the author's opinion, the most practical general rule (unless and until something better comes along) is this: If there is a rational and convenient way to avoid using "he" and its derivatives in referring to people generally, you should do it—in many bills (probably most) this is completely feasible. But if the effort to eliminate the problem (and do it consistently) would result in contorted sentences or would inescapably produce awkwardness or clutter, at any point in the bill you are working on, you should fall back and rely (throughout the bill) on the classic statutory principle that the masculine includes the feminine unless the context requires otherwise. Keep in mind that as a drafter your overriding objective is to express ideas clearly and readably, not to pursue a social ideology no matter how constructive and desirable it may otherwise be.

▶ **27.4   Abbreviations**

As a general rule, abbreviations should not be used in statutory language. It would always be a mistake, for example, to refer to a section—say section 5—as "sec. 5" in the text of a bill (even though the abbreviated form *is* used in the section's formal designation).

As you might expect, however, there are occasional exceptions to this rule. The most common involve parenthetical ("backup") citations to sources or locations of law. Thus, although a direct reference to a positive-law provision of the United States Code always spells out "United States Code", a parenthetical citation to a nonpositive-law provision of the

Code for informative purposes (see 24.6) always abbreviates it, as in "(45 U.S.C. 509)".

And the same is true in the case of parenthetical citations to the Statutes at Large, the Federal Register, the Code of Federal Regulations, and the treaty compilations; for example, "(89 Stat. 123, ch. 44)", "(19 Fed. Reg. 7521)", and "(49 CFR 571.208)".

It is also permissible to abbreviate the term "United States" when using that term as an adjective, as in "U.S. participation in [some international organization]", even though you would never abbreviate it when referring to the United States as a noun.

There is an increasing tendency to use acronyms in statutes, which is understandable and quite appropriate; obviously "NASA" is much more convenient than "the National Aeronautics and Space Administration" if you have to repeat it many times. But an acronym should be used in legislation only as a defined term, and not simply as an abbreviation; if you plan to use one you should use the full name once and define the acronym for subsequent uses, as in "The National Aeronautics and Space Administration (in this Act referred to as 'NASA') shall. . .".

Needless to say, this is another area in which you should be guided by the style manual of the jurisdiction in which you are working.

▶ **27.5** **Rounding**

Fractional quantities are almost always hard for administrators to deal with, and even harder for the affected persons to remember. In many cases the application of a formula in calculating such things as benefit amounts, pay rates, or allotments of funds, especially if it involves percentages, results in untidy figures like $75.13 or $237.54 (in a benefit or pay-rate case) or like $38,877.26 or $11,361,042.87 (in a per-State allocation case). The usual solution is to round the figure to some nice even quantity so that the odd cents or odd dollars are eliminated.

The rounding might be to a nearby even multiple of 10 cents (if the computed formula figure is very small), or to a nearby even multiple of $1,000 (if the computed figure is very large), or to anything in between. In some programs that start with an annual benefit or pay figure, that figure is rounded to the nearest $12 so that the monthly checks will be in even dollars.

Most often the figure involved is rounded to the nearest multiple of $1.

The necessary language of a rounding provision is very simple—it is often just the final part of the last sentence in the formula and is never more than a single short paragraph. There are, however, a few things to keep in mind:

(1) Whatever number your sponsor selects for the purpose—10 cents, $1, or $1,000—you can round a figure (up) to the next higher multiple of that number, you can round it (down) to the next lower multiple of that number, or you can just round it to the "nearest" multiple of that number.

(2) If you choose to round it to the nearest multiple, however, you must be careful not to leave an "undistributed middle". Remember that if the computed formula figure is $6.50, for example, $6 and $7 are equally "near", and you must deal with that case specifically.

Section 215 of the Social Security Act (which governs the computation of social security benefits) is a hotbed of rounding provisions and contains all the different varieties in several combinations—you might look at it if you are interested in the subject (although you should disregard everything but the rounding provisions themselves if you want to avoid a headache). Two of those provisions, however, will give you most of what you are likely to need in the way of models:

[(a)(1)(B)] (iii) Each amount established under clause (ii) for any calendar year shall be rounded to the nearest $1, except that any amount so established which is a multiple of $0.50 but not of $1 shall be rounded to the next higher $1.

(g) The amount of any monthly benefit computed under section 202 or 223 which [after various reductions and deductions] is not a multiple of $1 shall be rounded to the next lower multiple of $1.

The Railroad Unemployment Insurance Act (in connection with the first algebraic formula stated in 23.7) takes a slightly different approach:

(iii) Rounding Rule.—If the monthly compensation base computed under this formula is not a multiple of $5, it shall be rounded to the nearest multiple of $5, with such rounding being upward in the event the amount computed is equidistant between two multiples of $5.

One final comment. Obviously you should never even consider rounding if the figures involved must add up exactly to some particular amount (which would be the case, for example, if those figures represented allocations to States from a fund that has only a specified dollar amount for that purpose). In such a case the odd cents and odd dollars must be allowed to stand, whatever the administrative inconvenience.

▶ **27.6** **Bills and Acts**

The term "Act" (with a capital "A") is reserved for legislative measures that have actually been enacted into law, and is the only term that is ever used in a bill to refer to a specific enacted statute.

A bill is headed "A BILL" when it is introduced, and it remains a bill in fact until it is enacted (although by convention the heading changes to "AN ACT" as soon as one house passes it). Thus in speaking and writing about a bill you should call it a "bill" even after one house has passed it and its heading has changed to "AN ACT" (at least until the President signs it); but it should refer to itself as an "Act" even at the moment of its introduction. It should say, for example, "section 8(b) of this Act"—never "section 8(b) of this bill".

Note that a joint resolution (the other type of legislative measure that can actually be "enacted") is headed "H. J. RES." or "S. J. RES." both when it is introduced and after it becomes law—the heading does not change—and it always refers to itself as a joint resolution (lower case).

▶ **27.7** **Choosing the right antecedents**

It frequently happens that a basic term or concept that is expressed early in a section will have to be referred to (once or twice, or many times) later on in that section or in other provisions of the bill; and how you express it the first time often determines how much trouble you will have in referring to it later.

The simplest and most obvious example of a case in which the choice of the right antecedent will make your job easier is a purely mechanical one, involving the way you cite a particular provision of your bill or of existing law. If the provision in which you are interested is subparagraph (A) of paragraph (1) of subsection (b) of section 102, you would normally cite it as "section 102(b)(1)(A)" (see 24.8); but citing it instead as "subparagraph (A) of section 102(b)(1)" will make it possible in later references to say simply "such subparagraph", which is considerably clearer and more precise (though no more accurate) than "such section".

Other examples are less mechanical, but choosing the right antecedent can be just as helpful. Here is a very simple one:

If your intention in a bill is to confer a benefit of some kind on elderly individuals but only when they can demonstrate that they are physically disabled, you might confer that benefit in either of two ways:

> (1) The first time you mention the prospective beneficiary in the operative part of the bill (say in section 2), you might describe the beneficiary as "an individual who has attained age 65 and is under a disability", thus covering both requirements up front, as coequal aspects of eligibility.

> (2) Or you might describe the beneficiary as "an individual who has attained age 65, subject to section 3 [the section dealing with disability]", thus leaving the requirement of disability to be handled separately as a kind of special limitation.

Either course would do the job—the choice might depend on any of several factors—but a later reference to "such an individual" or to "an individual described in section 2" might have one meaning if you took the former course and another if you took the latter.

There is nothing complicated or esoteric about these thoughts, but you can ease your task (and avoid the necessity of periodically going back and revising the earlier expression) if you keep them in the back of your mind as you write.

Typography and
Typographical Terminology

▶ **28.1   Preliminary comments**

There are many ways in which material can be presented on a page. Some forms of writing involve more specialized typographical devices than others (consider the subscripts, superscripts, and symbols used in scientific writing, for example), but legislative drafting involves relatively few. By and large, legislative drafting (typographically) is just an ordinary form of prose composition.

The special typographical constraints that do exist in legislative drafting involve just two things:

(1) The way in which the various discrete pieces of a bill (the sections, subsections, paragraphs, and other subdivisions) are constructed on the page and located with respect to each other—most importantly their varying degrees of indentation. The specifications for this are set forth in detail in chapters 20 and 31 and are touched upon at several other places in the book; and the terminology is discussed in 28.2.

(2) The nature and placement of the headings to be used, and the characteristics of the type in which they are to be set—its size, font, and face. The specifications are set forth in detail in chapter 31, and the terminology is discussed in 28.3.

When drafting a bill, however, it is not enough that you get the specifications right; you must be able to describe the typographical aspects of what you do, so that you can talk about the bill to other technicians (committee staff, concerned agency staffs, and other specialists) while you are working on it and after it is finished, and so that you can accurately convey to the printer how you want the finished product to look. Remember that the public at large never sees your draft, and if the bill isn't printed the way you meant it to be no one will ever know what you wanted it to look like.

It is the purpose of this chapter to help you become comfortable with the typographical aspects of bills and laws at the Federal level. Sections 28.2 through 28.5 lay out the rules and symbols involved; 28.6 gives you an example of their practical application; and 28.7 and 28.8 show you how to mark your copy so as to apply them correctly.

▶ 28.2   Placement and structure

Centering and the left-hand margin.   All headings for a bill's senior components (and section headings in the "traditional" style) are centered on the line or lines on which they appear. Everything else in a bill, regardless of the drafting style being used, is based on the left-hand margin—that is, it begins either at the left-hand margin or at a point which is measured from the left-hand margin. The printer's shorthand mark for centered material is "ctr".

Full measure.   A subdivision or any other material in a bill is "full measure" when its left-hand margin coincides with the full left-hand margin of the page on which it appears. All sections and subsections are set full measure (as are most lesser subdivisions in the "traditional" and "United States Code" styles). The shorthand mark is "fm".

Paragraphing and flush material. A subdivision or any other material in a bill is "paragraphed" when its first line is indented 5 spaces (2 ems) from its left-hand margin, whether that margin is full measure or not. It is "flush" if it starts at the beginning of a new line and is not paragraphed, whether the new line is full measure or not. The shorthand marks are a backwards "P" with two stems ("¶") to denote a paragraph and "fl" to denote flush material.

"Cut-in" or indented material.   A subdivision or any other material in a bill is "cut in", or "indented" as a whole, when its left-hand margin is moved to the right of the page's full left-hand margin (or the left-hand margin of the matter immediately preceding it) by 5 spaces (2 ems). Indentations of this kind are often progressive; if the material immediately preceding a subdivision is itself cut in "once" (2 ems), that subdivision may be further indented or "cut in twice" by moving its left-hand margin two more ems to the right.

The shorthand mark to denote that material is to be cut in is a small box or circle with a figure inside it indicating the number of ems by which the material is to be indented (placed in the margin alongside that material, and preferably accompanied by a vertical marginal line indicating where the indentation starts and stops); for example, "②" in the case of material to be cut in once, or "⑥" in the case of material to be cut in three times.

"Run-in" and "dropped-down" material. Material is "run in" when it is a continuation of what precedes it and does not start on a new line. If the language immediately following the run-in material (or any other language for that matter) is to begin on a new line, it is "dropped down". Lines are never left blank, but it is always permissible to mark material "new line" (or even "new page") when necessary to make the arrangement clear. The headings of subsections and other inferior subdivisions in the "revenue" and "modified revenue" styles are always run in (immediately after the subdivision designation); and any designated subdivision that is run in is always called a "clause" regardless of how it is designated.

Placement of marks. As indicated in 28.8, all printer's marks (like regular penciled-in amendments) must be placed in the margin alongside the material to which they relate—not within the text itself—with a line drawn to (or around) the affected material if there could be any doubt about what that material is.

▶ **28.3   Characteristics of type**

Type size. Type comes in many sizes, of course, and these are measured in "points" (each of which, by the way, is equal to about 1/72 of an inch). The text of any bill is always printed in 14-point type, and so are the headings except for title and subtitle headings in revenue style (18-point), section headings in revenue or modified revenue style (10-point), and section headings in Code style (12-point). And occasionally the major headings in an omnibus bill are set in even larger type (that is, more than 18-point) in order to allow each of the principal components the full range of normal headings.

It should be emphasized, however, that (regardless of the drafting style involved) the size of the superior headings in a bill does not just gradually increase (and usually does not change at all) as you go up the scale of senior components. The important typographical variations between the several kinds of superior headings in a bill arise out of their different mixtures of large capital letters ("caps"), small capital letters ("small caps"), and lowercase letters and their different uses of boldface and lightface type.

(Note that there are specialized elements of a bill, such as tables of contents and columnar tables, that often use smaller (6-, 8-, or 10-point) type; but there are no established rules for them, and you should feel free to use whatever typographical devices seem appropriate. Note also that very massive bills have on occasion been printed in 8- or 10-point type in their entirety, with the lines set close together instead of double-spaced, in order to save space and avoid the sheer bulk that would be required if they were printed normally; but you are not likely to be confronted with this situation and should not consider it a viable option.)

The exact typographical specifications for all of the various headings that might be found in a bill in each of the accepted Federal drafting styles are set forth in chapter 31, along with literal examples.

Caps, small caps, and lowercase letters. At each level of size—14-point, 16-point, and so forth—there are three possibilities for each letter: It can be a full-sized cap (a "cap"), a small cap, or a lowercase letter. Caps at any level are obviously bigger than small caps and lowercase letters at that level (the latter two being of equal size); and caps, small caps, and lowercase letters at any level are obviously bigger than they would be at the next lower level. Numerals are printed the same size as caps.

You will occasionally have to mark your copy to specify the level of type size you want, but normally both you and the printer will know what level of type size is correct for the situation involved and marking for this purpose is unnecessary. It does sometimes become necessary, however, to specify whether you want caps, small caps, or lowercase letters in a particular case—not just in the headings but within the text as well—and the appropriate shorthand mark for a block of material would be "cap" or "caps", "sc", or "lc", or (for combinations of caps and either small caps or lowercase letters) "c+sc" or "c+lc". Single letters and individual words are simply underscored three times to indicate caps and twice to indicate small caps.

Typeface and font.   For the most part, all bills are printed in ordinary lightface (roman) type; no marking of the text is ever necessary to indicate this kind of type (except when returning to it after a lengthy segment of some other kind of type).

As has been mentioned and will be more fully discussed in chapter 31, however, headings are often printed in boldface type; and unless the face required is absolutely clear from the kind of heading that is involved (section headings are always boldface in revenue, modified revenue, or Code style, for example), you should mark it accordingly. The shorthand marks are "lf" and "bf", respectively.

And on those rare occasions when you want something in your draft to be set in italic type you should of course mark it accordingly; the frequently used device of simply underscoring language to indicate italicization would usually work but is too often ambiguous (except in the case of a proviso, where the need for italicizing *"Provided"* is understood by everyone). The shorthand mark is "ital".

Special typographical care is needed when you are working on a reported bill that contains amendments (see 30.7 and 30.8). Matter being eliminated is retained in the bill but printed with a line drawn through it ("line type" or "cancelled type"), and matter being added is shown in italics, with the unchanged portion remaining in roman type. A bill being reported with an amendment in the nature of a substitute shows the original language in line type (unless omitted altogether because of its length) followed by the substitute version in italics, which is easy enough. But a bill reported with cut-and-bite amendments often looks like it has measles, with bits and pieces of line type and italics scattered about indiscriminately; they must be marked ("lt" and "ital") with extreme care.

A bill as set forth in its conference report version has similar problems, although it is printed in "report style" (8-point type) rather than in bill style. The entire bill is shown in italic type in a conference report of the "complete substitute" variety, but heavy black brackets are used instead of line type to indicate stricken matter in the "numbered amendments" case. When it is of the "numbered amendments" variety, which is highly stylized and can be quite intricate (see 29.7

and 30.10), it must be marked ("bl.br.", "ital", and "roman") with care.

▶ **28.4   Other typographical terms and symbols**

The printer's mark for deleting something from the copy is a line with a hook or loop at the end, colloquially referred to as a "pigtail"; see 28.8 for examples. Cross out or encircle the word or phrase you want to eliminate, draw a line from it extending into the margin, and end the line with this mark. If you are deleting a large block of material, it is customary to do so by drawing a large "X" totally covering the material and enclosing it within a penciled box or circle, with a marginal pigtail attached to the latter.

When inserting something into the copy, write the material to be inserted in the margin (or staple it to the page if it is long), draw a line from that material (or from a marginal note referring to that material if it is attached) to the place where you want to insert it, and end the line (in the text) with a caret (an inverted "V"). Don't omit the caret; it helps to pinpoint the place of insertion. If the material being inserted is a comma, semicolon, colon, or period and nothing else, put an inverted "V" over it or circle it (and if it is a quotation mark or apostrophe put an upright "V" under it), so it will be recognized as the kind of punctuation mark it is.

The mark for showing that you want a blank space left between two words that have been inadvertently run together (or indeed for showing that you want a blank space left between two of anything) is the pound mark ("#"). And the mark for showing that you want to eliminate one or more blank spaces at some point (for example, to run two words together) looks like two parentheses (which can be of any length) lying on their sides, one over and one under the offending space—see 28.8 for an example.

The mark for reversing the order of two letters (or two words) that have been inadvertently transposed looks like an "S" lying on its side, with one of the offending letters (or words) within each of its curves—see 28.8.

The term "stet", alongside stricken matter, means "please ignore this deletion and retain the original matter".

Anything placed within parentheses is colloquially described as being "in the hole". The alphanumeric designations of the inferior subdivisions of a bill—the subsections, paragraphs, subparagraphs, clauses, and subclauses—are always placed "in the hole". Section numbers, and the alphanumeric designations of the senior components of a bill (the titles, subtitles, chapters, subchapters, parts, and subparts), are never "in the hole".

▶ **28.5   The Federal drafting styles**

Four different drafting styles are commonly used and accepted at the Federal level, and they are discussed in detail, with literal examples, in chapter 31. They are mentioned now, in passing, simply because the only mechanical differences between them involve the typographical matters discussed in this chapter—their headings and their systems of indentation.

Most of the things you are going to read in chapter 31 will thus be based on (and require a knowledge of) what you have read in this chapter; and conversely this chapter should be viewed as a kind of prologue to chapter 31.

▶ **28.6   Using the terminology**

It is important, as indicated earlier (and for the reasons given in 28.1), that you understand typographical terminology and feel comfortable with it so that you can communicate with others—the technicians with whom you are working and the printers who will have to deal with the product later—about what you have done or propose to do.

As a test of your comfort level in this area and an example of the sort of things that are involved, you might consider the typographical aspects of the following hypothetical provision, the text of which consists mainly of a single tabulated sentence written in "revenue" style (it would be the same in modified revenue style, but would vary somewhat in format if it were written in traditional or Code style):

SEC. 123. BENEFIT PROGRAM.

(a) In General.—The Secretary shall make a payment under this section to any individual who—

(1) files an application under subsection (b) and meets the eligibility requirements of section 124, and

(2) on the first day of the period for which the payment is made—

(A) is at least 65 years of age, and

(B) is needy (as determined under section 125),

unless the individual (i) is a dependent of another person receiving payments under this section or (ii) is unable to provide the assurances required by subsection (c).

(b) PROCEDURE FOR MAKING APPLICATION.—Any individual who . . . .

Subsections (a) and (b) (like all subsections) are full measure. Paragraphs (1) and (2) of subsection (a) are indented or cut-in; they are cut in "once" (2 ems). Subparagraphs (A) and (B) of paragraph (2) are also indented or cut-in, but they are cut in "twice" (2 more ems, for a total of 4). All of these are paragraphed, of course. The full-measure material beginning "unless" is flush (full measure), and clauses (i) and (ii) are run in.

The revenue-style section heading (which is full measure and flush) is set in 10-point boldface small caps. The subsection headings (which are run in) are set in 14-point (lightface) caps and small caps. Paragraphs (1) and (2) and subparagraphs (A) and (B) have no headings at all, since they are only parts of a tabulated sentence; they would have had run-in headings (set in 14-point small caps) if they were self-contained subdivisions or were prefaced by a colon (see 23.4).

▶ 28.7   Reproducing the typography

It should be obvious by now that what you write may actually appear in the printed bill in a number of different typographical formats, involving every conceivable combination of lowercase and capital letters in a dozen different sizes and typefaces along with various degrees of indentation, depending on the drafting style you are using, the complexity of the subject, and other factors. The typographical format that is indicated in any particular case will usually be clear to you after a reading of chapter 31, and you should always be familiar with it.

But unless your typewriter or computer is very sophisticated indeed, there is simply no way that you can reproduce many of a bill's headings and designations correctly on the typed page; and if you are writing in longhand, even the indentations can be hard to show precisely. And yet you do need to be certain that your bill will be printed exactly the way you want it. Chapter 31 only tells you what to do, not how to do it. What are your remedies?

In many cases, of course, there is no problem; the printer knows what the correct form is, and will get it right no matter what you do. For example, if your bill is clearly written in revenue style the printer will pay no attention to how you type your section headings and simply set them in 10-point boldface caps, full measure flush, because that's obviously what you meant to do. And if you type "Sec. 123." as a section designation in a bill that is clearly written in traditional style, or "(a) Secretary's Authority.—" as a subsection heading in a bill that is clearly written in revenue style, the printer will set it with caps and small caps, for the same reason.

In addition, if you do your typing carefully, most of your indentations will speak for themselves—the printer can just count spaces from the left-hand margin if necessary.

But whenever your typed characters do not accurately and precisely depict the exact typography that you intend, you should mark your copy so that the printer (and anyone else working on the project with you) will have no question about what you have in mind; this is the subject of 28.8 below. It is worth noting that many experienced drafters routinely mark every draft in this way—or at least the final version of the draft (the one that will actually be dropped in the hopper or filed)—as a kind of reflex action, even when there is no rational basis for uncertainty.

▶ **28.8   Marking copy**

The best way to mark copy is to use the terminology and shorthand marks described earlier in this chapter. All printers and most legislative technicians understand them. But if all else fails, don't hesitate to write a folksy note to the printer—for example, "Note to GPO: Please make this heading look exactly like the one at the top of the previous page", or "Please indent this paragraph 5 spaces more than the last one". Just do what you must to make your point absolutely clear, with all marks displayed in the margin and connected by lines and arrows to the places within the text where they are to have their effect.

Figure 28.8 on page 328 shows a sample page of draft language, liberally sprinkled with some of the more common typographical marks and showing how it ought to be done.

(b) Contents of Application. — —Any applicant for a _tion_

permit shall include in his application — —

② ¶ (1) the name and address of — —

¶ (A) the applicant (including the address of the
applicant which is nearest the site of the proposed
weather modification),

④ (b) any individual who will participate in the
activities involved, and   /≡/○

← ¶ (C) any person who secures the services of the _employs or otherwise_

← applicant; and

/c (2) ⧸ summary of the qualifications of any individual described in paragraph (1)(B), including his
education, training, and relevant experience in   /#

⊙ weather modification⧹

fm ←If the applicant has been issued a license by any State
fl- or local government as a specialist in weather modifica-
no tion, a certified copy of that license must accompany the
¶ application.

▶   Figure 28.8 Edited Text with Proofreader's Marks

Part VII

The Uniquely Federal Forms and Styles

Locations and Forms of Existing Federal Law

▶ **29.1   Preliminary comments**

If the bill on which you are working will be amendatory, you must of course locate and understand the relevant existing law in the field involved—in its most up-to-date form—before you can legitimately think about drafting at all. But even when your bill will be totally freestanding you will usually need to learn at least a little about the existing law in the field in order to determine the effect of the words you propose to use (and the effect of the existing law on those words). And very often you won't know until you have studied the existing law whether your approach should be amendatory or not.

In addition, even when there is no direct substantive connection between your bill and any definable body of existing Federal law, it will often be necessary (or at least desirable) that you locate and understand any existing laws that might—

1. bear upon specific aspects of your bill, such as those dealing with administrative procedures or involving the performance of existing functions by the relevant Federal officials,

2. overlap or be inconsistent with particular provisions of your bill, or

3. serve as useful models.

This chapter is designed to familiarize you with the various forms that Federal laws take, and to help you find them.

▶ **29.2   Slip laws**

The first official publication of any statute is in the form generally known as the "slip law". In this form, each law is published individually—as a separate document or pamphlet. Its heading indicates the public law number, the House or Senate number of the bill that was enacted, the date of enactment, and (since 1976) a citation to the volume and page of the Statutes at Large in which the law will appear.

In addition, each slip law contains marginal notes giving citations to any statutes mentioned in the text, and (since 1974) the U.S. Code classifications of the statute itself so that the reader can immediately determine where each of its provisions will appear in the Code. It also includes (since 1963) an informative guide to the legislative history of the law consisting of the names of the committees that handled it in each House, the committee report numbers, and the dates of consideration and passage in each House (with references to the *Congressional Record* by volume, year, and date). If it was passed over the President's veto or became law without his signature, a statement to that effect is included.

Figure 29.2 is an example of a recently enacted statute in its slip-law form (it is a short one, but contains all the essential pieces).

The slip laws are prepared by the Office of the Federal Register in the National Archives and Records Administration and delivered to the document rooms of both Houses— usually within a few weeks after enactment—where they become available to officials and the public. They may also be obtained by annual subscription or individual purchase from the Superintendent of Documents at the Government Printing Office. Under section 113 of title 1 of the United States Code they are competent evidence (of the laws involved) in all Federal and State courts, tribunals, and public offices.

Under the right circumstances slip laws are your best source of information about existing laws for two reasons:

1. They give you your earliest opportunity to see the laws

PUBLIC LAW 100-132—OCT. 16, 1987   101 STAT. 807

Public Law 100-132
100th Congress

An Act

To authorize the donation of certain non-Federal lands to Gettysburg National Military Park and to require a study and report on the final development of the park.

Oct. 16, 1987
[H.R. 797]

Be it enacted by the Senate and House of Representatives of the United States of America in Congress assembled,

SECTION 1. DONATION OF NON-FEDERAL LANDS.

16 USC 430g-3.

The Secretary of the Interior shall accept on behalf of the United States, the donation of approximately 31 acres of land known as the "Taney Farm" for administration as part of the Gettysburg National Military Park in Pennsylvania if such land is offered to be conveyed to the United States without cost to the United States by the Gettysburg Battlefield Preservation Association. Upon acceptance of title thereto by the United States, such property shall be subject to all laws and regulations applicable to the park.

Pennsylvania.

SEC. 2. ACQUISITION OF ADDITIONAL LANDS FOR GETTYSBURG NATIONAL MILITARY PARK; STUDY AND REPORT.

16 USC 430g note.

(a) ACQUISITION OF ADDITIONAL LANDS.—Except as provided in section 1 of this Act, until Congress receives the study under subsection (b), the Secretary of the Interior may not acquire by purchase, donation, exchange, or any other means any additional land for the Gettysburg National Military Park which is not within the boundaries of the 3,874 acre area depicted on the map dated July 25, 1974, numbered 305-92,004 and entitled "Gettysburg National Military Park".

(b) STUDY BY NATIONAL PARK SERVICE.—The Secretary of the Interior through the National Park Service shall conduct a boundary study and shall submit a report to Congress within one year of the date of enactment of this Act, with recommendations with respect to the final development of the Gettysburg National Military Park. In conducting the study, the Secretary shall consult with the people of the community and their elected representatives at all levels as well as with other interested individuals and groups.

Approved October 16, 1987.

LEGISLATIVE HISTORY—H.R. 797:

HOUSE REPORTS: No. 100-19 (Comm. on Interior and Insular Affairs).
SENATE REPORTS: No. 100-179 (Comm. on Energy and Natural Resources).
CONGRESSIONAL RECORD, Vol. 133 (1987):
        Mar. 10, considered and passed House.
        Oct. 1, considered and passed Senate.

▶ **Figure 29.2 Example of a Slip Law**

involved in their official form—the first available version of those laws, which contains all the requisite citations and references, and on which you can absolutely rely as to both form and substance.

2. They are the most convenient of all statutory forms to carry about and work with, since each slip law is a self-contained unit with no extraneous material in it, and is of a relatively manageable format (a mere 5½ by 8¾ inches, like a committee report).

Their usefulness is somewhat diminished, however, by two other factors:

1. They are less readily available to most drafters than the other statutory sources, since libraries tend to wait for the publication of the Statutes at Large or just to stock the United States Code (although, as indicated earlier, anyone who wants to obtain a slip law can usually do so with minimal effort).

2. They show only the statute as it was originally enacted and become out of date (from the drafter's point of view) as soon as they are amended by a later law. For this reason the utility of the older ones is limited.

If you can get your hands on the slip law setting forth the statute in which you are interested, you should choose it as your source whenever you can be sure (either because of its recency or because you have carefully checked and noted any subsequent amendments) that it is still reliable as a representation of the current state of the law. In any other case you should keep it handy and use it for stylistic guidance.

▶ **29.3   The Statutes at Large**

The United States Statutes at Large constitute a permanent collection of the laws of each session of Congress, printed in bound volumes. Each volume (which is also prepared by the Office of the Federal Register, and usually becomes available several months after the close of the session of Congress to which it relates) includes a complete index and table of contents, along with marginal notes referring to laws in earlier volumes and to other matters in the same volume.

You can think of the Statutes at Large as simply constituting chronological arrangements of slip laws, Congress by Congress. There is no attempt to arrange the laws according to their subject matter or to show the present status of earlier laws that have been amended on one or more occasions—that sort of thing is the function of the United States Code. And if you want to know what the slip law set forth in 29.2 would look like when it is printed in the Statutes at Large, just refer back to 29.2—the two versions are identical, down to the very last detail.

The Statutes at Large are legal evidence of the laws contained in them and will be accepted as proof of those laws in any Federal, State, or local court.

But their utility for the drafter is subject to the same two limiting factors that were mentioned in 29.2 with respect to slip laws: Lack of ready accessibility, and usefulness that diminishes with the passage of time. And their sheer bulk makes them harder to carry around and work with.

(Needless to say, the current state of any law can be determined from the slip laws or the Statutes at Large, by finding the original version of that law and then modifying it (by a cutting and pasting process) to incorporate all subsequent amendments as shown in later slip laws; but this can be a tedious and time-consuming process that is usually worth the effort only if you are preparing or updating a homemade compilation for regular personal use in the field of your specialty (see 29.6).)

In addition, you obviously need to know the particular Congress in which the law you are seeking was enacted in order to find that law quickly in the Statutes at Large, even if you do have a complete deskside set, because of their Congress-by-Congress arrangement.

▶ **29.4   The United States Code—positive-law titles**

The United States Code contains a consolidation and codification of the permanent laws of the United States, arranged according to subject matter under 50 title headings. It sets out the current version of those laws without repeating the vehicular language of the statutes that enacted or amended them. Its purpose is to present the laws in a concise, usable, and up-to-date form without requiring recourse to the many volumes of the Statutes at Large that might otherwise be involved.

For you as a drafter (whether or not the title you are interested in has become positive law) the Code has three great advantages over the slip laws and the Statutes at Large:

1. Its provisions are arranged by subject matter and are

comprehensively indexed, so that the provision being sought can readily be found.

2. It is kept up to date on a regular basis, with all amendments to existing provisions being periodically incorporated.

3. It is the most widely available, and far and away the most accessible, of all the possible sources.

The Code is prepared by the Law Revision Counsel of the House of Representatives. New editions (each of which contains about 15 very large volumes) are published every six years, and cumulative supplements are published after the conclusion of each regular session of Congress.

(The annotated version of the Code (the U.S.C.A.), which is the same sort of document but also contains references to relevant court cases and administrative rulings, is prepared and published by the West Publishing Company. Its main body occupies well over 50 volumes—one or more volumes for each title of the Code except in the case of a few of the shorter titles (which may be combined), so each volume is smaller and more manageable than its official counterpart—and it is brought up to date with quarterly pamphlets and annually issued pocket parts. One advantage of the annotated Code (in addition to the annotations themselves) is that you can buy any of its volumes (with updates) individually, which makes ownership feasible if most of your work is done within a single area.)

Originally the United States Code was intended simply as a convenience to individuals who might need to find, read, and understand particular provisions of existing law—it was not itself the law (although it has always been treated as "prima facie evidence" of the law, a treatment that is currently specified in title 1 of the Code). However, over the years selected titles have been revised and enacted into positive law, in a manner reminiscent of what was done in the Revised Statutes during the 1870s; and the process is continuing under the direction of the Law Revision Counsel.

But less than half of the titles have been rewritten and enacted, leaving the Code in a current state of considerable disarray; and work on some of the most difficult titles has not even begun. As of this writing 22 of the 50 titles of the United States Code have been enacted into positive law, one has been partly enacted into positive law, two have been eliminated altogether, and at least four others are in the process of preparation. In addition, title 26—the title dealing with revenue and taxation—is identical to the Internal Revenue Code of 1986 for all practical purposes (and indeed is entitled "Internal Revenue Code") although it has never actually been enacted as positive law. It is the hope of the Law Revision Counsel that eventually all of the titles of the Code will be enacted into positive law, and thereafter kept up to date by direct amendment.

If you are working from the United States Code (as most drafters must necessarily do, at least some of the time), it is critical that you know the status of the particular title in which you are interested (and of any other Code provisions to which you may have to refer). A positive-law title of the Code can be treated as gospel because it *is* the law—you can amend and cite it directly (ignoring the now-immaterial statute that enacted it), and you can absolutely rely upon its designations, style, and form. But if you are not sure you must be careful, since the titles that have not been enacted into positive law (and thus cannot be amended or relied on) have the same general appearance in the Code as those that have.

Figure 29.4 is an example of a provision in a positive-law title of the United States Code.

This provision of course reflects the established "Code style" (see chapter 31), which you would always follow when amending it (or writing a similar provision to be added anywhere in the positive-law titles of the Code). This format is used nowhere else in Federal statutes, and should not be used in *vehicular* language even when that language is adding a new section to a positive-law title of the Code.

For those who may be interested, Table 29.4 shows a complete list of the titles of the United States Code.

▶ **29.5   The United States Code—other titles**

As indicated in 29.4, the majority of the titles in the United States Code have never been enacted into positive law and are still primarily just a convenience to individuals seeking statutory provisions—they constitute prima facie evidence of the law but are not themselves the law. However, they remain invaluable to drafters (and others) because of the same three factors (arrangement by subject matter, regular updating, and ready availability) that apply to the positive-law titles.

§ 324. Removal of trustee or examiner

(a) The court, after notice and a hearing, may remove a trustee, other than the United States trustee, or an examiner, for cause.

(b) Whenever the court removes a trustee or examiner under subsection (a) in a case under this title, such trustee or examiner shall thereby be removed in all other cases under this title in which such trustee or examiner is then serving unless the court orders otherwise.

(Pub. L. 95–598, Nov. 6, 1978, 92 Stat. 2562; Pub. L. 99–554, title II, § 208, Oct. 27, 1986, 100 Stat. 3098.)

HISTORICAL AND REVISION NOTES

SENATE REPORT NO. 95-989

This section permits the court, after notice and a hearing, to remove a trustee for cause.

AMENDMENTS

1986—Pub. L. 99-554 amended section generally, designating existing provisions as subsec. (a), substituting "a trustee, other than the United States trustee, or an examiner" for "a trustee or an examiner", and adding subsec. (b).

EFFECTIVE DATE OF 1986 AMENDMENT

Effective date and applicability of amendment by Pub. L. 99-554 dependent upon the judicial district involved, see section 302(d), (e) of Pub. L. 99-554, set out as a note under section 581 of Title 28, Judiciary and Judicial Procedure.

SECTION REFERRED TO IN OTHER SECTIONS

This section is referred to in sections 703, 1104 of this title.

▶ Figure 29.4 Provision in a Positive-Law Title (title 11) of the United States Code

Even though the seeker must usually go further and consult more reliable sources (the Statutes at Large, the slip laws, or a literal compilation) when the title involved has not been enacted into positive law—an additional step not required in the case of the positive-law titles—they do provide a starting point, which is frequently half the battle.

In form and style the nonpositive-law titles of the Code are the same as the positive-law titles—a provision of one is indistinguishable on its face from a provision of the other. You could not tell just from looking at it, for instance, whether the example given in 29.4 is or is not positive law (which is why, in order to avoid serious drafting mistakes in

▶ **Table 29.4 Titles of the United States Code**

1. General Provisions [a]	(P.L. 80-278)
2. The Congress	
3. The President [a]	(P.L. 80-771)
4. Flag and Seal, Seat of Government, and the States [a]	(P.L. 80-279)
5. Government Organization and Employees; and Appendix [a]	(P.L. 89-554)
6. [Surety Bonds] [b]	
7. Agriculture	
8. Aliens and Nationality	
9. Arbitration [a]	(P.L. 80-282)
10. Armed Forces; and Appendix [a]	(P.L. 84-1028)
11. Bankruptcy: and Appendix [a]	(P.L. 95-598)
12. Banks and Banking	
13. Census	(P.L. 83-740)
14. Coast Guard [a]	(P.L. 81-207)
15. Commerce and Trade	
16. Conservation	
17. Copyrights [a]	(P.L. 80-281)
	(P.L. 94-553)
18. Crimes and Criminal Procedure; and Appendix [a]	(P.L. 80-722)
19. Customs Duties	
20. Education	
21. Food and Drugs	
22. Foreign Relations and Intercourse	
23. Highways [a]	(P.L. 85-767)
24. Hospitals and Asylums	
25. Indians	
26. Internal Revenue Code	
27. Intoxicating Liquors	
28. Judiciary and Judicial Procedure; and Appendix [a]	(P.L. 80-773)
29. Labor	
30. Mineral Lands and Mining	
31. Money and Finance [a]	(P.L. 97-258)
32. National Guard [a]	(P.L. 84-1028)
33. Navigation and Navigable Waters	
34. [Navy] [c]	
35. Patents [a]	(P.L. 82-593)
36. Patriotic Societies and Observances	
37. Pay and Allowances of the Uniformed Services [a]	(P.L. 87-649)
38. Veterans' Benefits [a]	(P.L. 85-857)
39. Postal Service [a]	(P.L. 86-682)
	(P.L. 91-375)
40. Public Buildings, Property, and Works	
41. Public Contracts	
42. The Public Health and Welfare	
43. Public Lands	
44. Public Printing and Documents [a]	(P.L. 90-620)
45. Railroads	
46. Shipping; and Appendix [a]	(P.L. 98-89)
47. Telegraphs, Telephones, and Radiotelegraphs	
48. Territories and Insular Possessions	
49. Transportation; and Appendix [a]	(P.L. 95-473)
50. War and National Defense; and Appendix	

[a] This title has been enacted as law (the enacting public law is noted to the right). However, any appendix to this title has not been enacted as law.

[b] This title was enacted as law and has been repealed by the enactment of Title 31.

[c] This title has been eliminated by the enactment of Title 10.

connection with any Code provision that you are dealing with, you must always check to confirm the category into which the provision falls if you don't already know it).

There is one difference between positive-law and nonpositive-law sections of the Code (in addition to the difference in their legal effect) that should not be over-looked. The parenthetical citations at the end of each section in a positive-law title of the Code, which refer to the statutes that enacted and amended it, are of historical interest only; but the corresponding parenthetical citations in a nonpositive-law title are critical—they tell you where to look to find the actual law that the provision involved reflects (and where to look to find all of the amendments that may have been made to it).

Consider, for example, the nonpositive-law section from title 12 of the Code in Figure 29.5.

---

§ 1701h. Advisory committees; payment of transportation and other expenses

The Secretary of Housing and Urban Development is authorized to establish such advisory committee or committees as he may deem necessary in carrying out any of his functions, powers, and duties under this or any other Act or authorization. Persons serving without compensation as members of any such committee may be paid transportation expenses and not to exceed $25 per diem in lieu of subsistence, as authorized by section 5703 of title 5.

(July 15, 1949, ch. 338, title VI, § 601, 63 Stat. 439; Aug. 2, 1954, ch. 649, title VIII, § 807, 68 Stat. 645; Aug. 10, 1965, Pub. L. 89–117, title XI, § 1106, 79 Stat. 503; May 25, 1967, Pub. L. 90–19, § 6(h), 81 Stat. 22; Oct. 17, 1984, Pub. L. 98–479, title II, § 202(c), 98 Stat. 2228.)

▶ **Figure 29.5 Provision in a Nonpositive-Law Title of the United States Code**

The parenthetical citations at the end of the section tell you that it came from section 601 of the Housing Act of 1949, and has since been amended by specified statutes in 1954, 1965, 1967, and 1984. Citations to all of these are given, and in the note that follows (not reproduced here) you are told what each of the amendments did.

These are critical pieces of information, because as a drafter you must go beyond the Code provision in your quest. Not only will a nonpositive-law provision's own section number always be wrong (1701h instead of 601 in this case), but such things as indentation, internal cross-references, and some of the key terminology will also have been changed (to fit the Code format) from the way they actually appear in the law.

You can (and should) use the nonpositive-law titles of the Code as convenient road maps, but you can't amend them, and you can't rely on them for drafting purposes. When you have found what you want to do you must almost always turn to the positive law to make sure that you do it right. And take the time to read the notes immediately following the provision involved—they will advise you of any other provisions of law (by reference to their Code citations) that may be relevant.

▶ **29.6   Compilations and looseleaf services**

You can always rely upon the United States Code for information about the current status of an existing law (at least if you have the latest supplement and properly use the *U.S. Code Congressional & Administrative News*—see 29.7 and 30.14), or even upon the slip laws and Statutes at Large if you are willing to make the effort; but without question the most valuable statutory source for everyday use by a drafter— although it is not an official source like the others—is the "literal" compilation.

A compilation of a statute shows that statute in its most up-to-date form. That is, it incorporates into the original statute all of the changes that have been subsequently made, with the amendments in place and the repealed provisions omitted (and it usually indicates in footnotes or otherwise the places where those changes appear). It is a "literal" compilation if it shows the statute exactly as it would appear in the positive law, faithfully reproducing its format, indentations, type sizes, typefaces, and its other stylistic features (including misspellings and typographical errors).

Compilations of significant Federal laws, which can be found in most major legislative fields, are generally prepared and kept up to date by the congressional committees or administrative agencies having jurisdiction over those laws or everyday responsibility for dealing with them. Such a compilation may or may not be "literal" (depending on whether its primary intended use is by drafters and other technicians or by policymakers), and may include a number of different laws when the field involved is broad.

These compilations are often regarded by the committees or agencies involved as "in-house" working documents that are not generally available to the public. But most of the important ones can be obtained simply by asking the committee or agency for a copy (which would be free) or by purchasing one from the Government Printing Office (which would be relatively inexpensive). Remember, however, that such a compilation will lose its currency as soon as the law involved is amended again, and you should be prepared to keep it up to date yourself until the next updated version is available.

Even better are the various commercially produced looseleaf compilations that are frequently available. The Commerce Clearing House and Prentice-Hall looseleaf services, for example, are best known for their compilations of the tax laws, but they produce similar compilations in many other fields. Along with the relevant statutes themselves (which are always presented in "literal" form) their compilations contain all of the relevant regulations, administrative rulings, and court decisions. And their compilations are kept more current than any others; subscribers typically receive their replacement pages within days after the enactment of amendatory legislation, even when that legislation has made massive changes in the statute or statutes involved. They tend to be bulky and expensive; but if you have access to such a service within your agency or organization you should use it.

Finally, you can of course make and maintain your own compilation, starting by making photostats of the original statute and all amendments to it from some reliable source and then keeping it up to date yourself by marking the changes in pencil or by a "cutting and pasting" process. (This is in fact what most professional drafters do; in the two Legislative Counsel's Offices each drafter maintains a personal compilation of the laws with which that drafter most often deals, and the Offices themselves (even though they subscribe to a broad spectrum of looseleaf services) maintain compilations of all major Federal statutes that they bring up to date by cutting and pasting almost daily.)

Bear in mind, however, that keeping any compilation current involves two separate activities—keeping abreast of any changes in the statute (which is not always as simple or clear-cut as it sounds), and then incorporating those changes (by marking or cutting and pasting) into the compilation—and either can consume a good deal of time and effort.

In any case, if you must deal regularly with an existing statute your first choice should be to work from a literal compilation if you can arrange it.

▶ **29.7   Interim sources**

One of the times when it is most crucial to know just what form a newly amended statute has taken is immediately after its enactment. At that time, however, nothing official has yet been published and the relevant compilations have not yet been updated. And the enrolled bill (the one the President actually signs) is almost never publicly available. What can you do?

Needless to say, if the bill has passed both Houses in exactly the same form, any copy of the bill as it passed either House will serve your purposes reasonably well. You can treat it as though it were the public law, and take it from there.

And if the final version of the bill resulted from a conference agreement of the complete substitute variety (see 30.10), the conference report, which is printed in both the House and the Senate, will set forth that version verbatim.

In any other case (unless one House or the other has gratuitously printed the bill in its final form, which occasionally happens), you must reconstruct it yourself:

1. If the final version of the bill resulted from a conference agreement of the numbered amendments variety (see 30.10), you will have to assemble a set of three documents—the bill as it passed the House in which it originated, the bill as it passed the other House (which will not be in bill form at all, but rather in the form of amendments to the first House's bill), and the conference report (which will show the action taken on each of the second House's amendments). By modifying the first House's bill to reflect all of the conference actions, you will arrive at the final version; this is not difficult in most cases, but it can be quite tedious.

If some of the second House's amendments were "reported in disagreement" in the conference report, and left to be dealt with on the floor of each House after the conference report is agreed to, you will need a fourth document—the record of the action taken on those amendments. For this you must turn to the *Congressional Record;*

and you must take what you find there with a grain of salt, since the *Congressional Record* (because of its multicolumn format) is not a reliable guide in matters of form and style and (because of its overnight printing) frequently contains typographical errors.

2. If the bill was never sent to conference and its final version resulted simply from amendments made on the floor of one or both of the two Houses—sometimes a bill bounces back and forth between the House and Senate several times before there is complete agreement—you have no recourse but to consult the *Congressional Record* to see what was done (bearing in mind the caveat stated in the preceding paragraph). The final version will consist of the bill as it passed the House in which it originated, modified to reflect all of these amendments.

Note that the only official version of what passed either House is the "engrossed" bill (or "engrossed" amendments) of that House—see 30.9—but this version is not easy to get hold of. (If you need a copy of a bill as it passed the House in which it originated but can't obtain the engrossed version, just get a copy of the bill as initially referred to committee in the other House—it can be safely treated as the exact equivalent of the first House's engrossed bill.)

Finally, on a somewhat different level, you should be aware that the *U.S. Code Congressional & Administrative News* (which is prepared by the West Publishing Company and consists of a series of softcover pamphlets that are published monthly) not only sets forth the text of the laws as they are enacted but includes periodically updated appendices that list all of the sections of the United States Code (positive law and nonpositive law) that are changed or otherwise affected by those laws. If you need to learn whether a particular provision of existing law has been recently amended (since your compilation was last brought up to date, for example), and you know the Code citation of that provision, a quick glance at those appendices will tell you. And if it has been recently amended, they will also direct you to the public law that did it.

▶ **29.8   Omnibus, appropriation, and reconciliation Acts**

The task of learning whether or not a particular provision of existing law has been recently amended, and locating the amendment if it has, is often complicated by the growing tendency of Congress to enact laws in bunches—multiple laws contained within a single bill.

Omnibus laws have always been with us, but until fairly recently they consisted of collections of provisions amending only related statutes and establishing only related programs. Today, however, a significant percentage of all Federal substantive legislation is enacted in omnibus bills that do not limit themselves to particular legislative areas. These take the form of appropriation bills (especially continuing resolutions) that are loaded down with substantive provisions and reconciliation bills (which are theoretically intended simply to bring the Federal budget into line but typically accomplish this by changing the scope and coverage of substantive programs).

The substantive provisions in appropriation bills and continuing resolutions have nothing to do with the appropriations process, of course, and many of the provisions in reconciliation bills actually have little or nothing to do with the budget process. They are put there in any particular case because time is running out and the appropriation or reconciliation bill is a convenient vehicle, because of political or intragovernmental divisions, or just because including them improves the sponsor's odds (since any such bill is almost certain to be enacted, in some form at least).

This is not the time or place to discuss the appropriations process or the budget process in depth. Suffice it to say (and it is the purpose of this subdivision simply to point out) that the increasing use of these omnibus bills makes it difficult for people in general and drafters in particular to know exactly what has been enacted—or even whether or not something has been enacted at all—until long after the fact. These bills are always massive, they are invariably enacted under extreme time pressure, and they can include anything under the sun. And their lack of any rational order or stylistic consistency often makes it next to impossible to find what you are looking for even when you know it is there.

In the case of reconciliation bills you have a fighting chance, since there is some order to them—the separate titles are at least arranged according to committee jurisdiction. And they are typically assembled by the Legislative Counsel's Offices, using material provided by the specialized committee staffs. But in the case of appropriation bills and continuing resolutions there is usually no order at all, since there is only limited participation by professional drafters and the specialized staffs of the legislative committees; there is no way that is both easy and practical to know what they contain, and you risk your sanity if you try to read one from cover to cover in order to see whether some provision in which you are interested has been included. (The bright side is that the Law Revision Counsel can't avoid doing this, and once that office has completed its work you can get your answer by simply consulting the United States Code.)

All you can do is remain alert to the fact that bills of this kind may contain material that changes or otherwise affects the laws you are working with, and be ready to look for it should the need become apparent.

▶ **29.9   Federal regulations**

Occasionally a sponsor may ask you to draft a bill to "undo" the effects of some government regulation. More often, the existence of a government regulation will have caused the problem you are being asked to solve, or simply needs to be taken into account in solving that problem. Whatever the reason, every drafter must from time to time consult government regulations, and it is important that you have a reasonably clear idea of how to find them.

Regulations formally prescribed by a Federal official, like Executive orders, first appear in the *Federal Register* (which is published more or less daily). They are subsequently codified in the Code of Federal Regulations (CFR), which is a multivolume set that is updated at least once a year and constitutes prima facie evidence of the text of the original documents. The 50 titles of the CFR (which represent broad areas of Federal jurisdiction but unfortunately are not numbered to conform with the 50 titles of the United States Code) are divided into chapters each of which usually bears the name of the issuing agency involved; and each chapter is subdivided into parts covering specific substantive areas. The subject index, which is revised annually as of January 1, appears in a separate volume entitled *CFR Index and Finding Aids.*

The CFR is kept up to date by the individual issues of the *Federal Register;* thus the two publications must be read together if you need to find the latest version of any given rule or regulation. To determine whether a CFR volume has been amended since its most recent revision you should consult the *List of CFR Sections Affected* (LSA), which is issued monthly, and the *Cumulative List of Parts Affected* in the Reader Aids section of the daily *Federal Register*. The two lists will provide you with the page number in the *Federal Register* of the latest amendment to any given rule or regulation.

▶ **29.10 Equipping yourself for the job**

As a drafter you will have to refer frequently to provisions of existing law, whether you are planning to amend that law (in which case you need a literal copy) or simply want a general understanding of it (in which case a nonliteral copy such as a nonpositive-law title of the United State Code is usually enough). And in either case you should be able to find what you want without bringing your other drafting activities to a grinding halt—that is, you need to know in advance where and how you will look for it.

What all of this means might be summarized this way:

1. Having on your desk at all times an up-to-date literal compilation of the laws to which you most often need to refer is the best way to avoid the necessity of looking further or of maintaining a large library, and will allow you to work with a document that is thoroughly familiar to you.

2. If the particular provisions in which you are interested are located in a positive-law title of the United States Code (see 29.4), you must know the location of the nearest set of the Code that will always be available when you need it.

3. In any other case, even though you will normally start with the United States Code, you should always check the Statutes at Large or the relevant slip laws (or at least look at a recently enacted law that amends the statute containing the provisions you are interested in, if you can find one) to ensure that the form and style you are using is the correct one. Remember that most of the titles of the Code are not positive law and never reflect the correct form and style of the laws they contain.

Beyond this, as a precautionary measure, you should make sure you know in advance how to get your hands on any of the documents discussed in this chapter on short notice—you never know when you will need them. And you should know where you can make photocopies, bearing in mind that some of them will require a machine that can handle large bound volumes.

Legislative Vehicles in Congress

▶ 30.1 Preliminary comments

There are four basic vehicles that Congress can use to accomplish its legislative objectives—the bill, the joint resolution, the concurrent resolution, and the simple resolution. Each has its own special purpose.

The four basic vehicles are described in 30.2 through 30.5; 30.6 sets forth and discusses the use of printed forms in drafting them for introduction; and 30.7 discusses the forms that amendments to them may take. The discussions in 30.2-30.7 bear upon what you are likely to be doing in your everyday drafting assignments. What remains in this chapter, 30.8-30.14, is largely for informational purposes, since most readers will seldom if ever be called upon to prepare the documents involved; they address the special forms that the basic vehicles may take at later stages of the legislative process (where new and different considerations may apply). In each case examples of the vehicles and forms are given.

Any bill or resolution can originate in either the House of Representatives or the Senate, except for tax bills ("bills for raising revenue"), which are required by the Constitution to originate in the House, and appropriation bills, which traditionally also originate in the House. (These exceptions are more matters of form than of substance, as a practical matter, since the Senate can always propose or concur with whatever amendments it chooses.)

The vast majority of legislative measures introduced in Congress are bills—most of them introduced in the House of Representatives—but all four of the basic vehicles go through the same stages (with a few exceptions which will be noted later) as they move through the legislative process, whether they are bills or resolutions and whether they originate in the House or the Senate.

One word of warning, however. Because it is one of the purposes of this chapter to distinguish between the various legislative vehicles, the broad definition of the term "bill" contained in 1.3 will be largely disregarded here—bills will be called bills, resolutions will be called resolutions, and amendments will be called amendments (although it should still be assumed that when reference is made to a House vehicle generically it could just as well have been made to the corresponding Senate vehicle).

▶ **30.2 Bills**

A bill is the vehicle used for most legislation, whether that legislation is permanent or temporary, general or special, or public or private. Once it is passed by Congress, and is signed by the President (or becomes effective without his signature in a veto-override or failure-to-return case), it becomes the law of the land.

If a bill originates in the House of Representatives it is designated by the letters "H.R." followed by a number, and it retains this designation throughout all of its parliamentary stages; thus the 123rd bill introduced in the House in any Congress is designated "H.R. 123", even when it is being considered in the Senate. (The letters signify "House of Representatives" and not, as is sometimes supposed, "House resolution".) A bill that originates in the Senate is designated by the letter "S." followed by a number indicating its chrono-

H.R. 3130

IN THE HOUSE OF REPRESENTATIVES

FEBRUARY 13, 1975

Mr. LaFalce introduced the following bill; which was referred to the
Committee on Merchant Marine and Fisheries

A BILL

To amend the National Environmental Policy Act of 1969
in order to clarify the procedures therein with respect
to the preparation of environmental impact statements.

1   *Be it enacted by the Senate and House of Representa-*

2   *tives of the United States of America in Congress assembled,*

3   That section 102 of the National Environmental Policy

4   Act of 1969 (42 U.S.C. 4332) is amended—

5   (1) by inserting "(a)" immediately after "Sec.

6   102."; and

7   (2) by adding at the end thereof the following

8   new subsection:

9   "(b) The preparation of any detailed statement re-

10   quired under subsection (a)(C)(i) may be accomplished by

11   the responsible Federal official or, at his discretion, may

▶ Figure 30.2 Short Bill Introduced in the House *(continued on next page)*

2

1 be delegated to an appropriate State agency or official or

2 may be prepared by a consultant to such Federal or State

3 agency or official. The preparation of any such statement

4 by any State agency or official or consultant shall not,

5 however, be construed as relieving the responsible Federal

6 official from full responsibility for the completeness, objec-

7 tivity, and content of such statement in approving and

8 adopting such statement."

9   SEC. 2. The amendments made by this Act shall take

10 effect January 1, 1970.

▶Figure 30.2 (continued)

logical place among the bills introduced in the Senate, but there are no other differences.

Figure 30.2 is an example of a short bill as introduced in the House. Except for its designation, this bill would look exactly the same if it had been introduced in the Senate. (You will see the same bill again, later on, in its reported, engrossed, conference, and public-law forms.)

Note that the enacting clause is identical in all bills regardless of where they originate, and mentions the Senate before the House even when the bill involved is a House bill.

▶ **30.3 Joint resolutions**

A joint resolution may be thought of as the equivalent of a bill, in that each becomes the law of the land upon its final approval. Both are subject to the same requirements and procedures and they are completely interchangeable (with one exception discussed below); statutes that originated as bills can be amended by joint resolutions and vice versa.

In practice joint resolutions are generally used for proposals that are narrower or more limited in scope, but this is not always true; the Balanced Budget and Emergency Deficit Control Act of 1985, for example—one of the broadest laws on the books—was enacted as part of a joint resolution.

If a joint resolution originates in the House of Representatives it is designated "H. J. Res." followed by its number, and it retains this designation throughout all of its parliamentary stages just like a bill. A joint resolution that originates in the Senate is designated "S. J. Res." followed by its number. The term "joint" does not signify that the resolution must be introduced in both Houses or be simultaneously considered by them.

Aside from their designations there are only a few relatively minor mechanical differences in form between bills and joint resolutions:

1. A joint resolution has a resolving clause instead of an enacting clause—that is, it begins with the word *"Resolved"* instead of with the words *"Be it enacted"*. The resolving clause (like the enacting clause in a bill) is identical in all joint resolutions regardless of where they originate.

2. The title of a joint resolution customarily begins with a verb in its gerundive form rather than its infinitive form—"Providing for" or "Authorizing", for example, instead of "To provide for" or "To authorize" as in the case of a bill—but this is not a requirement.

3. A joint resolution can contain a preamble (in the form of "whereas" clauses) if the sponsor wants to lead off with language justifying or explaining the need for the legislation; a bill cannot contain a preamble, and must do its justifying or explaining internally—usually in a separate "findings and purposes" section.

4. A joint resolution refers to itself internally as a "joint resolution" rather than as an "Act", even though it is "enacted" just like a bill.

Figure 30.3 is an example of a joint resolution as introduced in the House. Except for its designation, this resolution would look exactly the same if it had been introduced in the Senate.

There is one situation in which a joint resolution should not be thought of as equivalent to a bill. Joint resolutions are the vehicles used in proposing amendments to the Constitution,

101ST CONGRESS
1ST SESSION **H. J. RES. 218**

Disapproving the 1989 certification by the President with respect to the Bahamas under section 802(b) of the Trade Act of 1974.

IN THE HOUSE OF REPRESENTATIVES

MARCH 23, 1989

Mr. FEIGHAN introduced the following joint resolution; which was referred to the Committee on Ways and Means

JOINT RESOLUTION

Disapproving the 1989 certification by the President with respect to the Bahamas under section 802(b) of the Trade Act of 1974.

1   *Resolved by the Senate and House of Representatives*

2 *of the United States of America in Congress assembled,*

3 That the Congress hereby disapproves of the determination of

4 the President with respect to the Bahamas as contained in

5 the certification required by section 802(b) of the Trade Act

6 of 1974, received by the Congress on March 1, 1989.

▶ Figure 30.3 Joint Resolution Introduced in the House

and when used for this purpose they require a two-thirds vote in both Houses (a fact that is indicated in their resolving clauses). Upon their approval by such a vote they are signed by the Clerk of the House and the Secretary of the Senate and then sent directly to the Office of the Federal Register in the National Archives for submission to the States for ratification; they are not presented to the President.

▶ **30.4   Concurrent resolutions**

A concurrent resolution is not actually legislative in character. It deals with matters of concern only to the two Houses of Congress—matters involving their joint procedures or operations, or simply expressing facts, opinions, or purposes (the "sense of Congress") that both Houses want to get on the record.

It has to pass both Houses in identical form in order to be effective, just like a bill or joint resolution, but (unlike the latter) it stops there—it is not presented to the President for his signature, it does not become law, and it is not binding on anyone beyond the congressional establishment.

If a concurrent resolution originates in the House of Representatives it is designated "H. Con. Res." followed by its number. A concurrent resolution that originates in the Senate is designated "S. Con. Res." followed by its number. Upon approval by both Houses, it is signed by the Clerk of the House and the Secretary of the Senate and published in a special part of the Statutes at Large. The term "concurrent" does not signify that the resolution must be introduced in both Houses or be simultaneously considered by them.

Figure 30.4 is an example of a concurrent resolution as introduced in the House. Except for its designation and resolving clause, this resolution would look exactly the same if it had been introduced in the Senate. (A House concurrent resolution starts off "*Resolved by the House of Representatives (the Senate concurring)*", while a Senate concurrent resolution reverses the order and starts off "*Resolved by the Senate (the House of Representatives concurring)*").

▶ **30.5   Simple resolutions**

A simple resolution is like a concurrent resolution except that it deals only with matters of concern to the House in which it is introduced—matters involving the procedures or operations of that House, or expressing facts, opinions, or purposes which that House wants to get on the record. It is considered

101ST CONGRESS
1ST SESSION
H. CON. RES. 9

Expressing the sense of the Congress that tax legislation should not take effect earlier than 90 days after implementing regulations are issued.

IN THE HOUSE OF REPRESENTATIVES

JANUARY 3, 1989

Mr. NEAL of North Carolina submitted the following concurrent resolution; which was referred to the Committee on Ways and Means

CONCURRENT RESOLUTION

Expressing the sense of the Congress that tax legislation should not take effect earlier than 90 days after implementing regulations are issued.

1 *Resolved by the House of Representatives (the Senate*

2 *concurring)*, That it is the sense of the Congress that no

3 provision of law affecting the tax liability of any person

4 should take effect earlier than the day 90 days after the date

5 on which regulations implementing such provision are issued

6 by the Internal Revenue Service.

▶ Figure 30.4 Concurrent Resolution Introduced in the House

only by the House in which it is introduced; as soon as it is approved by that House the job is done, and it has no effect on anyone outside of that House.

The most important uses of simple resolutions involve matters with which the reader of this book is not likely to be concerned:

1. The organization of the House involved and its committees (at the beginning of each Congress).

2. The establishment of the formal rules of the House involved (at the beginning of each Congress), and their subsequent amendment.

3. In the House of Representatives, the establishment of the ad hoc "rules" (see 32.3) under which particular legislation is to be considered on the floor.

A simple resolution in the House of Representatives is designated "H. Res." followed by its number. A simple resolution in the Senate is designated "S. Res." followed by its number. Upon approval by the House involved, it is attested to by the appropriate official (the Clerk of the House or the Secretary of the Senate) and published in the *Congressional Record.*

Figure 30.5 is an example of a simple resolution as introduced in the House. Except for its designation and resolving clause (which of course mentions only the House of origin), this resolution would look exactly the same if it had been introduced in the Senate.

▶ **30.6   Using the forms**

Printed forms are available for use in preparing bills and resolutions for introduction in the House and Senate. These forms are not officially prescribed, they change from time to time, they are not always the same in both Houses, and with the development of computer-generated alternatives they may even disappear before long; but they have many virtues and you should use them whenever you can. They can be obtained from the House and Senate bill clerks (free but not generally available to the public) or from the Superintendent of Documents at the Government Printing Office (for a nominal price); and if you can beg, borrow, or steal a single copy of such a form you can of course make as many photocopies as you wish.

The four forms that make up Figure 30.6 are the forms

101ST CONGRESS
1ST SESSION

H. RES. 122

Requesting the Secretary of Labor to publish certain standards respecting
volunteer fire departments.

IN THE HOUSE OF REPRESENTATIVES

APRIL 6, 1989

Mr. DENNY SMITH submitted the following resolution; which was referred to the
Committee on Education and Labor

RESOLUTION

Requesting the Secretary of Labor to publish certain standards
respecting volunteer fire departments.

Whereas, volunteerism is an important facet of American life,
and

Whereas, volunteers comprise 80 percent of the fire service
work force in the United States,

Whereas, up to one million volunteers assist the operation of
more than 25,000 volunteer fire departments in this country, and

Whereas, the recent application of the Fair Labor Standards Act
of 1938 by the United States Department of Labor has
created confusion and brought added costs to volunteer fire
departments: Now, therefore, be it

▶ Figure 30.5 Simple Resolution Introduced in the House *(continued on next page)*

2

1   *Resolved*, That the House of Representatives requests

2   the Secretary of Labor to publish specific standards for the

3   application of the Fair Labor Standards Act of 1938 to vol-

4   unteer fire departments to assure that such departments have

5   specific rules by which to operate that will not restrict their

6   ability to provide fire prevention services.

▶ Figure 30.5 (continued)

currently used for the first pages of bills and resolutions in the House (all pages after the first are typed on plain paper).

If you remember what you read in 11.1, you will have noted that the space reserved for the title of the bill or resolution is in the wrong place on these forms—it should of course have been at the bottom of the page, immediately below the words "A BILL" (or their equivalent in the case of a resolution), where it belongs and where it will appear when the bill is printed. This is the result of a historical anomaly, and is not the case in the corresponding Senate forms.

You as the drafter fill in the Congress and session, the title, and the sponsor's name when you complete the draft; the sponsor signs his or her name; the appropriate legislative clerk (at the time of introduction) fills in the date and assigns the bill number; the parliamentarian adds a statement of the bill's committee reference; the printer adds a few mechanical touch-ups; and the deed is done. (Note that either document room can provide you with an official list showing the exact name by which each Member prefers to be called, including whether to use "Ms." or "Mrs." in the case of a female Member. It's a good idea to have one of these lists handy.)

If there are cosponsors, the blank for the sponsor's name is filled in "Mr. [Ms.] X [the primary sponsor, who introduces the bill], for himself [herself] and [the cosponsors]", although only the primary sponsor actually signs his or her name. And a cautious drafter, having no authority from the cosponsors, normally stops with the word "and"—just leaving it dangling

(Original signature of Member)

_____ CONGRESS

_____ SESSION

H.R._____

Insert
title
here
☞

IN THE HOUSE OF REPRESENTATIVES

_____, 19___

Insert
sponsor's
names
here
☞

A BILL

1   *Be it enacted by the Senate and House of Representatives of the United*

2   *States of America in Congress assembled,*

▶ Figure 30.6 Forms Used for First Pages of Bills and Resolutions in the House
(continued on next page)

and not actually naming them—and lets the primary sponsor
fill in the cosponsors' names before introducing the bill.

The form for a Senate bill is exactly the same (except that the
designation is "S." instead of "H.R.").

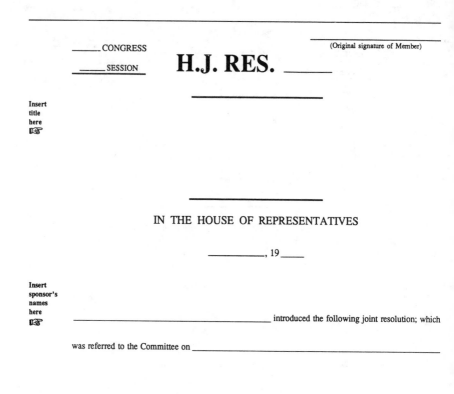

▶ **Figure 30.6 (continued on next page)**

Using the printed forms ensures that your front pages are correct, and simplifies the task of the officials and printers who will have to deal with the document after its introduction. But it is not necessary to use printed forms at all.

Bills and resolutions can be typed on plain paper, or even

_____ CONGRESS
_____ SESSION   **H. CON. RES.** _____

(Original signature of Member)

Insert
title
here
☞

IN THE HOUSE OF REPRESENTATIVES

_____, 19____

Insert
sponsor's
names
here
☞

CONCURRENT RESOLUTION

1   *Resolved by the House of Representatives (the Senate concurring),*

▶ **Figure 30.6 (continued on next page)**

written out in longhand (although that is not a good idea). If
you simply type the first page of a bill on plain paper, you
should place the sponsor's name at the indicated place
(upper left) and then go directly to the centered heading "A
BILL", locating your title immediately below that heading and
your enacting clause (or at least a paraphrase of it, such as

---

.... CONGRESS

.... SESSION

H. RES. ....

```
------------------------------------------
(Original signature of Member)
```

Insert
title
here
☞

IN THE HOUSE OF REPRESENTATIVES

-------------------, 19......

Insert
sponsor's
names
here
☞

RESOLUTION

1   *Resolved,*

▶ **Figure 30.6 (continued)**

"Be it enacted, etc.") below the title. The bill clerk of the House involved will fill in the rest of the blanks when it has been introduced.

For what it is worth, a good compromise (following the longstanding practice of the Legislative Counsel's Offices of

Congress) is to type your bills and resolutions on plain paper in this way, reserving the front page for the matters that would otherwise appear on the form and starting the actual text at the top of page 2, and then at the last minute substituting a filled-out form for your typed front page on one copy so as to create a "master" copy that has a properly formal look to it.

▶ 30.7   Amendments in committee and on the floor

Woodrow Wilson observed many years ago[1] that "Congress in session is Congress on exhibition, whilst Congress in its committee-rooms is Congress at work." This may be a slight overstatement, but it is certainly true that the most tangible manifestation of Congress's work on legislation is found in the amendments it adopts, and although some will come later, of course, most of them are adopted in its "committee-rooms."

An amendment offered to one of the basic legislative vehicles (a bill or resolution) is itself a legislative vehicle, in the sense that it is the recognized parliamentary device for changing what the basic vehicle does. The basic vehicle's message, more often than not, turns out to be (in whole or in part) the message carried to that vehicle by amendments that were offered to it at various stages of the legislative process.

But in terms of form amendments involve considerations that are quite different from those that apply to the bills and resolutions to which they are offered. As indicated earlier (in part V), there are two principal differences in form and style that you should keep in mind, both having to do with the form of the vehicular amendatory language.

First, an amendment to a bill is really nothing more than an instruction to the legislative official who will assemble and print the final product—the enrolling clerk of the House involved, for example—and is therefore always stated in the imperative mood, while an amendment to existing law in a bill is treated as being self-executing and is therefore always stated in the indicative mood.

And second, in a printed bill or resolution, every line (beginning with the first line of the enacting or resolving clause) is numbered; so the place in the bill where the amendment is to appear is normally identified simply by a reference to the relevant page and line number rather than by a descriptive reference to the provision being amended.

---

[1] *Congressional Government* 15th ed.; (Boston: Houghton Mifflin, 1900).

In a sense, the moment a bill or resolution is introduced, it comes into the custody of the House or Senate enrolling clerk, whose job during the legislative process is to keep up with it by incorporating any amendments that may be adopted from time to time. This job is initially handled at the committee stage by the professional staff of the committee involved, but in a practical sense every amendment made to a bill after its introduction is simply a way of telling the enrolling clerk how to make a specified change in it.

What this means to the drafter is that the formal requirements are relatively easy to satisfy. If the enrolling clerk can understand from reading an amendment exactly what you want him to do to a bill, the amendment meets the test. Shorthand devices are quite appropriate; thus, although a bill that inserts a new numbered paragraph in the middle of an existing subsection would have to explicitly renumber the subsequent paragraphs, an amendment that does the same thing in a subsection of a bill need only include the phrase "and renumber the succeeding paragraphs accordingly". (You can even add the words "and any cross-references thereto" if cross-references need to be conformed and you're short of time, although this is asking a little much of the clerk.)

Printed forms for amendments to bills and resolutions are often available, but there is no standard or required form. You can use plain typing paper, simply indicating the bill's or resolution's number and the Member's name and then stating the amendment in page-and-line terms. For example:

Amendments to H.R. 1234
Offered by Mr. [Ms.] X

Page 3, line 5, strike "four" and insert "seven".

Page 6, beginning on line 11, strike "but the Secretary" and all that follows through page 8, line 2, and insert a period.

Page 9, strike the paragraph beginning on line 4 [or strike lines 4 through 10].

Note that in some situations the document being amended has no line numbers (and occasionally no page numbers either), so you can't use the page-and-line-number approach. Such a situation might involve—

1. a draft bill that has not yet been introduced (committees and subcommittees often work from typed drafts, especially when they are developing substitutes for introduced

bills that have been referred to them);

2. an amendment that is to be offered to another amendment already offered by someone else (in the Senate the previous amendment will have sometimes been printed with line numbers, but usually not; and in the House amendments are never printed); or

3. an amendment to the long title of a bill or resolution, or to the preamble of a resolution, since those are matters that appear before the enacting or resolving clause and thus are never given line numbers.

In the first two situations you should simply identify the place where the amendment is to go as clearly as you can (usually by referring descriptively to the target provision—"In section 6...", for example), and if the enrolling clerk or his equivalent can understand your instruction you will have done your job. You can even get away with identifying the provision by its subject matter—"In the provision relating to eligibility...", for example—although again that is often asking a good deal of the enrolling clerk.

In the third situation, if the amendment is to the long title you should always state the new and revised title in its entirety (even if only a single word or punctuation mark would be changed):

Amend the title so as to read: "A Bill to promote good animal husbandry, and for other purposes.".

And if the amendment is to one of a resolution's whereas clauses you simply refer to it by its ordinal number—for example, "Amend the fifth clause in the preamble...".

(Note that amendments to the long title or preamble are never offered or considered until all amendments to the text have been disposed of. In the House they are not considered at all in the Committee of the Whole (where the other amendments are considered), but must wait until the Committee has "risen" and the action resumes in the "Whole House"—see chapter 32.)

▶ **30.8 Reported bills**

The first official printing of a bill is of course the introduced version, and the second official printing occurs when it is reported to the House involved by the committee to which it was referred. The reported version is easy to distinguish from the introduced bill by its report number, its calendar number, and a few other typographical legends that appear at the top of the front page. If the bill is reported unchanged there are no other differences; but if there were committee amendments they are incorporated into the bill.

The committee's amendments are shown in line type and italic; that is, any part of the introduced bill that would be stricken out is retained but printed with a line through it, and matter that would be added is printed in italic type. All unchanged portions of the bill remain in roman type. There is one exception: If the committee struck all of the text of the introduced bill and inserted a complete substitute and the stricken language was lengthy, the reported bill sometimes omits the stricken language altogether, starting off (right after the enacting clause) with the proposed substitute (entirely printed in italic) and simply referring readers who want to know what was eliminated to the introduced bill.

Note that the committee report itself (which "accompanies" the bill at this stage) will set forth all of the committee's amendments one by one, just as they were shown in the reported bill itself (except of course that they are individually listed by page and line instead of being incorporated into the bill at the places where they appear).

(Note also that it is a fairly common practice for a committee (or subcommittee), after making a number of amendments to a bill that was referred to it, to introduce a completely new bill (with a new number) incorporating all of the amendments and then report that bill without amendment (instead of achieving the same purpose by reporting the original bill with amendments). This often simplifies the process and avoids parliamentary problems; and the differences between the two bills can be explained in the accompanying committee report.)

To get a clearer picture of what the reporting process typically involves, you might take as an example the bill (H.R. 3130 of the 94th Congress) that was shown in its introduced form in 30.2. To see how it looked as reported with an amendment, see Figure 30.8A.

Note the additional legends at the beginning of the reported bill, and the line type/italic treatment of the committee's amendment.

As indicated earlier, the drafter's functions in connection with bills reported from committee may vary widely, depending in any particular case on the committee's procedures, the draft-

Union Calendar No. 62

94TH CONGRESS
1ST SESSION
H. R. 3130

[Report No. 94–144]

IN THE HOUSE OF REPRESENTATIVES

FEBRUARY 13, 1975

Mr. LAFALCE introduced the following bill; which was referred to the
Committee on Merchant Marine and Fisheries

APRIL 11, 1975

Reported with an amendment, committed to the Committee of the Whole
House on the State of the Union, and ordered to be printed
[Omit the part struck through and insert the part printed in italic]

A BILL

To amend the National Environmental Policy Act of 1969
in order to clarify the procedures therein with respect
to the preparation of environmental impact statements.

1   *Be it enacted by the Senate and House of Representa-*

2   *tives of the United States of America in Congress assembled,*

3   That section 102 of the National Environmental Policy

4   Act of 1969 (42 U.S.C. 4332) is amended—

▶ Figure 30.8A Reported Bill in the House *(continued on next page)*

2

1   (1) by inserting "(a)" immediately after "SEC.

2   102."; and

3   (2) by adding at the end thereof the following

4   new subsection:

5   ~~"(b) The preparation of any detailed statement re-~~

6   ~~quired under subsection (a)(C)(i) may be accomplished by~~

7   ~~the responsible Federal official or, at his discretion, may~~

8   ~~be delegated to an appropriate State agency or official or~~

9   ~~may be prepared by a consultant to such Federal or State~~

10   ~~agency or official. The preparation of any such statement~~

11   ~~by any State agency or official or consultant shall not,~~

12   ~~however, be construed as relieving the responsible Federal~~

13   ~~official from full responsibility for the completeness, objec-~~

14   ~~tivity, and content of such statement in approving and~~

15   ~~adopting such statement."~~

16   ~~SEC. 2. The amendments made by this Act shall take~~

17   ~~effect January 1, 1970.~~

18   *"(b) A statement prepared after January 1, 1970, shall*

19   *not be deemed to be legally insufficient solely by reason of*

20   *having been prepared by a State agency or official if the*

21   *responsible Federal official furnishes guidance and partici-*

22   *pates in such preparation and independently evaluates such*

23   *statement prior to its approval and adoption. This proce-*

24   *dure shall not relieve the Federal official of his responsibil-*

▶ **Figure 30.8A (continued on next page)**

3

1 *ities for the scope, objectivity, and content of the statement,*

2 *nor of any other responsibilities under this Act."*

▶ **Figure 30.8A (continued)**

er's personal relationship with the committee's professional staff, and the nature of the project.

The committee staff will always handle the bulk of the accompanying committee report—the committee's findings and recommendations, executive communications, the "bombast" (including the factual background, the reasons and justifications for the committee's actions, and the economics of the proposal), and the various declarations (on matters such as inflationary impact and estimated cost) that have to be included in order to satisfy the rules of the House involved.

As the on-the-scene drafter you would normally have three relatively specific functions:

1. The preparation of the reported bill itself, properly incorporating all of the committee's amendments.

2. The preparation of the first part of the accompanying report, which lists those amendments.

3. The preparation of the part of the report that is necessary to comply with the "Ramseyer rule" (see below) if it applies.

You may also be called upon to do the assembling of the committee's accompanying report—putting together the parts that you have written and the parts that the committee staff has provided; this function is particularly important when there are minority or dissenting views whose authors wish to keep the majority from seeing them in time to include an effective rebuttal in the main body of the report. And occasionally you might be asked to write a section-by-section analysis (as a technician, not as an advocate) for inclusion in the report.

The "Ramseyer rule", which was originally proposed by Congressman Christian Ramseyer and adopted in 1929, is a requirement in the House rules that whenever a committee reports legislation amending or repealing a provision of existing law (whether the amendment or repeal results from the introduced bill itself or from committee amendments), the accompanying committee report must show the changes by "appropriate typographical devices". Usually this is done by setting forth the existing law with the stricken matter in boldface brackets, the new matter in italics, and the remaining (unchanged) matter in roman type; occasionally it is done by showing the changes in parallel columns. The Senate has a similar requirement, which is known as the "Cordon rule" (although it too is often colloquially referred to as a "Ramseyer"). Compliance with the Ramseyer rule can be a massive job or a simple mechanical one, depending on the number and complexity of the changes in existing law that the bill makes.

(Note that the Ramseyer rule is one of the most important reasons why you should "narrow your target" as recommended in 16.1; read literally it requires that the report show all of any provision of existing law that is changed even slightly. Thus when you want to revise a sentence in paragraph (3) of section 6(b) of some existing law you should start off by saying "The third sentence in section 6(b)(3) [of the ABC Act] is amended. . .", rather than "Section 6 of [the ABC Act] is amended. . .", even though either could do the job, because in the latter case (in theory at least) the Ramseyer would have to show gratuitously a great deal of unchanged language from section 6 in addition to the target sentence itself.)

Figure 30.8B shows the front page of the report on H.R. 3130, setting forth the committee's amendment. (The remainder of the report, consisting of a description of the bill's purpose, a statement of what the bill does, the Ramseyer, the minority views, and a few other items, has been omitted. Note that the proposed new subsection (b) should have been surrounded by quotation marks, not because it is quoted in the report but because it was quoted in the committee amendment itself and the report should literally reflect the committee's action.)

A few final comments deserve to be made on the subject of committees and reported bills:

1. When a subcommittee reports a bill to its full committee no official printing of the bill occurs. However, if the

94TH CONGRESS	HOUSE OF REPRESENTATIVES	REPORT
1st Session		No. 4–144

STATE PARTICIPATION IN ENVIRONMENTAL ANALYSES

APRIL 11, 1975.—Committed to the Committee of the Whole House on the State of the Union and ordered to be printed

Mrs. SULLIVAN, from the Committee on Merchant Marine and Fisheries, submitted the following

R E P O R T

together with

MINORITY VIEWS

[To accompany H.R. 3130]

The Committee on Merchant Marine and Fisheries, to whom was referred the bill (H.R. 3130) to amend the National Environmental Policy Act of 1969 in order to clarify the procedures therein with respect to the preparation of environmental impact statements, having considered the same, reports favorably thereon with an amendment and recommends that the bill as amended do pass.

The amendment is as follows:

Strike line 9 on page 1 and all that follows and insert the following:

(b) A statement prepared after January 1, 1970, shall not be deemed to be legally insufficient solely by reason of having been prepared by a State agency or official if the responsible Federal official furnishes guidance and participates in such preparation and independently evaluates such statement prior to its approval and adoption. This procedure shall not relieve the Federal official of his responsibilities for the scope, objectivity, and content of the statement, nor of any other responsibilities under this Act.

▶ Figure 30.8B House Report Showing Amendment by a Committee (First Page Only) subcommittee has made amendments, an informal intermediate version with the amendments in place, or a detailed summary of the subcommittee's actions, is usually prepared for the full committee's convenience.

2. If the introduced bill was referred to more than one committee (either concurrently or consecutively), as often happens in the case of major bills that are broad in scope, there may be special problems for the drafter and others. Which committee files first? When the bill is taken up on the floor, can one committee amend another committee's amendments? Indeed, how do you distinguish one committee's amendments from another's on the face of the bill? The variations are infinite. Suffice it to say that the procedures to be followed in any particular case will be determined by the parliamentarian of the House involved on an ad hoc basis, and you should be very sure of what those procedures are before beginning work on committee amendments.

3. The committee amendments shown in a reported bill are only proposed amendments. Even though they may have more "steam" behind them (since they represent the collective product of an established body of specialized legislators) they still have to be offered and adopted on the floor just like any other amendments. To the extent that they have more dignity than amendments offered on the floor by individual Members, it is only because (A) they are actually printed in the reported bill, and (B) they are generally taken up (often en bloc) before the individual Members' amendments, which may give them a tactical advantage.

4. Published committee hearings are not legislative vehicles in the sense in which we have been using that term. Hearings, studies, and oversight reports may have real value for the policymakers, but they seldom concern the drafter directly.

▶ 30.9   **Engrossed bills**

There may be hundreds of amendments offered to a bill (and adopted) on the floor, or there may be none at all; but when the smoke clears and the bill has been passed it is the function of the enrolling clerk of the House involved to put together the "engrossed bill", which is the third official version of the bill and the only official version of what that

House did.

The engrossed bill is prepared by taking the reported bill, eliminating any of the committee amendments that were rejected on the floor, and incorporating into it all the other amendments (committee and individual) that were adopted on the floor. It looks and feels different from either of the earlier versions, and is recognizable by several changes in its form:

1. Most of the mechanical items at the front of the bill (including the name of the sponsor, the date of introduction, and the material relating to committee reference) have disappeared.

2. It now describes itself as "AN ACT" instead of as "A BILL" (even though it has of course not yet actually been enacted).

3. It is printed on heavier stock, and, if it is a House bill, on blue paper.

4. The attestation of the Clerk of the House (or the Secretary of the Senate in the case of a Senate bill) appears at the end.

Note, however, that the final action in the second body always takes the form of an amendment or amendments to the first body's engrossed bill, consisting either of a complete substitute or of cut-and-bite amendments; the resulting document is headed "AMENDMENT" or "AMENDMENTS", without an enacting or resolving clause, and is properly referred to as the "engrossed amendment" (or "engrossed amendments") of that body.

Figure 30.9A (without attempting to reproduce the blue paper) shows H.R. 3130 in its engrossed form, and Figure 30.9B shows the Senate's engrossed amendment.

As a drafter you should ideally use the engrossed version of a bill when working on amendments to the bill in the second body, simply because it is the only official version, but that may not be easy to do. Copies of engrossed bills and amendments are usually hard to come by, since they are printed in limited quantities and are not as widely distributed as other versions; many longtime Members of Congress and congressional staffers have never seen one, and do not know what they are.

As indicated earlier, the solution to this problem (at least if

H. R. 3130

AN ACT

To amend the National Environmental Policy Act of 1969 in order to clarify the procedures therein with respect to the preparation of environmental impact statements.

1   *Be it enacted by the Senate and House of Representa-*

2 *tives of the United States of America in Congress assembled,*

3 That section 102 of the National Environmental Policy

4 Act of 1969 (42 U.S.C. 4332) is amended—

5   (1) by inserting "(a)" immediately after "SEC.

6   102."; and

7   (2) by adding at the end thereof the following

8   new subsection:

9   "(b) A statement prepared after January 1, 1970,

10 shall not be deemed to be legally insufficient solely by rea-

11 son of having been prepared by a State agency or official

12 if the responsible Federal official furnishes guidance and

13 participates in such preparation and independently evalu-

14 ates such statement prior to its approval and adoption.

15 This procedure shall not relieve the Federal official of his

16 responsibilities for the scope, objectivity, and content of

▶ Figure 30.9A House Engrossed Bill *(continued on next page)*

2

1 the statement, nor of any other responsibilities under this

2 Act."

Passed the House of Representatives April 21, 1975.

Attest:

Clerk.

▶ **Figure 30.9A (continued)**

what you want is a copy of the bill as it passed the first House—that is, the House in which it was introduced), is to use the earliest version printed in the second House; the latter (which might be thought of as constituting the introduced bill in that House) is a copy of what was messaged over, and should be completely reliable.

Note that every bill that passes Congress goes through the same three official printings in both Houses—the introduced, reported, and engrossed versions—at least if you treat the "messaged over" version in the second body as that body's introduced version and the engrossed amendments of the second body as its engrossed bill.

▶ **30.10 Conference reports**

It is not enough that the House and Senate both pass the same bill—they must both pass it in identical form if it is to become law. Unless one body is willing to accept the other's version in its entirety, or a compromise between their two versions can be worked out entirely through amendments adopted on the floor, a committee of conference consisting of Congressmen and Senators must be appointed to iron out the differences. Those appointed are called the "conferees", or (more formally) the "managers on the part of the two Houses".

In the Senate of the United States,

May 22, 1975.

Resolved, That the bill from the House of Representatives (H.R. 3130) entitled "An Act to amend the National Environmental Policy Act of 1969 in order to clarify the procedures therein with respect to the preparation of environmental impact statements". do pass with the following

AMENDMENT:

Strike out all after the enacting clause and insert:

That section 102(2)(C) of the National Environmental Policy Act of 1969 (83 Stat. 852) is amended by striking the semicolon at the end thereof and inserting a period and the following new paragraph:

1   *"Any detailed statement prepared after January 1,*

2   *1970, on a major Federal action funded under a program*

3   *of grants to States shall not be deemed to be legally insuffi-*

4   *cient solely by reason of having been prepared by a State*

5   *agency or official which or who has statewide jurisdiction*

6   *and has the principal planning and decisionmaking re-*

7   *sponsibility for such action if the responsible Federal offi-*

8   *cial furnishes guidance and participates in such prepara-*

9   *tion and independently evaluates such statement prior to*

10   *its approval and adoption: Provided, That, in any state-*

11   *ment on any such action prepared after June 1, 1975, the*

▶ Figure 30.9B Senate Engrossed Amendment *(continued on next page)*

2

1 *responsible Federal official shall prepare independently the*

2 *analysis of any impacts of and alternatives to the action*

3 *which are of major interstate significance: Provided further,*

4 *That the procedures set forth in this paragraph shall not*

5 *relieve the Federal official of his responsibilities for the*

6 *scope, objectivity, and content of the entire statement or of*

7 *any other responsibilities under this Act;".*

Attest:

Secretary.

▶ **Figure 30.9B (continued)**

Although most bills are agreed to without the necessity of a conference, substantially all major bills go through this stage.

A conference report is simply the document that shows what the conferees on a bill have done. It sets forth the bill in its final form (either verbatim or by reference to the action taken on the individual items in dispute), and is accompanied (in the same document) by a "joint explanatory statement of the committee of conference" explaining what happened and why.

The terminology here may be a bit confusing. The term "conference report" is popularly used to describe the entire document filed by the conferees, but in a literal sense only the part of the document that contains the legislative language is the "conference report"—the remainder is the "joint statement". It is important to remember that the conference report itself is the bill, not a report like a committee report, and that only the joint statement resembles what would normally be considered a "report."

A few comments about conference organization and procedure may be in order before addressing the conference report itself:

1. With respect to any particular difference between the House and Senate versions of a bill, either House may surrender to the other, or the two Houses (within parliamentary limitations) may agree upon a compromise provision acceptable to both.

2. Each House determines for itself the number of conferees it will have. The number makes no difference (one House may have 17 and the other 3) because the conferees from each House collectively cast a single vote on any matter in disagreement, and both the conference report and the joint statement must be signed by a majority of them.

3. Conferees are usually chosen from the members of the standing committees that had jurisdiction over the bill (although occasionally a noncommittee member who sponsored an important amendment to it on the floor will be included). They elect their own chairman, who may be from either House; in cases where there are periodic conferences involving similar bills and substantially the same members (such as annual authorization Acts in a particular field), the chairmanship customarily alternates between the two Houses.

4. Separate conference reports are filed in the House and Senate—identical but each with its own report number— and once filed the conference report must be adopted as is in each House; it may not be amended on the floor. (There is a special procedure in the House for eliminating nongermane matter from a conference report, but it is very cumbersome and rarely used.)

The conference stage of a bill is generally considered the most important single stage because the small number of conferees makes it possible to actually address the substantive problems and negotiate the differences, the conferees are usually appointed from among Members who are particularly knowledgeable about the matters involved, and their final product is voted on by both Houses without amendment (and with very limited debate).

The terminology and variations of conference reports could be the subject of an entire book (the most common variations being those involving amendments to the title as well as the text, bills that have bounced back and forth between the two Houses before going to conference, and bills reported in disagreement—all discussed briefly below). Suffice it to say here that every conference report takes one of two forms:

1. **The complete substitute.** When one House has simply substituted its own text for the entire text of the bill as passed by the other, the conference report will do the same thing—it will treat the second House's text as a single amendment and will set forth in the report (as a single amendment) its own substitute for the entire text of both the House and Senate versions. This is by far the most common form of conference report, and the simplest; after the front page it is plain bill text (although printed in italic type), just like any other amendment that begins "strike all after the enacting clause and insert the following:".

2. **Numbered amendments.** When one House has made cut-and-bite amendments at specific places in the bill as passed by the other (rather than adopting a complete substitute), every amendment is assigned a number—there may be anywhere from one to 1,000—and the conference is very different. It must deal separately with each amendment (and may not deal at all, in theory at least, with any part of the bill that is not included within one of the amendments). In this case the conference report will not show the bill as a whole; instead, it will consist of—

A. a list of the numbers of the specific amendments on which the House surrendered outright;

B. a list of the numbers of the specific amendments on which the Senate surrendered outright; and

C. a series of paragraphs (referring to the remaining amendments in numerical order) each of which sets forth the conferees' compromise action on a particular amendment.

This form of conference report is mostly used on bills from the Ways and Means and Appropriations Committees, and tends to become complicated and largely incomprehensible; it is highly technical, and gives the casual reader no clue to what the bill is going to look like when the enrolling clerk gets through putting it together.

(There are printed forms for the front page of a "complete-substitute" conference report and for the front page of a "numbered amendments" conference report. There are also printed forms for the front page of a joint statement, but you would need them only if you are responsible for assembling the final product. These forms are the same in both Houses except for any necessary reversals of the terms "House" and "Senate", and are always used.)

Figure 30.10A shows the complete-substitute conference report on H.R. 3130 (the statement of managers is omitted). And just for purposes of comparison, Figure 30.10B is an example (entirely unrelated, of course) showing the beginning and end of a numbered-amendments conference report.

Finally, a word about a few of the more common variants that were mentioned a few pages back:

1. If the conference involves an amendment to the bill's title as well as one or more amendments to its text, the amendment to the title is treated separately—after the text has been disposed of. (Thus if the conference report on H.R. 3130 had included an amendment to the bill's title there would have been two amendments in disagreement, and the introductory language of the report would have referred only to the Senate amendment "to the text of the bill"; the amendment to the title would have been dealt with later—immediately before the conferees' signatures.)

2. If the bill has bounced back and forth between the two Houses one or more times before going to conference, it is the action of the last House from which it bounced that is the subject of the conference; the conference report might describe itself, for example, as being "on the amendments of the House to the amendments of the Senate to the bill H.R. 1234" instead of just being "on the amendments of the Senate to the bill H.R. 1234".

3. When the conferees are unwilling or unable to file a report in full agreement, one of three possible situations exists:

A. The conferees may actually be unable to reach any agreement at all (or to reach agreement on the really basic differences). In this situation they may just allow the bill to die without any formal action, possibly calling for another conference, or they may file a conference

AMENDING THE NATIONAL ENVIRONMENTAL POLICY ACT TO CLARIFY THE FEDERAL AND STATE ROLES IN THE PREPARATION OF ENVIRONMENTAL ANALYSES ON CERTAIN FEDERAL PROGRAMS

JULY 24, 1975.—Ordered to be printed

Mrs. SULLIVAN, from the committee of conference,
submitted the following

CONFERENCE REPORT

[To accompany H.R. 3130]

The committee of conference on the disagreeing votes of the two Houses on the amendment of the Senate to the bill (H.R. 3130) to amend the National Environmental Policy Act of 1969 in order to clarify the procedures therein with respect to the preparation of environmental impact statements, have agreed to recommend and do recommend to their respective Houses as follows:

That the House recede from its disagreement to the amendment of the Senate and agree to the same with an amendment as follows:

In lieu of the matter proposed to be inserted by the Senate amendment, insert the following:

That section 102(2) of the National Environmental Policy Act of 1969 (83 Stat. 852) is amended by redesignating subparagraphs (D), (E), (F), (G), and (H) as subparagraphs (E), (F), (G), (H), and (I), respectively: and by adding immediately after subparagraph (C) the following new subparagraph:

"(D) Any detailed statement required under subparagraph (C) after January 1, 1970, for any major Federal action funded under a program of grants to States shall not be deemed to be legally insufficient solely by reason of having been prepared by a State agency or official, if:

"(i) the State agency or official has statewide jurisdiction and has the responsibility for such action,

"(ii) the responsible Federal official furnishes guidance and participates in such preparation,

"(iii) the responsible Federal official independently evaluates such statement prior to its approval and adoption, and

"(iv) after January 1, 1976, the responsible Federal official provides early notification to, and solicits the views

▶ **Figure 30.10A House Complete-Substitute Conference Report**
(continued on next page)

2

of, any other State or any Federal land management entity of any action or any alternative thereto which may have significant impacts upon such State or affected Federal land management entity and, if there is any disagreement on such impacts, prepares a written assessment of such impacts and views for incorporation into such detailed statement.

The procedures in this subparagraph shall not relieve the Federal official of his responsibilities for the scope, objectivity, and content of the entire statement or of any other responsibility under this Act; and further, this subparagraph does not affect the legal sufficiency of statements prepared by State agencies with less than statewide jurisdiction.".

And the Senate agree to the same.

> LEONOR K. SULLIVAN,
> ROBERT L. LEGGETT,
> JOHN DINGELL,
> JOHN M. MURPHY,
> PHILIP E. RUPPE,
> EDWIN B. FORSYTHE,
> *Managers of the Part of the House.*
> HENRY M. JACKSON,
> FLOYD K. HASKELL,
> DALE BUMPERS,
> PAUL J. FANNIN,
> MARK O. HATFIELD,
> *Managers on the Part of the Senate.*

▶ **Figure 30.10A (continued)**

report "in disagreement" without addressing any of the issues involved. In the latter case the report simply states that the conferees "have been unable to agree"; and in either case the process reverts to the point to which it had progressed when the conferees were appointed.

B. With numbered amendments, the conferees may have reached agreement on most of the issues but be unable to reach agreement on all of them. In this case they usually file a normal conference report showing all the amendments that were agreed to, and report the bill with the remaining amendments still in disagreement; the latter are taken up one by one on the floor of each House immediately after it adopts the conference report.

| 101st Congress | HOUSE OF REPRESENTATIVES | Report |
| 2d Session | | 101–892 |

MAKING APPROPRIATIONS FOR THE DEPARTMENT OF TRANSPORTATION AND RELATED AGENCIES, FOR THE FISCAL YEAR ENDING SEPTEMBER 30, 1991, AND FOR OTHER PURPOSES.

OCTOBER 16, 1990.—Ordered to be printed

Mr. LEHMAN, of Florida, from the Committee of conference, submitted the following

CONFERENCE REPORT

[To accompany H.R. 5229]

The committee of conference on the disagreeing votes of the two Houses on the amendments of the Senate to the bill (H.R. 5229) making appropriations for the Department of Transportation and related agencies, for the fiscal year ending September 30, 1991, and for other purposes, having met, after full and free conference, have agreed to recommend and do recommend to their respective Houses as follows:

That the Senate recede from its amendments numbered 2, 3, 23, 28, 31, 35, 38, 41, 44, 46, 47, 54, 79, 85, 88, 99, 101, 105, 106, 107, 113, 126, 131, and 142.

That the House recede from its disagreement to the amendments of the Senate numbered 1, 5, 8, 9, 11, 12, 24, 26, 27, 36, 37, 89, 91, 95, 109, 111, 112, 114, 115, 116, 119, 121, 122, 125, 127, and 134, and agree to the same.

Amendment numbered 6:

That the House recede from its disagreement to the amendment of the Senate numbered 6, and agree to the same with an amendment, as follows:

In lieu of the sum proposed by said amendment insert: *$1,500,000*; and the Senate agree to the same.

Amendment numbered 16:

That the House recede from its disagreement to the amendment of the Senate numbered 16, and agree to the same with an amendment, as follows:

In lieu of the sum proposed by said amendment insert: *$406,331,000*; and the Senate agree to the same.

Amendment numbered 17:

That the House recede from its disagreement to the amendment of the Senate numbered 17, and agree to the same with an amendment, as follows:

▶ **Figure 30.10B House Numbered-Amendments Conference Report (First and Last Pages)** *(continued on next page)*

383

★ ★ ★

The committee of conference report in disagreement amendments numbered 4, 7, 10, 13, 14, 15, 18, 19, 22, 29, 32, 33, 45, 67, 68, 69, 70, 71, 72, 73, 74, 75, 76, 77, 78, 80, 81, 84, 93, 96, 97, 98, 104, 110, 117, 118, 129, 130, 132, 135, 136, 137, 138, 139, 140, 141, and 143.

WILLIAM LEHMAN,
WILLIAM H. GRAY III,
BOB CARR (except as to
   amendments 39 and 40),
RICHARD J. DURBIN,
ROBERT J. MRAZEK,
MARTIN OLAV SABO,
JAMIE L. WHITTEN,
LAWRENCE COUGHLIN,
SILVIO O. CONTE,
FRANK R. WOLF,
TOM DELAY,
Managers on the Part of the House.

FRANK R. LAUTENBERG,
ROBERT C. BYRD,
TOM HARKIN,
JAMES R. SASSER,
BARBARA A. MIKULSKI,
DANIEL K. INOUYE,
ALFONSE M. D'AMATO,
ROBERT W. KASTEN, Jr.,
PETE V. DOMENICI,
CHUCK GRASSLEY,
MARK O. HATFIELD,
Managers on the Part of the Senate.

▶ **Figure 30.10B (continued)**

(All of the remaining amendments must of course be agreed to in some form before the bill can be said to have passed.)

C. The conferees may have actually reached a complete agreement among themselves but cannot file a report incorporating that agreement because it would include matter outside the "scope" of the conference and would therefore be subject to a parliamentary challenge on the floor of either House. Here, too, the conference report is filed "in disagreement", but the disagreement is "technical"; it is anticipated that the offending provisions will in fact be agreed to in one form or another on the floor

of the two Houses (where there would be no problem
with scope), and the joint statement accompanying the
report will normally make clear both the problem and
the expected solution.

▶ **30.11 Enrolled bills**

When a bill has finally been agreed to by both bodies, it is
"enrolled" for presentation to the President by the enrolling
clerk of the House in which it originated.

In preparing the enrolled bill the clerk starts with the
engrossed bill and the engrossed amendments, and then
superimposes on them—

1. the conference report if there was one (along with the
subsequent floor actions if that report was filed in disagreement), or

2. the post-engrossment actions of the two Houses if their
differences were resolved without a conference, in order to
give full effect to the final compromise.

An enrolled bill is printed on parchment paper, and certified
by the Clerk of the House or the Secretary of the Senate
before being signed by the presiding officers of the two
Houses and sent to the President. There are no other copies
(except the enrolling clerk's working copies); most longtime
Members and staffers have never even seen one. For this
reason you should not expect to be able to get your hands on
a copy of any enrolled bill (and no copy of H.R. 3130 in its
enrolled form is included here).

But in the unlikely event that you have developed a genuine
concern about the ultimate fate of H.R. 3130, Figure 30.11
(which shows the resulting statute in its slip law form) may
reassure you.

▶ **30.12 Last-minute corrections**

It may be hard to believe, but occasionally a mistake is made
somewhere along the line in the text of a bill, and sometimes
that mistake is not discovered until too late to fix it in the
conference report. This is usually the result of the haste with
which the conference report was developed and filed; an
erroneous reference may not have been picked up in the final
proofreading, or the report may not accurately reflect some
action that was in fact taken by the conferees.

In such a case Congress may, if it acts in time and the mistake

Public Law 94-83
94th Congress, H. R. 3130
August 9, 1975

An Act

To amend the National Environmental Policy Act of 1969 in order to clarify the procedures therein with respect to the preparation of environmental impact statements.

Be it enacted by the Senate and House of Representatives of the United States of America in Congress assembled, That section 102(2) of the National Environmental Policy Act of 1969 (83 Stat. 852) is amended by redesignating subparagraphs (D), (E), (F), (G), and (H) as subparagraphs (E), (F), (G), (H), and (I), respectively; and by adding immediately after subparagraph (C) the following new subparagraph:

> Environmental
> impact state-
> ments, prepara-
> tion.
> 42 USC 4332.

"(D) Any detailed statement required under subparagraph (C) after January 1, 1970, for any major Federal action funded under a program of grants to States shall not be deemed to be legally insufficient solely by reason of having been prepared by a State agency or official, if:

"(i) the State agency or official has statewide jurisdiction and has the responsibility for such action,

"(ii) the responsible Federal official furnishes guidance and participates in such preparation,

"(iii) the responsible Federal official independently evaluates such statement prior to its approval and adoption, and

"(iv) after January 1, 1976, the responsible Federal official provides early notification to, and solicits the views of, any other State or any Federal land management entity of any action or any alternative thereto which may have significant impacts upon such State or affected Federal land management entity and, if there is any disagreement on such impacts, prepares a written assessment of such impacts and views for incorporation into such detailed statement.

The procedures in this subparagraph shall not relieve the Federal official of his responsibilities for the scope, objectivity, and content of the entire statement or of any other responsibility under this Act; and further, this subparagraph does not affect the legal sufficiency of statements prepared by State agencies with less than statewide jurisdiction.".

Approved August 9, 1975.

LEGISLATIVE HISTORY:

HOUSE REPORTS: No. 94-144 (Comm. on Merchant Marine and Fisheries) and No. 94-388 (Comm. of Conference).
SENATE REPORTS: No. 94-152 (Comm. on Interior and Insular Affairs) and 94-331 (Comm. of Conference).
CONGRESSIONAL RECORD, Vol. 121 (1975):
    April 21, considered and passed House.
    May 22, considered and passed Senate, amended.
    July 25, Senate agreed to conference report.
    July 29, House agreed to conference report.

89 STAT. 424

▶ Figure 30.11 Bill as Enacted in Slip Law Form

is serious enough, adopt a concurrent resolution instructing the enrolling clerk (actually the Clerk of the House or the Secretary of the Senate, who are the officials for whom the enrolling clerks work) to make the necessary corrections.

Figure 30.12 is an example showing the beginning and end of a concurrent resolution of this kind.

The mistakes that are correctable in this way are theoretically limited to those of a technical or mechanical nature, but the device has also been used to make substantive additions of compromise language that could not be agreed upon in the time available to the conferees (or deletions of substantive language about which last-minute misgivings have arisen). The concurrent resolution is considered on the floor of the House and Senate immediately after the conference report if it can be made ready in time, but may be considered later if it cannot.

Thus if you are involved as a drafter (on a major bill at least) you cannot yet relax when the conference report is filed; you will often begin receiving requests almost immediately for enrollment-correcting language (although a concurrent resolution incorporating that language will not be possible as a practical matter without the prior consent of the leadership and the principal legislative figures involved, and that consent is not always given).

Needless to say, concurrent resolutions to correct the enrollment of bills are very convenient devices and can cover a multitude of sins, since they bypass most of the regular steps in the legislative process, and (being cleared in advance) they are usually adopted without study or debate.

Note that a modified version of this kind of concurrent resolution can be used for the same purposes after the bill has been enrolled (in which case it would have to include language rescinding the enrollment), and even after the bill has been sent to the President (in which case it would request the President to return the bill and then rescind its enrollment), but these are relatively rare.

▶ 30.13 Committee prints

Before leaving the subject of legislative vehicles, it may be worthwhile to mention briefly the committee print, which is a totally informal and unofficial relative of a bill.

When a legislative committee (or a subcommittee or conference committee) is considering major legislation, it is fre-

H. CON. RES. 392

To correct technical errors in the enrollment of the bill H.R. 4653.

IN THE HOUSE OF REPRESENTATIVES

OCTOBER 26, 1990

Mr. FASCELL submitted the following concurrent resolution; which was considered and agreed to

---

CONCURRENT RESOLUTION

To correct technical errors in the enrollment of the bill H.R. 4653.

1   *Resolved by the House of Representatives (the Senate*

2   *concurring),* That, in the enrollment of the bill (H.R. 4653)

3   to reauthorize the Export Administration Act of 1979, and

4   for other purposes, the Clerk of the House of Representatives

5   shall make the following corrections:

6   (1) In the proposed subparagraph (C) of section

7   5(a)(4) of the Export Administration Act of 1979 (as

8   contained in section 103(2) of the bill), strike "re-

9   export" and insert "reexport".

10   (2) In the proposed subparagraph (D)(i) of section

11   5(a)(4) of the Export Administration Act of 1979 (as

▶ **Figure 30.12 House Concurrent Resolution to Correct Enrollment, Beginning and End**
(continued on next page)

★ ★ ★

1   (31) In section 442(e)(2) of the bill, strike "license

2   issued" and insert "license was issued".

3   (32) In section 523(c)(1) of the bill, strike "date of

4   enactment" and insert "date of the enactment".

5   (33) In section 523(d)(1) of the bill, insert a

6   comma after "in lieu of".

7   (34) In section 525 of the bill—

8   (A) in paragraph (1), strike "date of enact-

9   ment" and insert "date of the enactment"; and

10   (B) in paragraph (2), strike "date of enact-

11   ment" and insert "date of the enactment".

12   (35) In section 602(a) of the bill, strike "date of

13   enactment" and insert "date of the enactment".

14   (36) In section 602(b) of the bill, strike "date of

15   enactment" and insert "date of the enactment".

▶ Figure 30.12 (continued)

quently necessary to go through successive revisions over a
period of many days, weeks, or even months. Sometimes the
various proposals involved can be handled individually, and
then all put together at the last minute; but just as often the
provisions are too interrelated for that, and the drafters and
technicians (not to mention the committee members themselves) simply can't keep track of where they are at any
particular time without an up-to-date revised version of the
entire package to work with.

And sometimes a committee wants to junk the bill it started with and begin again from scratch, or is simply considering ideas before any bill at all has been introduced.

In these cases the most effective way to operate is to work from an informal draft (or a series of successive drafts) that incorporates all prior decisions (both final and tentative) as of any given time. The most efficient device for this purpose is the "committee print" in bill form, which can be printed overnight by the Government Printing Office to reflect the most recent changes in the product, and which looks exactly like a bill but is normally headed "COMMITTEE PRINT" (with a number and date when necessary to indicate its place in the series).

The bill that resulted in the medicare law in 1965, for example, required some 40 successive committee prints, running to several hundred pages each, over a three-month period; they were the documents actually considered by the Committee on Ways and Means in its deliberations. The Congressional Budget Act in 1974 required nearly as many. And most major bills go through several committee prints before the committee involved is ready to give its final approval to the legislation.

The point is mentioned here because committee prints often develop a life of their own—these totally unofficial documents, rather than the basic bills to which they relate, become the documents that are discussed, quoted, and argued about during the legislative process and even thereafter. Proposals are incorporated into them, debated, and then eliminated, only to reappear in later versions. To the drafter (and to anyone else who is interested in following the progress of the legislation involved) they can be the most important legislative vehicles in the whole process during most of the preenactment life of the legislation.

Note that some of the more ambitious committees like to prepare comparative prints to use when considering important legislation. These committee prints show for comparative purposes both the bill being considered and some other legislative document—either the existing law that the bill amends or another bill that incorporates a different approach to the same problem. The two documents may be shown in side-by-side columns, or they may be made into a single composite that reveals the similarities and differences by variations in typography. Conference committees use comparative prints regularly (the two documents in this case being the House bill and the Senate amendments or vice versa).

If you are working with one or more pieces of a major bill that is being considered or developed in a committee, you should expect to find that the versions of the bill you most often need to see are the unofficial committee prints. In many cases these prints are readily available to any legitimately interested person who can arrange to be present when they are being distributed and will just take the trouble to ask for one.

▶ **30.14 Tracking a bill through Congress**

There are a number of reasons why you might want to follow the course of a bill as it moves through the legislative process. You may be asked to work on it (or write amendments to it), so you need to keep abreast of its progress. Or you may want to follow it just because you are interested in what it does, particularly if it falls within an area in which you regularly work. And sometimes the progress of a related bill already under consideration will determine how you should draft your own.

It is the purpose of 30.14 to help you track a bill through Congress, and to indicate some of the information sources that may be available to you for this purpose.

The two tracking objectives. Most people who want to follow a bill through the legislative process are primarily interested in knowing when and where the various steps in the process will be taken, so they can be there to watch or just because they are interested in the legislation. This might be called "schedule" tracking, and may be either prospective (to discover where a bill is going) or retrospective (to learn where the bill has been).

But as a drafter you will need more than just dates, times, room numbers, summaries, and publicity handouts. Especially if you are (or expect to be) personally involved with the drafting of the bill or amendments to it, you will need literal copies of the bill in each of its forms (plus supporting documents) in addition to the schedule. The quest for these things, which might be called "substantive" tracking, is more difficult than the other—it requires pieces of paper that you can hold in your hand, not just general information.

The basic information sources. If you are "on the scene" and have congenial contacts all over Capitol Hill, you should normally have no problem in finding out what you need to know; but otherwise you must turn to whatever published information sources are available. Most of the latter are more useful for schedule tracking than for substantive tracking, and are better at telling you what has happened than at projecting future activities, but they can be helpful nonetheless. Among the most important are these:

1. **The *Congressional Record.*** This is the all-purpose information source, published daily while Congress is in session. It is widely available, and anyone can subscribe to it. Among many other things it includes each day—

A. a list of all bills introduced or reported in each body;

B. the full text of all bills taken up on the floor and of any amendments offered to those bills;

C. the full text of all conference reports;

D. a list of projected committee meetings; and

E. a Daily Digest, summarizing what has happened that day and indicating what is expected to happen on the next.

The *Record* is useful for substantive tracking as well as schedule tracking, subject to the caveat (discussed earlier) that you cannot rely on it for the niceties of form and style because of its format and typography (and, regrettably, because its overnight printing tends to result in typographical errors).

2. **The Calendars.**   The House and Senate each publish an official Calendar, which is brought up to date once a week. The Calendar lists every bill of the current Congress on which any postintroduction action has been taken and gives its legislative history to date, identifies all bills that are scheduled for conference, in conference, or through conference, and contains a great deal of other information of various kinds.

The Calendars are easier to use than the *Record* but are less current and less accessible for most people. And since they do not show the text of any bill or amendment, their use is largely limited to schedule tracking.

(Most committees publish their own calendars, which vary widely in their quality, coverage, and currency.)

3. **Looseleaf services.**   There are several companies that publish looseleaf volumes (some general and some limited to particular fields) expressly aimed at helping people

track bills through Congress. They are updated regularly and are very complete, although they rarely show any actual bill text. The *Congressional Index* (put out by Commerce Clearing House), for example, lists all introduced bills and resolutions with complete legislative histories along with other information such as committee memberships, hearings, voting records, and companion bills.

4. **Broader nongovernmental services.** There are several publicly oriented organizations that provide across-the-board tracking services. Probably the best of them is Congressional Quarterly, which puts out a number of different publications and newsletters aimed at helping its subscribers understand and follow congressional activities. These include the *Congressional Monitor* (which is published both daily and weekly, covers everything from projected committee hearings to floor action, and includes a telephone service to provide last-minute information), and *Congress in Print* (which is designed to help you get the congressional documents you need while they are still available).

5. **Electronic services.** Up-to-date information about the status and projected schedules of bills in Congress is provided electronically by LEGIS (through the Members' Information Network in the House) and by LOCIS (Scorpio) in the Senate through the Library of Congress. LEGIS is available only to Members and committees of Congress and to Federal agencies that have subscribed to it (although it does make bill status information available to the public by telephone). The Library of Congress permits the public to come in and search LOCIS's legislative information file on its own computer terminals, and even provides training.

Congressional Quarterly's Washington Alert is a very good electronic service that offers continuously updated information on congressional schedules, legislative actions, and congressional documents, with a variety of databases to choose from. Commerce Clearing House's electronic legislative search system provides up-to-date information on everything that happens to a bill in Congress (and in all 50 State legislatures as well), as it happens, although it does not include projections or future schedules. And a number of other services of this kind, designed for use by individual agencies or for sale to private persons and firms generally, have recently become available or are in the process of development.

Two other publications deserve to be mentioned in this subdivision, not because they are tracking sources in the strict sense but because they are invaluable sources of background information that no tracker should be without:

The *Congressional Directory* is the best available (and only official) source of general information about who's who and what's what in Congress—the names, office locations, and telephone numbers of all the Congressmen, Senators, committees, and major congressional staff members (along with the corresponding information for all Federal agencies and their officers), the membership of all congressional committees, and a vast amount of other useful information (even including maps of the various levels in the Capitol building). It can be purchased from the Government Printing Office.

And the *U.S. Code Congressional & Administrative News* (a monthly publication of the West Publishing Company) not only gives you the text of all new laws as they are enacted, in the literal form in which they will appear in the Statutes at Large—it contains cumulative tables that show the Code classification of each provision of law enacted during the current Congress and all Code sections (both positive and nonpositive law) that are mentioned in or affected by those provisions, along with recently issued Executive orders, Presidential messages, Federal regulations, and Federal court rules.

All of the publications and services mentioned in this subdivision are useful, of course, but the most valuable information-gathering device for any particular tracking operation is still the old familiar telephone. When you need a time, place, or schedule there is almost always someone, somewhere, who knows it and will be happy to tell you if you ask; and when you need a document there is always someone who has copies and will usually be willing to give you one, let you reproduce it, or tell you how to get a copy of your own. Crucial legislative events happen fast and schedules are always subject to change—often with little or no notice—and despite the yeoman efforts of the publishers, if you rely exclusively on the listed publications and services you risk being left at the starting gate. Make it your business to know whom to call, and arrange your contacts in advance if you can.

Tracking at different stages of the process. Needless to say, your ability to track a bill in Congress effectively (and the usefulness of the various information sources) will vary widely from stage to stage of the legislative process. In addition, special circumstances at any stage can sometimes make the task easy when it would normally be hard, and hard when it would normally be easy. The following offers a few brief comments about what your expectations should be at each stage.

Until a bill is introduced there is of course no way of knowing precisely what will be in it, or even (unless you somehow learn about the sponsor's plans in advance) of knowing that something worth inquiring about is going to surface. If you need to see the literal text of the bill or obtain a copy—and as a drafter you should never rely on anything else to tell you what it contains—you may have to wait a few days until the printed bill is available. The latter may be obtained from the House and Senate document rooms, from the committee to which the bill was referred, from the sponsor's office, or from GPO's Superintendent of Documents.

Any of the listed information sources can tell you about the beginning and end of the committee stage—that is, when a bill has been introduced and referred to a committee and when it has been reported—but most of them leave the actual committee stage shrouded in mystery. The Congressional Quarterly does make a continuing effort to tell you what is going on in committee, and several sources (including the *Congressional Record*) do notify you of scheduled committee meetings.

And this is one stage at which personal observation is a real plus. Almost all committee meetings are open to the public; and if you can afford the time and are a good notes-taker you should try to be on the scene when the committee is "marking up" the bill; you will understand better what is happening, and can often get copies of amendments and committee prints that will be hard to find later.

The committee stage really includes two separate stages— subcommittee and full committee. Tracking is often difficult when a bill is at the subcommittee stage, because the scheduling is more "iffy" and because the actions taken (being often informal and tentative) are less widely reported and sometimes harder to pin down. And you should remember that there are two separate staffs involved; when the bill in which you are interested is in subcommittee, it is the subcommittee staff that you should contact—the full committee staff is often not even aware of what the subcommittee is doing.

Committee hearings (though they may be of great interest to casual observers) are of little value to a drafter; professional drafters rarely go to them. You should concentrate on the committee markup sessions, which are where the action is; all of the committee's legislative and scheduling decisions are made in those sessions.

When a bill has been reported from committee it is placed on the appropriate Calendar, where it sits quietly until the leadership decides what to do with it and when. During this period plans are being made, of course, but no new information about it is likely to become available until Members begin to publicize their proposed amendments. And in most cases you cannot really be sure when the bill will be taken up on the floor until the weekly whip notice scheduling it comes out.

In the House the first concrete action on the floor is the adoption of the "rule" on the bill (see 32.3), which normally happens just before the bill is called up. You are not likely to have any interest in this except as an indication that the real floor action will soon begin (although bargains struck in the Rules Committee as a condition of its clearance can occasionally require some redrafting of the bill or the drafting of some agreed-upon amendments to be offered on the floor). The Senate has no corresponding step.

Several of the listed sources manage to keep their subscribers in touch with what is happening on the floor and what is expected to happen there, and provide summaries of the amendments offered—a few also provide the literal text of any amendments adopted. But for most people the best source is still the *Congressional Record,* which provides a verbatim transcript of the proceedings including the complete text of the bill and of all amendments offered (with a summary in the *Daily Digest*). Personal observation from the House or Senate galleries, though an occasionally pleasant spectator sport, is not likely to be of any value to you as a drafter or tracker.

As indicated earlier, the committee and floor stages in the second House are substantially the same as those in the first, although they may vary in their procedural details; and the information sources available to the tracker are also the same.

Sometimes, of course, the second House passes its own version of the bill (with its own number) rather than amending the first House's bill; parallel bills of this kind can help to get some of the early spadework done but they cannot produce a law, since sooner or later one House must take up and pass the other's bill or the process dies.

Sometimes, when the second House approves the first House's bill with changes, the easiest way to resolve the differences is to do so directly, by amendments offered on the floor of one or both Houses. Unfortunately, the compromise is usually worked out by informal negotiations between the leadership and relevant committee chairmen of the two Houses, and the floor actions necessary to adopt it are just "fitted in" where convenient. In most cases there is simply no way of learning from published sources just what is in the offing and when it will happen.

(You should check the proceedings in the *Congressional Record* each morning after the process starts; in a situation like this the majority leader in each House is often called upon by Members—usually toward the close of the day's session—to explain what is being planned for the next day, and he always responds if he knows the answer.)

Normally, however, when the House and Senate, after passing a major bill in different forms, have reached the "stage of disagreement" (a complicated parliamentary concept describing the point at which it becomes clear that the disputes cannot be settled directly as described earlier), a committee of conference is appointed to work out the differences.

As noted earlier, the conference stage is the most critical stage in the whole process. Unfortunately, though, it is also the most difficult stage to keep up with. Conference committees have no rooms of their own and conferees have their regular duties to perform, so the meetings must often be held wherever vacant space can be found and whenever the conferees (or at least most of them) have some free time. This causes problems for the tracker.

Many conferences do meet at regularly scheduled times and in obvious places (such as the main committee room of the standing committee of the House or Senate most directly concerned); in such cases you would usually have advance notice. But it would be equally typical for a conference (after a few hasty phone calls to summon the conferees) to meet at 10 a.m. in the Capitol attic, recess until 1:15, and reconvene in one of the House or Senate lunchrooms (hoping that the tables will have been cleared by then); and even the conferees and their staffs have trouble keeping up with all of this.

And the negotiations in a conference committee invariably involve a lot of private conversations between conferees, and a lot of caucusing behind closed doors to work out offers and counteroffers, so that nobody knows what is happening. Your best bet is just to stay in touch with someone on the scene who is personally involved, remembering that even that individual may have no advance notice until a few minutes before the gavel falls.

Once the conference report is filed it will be printed in the next day's *Congressional Record,* whether or not the report itself is available. Here again there are difficulties; conference reports are "in order at any time" on the floor—they do not have to be scheduled in advance like a bill or resolution— and they are customarily "fitted in" among the bills that are scheduled. But there is really no more tracking to do, since a conference report is presented to each House on a take-it-or-leave-it basis, and once passed by both Houses is enrolled for the President to sign. This is not trackable; there is literally no way for you to find out just when the enrollment will occur. The only possible complication arises when a concurrent resolution making corrections in the enrollment (see 30.12) is needed; but resolutions of this kind are not trackable either, since they do not go through committee and are almost always adopted (before they are even printed) along with the conference report itself.

The signing of the bill by the President is a tracking stage in a sense, but when and how he does it is somewhat beyond the scope of this subdivision. Unless he chooses to do it with great pomp and ceremony, it is highly unlikely that you could discover the time and place, or that you would be interested in it anyway.

Federal Drafting Styles

▶ **31.1   Preliminary comments**

Although what you do before you put pen to paper is generally more important than what you do afterwards, this chapter will for many readers constitute the core of the book. After all, thinking about and analyzing a problem is a familiar operation for anyone, but actually writing a bill is not. And the mystery is compounded by the fact that there are several different drafting styles in concurrent use at the Federal level with many others, obviously, being employed at the State and local levels.

"Drafting style" is the term used to describe the external characteristics of legislative language, and has nothing to do (directly) with what that language does or how the bill as a whole is organized. Some styles may be better than others for various reasons, a fact that will be discussed more fully in the succeeding subdivisions; but any legislative proposal could be legitimately expressed in any one of the currently accepted styles. You have no choice and must follow one of these styles if your sponsor is a Congressman or Senator, of course, and you would be well advised to do the same when drafting Federal legislation for a noncongressional sponsor if you don't want some other drafter deciding how the final version should be written.

For these purposes, bills will be treated as stylistically divisible into three parts:

1. *Sections*—the basic building blocks of a bill. All bills have them.

2. *Inferior subdivisions*—the subsections, paragraphs, subparagraphs, clauses, and subclauses into which the sections are divided. Most sections have inferior subdivisions; and most of the differences between the various Federal drafting styles involve them.

3. *Senior components*—the broader divisions (titles, subtitles, chapters, subchapters, parts, and subparts) into which most major bills are broken down and of which the sections are a part.

The bulk of this chapter will be devoted to an examination of the basic section and its subdivisions in each of the four principal Federal drafting styles (31.2 through 31.5). In the case of each such style the examination focuses on the same characteristics (headings, designation, and indentation), discussing in detail the specifications for the style involved and either setting forth an example of a section written in that style or indicating what it would look like by a comparative reference to one of the other styles.

The discussion of the various ways in which senior components and superior headings are handled under the four Federal styles (along with a detailed tabular comparison) is reserved for 31.6, since the differences between them are largely trivial.

After addressing a few collateral considerations in 31.7, the chapter then concludes (in 31.8) with a comparison and critique of the four styles.

Note that amendments are not regarded as a special case, or treated separately. The vehicular portion of an amendatory provision in a bill is written in the same drafting style as the rest of the bill, while the amendment itself is written in the drafting style of the law being amended—the two are usually but not always the same—and the vehicular language always takes the same form (see chapters 15 and 16) regardless of the drafting style or styles otherwise involved.

And remember, as you consider the descriptions contained in this chapter, that a section or inferior subdivision consists of two or three separate parts—its heading (if it has one), its designation, and its text. Any unqualified reference to a "section", "subsection", or other inferior subdivision encompasses them all; so if you wish to address one without addressing the others you must be explicit about it.

Two other preliminary comments about this chapter:

1. Differences in drafting style are largely a matter of typography, and in describing drafting styles this chapter uses a number of typographical terms that are not found in everyday conversation. These terms were discussed in detail in chapter 28, and examples of some of their descriptive uses were given in chapter 20.

2. In discussing each of the four Federal drafting styles, the example or comparative reference is given first to indicate how the style involved actually looks, and a statement of the detailed specifications for that style follows. To help you compare the four styles, the same section is used in each example; it is based on section 3121(u) of the Internal Revenue Code of 1986, which has however been rearranged, paraphrased, and shortened in order to focus on the purely stylistic aspects.

▶ **31.2 The traditional or classic style**

More existing statutes are written in the traditional style than in any other, largely because they were originally enacted before the other three styles came into widespread use (and their more recent amendments, under the Roman rule, have had to be written consistently). This style is the least demanding of all the accepted Federal styles, in that it has the fewest arbitrary technical requirements. Many of the older Members and longtime staff assistants still feel vaguely uneasy with any other style.

See page 402 for an example of a section written in the traditional style.

Headings. Section headings are optional in the traditional style (subject to the Roman rule), but are desirable for the reasons given in 20.5. If a heading is included it is centered, appears on a line of its own, and is printed in regular (lightface) small caps.

The inferior subdivisions are not usually given headings. The occasional subsection heading is centered on a line of its own, and printed in regular (lightface) caps and lowercase letters (with only the key words capitalized).

Designations. The section designation ("Sec. 123.", for example) is paragraphed on the first line of the text (the line immediately below the section heading if there is one), and is

MEDICARE COVERAGE OF GOVERNMENT EMPLOYEES

S<small>EC</small>. 123.(a) For purposes of chapter 21 of the Internal Revenue Code of 1986, the term "medicare qualified government employment" means service which—

(1) is employment (as defined in that chapter) with the application of subsection (b), but

(2) would not be employment (as so defined) without the application of that subsection.

(b)(1) For purposes of the taxes imposed by sections 3101(b) and 3111(b) of such Code, section 3121(b) of such Code shall be applied without regard to paragraph (5) thereof.

(2) For purposes of such taxes—

(A) except as provided in subparagraph (B), section 3121(b) of such Code shall be applied without regard to paragraph (7) thereof; and

(B) service shall not be treated as employment by reason of subparagraph (A) if—

(i) it is included under an agreement under section 218 of the Social Security Act, or

(ii) it is performed by an individual who is employed by a State or political subdivision to relieve him from unemployment.

set in caps and small caps—that is, the "S" is a large cap and the remaining letters are small caps. The section number is always an arabic numeral. The text itself begins immediately after the designation and is run in—it is not dropped down to the next line.

The designation of the inferior subdivisions follows the standard practice (see 20.3), with each such designation consisting simply of a letter or number enclosed in parentheses—"(a)" for a subsection, "(1)" for a paragraph, "(A)" for a subparagraph, "(i)" for a clause, and "(I)" for a subclause—and being followed immediately by the first word of the subdivision's text.

When a section is broken down into subsections, the designation of the first subsection ("(a)") is run in immediately after the section designation, not dropped down onto a new line. And the same principle—that the designation of an inferior subdivision is treated as part of the text of its parent and run in immediately after the parent's designation—applies when a subsection is broken down into paragraphs (or when any other inferior subdivision is further broken down). Note the designations "Sec. 123.(a)" and "(b)(1)" in the example.

Indentation. Inferior subdivisions are set full measure, just as the matter involved would be if the section had not been subdivided at all; each is paragraphed and given a designation, but it is not cut in (indented as a whole). Thus every section, except for its heading, its first line, and the first lines of its various paragraphed components, is set flush to the left-hand margin in its entirety, no matter how extensively it is broken down and subdivided.

And this applies to the paragraphed components within sections—the subsections, paragraphs, and paragraphed clauses—as well as to the sections themselves. But it does not apply, of course, to paragraphed components that are parts of a tabulated list or series or a tabulated sentence (see 23.4 and 23.5)—these are always cut in two ems more than their lead-in language—or to run-in clauses.

▶ **31.3   United States Code style**

As its name suggests, this style originated with the compilers of the United States Code, and is the style used in all the titles of the Code (both positive law and nonpositive law). It is not—currently at least—a bill-drafting style, since bills are always written in one of the other styles; even in a bill that consists of nothing but amendments to the Code, the vehicular language and overall format is traditional, revenue, or modified revenue in style, and only the amendments themselves reflect the Code style.

But Code style deserves an equal place among the accepted Federal drafting styles for two reasons. First, a substantial part of the Federal law is already embodied in positive-law titles of the United States Code, and the drafting of amendments to the Code has become a significant part of every drafter's work. Second, there is a good chance that the Law Revision Counsel's objective of converting all of the Federal statutory law into positive-law titles of the Code will be successfully achieved at some time in the future, and if and when that happens it is quite possible that Code style will become the only style, even for vehicular language and for freestanding bills.

The full example will not be repeated here, and it is not necessary to go through the detailed specifications again, because Code style is exactly the same as traditional style in all respects but two:

1. Every section must have a heading, which appears on a line of its own but (A) is set flush to the left-hand margin rather than being centered, (B) is printed in boldface lowercase letters with only the first word capitalized, and (C) is combined with the section designation, which uses a boldface "twist mark" before the arabic numeral instead of "SEC." or "SECTION". (Thus when the section is broken down into subsections, the designation of the first subsection ("(a)") cannot be run in immediately after the section designation as in the traditional style but appears instead on the next line at the beginning of the text.)

2. As in traditional style, subsection headings are seldom used; but when they are used they are run in between the subsection designation and the first word of the text, and printed in lightface caps and small caps followed by a period and a dash, as in revenue style (see 31.4). Subdivisions below the subsection level are never given headings.

If the example given in 31.2 were written in Code style instead of traditional style, its first few lines would read as follows:

---

§ 123. Medicare coverage of government employees

(a) For purposes of chapter 21 of the Internal Revenue Code of 1986. . .

---

but there would be no other differences.

▶ **31.4   Revenue style**

As its name suggests, "revenue" style is the style in which the tax laws of the United States (the Internal Revenue Code of 1986 and its predecessors) have been written for many years. It is a very disciplined style, and without question the most intricate and demanding of all the accepted Federal drafting styles. And with its mandatory use of headings for all subdivisions and its mandatory use of progressively increasing indentations below the section level, it is very different from the traditional and United States Code styles.

The example below sets forth the section shown in 31.2 as it would be written in revenue style (which of course is the style in which it was originally written). Note especially the headings and indentations.

Headings. Every revenue-style section has a heading, which is set flush to the left-hand margin rather than being centered,

---

SEC. 123. MEDICARE COVERAGE OF GOVERNMENT EMPLOYEES.

(a) MEDICARE QUALIFIED GOVERNMENT EMPLOYMENT DEFINED.—For purposes of chapter 21 of the Internal Revenue Code of 1986, the term "medicare qualified government employment" means service which—

(1) is employment (as defined in that chapter) with the application of subsection (b), but

(2) would not be employment (as so defined) without the application of that subsection.

(b) APPLICATION OF HOSPITAL INSURANCE TAX TO FEDERAL, STATE, AND LOCAL EMPLOYMENT.—

(1) FEDERAL EMPLOYMENT.—For purposes of the taxes imposed by sections 3101(b) and 3111(b) of such Code, section 3121(b) of such Code shall be applied without regard to paragraph (5) thereof.

(2) STATE AND LOCAL EMPLOYMENT.—For purposes of such taxes—

(A) IN GENERAL.—Except as provided in subparagraph (B), section 3121(b) of such Code shall be applied without regard to paragraph (7) thereof.

(B) EXCEPTION FOR CERTAIN SERVICES.—Service shall not be treated as employment by reason of subparagraph (A) if—

(i) it is included under an agreement under section 218 of the Social Security Act, or

(ii) it is performed by an individual who is employed by a State or political subdivision to relieve him from unemployment.

---

appears on a line of its own in combination with the section designation, and is printed in boldface 10-point caps with a period at the end.

All inferior subdivisions also have headings, no matter how far down the scale you go—subsections, paragraphs, subparagraphs, and paragraphed clauses and subclauses, except for those that are parts of a tabulated list or series or a tabulated sentence—although some drafters do violate the rule and omit them occasionally in the more trivial lower subdivisions. The mandatory use of headings for all inferior subdivisions is the first of the two major differences between revenue style and the others.

The heading of any inferior subdivision is "run in" between the subdivision's designation and the first word of its text. In the case of a subsection, it is printed in caps and small caps (with the former being used for the first letters of the key words), and in the case of a paragraph or other lower-level component it is printed entirely in small caps except for an initial large cap on the first word, followed immediately (in either case) by a period and a dash.

The dash leads directly into the text if the component involved is not further subdivided, but leads only into thin air if the component *is* further subdivided, because in revenue style—as explained below—each successive level of subdivision has to be "dropped down" and further indented.

Designations. As indicated in the preceding paragraph, the section designation in revenue style is printed in 10-point boldface caps and combined with the heading on a separate line, set flush to the left-hand margin.

The designation of the inferior subdivisions follows the standard practice (see 20.3), as in the other two styles, with each such designation consisting simply of a letter or number enclosed in parentheses—"(a)" for a subsection, "(1)" for a paragraph, "(A)" for a subparagraph, "(i)" for a clause, and "(I)" for a subclause—and being followed immediately by the heading.

If the section is not broken down into subsections, the text begins (paragraphed on the line just below the section heading) without a designation, as in the case of United States Code style.

But when a subsection is broken down into paragraphs (or any other inferior component is further broken down), the designation of the first such paragraph (or other lower-level component) is not treated as part of the text of its parent and run in immediately after the parent's designation as in the case of the other two styles. Instead, it is dropped down onto a new line (and indented two ems, or two additional ems); thus there can never be two designations juxtaposed in any component in revenue style. This produces the second major stylistic difference between revenue style and the others, and its discussion is continued in the following paragraphs.

Indentation. In revenue style, inferior subdivisions below the subsection level are progressively indented ("cut in") by multiples of two ems as you go down the scale; and none of the comments made about indentation in 31.2 and 31.3 will apply.

Thus all subsections are set full measure, all paragraphs are cut in two ems, all subparagraphs are cut in four ems, all clauses (other than run-in clauses) are cut in 6 ems, and so forth. And, of course, each of them has to be given a heading (see above).

The following sequence may serve to depict the progression more graphically:

SECTION 1. IMPOSITION AND RATE OF TAX.

(a) RATE OF TAX.—[subsection, full measure]

(1) IN GENERAL.—[paragraph, cut in 2 ems]

(A) SPECIAL RULES.—[subparagraph, cut in 4 ems]

(i) EXCEPTIONS.—[clause, cut in 6 ems]

(I) EFFECTIVE DATE.—[subclause, cut in 8 ems]

▶ **31.5   Modified revenue style**

In recent years there has been a concerted effort, spearheaded by the Legislative Counsel's Office in the House of Representatives, to come up with a uniform drafting style that incorporates the acknowledged virtues of revenue style without including what some people regard as its drawbacks (for these virtues and drawbacks see 31.8). The result is best described as "modified revenue style", which permits many of the characteristics of "full" revenue style to be either included or not included, at the drafter's option.

The full example will not be repeated here, and it is not necessary to go through the detailed specifications again, because modified revenue style is simply the old familiar revenue style (as described in 31.4) with three possible modifications:

> 1. Subsection headings are still required, but headings for the lower-level subdivisions—paragraphs, subparagraphs, clauses, and subclauses—are optional.

> 2. The lower-level subdivisions need not be progressively indented as in revenue style, but can be set full measure as in the traditional and Code styles so long as they are not given headings. If this were done, the first subdivision designation at any level would immediately follow the parent's designation (and heading if any).

> 3. The revenue-prescribed hierarchy of superior headings (which will be discussed in 31.6) can be modified as appropriate considering the nature and overall structure of the bill. For instance, the bill's titles could be set in 14-point caps and broken down into parts if 18-point caps and subtitles seem too ostentatious for the job at hand.

If the example set forth in 31.4 were written in modified revenue style rather than in "full" revenue style, it could conceivably differ in various ways—it might, for example, omit the paragraph and subparagraph headings in subsection (b) (and run in paragraph (1) immediately after the subsection heading)—but all the other specifications for full revenue style would apply. (For what it is worth, the author's personal preference would be to stay with full revenue style, since none of the extremes of that style—see 31.8—are present in the example.)

Whether you should adopt any of the modifications described in this subdivision or just go with straight revenue style is a matter of judgment, depending upon the size, scope, and nature of the bill and the context in which you are working. But if you do choose to adopt one of them in writing a particular bill you should use it consistently.

▶ **31.6**   **Superior headings**

When a bill is broken down into senior components—titles, subtitles, parts, subparts, chapters, or subchapters—their headings are always centered, and set in various combinations of different-sized lightface or boldface caps, small caps, and lowercase letters so as to distinguish them from each other and from the section headings.

Each of the four accepted Federal drafting styles has its own hierarchy of senior components, with its own typefaces and its own system of designation and headings. Fortunately, however, the four hierarchies are very similar, and can be thought of as simply four variations of a single standard arrangement. The designations and headings reflect a mixture of roman numerals, arabic numerals, and capital letters, and the typefaces often differ (revenue style uses only boldface type while the others use lightface (with a few exceptions), and revenue style ranks chapters above parts while the others do not). And except for title and subtitle headings (18-point) and section headings (10-point) in revenue style, and section headings (12-point) in United States Code style, all superior headings (like inferior headings and bill text) are set in 14-point type.

In revenue style the established system for naming and designating senior components, and for setting their headings in type, is faithfully and consistently followed. And in modified revenue style the revenue-style system for senior components is faithfully followed unless a specific modification is consciously adopted.

In the traditional style, however, the prescribed system is honored more in the breach than in the observance. The first breakdown of a bill into senior components is always into titles, of course; but if a further breakdown is necessary there is very little discernible consistency in actual practice (see chapter 20).

And in United States Code style (which otherwise faithfully follows its prescribed system) there are a couple of special considerations:

1. The chapter is the basic senior component in the Code, and every title is broken down into chapters even if that means omitting several of the intermediate levels that are otherwise prescribed.

2. At several levels of senior components in the Code there is a choice or potential choice between using roman numerals or capital letters as designations. This choice in any given case is distributive—it depends upon what other senior components are included in the title involved and what form of designation is available taking into account the needs of those components. Accordingly, you should always look first at the particular title you are proposing to amend, and follow its style.

Table 31.6 shows in tabular form the accepted hierarchies of

▶ Table 31.6 Superior Headings

Traditional Style	U.S. Code Style	Revenue Style
Title I, II, III . . . 14-pt caps	**Title** 1, 2, 3 . . . 14-pt caps	**Title** I, II, III . . . 18-pt bf caps
Subtitle A, B, C . . . 14-pt c+lc	**Subtitle** I, II, III . . . (or A, B, C . . .) 14-pt c+lc	**Subtitle** A, B, C . . . 18-pt bf c+lc
Part 1, 2, 3 . . . 14-pt c+sc	**Part** I, II, III . . . 14-pt c+sc	**Chapter** 1, 2, 3 . . . 14-pt bf caps
Subpart A, B, C . . . 14-pt c+lc	**Subpart** A, B, C . . . 14-pt c+lc	**Subchapter** A, B, C . . . 14-pt bf c+lc
Chapter 1, 2, 3 . . . 14-pt bf caps	**Chapter** 1, 2, 3 . . . 14-pt bf caps	**Part** I, II, III . . . 14-pt bf caps
Subchapter I, II, III . . . 14-pt caps	**Subchapter** I, II, III . . . 14-pt caps	**Subpart** A, B, C . . . 14-pt bf c+lc
Section 1, 2, 3 . . . 14-pt sc ctr	**Section** 1, 2, 3 . . . 12-pt bf lc fl	**Section** 1, 2, 3 . . . 10-pt bf caps fl
Subsection (a), (b) . . . 14-pt c+lc ctr	**Subsection** (a), (b) . . . 14-pt c+sc run-in	**Subsection** (a), (b) . . . 14-pt c+sc run-in
		Par., etc. (1), (2) 14-pt sc run-in

all the components under the various Federal drafting styles (with modified revenue style being treated as a part of revenue style for this purpose), along with their designations and the kinds of type in which they are set. Figure 31.6 gives literal examples of the superior headings in each drafting style as they would appear in a bill.

▶ ## 31.7   Maverick styles

It should come as no surprise that sometimes bills are drafted and introduced (and even enacted) in a style that bears little resemblance to any of the four Federal styles discussed in this chapter. This can happen in several ways.

There are cases in which whoever drafted the bill paid no attention to style at all, and simply wrote down the ideas as

Traditional style

TITLE II—TITLE HEAD

Subtitle A—Subtitle Head

PART 3—PART HEAD

Subpart A—Subpart Head

CHAPTER 2—CHAPTER HEAD

SUBCHAPTER II—SUBCHAPTER HEAD

United States Code style

''TITLE 10—TITLE HEAD

''Subtitle II—Subtitle Head

''PART II—PART HEAD

''Subpart A—Subpart Head

''CHAPTER 2—CHAPTER HEAD

''SUBCHAPTER II—SUBCHAPTER HEAD

Revenue (and modified revenue) style

TITLE II—TITLE HEAD

Subtitle A—Subtitle Head

CHAPTER 2—CHAPTER HEAD

Subchapter A—Subchapter Head

PART II—PART HEAD

Subpart A—Subpart Head

▶Figure 31.6 Literal Examples of Superior Headings

they surfaced without regard to form or arrangement, as if taking notes at a lecture. This is inexcusable, of course, but seldom has any permanent bad effect. It most often happens when a Member introduces a constituent's draft without having had it reviewed by an experienced drafter; and if it were actually taken seriously it would be reviewed.

There are cases in which the drafter clearly paid a great deal of attention to style, but elected for some reason to invent and use unusual stylistic features. In the Atomic Energy Acts of 1946 and 1954, for example, the subsection and paragraph designations were not enclosed in parentheses but each included a period—thus "a." or "1." instead of the more familiar "(a)" or "(1)"—which was perhaps tolerable in the designations themselves but a disaster in the cross-references (since it resulted in periods being scattered about in the middle of sentences). The author has no idea why it was done this way; but it may be significant that the Joint Committee on Atomic Energy never used on-the-scene drafters (except as after-the-fact editors, when it was too late to make sweeping stylistic changes) since they never seemed to have the required security clearance.

And there are cases in which the drafter followed one of the accepted styles but incorporated into it one or more features of another style. The Congressional Budget Act of 1974, for example, was written in the traditional style, but included revenue-style subsection headings; this happened because the desirability of the headings did not occur to the committees' professional staffs (or the drafter) until too late in the game for a general stylistic overhaul. There is nothing really wrong with this kind of stylistic combination (although it would have been better if the bill had been written in revenue or modified revenue style in the first place).

A similar case arises when a major block of new material being added at the end of an existing law is considered sufficiently separate from the rest of that law to justify the use by the drafter of a different style despite the apparent violation of the Roman rule. This would produce a stylistic combination that is sequential rather than interwoven. Continuing the example given in the preceding paragraph, when two new titles were added to the Congressional Budget Act in 1990 they were drafted in full revenue style despite the fact that the existing titles of that Act were written in (slightly modified) traditional style.

One final comment: As mentioned earlier (12.12), the most

common (and most important) example of a major bill that uses a maverick style is the typical general appropriation bill, which is sometimes described by uncharitable persons as having no style at all. It has some superior headings (which are not used consistently, and follow no consistent typographical pattern even when they are), but the bulk of it—everything except the miscellaneous provisions that appear toward the end of the bill—does not even have section numbers. Such bills are exhausting to read and almost impossible to find anything in. Fortunately, it is unlikely that you will ever have to work on one.

▶ **31.8   Comparison and critique**

If you have a choice, which of the four styles should you use?

Again, there is nothing really wrong with any of the four styles; a perfectly good statute can be constructed out of any of them, and their purely typographical differences are largely trivial.

The differences that matter have to do with the way in which the various elements of a bill's sections are set apart from each other and their place in the hierarchy of ideas identified. On the basis of these differences (to jump the gun a bit), it is the author's judgment that

1. revenue style and modified revenue style should be preferred over the traditional and United States Code styles, other things being equal; and

2. modified revenue style has advantages over straight revenue style because it is more flexible and usually more readable.

The traditional and Code styles are relatively bland; the inferior subdivisions are set apart from each other only by their designations, and they are otherwise written as a more or less continuous narrative in the style of everyday prose composition. There are very few technicalities to learn.

Revenue style, on the other hand, makes extensive use of technical devices such as headings and indentations to set the inferior subdivisions apart from each other and indicate their place in the hierarchy. As indicated earlier, these devices (along with the more typographically prominent section headings) not only help you as a drafter to organize your thoughts, to unearth gaps, overlaps, and other problems, and in general to handle complicated assignments efficiently—

they also help sponsors and staffs to find their way through the maze. And the slight additional effort needed to master them is well worth it even if you will be normally using another style.

Modified revenue style has all the virtues of straight revenue style, without some of its faults:

> 1. The headings required by straight revenue style for all inferior subdivisions of a section are sometimes counter-productive in the case of the lower-level components. A heading for a two-line clause that simply clarifies some minor point made in the preceding provisions of its parent subparagraph, for example, often appears artificially technical and can make the subparagraph harder rather than easier to read and comprehend. Modified revenue style allows such headings to be omitted when the parent provision can best be read smoothly as a unified whole—without the distracting pauses that result from the too many minor headings.

> 2. The progressive indentation required by straight revenue style for lower-level subdivisions is sometimes counterproductive for the same reasons. A section containing several levels of inferior subdivisions can have a very odd appearance; a page from a tax bill can often be recognized from clear across the room by the large amount of empty space it contains (which may explain the fervor with which tax drafters claim to abhor clauses and subclauses even while using them liberally). Modified revenue style allows the lower-level subdivisions to be set full measure, as in the traditional or Code style, when that will make the overall text read more naturally.

To paraphrase *HOLC* (page 9), modified revenue style provides you with more options and flexibility than any other, with the widest range and variety of drafting tools and conventions. On the one hand it can be used full-bore (straight revenue style) to promote the clear expression of complex policies, and on the other it can be applied in a limited way (modified style) in the expression of less complex policies.

Modified revenue style quickly became the style of choice in the two Legislative Counsel's Offices following its introduction in the late 1980s. It is only fair to mention, however, that both Offices (after an initial burst of enthusiasm) are today tending more and more to ignore the optional modifications and stay with straight revenue style.

At any rate, you should know how to use any of the four accepted styles when the occasion calls for it. And when there is no reason (Roman rule or otherwise) to choose one style over the others, you should use the one you are most comfortable with. But if you like to "go with the flow," you should use the revenue and modified revenue styles, which are without question the Federal drafting styles of the future.

Federal Parliamentary Considerations

▶ **32.1 Preliminary comments**

Parliamentary pitfalls abound in every legislative setting. You cannot wish them out of existence, of course, and you cannot control what other people do with your product after you have turned it loose; but you are not doing your job unless you consciously do everything you can to avoid them. Many a beautifully drafted bill comes to naught because the drafter was unaware of (or just plain forgot) some parliamentary obstacle that could have been circumvented or some parliamentary requirement that could have been met.

This does not mean, however, that you should try (or expect) to become a full-blown parliamentarian. In the first place, every legislature has one of those, whose word is law on parliamentary points and whose rulings may be technically appealable but as a practical matter are almost never successfully challenged. And in the second place it would be a futile effort; the subject is so broad and complicated that only a person who has studied it full-time over a period of many years could claim real expertise.

What it does mean is that you must always be aware of the potential for such problems. You should know and understand the most common ones, and should know where to go for information on the others. And you must always warn the sponsor of any parliamentary problems you can foresee. Sponsors can usually live with losing on the merits, but are understandably piqued when their proposals are unexpectedly shot down on technicalities.

The restrictions and prohibitions that parliamentary requirements impose come primarily from three sources (in addition to the ad hoc rules that apply in particular cases—see 32.3):

1. The published rules of the legislative body involved (the Rules of the House of Representatives and the Standing Rules of the Senate, at the Federal level). Note that *Jefferson's Manual,* dating from 1797, still governs the House to the extent not inconsistent with the regular rules, and is printed in the same volume as the House Rules. These rules may be either substantive (flatly prohibiting the consideration of certain kinds of bills) or procedural (limiting the circumstances under which certain kinds of bills may be considered).

2. Statutes (such as the Congressional Budget Act and the Emergency Deficit Control Act, which contain many similar prohibitions and limitations). Note that the procedural provisions of these statutes are treated as rules of the two Houses (see 12.13) even when they are not cast in that form.

3. The precedents of the legislative body involved—that is, the sum total of all the rulings made and interpretations given over the years by its parliamentarians. In theory these are nothing but explanations of what the rules mean, but they "fill in the chinks" in cases where the application of the rules is not clear, and the chinks are often large enough to give the precedents a very important life of their own.

Of course, parliamentary rulings and interpretations are actually made by the presiding officer of the House involved—not by the parliamentarian—but the presiding officer always acts on the basis of the parliamentarian's recommendations if the case is clear-cut, and relies on the parliamentarian's advice when there are conflicting precedents and strategic reasons might dictate choosing one over the other.

Compliance with parliamentary requirements is usually enforced through parliamentary means. That is, the rule involved simply says that "it shall not be in order" to consider a bill or take a specified action if the requirement has not been complied with; any single Member, however deeply imbedded in the minority, can defeat that bill or prevent that action by simply raising a point of order against it. When a more direct form is used (as when the rule or statute says that "no bill [of a specified type] shall be considered unless. . ."), the proscription is absolute on its face, and the officials of the House involved—raising their own point of order, as it were—have been known to apply it without waiting to see whether anyone else has an objection.

It may be true (as you are doubtless well aware) that almost any parliamentary requirement can be waived by unanimous consent, and that possible points of order are sometimes overlooked (or voluntarily withheld for one reason or another). But such things are totally unpredictable, and you should never proceed on the assumption that they will happen.

This chapter makes no pretense of being exhaustive; it merely endeavors to alert you to the kinds of parliamentary proscriptions that bear upon what a drafter does at the Federal level, and to familiarize you with some of the most commonly arising requirements. It uses the House of Representatives as its model because the House (largely because of its 435 Members) must adhere much more strictly to parliamentary procedures than the Senate (with only 100 Members) in order to function effectively as a legislative body. However, the parliamentary rules in different legislative bodies resemble each other to a surprising extent.

▶ **32.2   Committee referral and jurisdiction**

Before 1975, introduced bills were referred to committees (in the House, at least) according to completely arbitrary standards, and every bill was referred to a single committee regardless of how many different subject matters were involved. Thus a Member serving on the Agriculture Committee could have a military construction bill exclusively referred to that committee, by simply casting it in the form of an amendment to an existing agricultural law or somehow attaching it to an agricultural bill already under consideration; the Armed Services Committee could usually block the bill's passage in that form, of course, but at least it gave the Member a friendly forum in which to express views and possibly to hold some hearings and exert a little pressure.

Irrational committee references of this kind are no longer possible. Bills today are referred to the committee or committees legitimately concerned with their subject matter, and you cannot avoid this. The relevant provision in the House Rules (clause 5 of Rule X), after specifically nullifying the old rules and precedents, provides as follows:

> (b) Every referral shall be made in such manner as to assure to the maximum extent feasible that each committee which has jurisdiction under clause 1 over the subject matter of any provision thereof will have responsibility for considering such provision and reporting to the House with respect thereto. . . .

> (c) In carrying out paragraphs (a) and (b) with respect to any matter, the Speaker may refer the matter simultaneously to two or more committees for concurrent consideration or for consideration in sequence (subject to appropriate time limitations in the case of any committee), or divide the matter into two or more parts (reflecting different subjects and jurisdictions) and refer each part to a different committee, or refer the matter to a special ad hoc committee . . . , or make such other provision as may be considered appropriate.

What this means is that if your sponsor wishes to have a bill referred to a particular committee, you must try to draft it in a way that clearly invokes an established jurisdictional basis of that committee (and you should always read the listing of that committee's jurisdiction in the Rules of the House involved before you begin drafting). Sometimes there is nothing you can do to influence a bill's referral. But the way you characterize the things you are doing, by the careful and repeated use of key jurisdictional words and phrases (taken from the Rules), can often get the desired result.

For example, if your sponsor is a member of the Committee on Science, Space, and Technology who wants to provide for the construction of scientific laboratories and have the bill considered by that committee, you might characterize the bill as one designed to promote "scientific research" (a subject exclusively within that committee's jurisdiction)—displaying that term prominently in the title and throughout the text and treating the actual construction of the laboratories (if you mention it at all) as more or less incidental. Emphasizing the construction aspect of the bill is likely to get it referred to another committee altogether, with a concurrent referral to the Science Committee the best you can hope for.

And if the sponsor would like to have the bill considered first by a particular subcommittee—each committee can divide its jurisdiction among whatever subcommittees it chooses to establish—you should draft the bill with similar emphasis on matters within the jurisdiction of that subcommittee.

The thing to remember is that if you include anything at all that impinges on the jurisdiction of another committee, the bill may also be referred (concurrently or sequentially) to that committee. If the impingement is minor or only technical, joint referral is usually made only when formally requested by the other committee; but if it is clear-cut and obviously significant (and there are quite a few areas in which two or more committees are expressly given joint jurisdiction by the Rules), the joint referral will be made automatically, at the time the bill is introduced. Joint referrals not only cause procedural complications in reporting and on the floor—they also invite obstruction of the primary objective on unrelated grounds.

Finally, it is worth mentioning that a number of committees have rules that bar the consideration of specified types of bills referred to them—usually to avoid discrimination or on the grounds that adequate administrative or judicial remedies are available. (The Rules of the House flatly prohibit even the introduction of private bills of several kinds.) It is the drafter's job to be aware of these obstacles and to warn the sponsor so that the sponsor will not unexpectedly run into a stone wall after having made promises to constituents.

▶ **32.3**   **Procedure generally (on the floor and in committee)**

Floor procedure.   The rules that determine how a bill is considered on the floor are numerous, often complicated, and occasionally obscure. Their details are beyond the scope of this book, and the parliamentarians of the House and Senate will not advise the public; so you should try to maintain contact with some person experienced in parliamentary procedure to whom you can turn when you need advice.

A few general comments about the usual floor procedure in the House of Representatives may be helpful, however. Bear in mind that variations are possible, and that the special ad hoc rule on the bill (see below) will normally determine many of the details.

When a typical bill is called up for consideration (after the adoption of the rule on the bill), the House resolves itself into the "Committee of the Whole House on the State of the

Union", which is chaired by a Member appointed by the Speaker. The bill then goes through three stages.

The first stage consists of general debate, in which Members are supposed to discuss the bill in general terms but which they often use to talk about the specific amendments they plan to offer later. The amount of time allowed for general debate (for and against the bill) is always specified in the rule; it can range from one hour to 50 hours.

Upon completion of general debate, the bill is read for amendment (the second stage). All amendments (except title and preambular amendments) are offered and dealt with in the Committee of the Whole, and their consideration is made easier because in that Committee it takes only 100 Members (instead of 218) to make a quorum. The bill is customarily read section by section or title by title, under the five-minute rule (which technically limits debate on each side of any amendment to five minutes but is easily circumvented by the use of pro forma amendments); once a particular section or title is finished it cannot be returned to. When all amendments have been acted on, the Committee reports the bill as amended to the full House and "rises"; and the Speaker resumes the chair.

The bill with its amendments is now "back in the House" (the third stage). After considering and acting on any amendments to the title or preamble, and usually one motion to recommit (see below), the House approves the bill; this constitutes final passage.

Several aspects of this procedure deserve special mention for their parliamentary implications:

1. **The "rule".** If you are interested in knowing how a particular bill is going to be handled on the floor, you should get a copy of the special ad hoc rule on that bill (usually just called the "rule" on the bill) or contact the Rules Committee to find out what it provides. Rules are public documents—ordinary simple House resolutions—but they spring full-blown from that committee without ever having been introduced and are often unavailable in advance.

The rule prescribes the floor procedure to be followed, and the bill cannot even be considered until it is adopted. It not only specifies the procedures that are to be followed (as described above and elsewhere)—it will frequently also waive or modify particular parliamentary requirements, making amendments possible when they would otherwise be forbidden by the House Rules or forbidding amendments that would otherwise be in order. Rules that forbid amendments altogether are called "closed rules", and those that permit only specified amendments are called "modified closed rules"; both are common in the tax area, and are occasionally found elsewhere. (There is nothing like this procedure in the Senate, where the corresponding determinations are typically made by leadership fiat or by unanimous consent.)

Some rules are short and simple, consisting almost entirely of boilerplate, while others are long and complicated—it depends on the nature of the legislation involved and on tactical considerations. Figure 32.3 is an example of one that falls somewhere in the middle.

Note that methods are available for discharging the Rules Committee and bringing to the floor a bill that is "bottled up" in that committee, but they very seldom work and are rarely even tried.

2. **Order of amendments.**   The order in which amendments to a given provision may be offered and considered, as discussed more fully in 32.4, can be tactically significant. It can prevent your amendment from being offered at all if your sponsor is not sufficiently alert; and (because it determines what other amendments your own will become entangled with) it materially affects the odds for success. Make sure you understand it.

3. **Recommittals.**   A motion to recommit usually represents the last gasp of the losing side—it has to be made by someone opposed to the bill—but it is sometimes a politically attractive alternative to a "no" vote on final passage (and often succeeds for that reason) because it can be viewed as a technical device that simply returns the bill to the committee from which it came (presumably for further consideration there) rather than actually killing it. Adopting a simple motion to recommit (without instructions) does effectively defeat the bill, and as a practical matter is equivalent to a "no" vote on final passage; but a motion to recommit with instructions sometimes has a better chance of success because it is selective about its targets—isolating and attacking the weakest links—and permits the bill (with those targets destroyed) to be passed immediately.

House Calendar No. 62

101ST CONGRESS
1ST SESSION

H. RES. 255

[Report No. 101–267]

Providing for the consideration of the bill (H.R. 1495) to amend the Arms Control and Disarmament Act to authorize appropriations for the Arms Control and Disarmament Agency, and for other purposes.

IN THE HOUSE OF REPRESENTATIVES

OCTOBER 3, 1989

Mr. DERRICK from the Committee on Rules, reported the following resolution; which was referred to the House Calendar and ordered to be printed

---

RESOLUTION

Providing for the consideration of the bill (H.R. 1495) to amend the Arms Control and Disarmament Act to authorize appropriations for the Arms Control and Disarmament Agency, and for other purposes.

1   *Resolved,* That at any time after the adoption of this

2   resolution the Speaker may, pursuant to clause 1(b) of rule

3   XXIII, declare the House resolved into the Committee of the

4   Whole House on the State of the Union for the consideration

5   of the bill (H.R. 1495) to amend the Arms Control and Dis-

6   armament Act to authorize appropriations for the Arms Con-

---

▶ Figure 32.3 "Special Rule" for Consideration of a Bill in the House
(continued on next page)

1 trol and Disarmament Agency, and for other purposes, and

2 the first reading of the bill shall be dispensed with. After

3 general debate, which shall be confined to the bill and which

4 shall not exceed one hour, with thirty minutes to be equally

5 divided and controlled by the chairman and ranking minority

6 member of the Committee on Foreign Affairs, and with thirty

7 minutes to be equally divided and controlled by the chairman

8 and ranking minority member of the Committee on Armed

9 Services, the bill shall be considered for amendment under

10 the five-minute rule by titles instead of by sections and each

11 title shall be considered as having been read. All points of

12 order against the bill for failure to comply with the provisions

13 of clause 5(a) of rule XXI are hereby waived. It shall be in

14 order to consider en bloc as amendments to title II the

15 amendments recommended by the Committee on Armed

16 Services now printed in the bill. At the conclusion of the

17 consideration of the bill for amendment, the Committee shall

18 rise and report the bill to the House with such amendments

19 as may have been adopted, and the previous question shall be

20 considered as ordered on the bill and amendments thereto to

21 final passage without intervening motion except one motion

22 to recommit.

▶ **Figure 32.3 (continued)**

The traditional form for a motion to recommit without instructions is as follows:

> Mr. [Ms.] _____ moves to recommit the bill (H.R. 1234) to the Committee on _____.

A motion to recommit with instructions simply adds a few words, followed by whatever amendments to the bill the offeror of the motion chooses to include—one or two short amendments or many pages of them. Thus:

> Mr. [Ms.] _____ moves to recommit the bill (H.R. 1234) to the Committee on _____ with instructions to report the bill back to the House forthwith with the following amendment [or amendments]:....

The amendments are written in the usual form (like other amendments to bills as described in 14.6 and 30.7). It is assumed that someone—the parliamentarian, the relevant committee staffs, or the drafter—has been alerted and has the necessary amendments ready, so that the committee to which the bill is recommitted can hold a pro forma meeting and report it back immediately.

You should understand the uses and forms of these motions (whether or not you ever have to write one) simply because they are legislative vehicles in every sense, requiring (in the case of a motion with instructions) the same drafting skills as ordinary amendments.

4. **Suspensions.** One frequently used parliamentary shortcut that you ought to be aware of is the passage of bills in the House "under suspension of the rules". The procedure is activated by a motion made on the floor; adoption of the motion requires a two-thirds vote and the procedure is only available at specified times, but it has real advantages when a bill that could easily pass is having trouble finding a time-slot sufficient for its full-scale consideration.

A bill taken up "under suspension" can have as many amendments in it as the sponsor desires, already marked in place on the copy that accompanies the motion. No amendments to it can be offered on the floor, and debate is limited to 40 minutes, evenly divided between the pros and cons. And all parliamentary requirements that would otherwise apply are waived. This sounds as though it would invite widespread abuse; but in practice the whole procedure is always cleared with both sides (as well as with the leadership) in advance, and any Member who attempted to conceal a noncleared provision in the document is unlikely to be given another opportunity to try.

To prepare a motion to suspend is relatively simple:

A. Just get a copy of the bill as it was reported (with rare exceptions only reported bills are passed under suspension).

B. Clearly mark in the bill all amendments your sponsor may wish to include (in addition to any committee amendments already shown in the reported bill, which would be automatically included unless you choose to strike them out).

C. Type at the top of the first page (or on a separate sheet of paper) the following:

Mr. [Ms.] ⸻ moves to suspend the rules and pass the bill H.R. 1234 [as amended]:

You should make copies of the finished product for the various House officials and for representatives of both the majority and the minority on the floor.

Committee procedure. The Rules of the House "are the rules of its committees and subcommittees so far as applicable", with one or two minor exceptions (Rule XI, clause 1); and subcommittees are subject to the rules of their parent committees "so far as applicable". Each committee has its own rules, and in most parliamentary respects they follow the Rules of the parent body closely.

But in fact there are many differences between House procedures and committee procedures—some based on obviously sound ground (committees have nothing resembling the Committee of the Whole House on the State of the Union, for example, and must therefore make their own way in this area) and some quite inexplicable. There is no definitive body of parliamentary law on what "so far as applicable" means in this context; when a question arises on the floor about the validity (under the Rules) of some committee action, the parliamentarian decides.

To the best of the author's knowledge, no one has ever tried to enforce complete procedural conformity among committees (although most committees do insist on conformity among their subcommittees). The only thing that can be safely said is that committee rules and procedures bear a noticeable resemblance to those of the parent body, but tend to be a good deal looser in actual practice. You usually can assume that committee parliamentarians will impose the same requirements and interpret the rules in the same way as their House (or Senate) counterpart, but you should not totally rely on that assumption. And you should of course have a well-thumbed copy of the rules of any committee you deal with regularly.

It should be mentioned again that the Rules of the House require all committee reports on bills to include a number of specific items—various budgetary findings, oversight summaries, and economic statements as well as the "Ramseyer" (see 30.8). Preparing most of these items is up to the committee staff (although the Ramseyer is normally left to the drafter); but if you are responsible for assembling the final report you should remember to make sure that all the pieces are there. The bill may be subject to a point of order on the floor if they are not.

▶ **32.4   Amendments**

Degree.   Both in committee and on the floor, there is a limitation on the number and kind of proposed amendments to a provision of a bill that may be pending at any one time. It is usually put this way: Amendments in the "first degree" and "second degree" are permissible, while amendments in the "third degree" (or any higher degree) are not.

Under this limitation there can be as many as four amendments pending at the same time:

1. An amendment to the text of the bill (first degree). This can be either a simple amendment or an amendment "in the nature of a substitute".

2. A substitute for that amendment (also treated as first degree). This must be called a substitute—headed either "Substitute Offered by Mr. [Ms.] Y for the Amendment Offered by Mr. [Ms.] X" or "Amendment in the Nature of a Substitute Offered by Mr. [Ms.] Y to the Amendment Offered by Mr. [Ms.] X".

3. An amendment to the original amendment (second degree)—"Amendment Offered by Mr. [Ms.] Z to the "Amendment Offered by Mr. [Ms.] X".

4. An amendment to the substitute (also second degree)—

"Amendment Offered by Mr. [Ms.] Z to the Substitute Offered by Mr. [Ms.] Y".

Any amendment offered to either of the latter two amendments would be "in the third degree", and would be out of order.

Committee amendments included in the printed bill as reported are counted as amendments on the floor, so that if there is a committee amendment to a particular section of the bill only three additional floor amendments to that section can be pending at any one time. It should be noted, however, that when a committee has reported a bill with an amendment in the nature of a complete substitute (striking out the entire text of the bill and inserting a new text), the rule on the bill frequently provides that the committee substitute is to be treated as the original text for purposes of amendment, which restores the four-amendment possibility.

When the time comes to act on the four pending amendments, the first one voted on is the amendment to the amendment (clause (3)), followed in order by the amendment to the substitute (clause (4)), the substitute itself (clause (2)), and the original amendment (clause (1)). Members waiting in the wings with amendments that would have been in the third degree can offer them as soon as slots become available; for example, a Member who has another amendment to the substitute can offer it as soon as the first amendment to the substitute has been disposed of.

Needless to say, all of this poses real problems for the absentee drafter (and even for an on-the-scene drafter), who must tailor amendments to fit a scenario that changes by the minute. And when the smoke clears it may be too late to offer them.

The rules governing amendments in committee and on the floor have been simplified and condensed in what is sometimes called the basic amendment tree (see Figure 32.4).

Germaneness.   Any amendment offered to a bill in committee or on the floor must be "germane" to that bill and to the particular provision or provisions affected. The dictionary defines germaneness as the quality of being "closely related, appropriate, pertinent, to the point, akin, relevant". The Rules of the House (Rule XVI, clause 7) put it this way: "No motion or proposition on a subject different from that under consideration shall be admitted under color of amendment".

The requirement is absolute and must be complied with; but

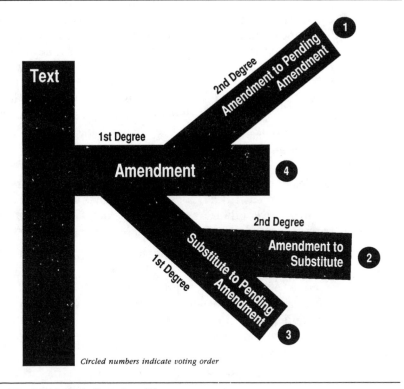

Circled numbers indicate voting order

▶ **Figure 32.4 Basic Amendment Tree**

you don't have to be a genius to recognize that "germane-ness" is a very slippery term. How far afield can you go before your amendment can be said to involve "a subject different from that under consideration"?

If the bill involved, for example, is one that increases widows' insurance benefits under the social security program, an amendment to change the amount of the increase is clearly germane, and an amendment to provide military assistance to Pakistan is clearly not. But what about an amendment to decrease widows' benefits instead, or to change the amount of other types of benefits, or to change eligibility requirements for widows, or to improve related administrative procedures? What if it goes further and increases disability benefits, or benefits under the SSI program? All of these contain subject matter that could be characterized, in varying degrees, either as "related to" or "different from" the bill.

You might take a sabbatical and read the several thousand

existing precedents on the subject of germaneness, starting with the parliamentarian's notes following the cited clause in the bound volume of the House Rules. The author would not recommend this, although the parliamentarian's notes (which could be read through and digested in an hour or so) would give you a good feel for the subject and might be worth the effort. If you do read the precedents you will quickly learn that most of the legitimate germaneness questions that have been raised in the past have been decided in different ways at different times.

In most cases, however, it isn't really that difficult—after all, the meaning of the term is clear in a general sense even if its application to particular cases can sometimes be troublesome. And in any event there are several considerations that may be helpful:

1. In dealing with questions of germaneness you should apply four basic tests—the subject matter, the breadth or scope of the bill (or provision) being amended, the fundamental purposes of the bill (or provision) and of the amendment, and the jurisdiction of the committee that is considering or has reported the bill. These tests are not exclusive.

2. To the extent possible, in doubtful cases, you should look for ways to tie your amendment to what is already in the bill—make it look like an exception, a special rule, or a conforming change, rather than like a freestanding and apparently separate provision.

3. If you are responsible for the bill, and the sponsor (for tactical reasons) wants to make it harder for others to amend, keep its scope and apparent purpose narrow, and include language reflecting that narrowness wherever possible. A bill "to amend section 202(e)(2)(A) of the Social Security Act to provide a 10-percent increase in widow's insurance benefits" is better in this respect (though unnecessarily cumbersome for most purposes) than a bill "to amend title II of the Social Security Act to improve the benefit structure of the OASDI program"; and either is better than a bill "to provide greater financial security for aged individuals".

▶ **32.5   Prohibited appropriations**

The Rules of the House prohibit appropriations in two types of cases that occasionally rise up to trouble well-intentioned legislators. You will probably never have to draft a bill making appropriations, but if you are called upon to draft an amendment doing that you should understand what is involved so you can advise your sponsor properly.

Appropriations without previous authorization. No appropriation can be made unless it has been authorized in a previously enacted statute. The pertinent language is in Rule XXI, clause 2(a): "No appropriation shall be reported in a general appropriation bill, or shall be in order as an amendment thereto, for any expenditure not previously authorized by law. . .". This requirement was discussed in 12.5.

Most bills creating major programs include a provision explicitly authorizing appropriations in specified amounts and for specified periods. When confusion arises it is usually because the program involved does not include such a provision, which sometimes makes sponsors nervous about whether or not the program can be funded. But it is well established that any law that creates a function or requires an action to be taken is in and of itself an authorization of whatever appropriations may be necessary for that function or action, without limit as to amount or time.

Thus an explicit authorization of appropriations is necessary only to place limitations upon the amount of the appropriations or the period for which they can be made. The prohibition against unauthorized appropriations is aimed at appropriations in amounts or for periods exceeding those limitations, or for programs or functions that have not yet been created at all. (A related provision of the Rules prohibits reappropriations of unexpended balances from prior years, except for the continuation of public works.)

Appropriations in legislative bills. No appropriation can be included in a "legislative" bill (that is, in a bill not originating in the Appropriations Committee), or in any amendment to such a bill. The pertinent language is in Rule XXI, clause 5: "No bill or joint resolution carrying appropriations shall be reported by any committee not having jurisdiction to report appropriations, nor shall an amendment proposing an appropriation be in order during the consideration of a bill or joint resolution reported by a committee not having that jurisdiction.".

For the most part this is an easy requirement to comply with, since appropriations are usually recognizable as such on their face.

There is one situation, however, where the prohibition applies but the offending provision may not be recognizable on its face as an appropriation. When funds have been properly appropriated for a specified purpose, a legislative bill that subsequently makes a sufficiently basic change in that purpose may sometimes be viewed as diverting the previously authorized and previously appropriated funds from the old purpose to a totally new one. If it is so viewed (whether or not the bill explicitly says that the existing funds are to be available for the new purpose) it will be treated as constituting a new appropriation, and requires a new authorization.

Obviously the dividing line between a completely new purpose and a merely modified or expanded one is not always easy to spot. Adding new features to an existing program or increasing its size is everyday stuff for the drafter, of course, and creates no problems; but substituting an entirely new program for the old one (using the money already available) will fall before a point of order every time. And any overhaul of the old program may be suspect if it is extensive enough to constitute a basic change in the program's purpose.

You should be alert to these possibilities, and if you think you have a problem (after reading the operating and funding provisions of both the existing law and the proposed bill as well as the previous appropriation), you should raise with the sponsor the possible necessity of explicitly writing the bill as an authorization only (like any other bill establishing a new program) and obtaining the funding through new appropriations in a separate bill to be enacted later.

▶ **32.6   Legislation in appropriation bills**

The other side of the coin is that the House Rules also prohibit the inclusion of "legislation" in an appropriation bill. The pertinent language is in Rule XXI, clauses 2(b) and (c): "No provision changing existing law shall be reported in any general appropriation bill . . . [and no] amendment to a general appropriation bill shall be in order if changing existing law.". (Exceptions are provided for "germane provisions which retrench expenditures" and for rescissions.)

If this prohibition were uniformly applied according to its terms, your options would be clear; and appropriations riders—the devices commonly used to legislate in appropriation acts (see 12.12)—could hardly exist. In fact, however, it is riddled with major exceptions.

The most important method of circumventing the prohibition

is based on the so-called principle of "limitation". That principle (which is well known to all Members of Congress but not fully understood by many of them) provides in essence that, since Congress is not obliged to appropriate anything just because there is an authorization of appropriations on the books, it is permissible for Congress to limit the use of any appropriation it does make. The limitation is usually accomplished by simply providing that no part of the appropriation involved shall be used for certain specified purposes.

Thus, for example, if the Appropriations Committee disapproves of an agency's (legally authorized) practice of awarding contracts in some cases to persons who were not the low bidders, it could provide in that agency's annual appropriation bill that "no part of any amount appropriated for a project in this Act shall be used to carry out a contract with a person who was not the low bidder on that project".

And the long-established practice of Treasury borrowing to finance major Federal programs ("backdoor spending"), which was finally put to death by the Congressional Budget Act of 1974, was actually brought to a grinding halt around 1960 by a rider (placed in every general appropriation bill) that simply said in effect "No part of any amount appropriated in this Act for salaries and expenses shall be used to pay the salary or expenses of any officer or employee who is engaged in carrying out a program or activity funded in whole or in part from sources other than appropriations".

Such a limitation does not literally terminate the offending program or activity, of course; it only cuts off the funds. The officials involved could theoretically continue the program or activity and pay for it out of their own pockets, but somehow they never do.

The question of what constitutes a permissible "limitation" is a very complicated one, and there are hundreds of precedents (often conflicting) that bear on it. But if the language does not give affirmative directions, does not impose new duties, and does not directly interfere with anyone's discretionary authority—that is, if the job can be done by a simple negative on the use of the appropriation—the device can be (and regularly is) used freely.

Recent changes in the House Rules (intended to discourage appropriations riders by imposing restrictions on when and how they can be offered and by giving the Appropriations

Committee the right to effectively prevent their consideration in some cases) have cut down on the practice considerably but have not altogether eliminated it. If you are called upon to write an appropriations rider you should have no misgivings about it; just be sure that it meets the tests given above and that the sponsor is aware of the practical difficulties.

▶ **32.7   The budget process**

The Congressional Budget Act of 1974 imposes a number of limitations on the way in which (and the times at which) bills and amendments having budgetary impact can be considered. Some of these limitations must be taken into account in the actual drafting process; the rest do not directly concern you as a drafter but are important nonetheless, because you will often be called upon to advise your sponsor on the best legislative route to take and on the obstacles that route is likely to contain.

This body of law—the Budget Act and its confederates (the Emergency Deficit Control Act of 1985, the Budget Enforcement Act of 1990, and a few others)—makes up a tapestry that is far too complicated and mysterious to address in detail here. But the limitations that are likely to concern you as a drafter are reasonably clear; and without attempting anything exhaustive it is the purpose of this subdivision to remind you of a few of the more important ones (as they currently exist—new ones are added and old ones changed on a regular basis):

1. No bill or amendment having budgetary impact in any fiscal year can be considered in either House until the budget resolution for that year has been agreed to (section 303). For this purpose "budgetary impact" means new budget authority, changes in revenues, changes in the public debt limit, new entitlement authority, credit authority, and (in the Senate) outlays and other new spending authority.

2. After the budget resolution for any fiscal year has been agreed to, no bill or amendment can be considered in either House if it would have the effect of increasing outlays or reducing revenues, within any committee or subcommittee allocation, beyond the applicable levels permitted by that allocation (section 302). And any reported bill providing entitlement authority beyond those levels must be re-referred to the Appropriations Committee

before it can be considered (section 401(b)(2)).

3. No amendment to a reconciliation bill can be considered if it would have the effect of increasing outlays or reducing revenues, unless it makes offsetting reductions in other outlays or offsetting increases in other revenues (section 310).

4. After the budget resolution for any fiscal year has been agreed to, no bill or amendment can be considered in either House if it would have the effect of increasing outlays or reducing revenues beyond the level specified in the resolution (section 311).

5. No bill or amendment providing Treasury borrowing authority or advance contract authority, or providing new credit authority, can be considered in either House unless it also specifically provides that such authority "is to be effective for any fiscal year only to such extent or in such amounts as are provided in appropriation Acts" (sections 401(a) and 402). (This allows the practice but maintains control within the appropriations process.)

6. No bill or amendment can be considered in either House if it provides entitlement authority that would become effective before the first day of the upcoming fiscal year (section 401(b)(1)).

And a number of esoteric violations of the Emergency Deficit Control Act are treated in a similar way.

Bear in mind that this list is provided only to help you understand the kinds of parliamentary obstacles your bills will face on the budgetary front—a complete mastery of the budget field is more than the author would try to impose on anyone. Any problems you may have in this area will most likely involve uncertainty about the meaning of the key terms; you should read the definitions carefully and consult an expert if you can find one, but actually reading the entire Budget Act and its confederates is something you should do only as a last resort if you hope to maintain your sanity.

▶ **32.8   Conference limitations**

Every drafter should be aware, in general terms at least, of just how far conferees can go in resolving differences between the two Houses.

The basic rule in the House, which is stricter than the

corresponding rule in the Senate (and governs in any case, as a practical matter, because both Houses must be able to agree to whatever the conferees come up with), is found in Rule XXVIII, clause 3:

> Whenever a disagreement to an amendment in the nature of a substitute has been committed to a conference committee it shall be in order for the Managers on the part of the House to propose a substitute which is a germane modification of the matter in disagreement, but the introduction of any language in that substitute presenting a specific additional topic, question, issue, or proposition not committed to either House shall not constitute a germane modification of the matter in disagreement. Moreover, their report shall not include matter not committed to the conference committee by either House, nor shall their report include a modification of any topic, question, issue, or proposition committed to the conference committee by either or both Houses if that modification is beyond the scope of that specific topic, question, issue, or modification as so committed to the conference committee.

As in the case of most major parliamentary problems, the questions that arise in the conference area can often be answered in different ways by different people, and there are hundreds of precedents (frequently conflicting) that bear upon what is permissible and what is not. But it is in the application of the parliamentary requirements to particular cases that the difficulties arise—the requirements themselves are fairly straightforward.

This subdivision will not attempt to address all the intricacies, but will limit itself to a few of the more fundamental considerations that every drafter should understand.

Complete substitutes versus numbered amendments. As indicated earlier, a conference report can take one of two forms:

1. If the Senate amendment was a complete substitute for the House bill (or vice versa), the conference report will be a complete substitute for both of them. The entire document will have been committed to the conferees, as a single amendment in disagreement, and is "in conference".

2. If the Senate instead made cut-and-bite amendments at specific points in the House bill (or vice versa), each of

those individual amendments is given a number, and only the numbered amendments are "in conference".

The requirements of germaneness and scope (discussed below) apply equally in either case, but the practical limitations on what the conferees can do may be quite different, because technically conferees have no power to consider anything that is not before them ("in conference").

To take a trivial example, if the conferees decide to eliminate the next-to-last section of the bill in a complete-substitute case, they can redesignate the succeeding section to close the gap (and can conform any cross-references) without transgressing the rules, because the entire bill is before them. But if they decide to do it in a numbered-amendments case, where the offending section was added (say) by Senate amendment numbered 12, they would not technically have the power to make the conforming redesignation (unless the section number of the succeeding section were the subject of Senate amendment numbered 13), because that section is not before them. (In fact, in the latter case, they would make the conforming redesignation, but in less mechanical situations it often takes some bobbing and weaving to do it.)

A related consideration is that the complete-substitute conference report, like a complete-substitute amendment in committee (see 15.2 and 15.3), effectively conceals from the casual reader just what has been done (although it has the advantage of showing the final product in its entirety), while a numbered-amendments conference report, like cut-and-bite amendments in committee, highlights what has been done. The author would not want to be seen as counseling deception, of course, but the former can cover a multitude of parliamentary sins while the latter cannot—a point that can be of great significance when dealing with the unavoidable last-minute parliamentary snags.

Germaneness. Whether or not one proposition is "germane" to another is of course a matter of subjective judgment in close cases. Enough has been said about the elusiveness of the concept (see 32.4); but you should never forget that it is an absolute requirement in conference reports.

Not only must every conference action be germane to the provisions of either the House or Senate version of the bill when that action is taken during the conference, but when the conference report is subsequently considered in the House all of its provisions (including, for example, any

Senate provisions that were agreed to by the conferees) must meet the same test of germaneness that they would have to meet if they had been offered as amendments to the bill when it was originally being considered on the House floor. The entire report will fall if a single one of its provisions is ruled nongermane. (The special House procedure for eliminating nongermane Senate amendments that were included in the conference report, and then adopting the rest of the report, is a difficult and cumbersome one and is seldom even tried.)

Scope.   A somewhat more tangible requirement involves the "scope" of the conferees' powers. When the difference between the House and Senate versions of a particular provision is measurable on some objective scale, the conferees must adopt one of the two versions or come down somewhere between them.

Thus if one House authorized $1,000,000 for benefits to be paid in or after 1992 to individuals age 65 or over, and the other House authorized $3,000,000 for benefits in or after 1994 to individuals age 62 or over, the conferees could agree upon an authorization of $1,000,000 or $3,000,000 or any figure in between, upon a starting date of 1992, 1993, or 1994, and upon an age limit of 62, 63, 64, or 65 (and they could do this in any combination unless the parliamentarian chose to regard the three differences as part of an indivisible whole). But they would have no power to go higher than $3,000,000 or lower than $1,000,000, or to start earlier than 1992 or later than 1994, or to specify an age above 65 or below 62—if they did a point of order would lie against their entire report.

Obviously most scope measurements are not this easy. Usually the two versions are at least comparable in substance, however, and the conferees must try to find the outer limits of each in order to comply with the scope requirement. In the relatively rare cases where they are not comparable at all—for example, a House provision imposing capital punishment for some crime, replaced in the Senate by a provision for the appointment of additional judges to hear cases of the kind involved—it would be futile to try and measure the scope of the difference; the two versions would have to be treated as containing totally unrelated provisions, and by default the question becomes one of germaneness only. (In the example given the conferees could probably agree on either or both provisions, with or without germane changes, or on neither.)

If you become involved in very many conferences you will soon have your fill of scope and germaneness questions, many with no clear-cut answer. Just be alert for them, and hope that someone at the conference has the ear of the official parliamentarians (who always have the last word on such matters) so that they can be settled on the spot; waiting for a ruling until after the conference report has been filed is unsatisfactory for obvious reasons.

But remember that scope and germaneness allegations are tactical tools commonly used by conferees seeking to win the battle on technical grounds rather than compromising on the merits; so don't rock the boat too soon.

Index

Index

Augustus F. Hawkins-Robert T. Stafford Elementary and Secondary School Improvement Amendments of 1988, as a poor short title, 11.4
Authorization of funds, 12.5. *See also* Appropriations bills
annual amendments, 18.5
end of bill, 13.1
entitlements, 12.6
models, 10.4
questions concerning, p. 44

Backdoor spending
legislative committees, 21.5
prohibition, 32.6
Backup citations. *See* Parenthetical expressions, abbreviated; Parenthetical expressions, citations
Balanced Budget and Emergency Deficit Control Act, 11.1, 11.4
joint resolution, 30.3
Beaman, Middleton 1.1
Bell, John A., 19.2
Bills. *See also* Organization of bills
becomes "An Act", 30.9
committee reference, 30.6
enacted, 26.1
engrossed, 29.7, 30.9 and example, pp. 374-375
enrolled, 30.7, 30.11
existing federal law, 29.1
introduced in House, 1.3, example, pp. 350-351
key provisions, alphanumeric designations, 2.3, 8.4
legislative vehicle, 30.1, 30.2
number assigned, 30.6
references to, 24.8
reported, example, pp. 367-369, with amendments, 30.8 and example, p. 367
subdivisions, 20.1, 28.1
titles on printed forms, 30.6
typography, 28.1
Boilerplate
authorization of funds, p. 156
begin writing, 10.5
bill provision, 10.4
existing law examples, 12.4
Rules of House and Senate altered by statute, p. 153
savings clauses, 13.4
severability clauses, 13.6
Buckely v. Valeo, validity of separability clauses, 13.6
Budget Enforcement Act of 1990
limitations, 32.7
Budget and Impoundment Control Act of 1974
short titles, 11.4

Budget reconciliation bill, 11.4, 29.8
"Budgetary Systems and Concepts" (U. S. Budget), 12.6

Calendar year, use of, 22.9
Calendars, official and committee, 30.14
Capitalization, 21.7, 28.3
Central provisions, 12.1
Chapters, United States Code Style, 31.6
Civil penalties, 4.3, 4.8, 12.9
Classic drafting style. *See* Traditional style
Clayton Act, 4.8
Clerk of the House of Representatives
attestation of bill, 30.9
certification for enrollment of bills, 30.11
constitutional amendments signed, 30.3
Closed rules, for floor debate, 32.3
Closing provisions, 10.4
Code of Federal Regulations. *See also* Regulations
citations to, 25.2
codification of regulations, 29.9
Codification, 9.2
Collateral provisions, 22.5
implicit amendments, 18.2
Colons, 16.2, 21.6
Commas, 21.6
versus parenthetical expressions, 23.6
Commerce, Department of, 9.5
Commerce Clearing House. *See* Law, compilations of; *Congressional Index*
Committee hearings, and drafter, 30.8
Committee prints, in bill form, 30.13
Committee procedures, differences with House, 32.3
Committee reports
amendments explained, 30.8
legislative history provided, 19.6
Committee reports, content, 32.3
Committee veto, 12.13
Committee of the Whole
amendments considered, 30.7
consideration of bills, 32.2
Committee of the Whole House on the State of the Union, 32.2
amendments, 30.7
Committees. *See also* Amendments; Subcommittees, reporting bills with amendments
competing jurisdictions, 30.8
referral of bills, 32.2
rules, 32.2
substantive amendments, 12.11
Companion (identical) bills, 10.4
Comparative prints of bills, 30.13. *See also* Committee prints, in bill form
Compilations, and tables of content, 11.5. *See also* Law, compilations of
Composite reference, 24.8
excluding senior components, 24.11

442

Compound sentences, 7.3. *See also* Writing, rules
Concurrent resolutions
adopted or agreed to, 11.2
corrections of errors, 30.12 and example, pp. 388-389
introduced in House, example, p. 355
legislative vehicle, 30.1, 30.4
printed forms, 30.6
Conference bills
interim source, 29.7
"report style" for, 28.3
"reported in disagreement", 29.7, 30.10
Conference limitations, 32.8
Conference reports, 30.10
complete-substitutes, 32.8
numbered-amendments example, p. 383
scope of conferees powers, 32.8
Confidentiality and privilege, 2.5
Congress in Print, 30.14
Congressional Budget Act, 5.2, 11.4, 12.6, 12.13, 22.8
backdoor spending prohibition, 32.6
committee prints used, 30.13
House and Senate rules, 32.1
limitations on consideration of bills with budgetary impact, 32.7
mixture of drafting styles, 31.7
Congressional Directory, 30.14
Congressional Index, 30.14
Congressional Monitor, 30.14
Congressional Quarterly. *See Congress in Print, Congressional Monitor,* Washington Alert
Congressional Record, 30.14
interim source of law, 29.7
slip laws citations, 29.2
Conjunctions, 21.10, 22.18
"Consider", indicates discretion, 22.11
Consolidated references, 16.1
convention, 24.10
Constitution
Constitutional amendments, as joint resolutions, 30.3
rules of House and Senate, 12.13
Context, and use of definitions, 11.7
Continuing resolutions, 12.12, 13.5
Convention on the Territorial Sea and the Contiguous Zone, proper citation, 25.3
"Cookbook formula". *See* Formulas
Courts
findings and purpose statements, 11.6
jurisdiction, 6.2
Criminal provisions
changes in law, 29.8
criminal penalties, 4.3, 4.8, 12.9
effective dates, 26.1, 26.4
Cross-references, 3.6, 5.4, 6.2, 6.6, 7.5, 12.3
clarity, 23.8

correct after redesignation of provisions, 18.1
explicit, 22.4
incorporate provisions, 23.3
Cumulative amendments. *See* Amendments
Cut-and-bite. *See also* Amendments
amendatory tool, 15.1, 15.2, 15.4
use for margins, 16.4
with serial amendments, 17.2
Cut-in material, 28.2. *See also* Margins
revenue style, 31.4

Daily Digest. See Congressional Record
Dashes, 21.6
tabulated lists, 23.4
Debate, general on floor, 32.2
Debt limit, amendments to bills, 17.4
Definitions, 3.6, 6.2, 10.4
analyzing complex concepts, 23.2
federal statutes, 19.5
forms, 11.7
partial, 11.7
Degree, of amendments, 32.4. *See also* Amendments
Descriptive phrases, when striking or adding, 16.1
Designation clauses
mentioned, 31.1
revenue style, 31.4
simple resolutions, 30.5
traditional style, 31.2
Dickerson, Reed
ambiguity, vagueness, generality, 19.4
conjunctions, 21.10
definitions, 11.7
drafters, 1.1, 2.1, 2.2
form and style, 3.3
imperative mood, 21.5
incorporation through reference, 23.3
on modifiers, 22.5
organization of bills, 6.2, 6.4, 10.1
positive expressions, 22.12
prohibitions, 22.2
specialized assistance, 3.6
Drafters
anonymity, passion for, 2.5
audience 1.3, 3.3, 7.1, 9.3
classification as occasional or professional, 1.3
in-house professionals, 3.1
institutional, 3.4
lack of time, 4.9
problems for occasional, 14.5
professional responsibility, 4.6
need for substantive expertise, 4.9
setting and context, 1.3
sponsors, relationships, 1.3, 2.1, 4.1, 4.2, 4.3, 4.9
stages in the legislative process, 3.5

Peacock, James Craig, 9.3, 18.1
Penalty provisions, 10.4
Percentages, 22.22
Period, with quotation marks, 16.2
Periodic reports to Congress, 12.7
Permanent provisions, 6.2, 10.1, 14.4
"Permissible limitations", language in
 appropriations bills, 27.2
Person versus individual, defined, 22.7
Place, with location, 16.1
"Plain language". *See* Judicial review, inter-
 pretation of statutes
Plural nouns, and ambiguity, 21.2
Points. *See* Fonts, typeface, and points
Points of order, 32.1
Policy
 development, 2.1, 2.3
 main thrust, subsidiary, collateral, 1.3,
  3.2, 4.3, 4.5, 4.6, 5.1, 11.1, 12.2, 13.3
 models, 10.5
 types of policy questions, 4.3
Policymakers, 1.3, 3.5, 10.5, 12.11
Positive law
 enacting code revision into, 9.2, p. 337
 references to, 24.2
 U.S. Code, 17.1, 29.4, example, p. 338
Poultry Products Inspection Act, as hidden
 amendment example, p. 205. *See also*
 Hidden Amendments
Preamble, 11.6
Preliminary stage, 3.3
Prentice-Hall. *See* Law, compilations of
President, signing of bills, 26.1
Printer's marks, 28.2, 28.4
Private relief bills, 2.2, 10.4, 11.1
Procedures, congressional, 2.3, 4.9, 12.13.
 See also Rules, House and Senate
Program models, 10.4. *See also* Models
Prohibited acts and exclusions, 6.2
Prohibitions, 4.3, imposition of, 22.2
Proofreader's marks, example, p. 328. *See
 also* Printer's marks
"Provided". *See* Provisos
Provisos, 27.2
 typeface, p. 323
Public documents citations, 25.5
Public Law 204, 3.1
Public law numbers, references to, 24.4
Punctuation, 7.1
 accepted rules, 21.6
 amendatory, 16.2
Pursuant to, 22.17

Quotation marks, 11.5, 16.2

Racketeer Influenced and Corrupt Organizations (RICO), 4.8
Railroad Retirement Act, 5.4
 rounded numbers in, 27.5

Railroad Retirement Board, 12.3
Railroad Unemployment Insurance Act,
 23.7
Ramseyer rule
 amendments to existing law, 30.8
 committee reports, 32.3
Readability and clarity, 1.3, 2.1, 3.3, 4.4, 6.5,
 7.1, 7.2, 7.3, 9.1, 9.4, 11.7
Recommittals, 32.3
Redesignations of provisions in existing
 law, 18.1
Redundancies and circumlocutions, 22.13,
 22.15
Reference sources. *See* Law, compilations
 of
Reform bills, 6.7
Regulations, 2.2, 3.2
 citations to, 25.3
 event-related effective dates, 26.4
 retroactive changes, 26.3
Regulatory bills, 13.3, 13.4, 29.9. *See also*
 Bills
"Relating to" clauses, 9.4
Relative pronouns "that", "which", "who",
 "whose", 21.8, 21.9
Repeal, use in amendatory tools, 15.2
Repealers, 15.5. *See also* Striking text
Reported bills. *See* Bills, reported
Reports to Congress, 6.2
Resolutions. *See* Concurrent resolutions,
 Joint resolutions, Simple resolutions
Resolving clauses, 11.2
 simple resolutions, 30.5
Restatement, amendatory tool, 15.1, 15.3,
 15.4
Restrictions, parliamentary and constitu-
 tional, 3.2. *See also* Constitution
Revenue bills. *See* Tax bills.
Revenue style, 8.5, 31.4. *See also* Drafting;
 Internal Revenue Code
 advantage over traditional and U.S. Code
 styles, 31.8
 use with senior components, 20.4
Revenues, statutory limits, 12.5
Revised Statutes, p. 336
Revisions, 3.6
Richards, Ivor A., 7.4
Riders, on appropriations bills, 12.12. *See
 also* Appropriations bills
Rights conferred, 22.2
Roman rule, 8.1, 8.3, 8.5, 9.2, 9.4, 12.13
 citations, 25.5
 drafting styles, 31.2, 31.7
 literal sense, 16.3
 mentioned, 31.8
 senior components, 20.4
 subdividing bills, 20.1
 superior headings, 20.5
Rulemaking and authority, 12.8

Index

Rules, House and Senate, 32.1
  ad hoc on bills, 30.5, 32.3
  amendments to 12.13
  citations, 25.4
  consideration of legislation, 32.1
  "enacted", use of, 11.2
  Ramseyer rule, 30.8
  referral of bills, 32.2
  simple resolutions to establish, 30.5
  statutory provisions influence, 32.7
Rules Committee, discharging, 32.3
Run-in material, 28.2
  revenue style headings of inferior subsections, 31.4

S. Con. Res. *See* Concurrent resolutions
S. J. Res. *See* Joint resolutions
S. Res. *See* Simple resolutions
Sanctions, 6.2, 12.9
Savings provisions, 6.2, 10.4, 13.3, 13.4
Schedule tracking. *See* Tracking bills
Science, Space, and Technology, House committee veto, 12.13
Seabed Arms Control Treaty, proper citation, 25.3
Secretary of the Senate
  attestation of bill, 30.9
  certification for enrollment of bills, 30.11
  constitutional amendments signed, 30.3
Self-sufficient text, 20.3
Senate, introduction of bills, 30.2
Senate engrossed amendment, example, pp. 376-377. *See* Amendments, engrossed
Senate Office of Legislative Counsel
  printed forms, 30.6
  provisos, 27.2
Senior components of bills, 20.2
  drafting styles for, 31.1
  references to, 24.9
Sense of Congress, 4.1
Sentence structure, 7.1. *See also* Tabulated sentences
  order of thoughts, 22.14
  short or declarative, 7.3, 9.5
  undistributed middle, 22.23
Separability clauses, 10.4, 13.6
Serial amendments, 16.1, 17.2. *See also* Amendments
Severability clauses. *See* Separability clauses
"Shall be effective" (date), 21.3. *See also* Effective dates
  granting rights and authorities, imposing duties, 22.2, 22.7
Short titles, 11.3
  amendatory bills, 16.5
  references to, 24.3
Simple resolutions
  adopted, 11.2

introduced in House, example, pp. 357-358
legislative vehicle, 30.1, 30.5
printed forms, 30.6
Singular nouns, 21.2
Slip laws, 29.2, example, pp. 333, 386. *See also* Law
Social Security Act, 2.2, 4.6, 5.4, 6.6, 7.3, 9.3, 11.4, 13.3, 15.5
  germaneness example, 32.4
  resignation of provisions, 18.1
  rounded numbers in, 27.5
  undesignated sections, 20.3
Sounding board, 3.6
Special rules, 4.9, 6.2, 6.6, 12.3
  consideration of bill in House, example, pp. 423-424
Specialized assistance, 3.6, 4.1, 4.2
Specific provisions, 10.1, 10.4
Split amendments, 6.6
  and provisions, 13.3, 13.4, 22.4
Split infinitive, uses, 21.11, 22.6
Sponsors. *See* Bills; Drafters
State governments and legislatures, 2.2, 3.1, 4.9, 6.3, 9.2
  amendatory tools, 15.4
  cross-references in statutes, 23.3
  designation systems in state statutes, 20.1
  effective dates, 26.1
  person defined in statutes, 22.7
  state plan model, 10.4, 11.1, 11.7, 12.8, 12.9
Statutes, 3.6, 4.1, 6.2, 14.1
  citations, 24.1
  congressional procedures, 12.13
  drafting styles for, 31.1
  format, 10.2
  language, 2.2, 4.6, 9.4, 9.5
  literal compilations, 29.6
  numbered sections, 6.5, 6.7, 11.3, 11.5, 20.2
  renumbered, 17.1
  renumbering provisions, 5.4
Statutes at Large
  abbreviated citations to, 27.5, 29.3
  mentioned, 24.7
Statutory construction, 19.5
  formats, 10.2
Striking text. *See also* Adding text; Inserting text
  amendatory tools, 15.2
  stylistically, 16.1
Structural provisions, 12.4, 22.6
Strung-out references, 24.8
Stylistic consensus, 7.6
  consistency, 7.6, 8.2, 10.2, 19.2
Subcommittees, reporting bills with amendments, 30.8. *See also* Amendments; Committees

Index